PATHWAYS AND PARTICIPATION IN VOCATIONAL AND TECHNICAL EDUCATION AND TRAINING

ORGANISATION FOR ECONOMIC CO-OPERATION AND DEVELOPMENT

ORGANISATION FOR ECONOMIC CO-OPERATION AND DEVELOPMENT

Pursuant to Article 1 of the Convention signed in Paris on 14th December 1960, and which came into force on 30th September 1961, the Organisation for Economic Co-operation and Development (OECD) shall promote policies designed:

- to achieve the highest sustainable economic growth and employment and a rising standard of living in Member countries, while maintaining financial stability, and thus to contribute to the development of the world economy;
- to contribute to sound economic expansion in Member as well as non-member countries in the process of economic development; and
- to contribute to the expansion of world trade on a multilateral, non-discriminatory basis in accordance with international obligations.

The original Member countries of the OECD are Austria, Belgium, Canada, Denmark, France, Germany, Greece, Iceland, Ireland, Italy, Luxembourg, the Netherlands, Norway, Portugal, Spain, Sweden, Switzerland, Turkey, the United Kingdom and the United States. The following countries became Members subsequently through accession at the dates indicated hereafter: Japan (28th April 1964), Finland (28th January 1969), Australia (7th June 1971), New Zealand (29th May 1973), Mexico (18th May 1994), the Czech Republic (21st December 1995), Hungary (7th May 1996), Poland (22nd November 1996) and the Republic of Korea (12th December 1996). The Commission of the European Communities takes part in the work of the OECD (Article 13 of the OECD Convention).

Publié en français sous le titre :

ITINÉRAIRES ET PARTICIPATION DANS L'ENSEIGNEMENT TECHNIQUE
ET LA FORMATION PROFESSIONNELLE

FOREWORD

In 1990, the OECD launched a project on "The Changing Role of Vocational and Technical Education and Training" (VOTEC). The cross-country study of training paths and youth participation in this system was one of the themes of the conference entitled "Vocational and Technical Education and Training for the 21st Century: Opening Pathways and Strengthening Professionalism" (28-30 November 1994).

The notion of participation covers all data on pupils and their entry, transition, and exit from different programmes, which are the result of the choices young people make with respect to the different educational possibilities offered to them. Ten countries participated in this study: Australia, Austria, Canada (Quebec), Denmark, France, Germany, Italy, the Netherlands, Switzerland and the United Kingdom.

At the beginning of the study, a number of hypotheses were formulated on the factors that can influence participation, and it was suggested that each country envisage their plausibility in their respective systems (these hypotheses are stated in the annex of Chapter 1).

OECD countries have very different traditions concerning initial vocational education and training. The goal of this study is to improve the understanding of the internal organisation and workings of these different systems. It identifies, quantifies, and tries to explain the patterns of participation in VOTEC, and their changes over time. The diversity of the existing systems is expected to shed light on the ways in which different policies encourage, or discourage, young people to participate in VOTEC, and explains how such policies influence their choices and how other factors, such as the situation of the job market, gender, socio-cultural origin, etc., impact their decisions.

Nevertheless, the evolution of VOTEC can be studied only with reference to the other sectors of the educational system. Therefore, only the entire secondary school and higher education systems provide an adequate framework for the study of the relative attractiveness of VOTEC, compared to other pathways, which are often qualified as "general".

For the purposes of this study, education and training systems can be considered as different and intertwined *pathways*, themselves made up of a series of *programmes*. The programmes can be described in terms of training location (school, business, etc.), level of education and qualification sought,* certification or qualification obtained, entry requirements, length and nature of training, degree of differentiation and "modularisation", the possibility to further studies, etc. Another important dimension concerns the value that different packages and pathways have on the labour market.

The synthesis of country reports, which outlined some of the answers to the questions raised, was prepared by Professor Claude Pair from the *Institut universitaire de formation des maîtres* of Nancy (France).

The country reports provide information on the respective educational systems, in particular the training streams that come under VOTEC, data on the participation in different kinds of instruction and training, and show the first attempts to analyse and explain the systems, which may reflect the impact of recent reforms.

The concluding chapter, prepared by David Raffe, who played a key role from the start in establishing this study on pathways and participation, develops the lessons to be learned from this work. It stresses the importance of basic concepts and the methods used, as well as the consequences for future research. This work still must be improved in order to make the information more usable and more comparable, and above all to draw conclusions about the factors influencing young people to participate in VOTEC training and their transition to employment. The idea is to help national policy-makers distance themselves from ready-made, ideological responses and rely on experiences, adapting them to the traditions of their countries. The OECD has decided to play a role in this endeavour.

It should be noted that the studies in the ten countries were spread out over several years. The statistical data and the reforms analysed relate, for most countries, to developments in the 1980s and early 1990s. Since the purpose of this book is to elaborate a common conceptual and methodological approach to the study of young people's pathways and choices and of their evolution over time, the data presented here, even though somewhat dated, are still very relevant for illustrative purposes.

Within the Secretariat of the OECD, Ms. Marianne Durand-Drouhin, assisted by Ms. Anastasia Fetsi, was responsible for the organisation and management of this project. This report is published on the responsibility of the Secretary-General of the OECD.

---

* There is an international classification system of different educational levels (International Standard Classification for Education, ISCED), but some countries use their own classification system.

TABLE OF CONTENTS

SYNTHESIS OF COUNTRY REPORTS

by

Claude Pair, former Rector and Professor,
Institut universitaire de formation des maîtres, Nancy

I. SCOPE OF THE STUDY

The acronym VOTEC comes from the two adjectives "vocational" (*professionnel* in French) and "technical" (*technique* or *technologique* in French), which do not mean the same thing in different countries. Here we intend to consider that these two adjectives refer to the targetted level of employment, with the first word covering skilled operative jobs, blue- and white-collar, and the second concerning intermediate-level jobs, in particular those of technicians and middle managers. The corresponding training paths form part of the study. However, training for design work, higher management and the professions, which can all be designated professional-level in English, lies outside the scope of this study.

The title of the VOTEC project also contains the words "education" and "training". The first refers more to school activities exercised in establishments coming under the Ministry of Education, while the second has a less academic connotation, the emphasis being on the world of work: enterprises, services, administration. However, there is here a bipolarity rather than a sharp boundary, and both sites are becoming increasingly associated in what we shall call here "vocational and technical training".

The word "training" thus covers both initial training, which takes place at the beginning of adulthood and before entry into the labour market, and continuing training which goes on throughout working life. This study is concerned with young people, not adults, and hence initial training. However, here again the boundary is not clearly defined, and the place of apprenticeship or training courses for the unemployed is open to discussion. In certain countries, in fact, such as the United Kingdom, Australia, Canada and the Netherlands, initial training and continuing training are interrelated and delivered by the same establishments, and it is not easy to separate them. Over and above questions of organisation is the conception of training as a continuum.

From the standpoint of the school career, the training considered here comes in all countries after middle school or lower secondary, and hence for the most part after compulsory schooling. Vocational training is at upper secondary level. Technical training may also start at this level and continue at post-secondary, in what many countries call higher education or tertiary education: this includes the universities, of course, but also other institutes and colleges.

However, some of the national reports give little coverage to that part of VOTEC which comes under higher education. This is no doubt due to the difficulty of tracing the upper boundary of VOTEC, since the term "technical" is understood in different ways, depending on the country: certain countries use different adjectives, such as "para-professional" in Australia; it even happens that the word "technical" is used for training oriented towards the industrial production sector as opposed to the service sectors.

The fact is that the jobs in intermediate positions between the formerly clearly distinct categories of operatives and managers are many and varied, and categorisation is often somewhat fuzzy. Such jobs may be those of highly-skilled workers or supervisory staff (and the boundary with skilled workers is difficult to trace) or people responsible for project studies or control (and here the difference between them and engineers, for example, is not always clear). A nurse or a physiotherapist may occupy a post in a hospital or have his or her own professional practice, whereas the training is the same in both cases. The Australian report distinguishes between eight levels of competence, four of which appear to belong to this intermediate category.

Access to these intermediate jobs is generally through internal promotion or through the recruitment of young people, depending on the case, sector of activity or country. The corresponding training thus varies, but it is neither the traditional training for skilled workers (on-the-job, through apprenticeship or in basic vocational education schools) nor the traditional training of senior managers (based on an academic secondary education followed by university). This is a new situation which has come about in the past ten or twenty years. It has not yet become stabilised, but it certainly has a promising future.

The initial aim of the study was to explain the greater or lesser quantitative importance of initial vocational and technical training in different countries – what is known as young people's "participation" in this training – and its changes over time. Do the different policies governing the structure of education systems encourage young people to participate in VOTEC? How do they influence their choices – in connection with what other factors and notably the signals coming from the labour market?

The first stage is to identify, for each country, the *programmes* which comprise VOTEC and the *pathways* which young people take through these programmes, then to provide statistical information on student numbers and flows. It is this first stage with which the reports are above all concerned. Even though the statistical information given is not always equally rich and recent, it constitutes a first step towards a common language to enable us to describe and analyse the existing systems and young people's *participation* in the various possible pathways. In addition, some of the reports give certain elements of explanation, which by comparing them enables a number of observations to be made and certain hypotheses to be formulated.

2. PROGRAMMES AND PATHWAYS

In all countries, secondary education used to be limited to a general academic curriculum intended to educate the future elites of society. Today, while lower secondary education is open to all and has become compulsory, this traditional education has an heir at upper secondary level, a pathway which, after the final diploma (A*bitur*, baccalaureate, General Certificate of Education, *matura*, *maturità*, etc.), leads the great majority of young people into higher education.

Alongside this academic path various forms of VOTEC training have developed since the second world war. They now begin usually at upper secondary level. While the transition to higher education has become possible, it is less normal and more difficult than in the case of the academic pathway.

Everywhere there is a hierarchy established between academic education and VOTEC training, and also between the various forms of VOTEC training. This hierarchy is reflected in the educational level and sociocultural origin of the young people entering the different programmes.

Apart from these constants, there are differences in the systems of each country. The first comes prior to VOTEC and concerns the structure of middle or lower secondary education. While it is unified in the majority of countries (with the exception of special education which concerns 3 or 4 per cent of pupils), it is divided into distinct programmes in Germany, Austria (where this separation was made less rigid during the 1980s), the Netherlands (where the situation has been reviewed since 1993) and Switzerland. One of the programmes is then the beginning of the academic pathway, while the others lead essentially to VOTEC. France is in an intermediate situation with, for a small proportion of pupils, a programme which leads above all to vocational training. It was introduced in 1984 to delay entry to vocational training which began for some pupils before the end of lower secondary education.

Another difference concerns the relative numeric importance of the VOTEC and academic pathways in upper secondary education. This criterion leads to a clear division of the ten countries into two groups: those of the British Commonwealth – Australia, Canada and the United Kingdom – where the academic pathway is very much in the majority, and those of continental Europe, where it is VOTEC which dominates: Austria (about 80 per cent), Switzerland (75 per cent), Germany and the Netherlands (about 70 per cent), Denmark, France and Italy (about 60 per cent), the figures possibly varying a little according to whether pupil numbers or flows are considered.

This difference is partly connected with the various modes of access of young people to skilled jobs and more generally to positions in the hierarchy of enterprises. This may occur at a certain time after recruitment, when the young person has proved himself; after a fixed and codified period of service, according to a specific labour contract; or on recruitment, depending on the qualifications previously acquired.

For vocational training, these three modes of access lead to three broad traditions: *on-the-job training, formal apprenticeship, school training*. While these practices continue to coexist in the different countries, their weightings vary: frequently one of them dominates and orients training policy, definition of programme contents, and certification requirements.

Where, as in the United Kingdom or Australia, on-the-job training was predominant until recent years, governments became concerned about the risks of this situation in the face of the rapid changes in the skills required by employers and in the labour market. They introduced various types of training schemes, associating the initial training of young people and the continuing training of adults; and they sought to guide all this by means of a general and modular system of certification. Reforms along these lines have been introduced, essentially since the beginning of the 1990s. Thus in England and Wales, the National Vocational Qualifications (NVQs), created in 1988, recognise work skills; and in 1992 the General Vocational Qualifications (GNVQs) were introduced, essentially for young people studying full-time in schools and colleges: these may lead either to employment or to higher education.

In the countries of continental Europe, apprenticeship and school training coexist with different weights. In Switzerland, apprenticeship is clearly dominant: it was codified by a law of 1930 which was last amended in 1978. The situation is similar in Germany (law of 1969, last amended in 1981), though a significant proportion of young people complete full-time upper secondary education, either in VOTEC (various kinds of vocational schools) or outside it (*Gymnasium*), before entering the dual system. In Austria, the dual system of apprenticeship was the tradition too, but over the years school training has become dominant in terms of student numbers. In the Netherlands, training is mainly in schools but there are also many young people in apprenticeship. In France, the school system is dominant and apprenticeship is mainly limited to the craft trades. In Italy, training is essentially in schools and apprenticeship receives those who have left school early. Denmark constitutes a particular case where, rather than coexistence or even competition, we should speak of a system where school training and work training are articulated in a balanced way: this system was reviewed in 1989. As for Quebec, where access to higher education is very developed, it has a school training system which is situated for the most part at the post-secondary level of the *collèges*.

The concepts of *programme* and *pathway* adopted by the OECD as bases for the study apply differently in English speaking countries on the one hand and continental Europe on the other.

Programmes tend to multiply in a modular system where enterprises and various types of training establishments are invited to participate and compete with one another in initial and continuing training markets which are essentially regulated by the recognition of qualifications. It is difficult to talk of them other than in terms of levels. Thus the United Kingdom defines five levels (foundation, craft, technician, higher technician, professional) for the NVQs, the GNVQs being limited at present to the first three. In Australia, where the federal aspect of the country further complicates the situation, there are eight levels. In these two countries, the situation does not yet appear to have stabilised.

The concept of pathway is then difficult to identify, except by noting the great multiplicity and by remaining at the level of generalities. In England and Wales there are three principal pathways from age 16 – General Certificate of Education, GNVQ, NVQ, all of which may in fact exist in the same institution.

VOTEC *training at secondary level* leads to two possibilities: employment or further studies, notably technician training. The countries of continental Europe distinguish between these two by separating two types of VOTEC programme at this level: the first, which may be called "vocational", is directed above all to employment at skilled-worker level, while the second, which may be called "technical", keeps both options open, with possible employment at technician level but also leading increasingly to post-secondary studies.

Thus Austria has full-time vocational schools and technical schools; France has a vocational pathway and a technical pathway; Italy has vocational schools and technical schools; Denmark distinguishes between vocational training by means of sandwich courses after which the majority of young people go straight into employment, and technical and commercial courses, entered after one year of vocational training, which also prepare pupils for higher education; in Germany, certain schools prepare pupils for the *Fachhochschulreife* which gives access to higher technical colleges (*Fachhochschulen*); Switzerland, where there used to be little differentiation in levels, has just introduced the vocational *maturité* to reinforce general training and so prepare entry to higher vocational schools. In Quebec, VOTEC at secondary level comprises only vocational programmes which lead above all to employment.

Some countries distinguish between two levels of *vocational programme*. This is the case in France where, after the first level which leads to a certificate, young people can either go straight into skilled work or enter the second level, introduced in 1986, which leads to the *baccalauréat professionnel* and then normally to employment. In the Netherlands, the long cycle of three or four years begins either directly on completion of lower secondary schooling or after a two-year short cycle introduced in 1979 to favour access to vocational training for young people who experience difficulty with school work.

Technical programmes are at post-secondary level. Entry is then either from the general secondary pathways or from VOTEC.

In Quebec, virtually all students in the technical pathways of colleges come from the general pathway, both because this is dominant at secondary level and because the pupils in the vocational pathway rarely go on to further studies. In Austria, the post-secondary colleges award the same kind of qualifications as the technical colleges and thus receive students coming from the general pathway, even though pupils from technical schools enter them also to acquire additional skills. Increasing numbers, however, also go on to university; and higher technical schools (*Fachhochschulen*) are being set up as from 1994. In the Netherlands, there is a well-identified higher technical education where the intake comes partly from the general pathways, notably that which is not considered to be pre-university, while one-quarter of entrants come from vocational secondary schools (and as much as 35 per cent if we consider only direct entry from schools) and a smaller proportion from apprenticeship. In France, short-cycle higher technical education entrants are holders of the general or technical baccalaureate in roughly equal numbers. In Germany, entrants to the higher technical schools come above all from full-time technical secondary schools. In Switzerland, certain colleges are reserved for students who have served an apprenticeship, and *Fachhochschulen* (higher specialised schools) are being established to receive holders of the vocational *maturité*.

It is thus possible to identify vocational pathways, sometimes with two levels (France and the Netherlands), and technical pathways with a programme at secondary level possibly followed by a higher education programme, or with a general secondary education followed by a technical higher education programme. In addition, a pathway may begin with a vocational programme and then continue with one or two technical programmes. Thus in France the first-level vocational programme may give access to one leading to the technical baccalaureate and then to higher technician training; in the Netherlands a vocational programme gives access to higher technical education.

More generally, an effort has been made in most countries to build *bridges* between the different types of training, and in particular between vocational and technical training. This situation is in fact traditional in Germany, where the

◆ Figure 1. **Bridges between general education and vocational training**

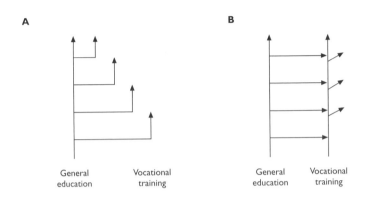

Source: OECD.

pathways are many and flexible. In particular, entry to the dual system can be made at various levels of secondary education and sometimes even after starting higher education. Only Italy, where the pathways are fairly rigid, appears to be an exception. Regions responsible for apprenticeship or training accept drop-outs from state technical and vocational schools.

The systems of the different countries can be seen as operating between two poles: in the one (Figure 1A), there are several ranked levels of vocational and technical training, all with their intake coming from general education; in the other (Figure 1B), there is a vocational and technical pathway which it is possible to enter at various levels from general education and to exit at different levels of initial or continuing training. Neither of these models is found in its pure form in practice, but over time the trend has been to move from the first towards the second, and individual countries have advanced to greater or lesser extents in this direction.

3. PARTICIPATION: QUANTITATIVE TRENDS

It is difficult to be very precise here because the national reports are not compatible as regards either the information provided or the period covered. In order to make comparisons, we have taken a period of some ten years starting at the beginning of the 1980s, a period in which the structure of education systems remained relatively stable. A comparison reveals many convergences and some significant differences.

The clearest convergence concerns the *general raising of the level of training* through extending the duration of schooling – not, during the period considered, as the result of policy decisions but spontaneously.

The proportion of a cohort completing secondary education increased in Australia from 45 per cent in 1985 to 72 per cent in 1992, in France from 34 per cent in 1981 to 63 per cent in 1993 and in Denmark from 70 per cent in 1983 to 77 per cent in 1993. In Germany, the proportion of secondary school leavers obtaining the final diploma (*Hochschulreife*) increased from 21 to 26 per cent between 1984 and 1991. The proportion of young people of age 17 in education in Switzerland increased from 80 per cent in 1980 to 87 per cent in 1990; the proportion of 18-year-olds in education in the Netherlands increased from 55 per cent in 1979 to 77 per cent in 1990 (full- and part-time); in the United Kingdom, from 32 per cent in 1980 to 45 per cent in 1992 (15 to 33 per cent for full-time alone). In Italy the number of pupils in upper secondary education increased by 400 000 between 1982 and 1991.

In higher education, student numbers increased by almost half in Australia between 1981 and 1990, and by two-thirds in France between 1980 and 1992. In Denmark the proportion of a cohort entering higher education increased from 34 to 44 per cent between 1983 and 1993. In Germany the proportion of holders of a final secondary diploma going on to higher education increased from 41 to 47 per cent between 1984 and 1990. In the Netherlands, the proportion of young people leaving the education system who were in general or technical higher education increased from 21 per cent in 1978 to 29 per cent in 1990.

It may be added that in those countries where lower secondary education is differentiated, the tendency is for those sections which lead mainly to the longest training to develop.

At *upper secondary level* the increase is divided between the general and VOTEC pathways in different ways, and two broad groups of countries can be distinguished here.

The relative share of VOTEC increased in the Netherlands, and to a lesser extent in the United Kingdom and Austria. In the Netherlands, VOTEC was responsible for all the growth, the proportion of a cohort in general education remaining virtually constant. In the United Kingdom, the increase of the number of young people in VOTEC appears substantial in percentage terms, but absolute numbers are low. In Austria the increase was slight.

In all the other countries the increase was more in favour of general education. In Denmark the proportion of the cohort entering VOTEC increased, but less than for general education from the mid-1980s. In Australia, France and Italy the increase was entirely in general education, the numbers in VOTEC remaining stable or falling slightly. In Germany the proportion of a cohort entering general education increased, whereas that entering the dual system remained stable after lower secondary education; it fell after the *Gymnasium* to the benefit of higher education, and after the other forms of schooling to the benefit of employment. All this in the context of a marked fall in the population in Germany. In Switzerland, general education increased and VOTEC decreased but the variations were not great. In Quebec, VOTEC is disappearing for young people at secondary level: 32 000 enrolled (full-time equivalents) in 1985, but only 7 000 in 1992; this decrease coincides with the reform of 1987 which requires more complete foundation training before entry to VOTEC.

Within VOTEC *programmes at secondary level*, two trends should be noted: the proportion of technical programmes increased at the expense of vocational programmes where they were distinct. The importance of apprenticeship, though fluctuating sometimes when political attempts revive it, is tending to decrease as compared with school training.

Thus, in Austria between 1980 and 1990 the technical school share of upper secondary pupil numbers increased from 18 to 26 per cent, that of vocational schools fell slightly from 18 to 17 per cent, and apprenticeship fell from 46 to 39 per cent. In France between 1981 and 1992, numbers in the technical pathway increased from 257 000 to 374 000, while those in vocational *lycées* fell from 844 000 to 735 000 and those in apprenticeship from 250 000 to 218 000, at the same time as training courses in vocational *lycées* and apprenticeships were made longer.

In Denmark, entry into full-time technical programmes increased most (9 per cent of the cohort in 1983, 16 per cent in 1993). In Italy, while the variations in numbers were small, entries to technical schools remained stable between 1982 and 1991 whereas they fell in vocational schools.

In the Netherlands, numbers increased in both vocational secondary education and apprenticeship, but the increase was greater in the former. In Switzerland the slight reduction in VOTEC concerns apprenticeship only, while full-time vocational schools tended to see pupil numbers increase, even though they remained very much in the minority. The situation is more difficult to assess in Germany, where entry to the dual system may be preceded by full-time vocational training. But trends in VOTEC cannot be judged by considering the secondary level alone.

At *post-secondary level* the increase appears more marked in those cases where this point is dealt with in the country reports. In France the student numbers in programmes training higher technicians increased by a factor of over 2.5 between 1980 and 1992 – much more than the overall increase in higher education – and they now make up almost 20 per cent of the total VOTEC training population. In the Netherlands, entries to higher technical education increased by 40 per cent between 1980 and 1990. In Australia, while overall student numbers in VOTEC were stagnating, those training for higher technician status increased by 11 per cent in three years. In Germany, the number of students in higher technical schools increased by over 4 per cent a year between 1984 and 1990, though this was partly due to the increase in the average duration of studies. In Quebec, in initial training, VOTEC now exists mainly at post-secondary level, but while student numbers increased slightly during the 1980s, their share with respect to general education in the colleges, which amounted to half in 1980, fell by 3 per cent.

The development of post-secondary technical education now permits VOTEC students at secondary level more easily to pursue their studies, something which was virtually impossible in most countries just a few years ago.

In France, 70 per cent of those leaving the secondary technical programme went on to higher education in 1992, as against only 44 per cent in 1980, and a far from insignificant number of holders of the vocational baccalaureate, in the order of 20 per cent, did so too. In the Netherlands, the proportion of students in higher technical education originating from vocational schools increased by a factor of 2.5 between 1980 and 1990. In Austria, 40 per cent of those obtaining technical school diplomas now go on to university. In the United Kingdom, 36 per cent of entrants to higher education do not hold the traditional General Certificate of Education at A-level, and the majority of them have completed vocational training. In Germany, as already mentioned, entrants to higher technical schools come in particular from full-time secondary technical education; conversely, the dual system does not generally give access to higher education but rather to employment, and this percentage has increased in recent years.

In particular, the development of VOTEC, and notably of technical programmes, favours increased participation in formal education by young people of the lower social categories.

Some of the country reports discuss differences according to gender. The conclusions are similar everywhere. Where girls formerly had lower participation rates, they have now caught up, except in Switzerland, though they are no longer far behind here either. Young women succeed academically better than their male counterparts and are found in greater numbers in the more academically esteemed programmes and a little less in VOTEC, except in Quebec. They are very much in the minority in apprenticeship. Their share in VOTEC is increasing however, as it is in employment, with the development of the tertiary sector. The increase often tends to be concentrated somewhat in the highest levels of training: a striking example is that of going on from vocational education to higher technical education in the Netherlands, where the proportion of young women increased fivefold between 1980 and 1990.

But while there is a tendency for greater similarity of behaviour between young men and women, with comparable participation rates in the broad categories of training, this is true only of the global situation, and the specialities chosen remain very different; women are significantly represented in only a small number of occupational fields: administration, health, social services and personal services.

4. HYPOTHESES CONCERNING THE DEVELOPMENT OF VOTEC PARTICIPATION

The conclusion which can be drawn from the above analysis is that VOTEC is part of the general movement of increasing participation in education. In order to be more precise, we can compare the situations in the different countries to see in which cases VOTEC participation increased during the period considered.

Overall, VOTEC participation increased significantly at upper secondary level only in the Netherlands. The growth of VOTEC, particularly strong in school training, coincides there with an increase in progression to higher technical education; in addition, a short-cycle vocational education programme was introduced in the same period, giving a second chance to those who had done badly in earlier schooling; they subsequently have the possibility of joining a four-year training course, without this course being devalued.

In Austria, where the VOTEC share has increased slightly, it is the technical schools which have benefited, while numbers have fallen in vocational schools and above all in apprenticeship. In Denmark, the technical and commercial programmes, which give easier access to higher education, are the ones that have developed most. In France, where VOTEC has seen its share fall and its overall numbers stagnate in secondary education, the technical pathway has developed at the expense of the vocational pathways, which have resisted only thanks to the rapid growth in preparation for the vocational baccalaureate which leads to a better level and raises hopes, often unfulfilled, of the possibility of going on to further studies. The variations have been less marked in Italy, where however the technical schools, which permit limited access to higher education, have resisted the erosion better than the vocational schools, and in Switzerland where there has been a certain decline in apprenticeship but where the vocational *maturité* has recently been introduced. In Quebec, where vocational training at secondary level does not generally permit further studies, it is tending to disappear.

The conclusion seems clear: at secondary level, VOTEC is developing through pathways which give access to post-secondary education, in particular technical education, for a significant proportion of students. The Italian report in fact points out that it is in the passage to higher education that the relative esteem attached to general and vocational training is reversed. The same is true in France.

Otherwise, VOTEC training at post-secondary level developed in almost all countries whose reports mentioned it – the one exception was Quebec, where participation in post-secondary education is very high and now constitutes virtually the first level of VOTEC and where it suffers at secondary level from the competition of pre-university training. This example may thus give reason to fear that the above conclusion could be only provisional.

This conclusion may be compared with the hypotheses formulated on VOTEC at the beginning of the study and which are recapitulated in the annex. It clearly concords with Hypothesis 4 (long pathways): "participation in VOTEC is higher, the greater the possibility given to young people to increase their level of qualification both at the secondary level and in post-secondary vocational and academic education".

One way to provide access to such VOTEC pathways leading to higher education, those we have called "technical", is to permit entry at various levels for young people from general education and vocational training. These possibilities are present in the countries cited above as having improved VOTEC participation, or in any event in the technical pathways. This confirms Hypothesis 3 (flexible pathways) as regards transfer from general education to VOTEC and from one VOTEC programme to another at a higher level. However, transfer from general education to VOTEC scarcely appears in the reports, no doubt because it is more difficult to manage.

As we have already said (cf. Figure 1B), pathways are appearing which can be entered at various levels from general education and exited at various levels, in initial training and in continuing training (cf. Hypothesis 5: segmentation of pathways within VOTEC). This, as pointed out in the Italian report expressing regret that this flexibility does not exist in Italy, frees young people from having to decide in advance "the length of the pathway to follow" according to their performance at school and the financial possibilities of their family.

Hypothesis 2 (delayed divergence of pathways) goes in a different direction and is in fact not confirmed by the observations. The three countries where the VOTEC share is greatest at secondary level – Austria, Switzerland and the Netherlands – are those where the pathways diverge already in middle school. The decline of VOTEC in secondary schools in Quebec coincides with the raising of the age and required level for entry, and this in a country where, for the majority of young people, pathways do not diverge until post-secondary level. In France, initial entry to vocational education was delayed for two years and this coincided with a fall in numbers in the corresponding programmes. An observation of the same kind is made in the Australian report.

Hypothesis 9 (*work-based pathways*) seems disputable in the light of the results obtained. Admittedly, the countries where the VOTEC share is the greatest all have a strong tradition of apprenticeship; but the apprenticeship share appears to be falling everywhere, even in these countries, perhaps because the apprenticeship system is not suited, or has not been adapted, to raising levels of qualification.

The country reports scarcely permit any conclusions on Hypotheses 1 (*new pathways*) or 6 (*preparation for broad occupational fields*) which appear contradictory if we understand Hypothesis 1 as leading to a high degree of specialisation of programmes and pathways; it can in fact be observed that in most countries the trend is rather towards the merging of programmes preparing for related occupations and that Hypothesis 6 appears more compatible with the upward extension of pathways and multi-level pathways. The Austrian report suggests choosing between the different possible meanings of Hypothesis 1: it can also be understood as meaning the diversification of training methods and institutions, as is happening in Australia and the United Kingdom.

The extension of training pathways and the establishment of multi-level pathways are credible only if there is a formal and coherent system of recognition of the qualifications, as envisaged in Hypotheses 7 and 8. The reports show that the majority of countries have such a system and that those which do not are setting one up.

Hypothesis 10 (*value of qualifications*) is also connected with the existence of this system. It refers to the labour market, whose influence is touched upon in several national reports. The French report shows that the signals coming from the labour market encourage young people to continue their studies. The Netherlands report mentions the favourable situation during the 1980s of secondary and tertiary VOTEC qualifications, which were two growth sectors, as against general educational qualifications. The Austrian report points to the recruitment conditions as being among the possible causes of the decline of apprenticeship. The Quebec report points out that the pursuit of studies by young people qualifying in technical programmes fluctuates in parallel with the unemployment rate among the holders of these qualifications. The German report shows that access to employment after VOTEC training improved between 1984 and 1990, which reduced the continuation of studies in some fields. It can thus be seen that VOTEC participation does not depend only, and perhaps not primarily, on the structures of the education system.

5. CONCLUSION

This study on trends in participation in the various programmes and pathways enables us to identify certain correspondences and reject certain hypotheses, but not to make conclusions regarding causalities.[1]

This is first of all because in certain reports the figures appear fragile. They are also very global, and analyses by occupational field, gender or social origin being rare. It would appear necessary to develop statistical studies on trends over time, with international co-ordination to ensure the comparability of data.

A more fundamental reason, however, is that training structures are not the only explanatory factor, and no doubt not the essential factor. The situation results in effect from the interaction of many actors, enumerated in the French report:

– employers, who in most countries asked for a raising of the level of training in order to respond to changes in the economy and employment, most often through the intermediary of the recruitment conditions;

– unions, who have to deal with the competition between adults and young people in the labour market;

– young people, who want their training to protect them from unemployment and provide them with satisfactory access to working life, with upward social mobility, something which appears difficult today; in OECD Member countries they are now less limited in their ambitions by the financial resources of their family than in the past;

– public authorities, who have to define education and training policy: they seek to reconcile economic demand and social demand but sometimes see VOTEC primarily as a way of stemming the rush to universities;

– training and education establishments, which have a real influence on the esteem in which different types of training are held.

It is the interaction between all these actors which has led to the situation described above. There has been a convergence between them in the direction of a general raising of the level of training, which inevitably leads to the conclusion set out above: VOTEC is developing through pathways which give access to post-secondary education. It remains to be seen under what conditions, as regards both the organisation of VOTEC and the labour market, and this conclusion will make it possible in the longer term to satisfy the needs of the economy and the aspirations of individuals, as pointed out by the Australian report. For the development of VOTEC participation is not an end in itself.

Lastly, the real decision-makers are increasingly the young people themselves, and this fact cannot be considered regrettable even if it creates difficulties for the other decision-makers. The democratisation of education, progressing in all countries – often despite a certain slowing due to economic difficulties – is leading to more information, greater freedom of choice and a fight against the sociocultural determinism which predestines some for management positions prepared for through academic training and others for operational tasks requiring vocational training.

Contrary to what is often said, young people's behaviour appears quite rational, even though it is based more on current situations than on a future which is in any case difficult to foresee with any precision. If young people do not always follow conventional wisdom that there should be more vocational training, this is probably because this view seems not to accord with job prospects. It would be useful to have additional studies on this issue.

VOTEC is faced with a twofold challenge:[2]

– to reconcile education and training, *i.e.* individual, social and economic goals;

– to ensure, in a democratic society, a balanced distribution of persons between socially unequal functions.

It should be added that these challenges have to be taken up in a context of change and uncertainty which requires both adaptability of the persons trained, in the course of their career, and adaptability of the training system itself, but the fact is that its historical roots and the multiplicity of actors makes any kind of change a long and difficult process.

Taking up the first challenge means becoming aware that the acquisition of occupational skills forms part of the constitution of a personal identity and that the economic goals have to be present right throughout the education process, but that conversely they cannot be pursued on their own without regard to forming complete and well-developed personalities. All this means that there should not be complete separation between general education and vocational training, and that as far as possible general education should continue during vocational training.

Another response to the requirement of adaptability lies in continuing training, throughout working life, with one of the aims of initial training being to favour "learning to learn". It is therefore a matter of thinking in global terms of lifelong training, of a continuum between initial and continuing education and training.

As regards the second challenge, part of the solution concerning training structures lies in the definition of multi-level pathways (Figure 1B), finally leading to the training of "professionals" (in the English sense of the term) but also supplying the whole of the economic fabric, including what are now considered to be operative occupations.[3]

The transformation of training structures thus makes sense only in interaction with changes in the organisation of work in enterprises, and the quality and number of jobs available.

NOTES

1. See David Raffe's text study in the final chapter.
2. C. Pair, "The changing role of vocational and technical education and training: context, actors, challenges", November 1994.
3. B. Lutz (1994), "The difficult rediscovery of professionalism", *Apprenticeship: Which Way Forward,* OECD, Paris.

Annex

WORKING HYPOTHESES

FACTORS EXPLAINING PARTICIPATION IN VOTEC

Hypothesis 1: diversification of programmes and pathways. Participation in VOTEC is higher when the number and diversity of possible programmes and pathways increase.

Hypothesis 2: delayed divergence of pathways. Participation in VOTEC is higher, the later pathways diverge (delayed provision/starting point of VOTEC programmes).

Hypothesis 3: flexible pathways. Participation in VOTEC is higher, the greater the opportunities for transfer:

- from VOTEC to general education;
- from general education to VOTEC;
- among programmes and pathways within VOTEC.

Hypothesis 4: long pathways. Participation in VOTEC is higher, the greater the possibility given to young people to increase their level of qualification both at the secondary level and in post-secondary vocational and academic education.

Hypothesis 5: segmentation of pathways within VOTEC. Participation in VOTEC is higher when different programmes and pathways provide exit points at different levels of recognised qualification.

Hypothesis 6: preparation for broad occupational fields. Participation in VOTEC is higher, the wider the range of occupations to which any vocational programme may lead.

Hypothesis 7: formally recognised qualifications. Participation in VOTEC is higher when students/apprentices have access to a widely recognised certification.

Hypothesis 8: one coherent national system of qualifications. Participation in VOTEC increases if all general and vocational certificates are part of one and the same national system of certification.

Hypothesis 9: work-based pathways. Participation in VOTEC is higher if pathways lead into internal labour markets.

Hypothesis 10: value of qualification. Participation in VOTEC depends on the value of obtained qualifications in the labour market.

2

AUSTRALIA

by

Department of Employment, Education and Training (DEET), Canberra*

1. INTRODUCTION

Australia's vocational education and training system is, in fact, a composite of eight state and territory systems, so that any description of a national system involves a certain abstraction of general patterns from a varied reality (Box 1). However, to a degree that is unusual in countries with federal constitutions, Australia in recent years has been endeavouring to develop consistency between practices in the eight states and territories, in order to reduce artificial distortions in national markets for goods and services, and to improve the country's international competitiveness.

The term VOTEC, used throughout this chapter, although not in general use in Australia, corresponds with current Australian usage for vocational education and training (VET), which encompasses vocational courses in upper secondary schooling, public, industry, enterprise, commercial and community education providers. "TAFE" is an Australian acronym for Technical and Further Education, the government-funded public providers of VOTEC. In Australia, "further education" is understood to encompass adult education.

This chapter explores patterns of participation in terms of programmes and pathways. Young people have been defined here as those undergoing initial VOTEC for entry into the workforce, and the age cohorts for 15-24 have been used. Participation patterns are examined on a national basis over a 15-20-year period.

---

* The Department was renamed the Department of Employment, Education, Training and Youth Affairs (DEETYA) after the election of a new federal government in March 1996. Some of the reforms to vocational education and training described in this chapter have been modified in the past two years, and new programmes have been launched. However, the changes are essentially consistent with the policy objectives and operating principles outlined here.

Box 1. **States' systems of vocational education and training**

Each of the four States (New South Wales, Victoria, Tasmania and the ACT) has 13 years of schooling, with a kindergarten or pre-school year, six years of primary and six years of high school. In Tasmania and the ACT, high schools operate through Years 7-10, with the two post-compulsory years (Years 11 and 12) being provided by secondary senior colleges, except in the case of a few private schools. The ACT and Tasmania senior colleges offer considerable flexibility in the programming of general and vocational courses. ACT schools also offer a mix of university and non-university entrance courses. In the ACT, the Technical and Further Education (TAFE) has a single, multi-campus Canberra Institute of Technology, with a strong emphasis on ASF Levels 4-5 qualifications. The Tasmanian TAFE colleges are relatively consolidated, but they cover a more typical mix of programmes.

Two States (South Australian and the Northern Territory) have a kindergarten or pre-school year which the remaining two States (Queensland and Western Australia) generally do not offer. These four jurisdictions have seven years of primary and five years of secondary school. Victoria, the Northern Territory, Western Australia and Queensland have a few senior colleges, and a private one operates successfully in South Australia. Otherwise, schools in Victoria, the Northern Territory, Western Australia, Queensland and South Australia offer conventional Year 8-12 high schools (public and private) with a mix of general and vocational programmes. Vocational programmes are increasing in all cases. In South Australia, vocational programmes are a small proportion of upper secondary provision. In New South Wales, South Australia, Queensland and the Northern Territory, TAFE colleges have been consolidated into a few large institutes, although in New South Wales, institutes are decentralised administrative units. Creation of institutes has not usually involved physical consolidation. Victoria and Western Australia still have a relatively large number of TAFE colleges.

New South Wales post-compulsory education is being organised into four "pathways". The four streams are a general university-preparation stream, a vocational school-based stream, a Year 12 school certificate programme delivered by TAFE, and a work-based pathway which articulates into vocational courses but does not provide a Year 12 certificate. Queensland, New South Wales, Western Australia and Tasmania are developing dual recognition arrangements for TAFE courses delivered to school students. The Tasmanian Certificate of Education (Year 12) offers a choice of 271 syllabi, of which only 41 are for university entrance; the rest have a VOTEC orientation.

This national emphasis is necessary, but major differences in pathways and patterns of participation between states and territories are indicated where appropriate.

Three critical points in time – 1989, 1992 and 2001 – have been chosen to explore changes in participation with reference to longer-trend data for major developments. The points chosen represent a phase in the development of VOTEC. Each point will be examined in terms of the changing programmes, pathways and patterns of participation. The "target scenario" for the year 2001, developed in the Finn report (Finn, 1991) to illustrate the effects of participation and outcome targets recommended in that report, will provide a future perspective.

The publication of the Australian Committee on Technical and Further Education report, TAFE *in Australia* (Kangan, 1974 and 1975) (discussed in Section 2 below), made 1974 a year of major significance in the development of the Australian VOTEC system, and so it is a convenient starting point for our 20-year perspective. The Kangan report initiated substantial federal funding for VOTEC and saw a degree of national consistency develop around the concept of a tertiary TAFE system. In 1985, the *Report of the Committee of Inquiry into Labour Market Programs* (Kirby, 1985*a*) prepared a further shift of emphasis in the consolidation of labour market programmes.

After the Kangan and Kirby reports, the next major period of change in VOTEC developed as from 1989, the first "critical" year, with the first of two special national ministerial conferences. These two conferences of federal, state and territory ministers defined the fundamentals of what has become known as the national training reform agenda. The conferences endorsed the basic issues of previous work done in government advisory bodies and leading private sector peak councils, such as the Australian Council of Trade Unions (ACTU), the former Confederation of Australian Industry (now the Australian Confederation of Commerce and Industry) and the employer and employee organisations of the metal industry (Australian Council of Trade Unions, 1987; BCA, 1990; Confederation of Australian Industry, 1991). The national training reform agenda is discussed in Section 3 below.

Since 1989, then, there has been a consistently vigorous reform of VOTEC in Australia. The 1991 Australian Education Council Review Committee report on *Young People's Participation in Post-compulsory Education and Training* (Finn, 1991) emphasized the importance of VOTEC and recognised its increasing convergence with general education. Over the last decade, the role of young people in education and training has grown significantly, owing largely to an increase in participation in schools and higher education; but teenage participation in VOTEC, including TAFE colleges, remained fairly constant over the same period (see Section 3). The Finn report used this concept of pathways to describe "the processes associated with movement from compulsory education, through post-compulsory education and training, and between education, training and employment" (Finn, 1991, Vol. 1, p. 13).

The second "critical" year, 1992, saw the Employment and Skills Formation Council's Carmichael report on *The Australian Vocational Certificate Training System* (Carmichael, 1992) and the Mayer committee report on *Putting General Education to Work: The Key Competencies Report* (Mayer, 1992). The Carmichael report specified a national framework for a new integrated, entry-level training system, the Australian Vocational Certificate Training System (AVCTS). In November 1990, federal, state and territory ministers had agreed in principle to pursue that objective, and in June 1992 a joint meeting of the Australian Education Council and the Ministers of Vocational Education, Employment and Training agreed to "a phased implementation approach placing heavy reliance on pilots and further development of detailed implementation arrangements in further consultation with relevant groups" (AEC and MOVEET, 1992).

The AVTS (Austalian Vocational Training System), as the AVCTS was later renamed, is intended to greatly increase the amount of recognised vocational education and training done in Australia, and to focus such training upon increased effectiveness at work. The AVTS embodies the concept of a broad range of pathways combining education, training and work placement. All pathways not proceeding to higher education provide credit for prior learning and formally link different levels of courses or training programmes. The AVTS seeks to ensure that virtually all school-leavers obtained structured training and gained formally recognised qualifications for work. Following the evaluation of extensive pilot schemes, ministers decided in 1996 to implement the AVTS. The AVTS and other reforms are considered in Section 4.

2. A BRIEF HISTORY OF VOTEC IN AUSTRALIA UP TO 1989

Australian historians generally accord the Ballarat School of Mines, which was established in 1871, the honour of being Australia's first technical college. By 1900, technical colleges or mechanics institutes had been established in all the country's major cities. They were originally local community-based bodies in which 19th century colonial and 20th century state governments were rather slow to take interest. Despite this, technical colleges played an important role in the education of the Australian workforce, and several of them have evolved into universities (Murray-Smith, 1971). VOTEC has gradually developed a stronger sectoral identity since World War II. Most of the progress has occurred since the 1974 Kangan report, which led to significantly increased federal funding for VOTEC.

The 1950s and 1960s

The development of VOTEC was linked with post-war industrialisation, some-times construed rather narrowly as "the training of persons for engagement in trades, technical occupations or agricultural or other rural occupations" (Fraser, 1972, p. 4). World War II and post-war industrialisation provided a considerable stimulus, but the immediate post-war years also saw a large rise in the birth rate and this created severe stresses upon the primary and secondary education structures. VOTEC funding was constrained because the states and territories struggled to meet the financial responsibilities for expanding primary and secondary, as well as higher, education.

During the 1950s and 1960s the labour market for unskilled or semi-skilled workers was usually quite buoyant. Less than a third of young people completed secondary education, since the majority entered the labour force and received training on the job in what were largely unskilled or semi-skilled occupations. Skilled labour was provided through an apprenticeship system which targeted a narrow band of occupations, and was substantially supplemented by immigration. However, the 1950s saw a large expansion in white-collar employment, and entry to these occupations required a secondary education. This led to some increase in the number of young people completing secondary education as a means of entering these vocations.

VOTEC was regarded as each state's responsibility and they thus had the task of financing the institutions. These developed their own individual structures which reflected the different social, economic, demographic, geographic and political characteristics of each state. However, while interest in technical education expanded rapidly, the financing of institutions failed to keep pace. Funds tended to be diverted towards the university sector, which expanded considerably. The financial burden of this growth therefore led the states to seek Commonwealth assistance for technical education.

The 1960s saw the development of a more vocational type of higher education institution, modelled on other institutes of technology in several states. Following pressure from many professional groups seeking more status, in 1966 the first colleges of advanced education (CAEs) were formed to become "diploma colleges". The colleges of advanced education were established to provide practical courses to students with appropriate aptitudes. A number developed from teachers' colleges, which were single-purpose bodies with a similar status and role. Diploma programmes, such as commerce, were transferred from the technical colleges and some upgraded to degrees awarded by institutes of technology and CAEs.

Despite this appropriation of diploma courses, the rest of VOTEC saw a rapid growth in enrolments of over 1 per cent between 1953 and 1962 (Barcan, 1981, p. 337). This pace of growth continued during the 1960s, and the strain upon state governments to fund such growth was readily apparent. Conditions in technical colleges were quite poor compared to the standard of facilities and working conditions available in the universities. Libraries were old and often not open because of lack of staff, and buildings were overcrowded and run-down. The constraints on state funding led a number of state governments again to approach the Commonwealth for assistance for technical colleges.

In 1964, the Commonwealth government made available special-purpose grants to the states for the provision of buildings and non-consumable equipment for VOTEC. Funding was provided to the states on the grounds that they agreed to maintain their current levels of expenditure on VOTEC. The result of this action was that total capital expenditure more than doubled and an impetus was given to the states to increase their own spending. States were more able to plan the provision of facilities to meet the areas of greatest need and to supply special training facilities for emergent occupations.

In spite of the expansion of construction programmes for technical colleges, dissatisfaction about funding of VOTEC amongst students, parents and teachers arose during the late 1960s. Teacher associations lobbied government and were successful in making education an issue at federal level. The dissatisfaction was not confined to VOTEC but was driven by schools and universities. Australia was reproved by an OECD review in 1968 as having education and training arrangements based on "obsolete notions of an industrial economy requiring few professional and trade workers and a large number of semi-skilled workers". In that environment, VOTEC lobbies tended to be less effective than school and higher education lobbies.

The 1970s

In 1970, a report by an *Australian Tripartite Mission to Study Methods of Training of Skilled Workers in Europe* tried to bring more attention to the needs of VOTEC. The mission investigated methods of training skilled workers in Europe and noted that Australia could no longer rely upon migration to overcome skills shortages. Steps were recommended to update methods of training: they should be co-ordinated nationally, with uniformity in standards and common acceptance of qualifications. The report seemed to be largely ignored, but two decades later similar recommendations generated a strong national response.

In the run-up to the 1972 election, the Labour opposition had focused upon education as a means of addressing many inequalities which were apparent in society. Immediately upon winning office, the Labour Party quickly established advisory commissions for pre-schooling and for primary and secondary and higher education. A year of intense lobbying by teacher associations saw an inquiry established to look into conditions within VOTEC. The new government set up the Australian Committee on Technical and Further Education led by Myer Kangan, Deputy Secretary of the Department of Labour and Immigration in 1973. The

Committee essentially picked up the loose ends of education not covered by the other enquiries.

In 1974, each state and territory had a structure of technical colleges that was the main agency for the provision of vocational TAFE programmes to school-leavers and existing workers (by part-time study), and adult education for personal enrichment and development (Department of Education, 1976, p. 96). There were 836 institutions providing TAFE in six states. Of these, 167 were classified as principal institutions, while the remaining 669 were branches, annexes or centres. The average enrolment of the principal institutions was 2 500, with the others averaging 200. The larger institutions provided a full range of TAFE courses, whereas the smaller institutions tended to be more restricted, with an emphasis upon specialised facilities. These institutions provided about 2 300 courses ranging in length from 25 to 4 750 hours of study. The courses were established according to six academic streams covering ten major fields of study (see Box 2). There was a large division between the students in adult education and the other

---

Box 2.   **Courses and fields of study in TAFE (1974)**

Six academic streams:

- Academic Stream 1 (Professional) – courses which lead to professional status or which enable professionals to update or specialise.
- Academic Stream 2 (Para-professional) – courses which lead to middle level or technician occupations.
- Academic Stream 3 (Trades) – all apprenticeship courses and post-apprenticeship courses not covered in Stream 2.
- Academic Stream 4 (Other skilled) – all other skilled and vocational courses not included in Stream 3.
- Academic Stream 5 (Preparatory) – all courses which prepare the way for further study, including matriculation and diploma entrance courses, remedial courses and vocational courses not included elsewhere.
- Academic Stream 6 (Adult education) – all courses in home handicrafts, hobbies, self-expression and cultural appreciation.

Fields of study were divided into ten major specialisations: applied science, art and design, building industry, business studies, engineering, rural and horticultural, music, paramedical services, services and miscellaneous, general studies.

streams which were referred to as "technical education". As adult education consisted predominantly of home handicrafts, hobbies, self-expression and cultural appreciation it was regarded as having little or no direct vocational application and thus not a professionally relevant avenue of education.

Not only was there a great diversity of courses available but the duration of such courses also varied widely. Professional-stream courses had an average duration of 2 870 hours, while paraprofessional courses were between 1 200 and 1 500 hours in duration or approximately half that of a professional course. A trade course was shorter again, being almost a third in length to that of a professional course. The nature and duration of a course was a significant factor in the availability of full-time study. Generally, only the professional courses were available on such a basis, but increasingly, paraprofessional courses were becoming available for full-time study. Most students, however, attended on a part-time basis. For the trade courses, apprentices attended for one day per week for approximately three years. The paraprofessional courses available on a part-time basis were four years in duration, allowing for full- or part-time work combinations (see Section 3).

Although the apprenticeship system enjoyed general support in principle, there was considerable criticism of its operation and effectiveness. In 1973, the National Apprenticeship Assistance Scheme, which provided assistance to employers, was established. The scheme saw the intake for apprentices rise by over 29 per cent in 1973/74, but in 1975/76, numbers fell by over 17 per cent (Department of Education, 1976, p. 108). There was concern over the difficulties experienced by small and medium firms in providing satisfactory practical training for apprentices and about their ability to absorb rising costs despite Commonwealth subsidies.

Some groups expressed their disquiet over the narrowness and task-specific orientation of many of the TAFE courses. Given the low funding and the poor level of equipment and facilities, curriculum development was often considered inadequate. The Kangan report noted briefly criticisms by some employers that the secondary education system pays too little attention to preparing young people for vocational education. The committee noted that employers have a substantial role in the training of their employees, but a large section of the labour force is employed in small and medium businesses, many of which did not have the facilities to provide adequate training. The committee argued that the full-time option for study should be expanded, without reducing part-time courses. The response of the Kangan report was to suggest that the most important development needed in the training of apprentices was a substantial period of full-time attendance at a technical college. This implied a review of the current indenture system, which was seen as increasingly irrelevant, and the need for greater financial support for young people undertaking such full-time study.

The Kangan report gave a new impetus to the formation of a national institutional structure and the recognition of TAFE as a sector of education, and made 1974 a seminal year in the development of vocational education and training in Australia. The report not only led to significantly increased financial support for technical education by the Commonwealth, it gave VOTEC a national identity and purpose such as that of TAFE. The report also argued that the best way for TAFE to meet industry's manpower needs was to focus on meeting the needs of people as individuals. Ideas and concepts about lifelong learning and re-entry into education for adults were concepts adopted from the International Labour Office, UNESCO and the OECD. The idea of broadening access to TAFE received unprecedented attention.

While the Kangan report was very important, its significance cannot be separated from reforms in other education sectors during the early 1970s. The report signalled that the Commonwealth had a role to play in all sectors of education, which was consistent with the approach of the government. The schools sector saw a very large increase in federal funding, especially for private schools, on the basis of the 1973 report by the Interim Committee of the Australian Schools Commission, known as the Karmel report. In terms of higher education, the Commonwealth substantially took over public funding from the states in 1972. Importantly, higher education tuition fees were abolished and the scholarship system replaced with allowances based upon a means test rather than academic merit.

The reduction of financial barriers and the expansion of full-time courses saw immediate results. TAFE enrolments increased from 400 700 in 1973 to 671 013 in 1975, compared to a small increase for higher education. The Kangan report's recommendation that TAFE tuition fees be abolished was a factor in this growth. TAFE continued to enjoy a rise in expenditure, owing to its direct involvement with industrial development. TAFE was seen as a means of increasing labour force skills and picking up the casualties from the growth in unemployment. It was because of this direct economic involvement that TAFE avoided the cuts, rationalisation and amalgamations and funding ceilings that were experienced by schools and universities.

Inquiries into post-compulsory education were held in all states, defining a role for TAFE by examining the relationship between all sectors of education. Following this, those states which had not already done so formed a separate department to administer the TAFE system. Commonwealth grants assisted TAFE colleges to become more financially and operationally independent. The Commonwealth expectation that the states would administer federal programmes through the TAFE system was to be an ongoing source of tension between the levels of government.

The 1980s

The 1980s saw a further change in direction for TAFE. Following the 1983 election, when the Labour Party was returned to federal government, economic policies shifted significantly, with great repercussions for TAFE. New economic policies which sought to enhance industrial competitiveness and productivity with reduced public spending had the support of both the business community and the union movement. Higher education was seen as a vital component producing graduates with research skills geared to the needs of industry, and TAFE was seen as a vehicle for improving skill levels within the labour force.

The structural problem of youth unemployment and the cyclical skill-shortage aftermath of the 1982/83 recession led the Commonwealth, state and territory governments to pay increasing attention to vocational education and training. A range of labour market programmes such as the Transition from School-to-Work Program, the Community Youth Support Scheme and the Youth Training Program were adopted in quick succession. Federal policy maintained a strong employment focus concentrated upon short, intensive courses that provided a narrow range of vocationally specific skills. The TAFE system, which administered the training component of these programmes, saw its function as delivering a broad vocational education package providing skills and knowledge that enable mobility between enterprises in a given occupation.

The tension that existed between the Commonwealth (principally through the then Department of Employment and Industrial Relations) and the states and territories was exacerbated as TAFE argued that it largely subsidised these programmes. As the respective governments took an interest in the scope and the quality of training, the lack of data and research on training beyond the formal education system and apprenticeship became apparent. In late 1983, a Committee of Inquiry into Labour Market Programs, chaired by Peter Kirby, was established to develop a coherent framework for government intervention in the form of labour market programmes.

The Kirby report signalled a recognition of the inadequacies of the labour market programmes of the early 1980s which had neglected the role of training. The need for reform had come through a dramatic decline in pathway opportunities for young people. Kirby noted that at one time a variety of exit points had existed for secondary school at Years 10, 11 and 12, with each giving access to reasonable jobs or post-secondary courses but that "this situation has changed dramatically" (Kirby, 1985a, p. 20). He also noted that the committee had estimated that "up to 100 000 young Australians still seek to enter the labour market each year without completing a full secondary education and with no substantial vocational preparation" (p. 21).

Substantial public funds through wage subsidies and off-the-job training had provided young apprentices with an alternative to higher education. Yet the apprenticeship system still catered for a small number of young men and far fewer women, in a limited number of occupations. Table 1 provides data on participation in apprenticeships. Part of the solution was to ensure that young people had a sufficiently high level of basic education, training and work experience, and this meant raising the participation and retention rates within secondary and post-secondary education. It was becoming apparent that a new training system for the young which combined continued education off the job with work experience was necessary.

The apprenticeship system has been a highly legislated environment where, in most cases, the only legal means of entry into trades and crafts is the completion of an apprenticeship. The systems of apprenticeship have varied from state to state, since they are governed by state legislation and industrial awards. However, it is a customary arrangement that the apprentice enters a binding contract for an average period of four years, which can be extended to five, with an employer who will teach him a trade. Approximately 90 per cent of total training received by apprentices is on the job (Department of Employment, Education and Training, 1992, p. 3).

As part of the contract, apprentices attend courses, usually provided through a TAFE college, that are designed to teach the theoretical components of training and that cover the practical application of theory. Course work usually occupies about 10 per cent of apprentices' total time in training, which was and is commonly carried out in three stages over the first three years of the apprenticeship. Attendance at the college is usually compulsory and is arranged through release from an employer either for one day per week or through block-release arrangements lasting up to seven weeks at a time. The terms of an apprenticeship may be reduced, in which case it usually occurs through pre-employment training

Table 1. **Apprenticeships completed, 1972-73 to 1992-93**

1972-73	1973-74	1974-75	1975-76	1976-77	1977-78	1978-79	1979-80	1980-81	1981-82
22 067	21 160	27 186	25 766	29 268	32 902	30 632	30 814	34 349	32 014

1983-84	1984-85	1985-86	1986-87	1987-88	1988-89	1989-90	1990-91	1991-92	1992-93
35 102	36 537	38 156	26 532	29 916	30 436	32 148	32 202	36 066	39 681

Source: DIER/COSTAC, *Apprenticeship Statistics, 1972-73 to 1981-82.*
DEET/COSTAC, *Apprenticeship Statistics, 1983-84 to 1992-93.*

provided by TAFE colleges. This training is offered to young people who are not apprenticed but wish to commence trade training. The courses usually cover one or two stages of the technical education undertaken by apprentices.

Labour market programmes had failed to recognise the place of structured training for young people. They had been designed as counter-cyclical employment-promotion measures, not as stable long-term arrangements for more extensive provision of entry-level training. The Kirby report of 1985 proposed the introduction of the Australian Traineeship System (ATS) to meet the need for structural reforms in training for young people. Like the apprenticeship system, the traineeship provides a combination of on- and off-the-job training for those entering the workplace.

The Kangan committee believed there should be more options combining education and work as the means for enhancing prospects for individuals. The introduction of the ATS in 1985 was a notable advance in terms of extending the VOTEC system to certain industries and occupations not previously involved in the apprenticeship system, such as retail and administration/clerical occupations. The ATS borrowed the strengths of the apprenticeship system, without the detailed legislation. Arguably, in the ATS scheme, periods of work and study are more co-ordinated than they have been in most apprenticeships. Off-the-job ATS training, such as the apprenticeship system, was to be provided through the TAFE structure, combining generic and occupationally-specific skill development.

The ATS traineeships seek to give the trainee closely-linked on- and off-the-job training which is relevant to industry needs, thus improving their long-term employment prospects, especially those of the disadvantaged. Traineeships are of at least 12 months' duration with a minimum of 13 weeks' off-the-job training spread throughout the year in a TAFE college or another approved training centre. In general, people up to 19 years old are eligible to participate, with those who left school before completion of Year 12 being given preference. On successful completion of the traineeship, an Australian Traineeship System certificate is awarded by the state training authority, which attests to the training undertaken and the skills acquired. The certificate provides the trainee with documented qualifications for future employment which are recognised widely by employers and industry. It is also a basis to further education and training opportunities. The training is being anchored in the competency-based approach to learning. Figure 1 provides data on ATS commencements by financial year since the scheme started in 1985/86. Although the scheme was intended to grow to around 75 000 participants, it has not exceeded 17 000 annual commencements.

In TAFE during this period, the trades structure via the apprenticeship system attracted nearly a quarter of the enrolments but received more than two-fifths of the total teaching effort. The 1980s had seen some big changes to the appren-

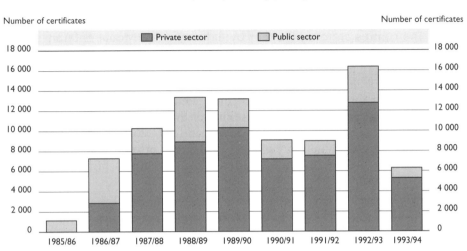

◆ Figure 1. **Australian traineeship system**
Number of certificates by fiscal year

Source: DEET.

ticeship structure and there was growing pressure for more. Changes were made to the duration of the apprenticeship, to wages and conditions, and to the intro-duction of compulsory attendance at TAFE during working hours. TAFE authorities generally play the major role in the development and review of trade-course curricula, although in most cases state training authorities have powers to monitor and approve course content. Generally, TAFE and training authorities co-operate in the development of formal courses in trade theory.

Apprenticeships are regulated by state and territory authorities. The Commonwealth's interest in apprenticeships has stemmed from the concern over the impact of skilled labour upon the state of the economy. The Commonwealth continues to assist in the financing of TAFE through supplementary funding of TAFE institutions and through assistance. A range of aids to apprenticeship was available through the Commonwealth Rebate for Apprentice Full-time Training scheme. Employers were entitled to a series of financial incentives, and a mea-sure of financial assistance is available to apprentices.

Structured workplace-learning in Australia has also improved considerably since the early 1980s. Since that time, the Commonwealth has developed a range of approaches to improve the level of training beyond the institutions of TAFE. The assistance has come through the following programmes:

- *Skill centres* established in 1987-88 have been well accepted by industry. The centres are owned either by industry or individual enterprises, and have met government standards in terms of training curriculum and delivery requirements. The federal government has encouraged industry and individual firms to develop their own training centres through one-off grants of up to 50 per cent of their establishment costs. The ongoing operating costs are the responsibility of the management group. Many of the centres provide training in advanced technology to enable Australian workers to be trained in the latest local and overseas trends and developments in their industry. The federal government has provided funds for over 84 skill centres in 23 industries.

- *Group training* arrangements aim to increase structured training opportunities for apprentices and trainees. They achieve this primarily through rotation with a range of host employers; many of these are small companies that do not have the capacity to recruit and train apprentices and trainees in their own right.

Industry involvement has been instrumental in the restructuring of VOTEC, and a number of avenues were developed as from the mid-1980s. Industry was encouraged to take a more active role in the development of VOTEC through a number of key fora. Employer and industry involvement in training had traditionally been limited to the provision of unstructured and informal training in the workplace. Industry has been able to participate through a number of tripartite bodies, involving union and both federal and state representation, and to collaborate in the reform process.

In 1986, all TAFE courses underwent a reclassification. The two-dimensional classification of streams and fields were retained, with the system being streamlined into four major categories consisting of 19 sub-categories. The structure finally adopted is summarised in Box 3. The educational prerequisite for TAFE courses depended largely upon the particular stream. For the trades courses, the educational prerequisite was Year 10 of secondary school, and in many instances lower standards were specified. For paraprofessional courses, a minimum of ten years' education was required for many, while a fifth of such courses required completion of eleven years of education. Only professional courses had a requirement of 12 years of general education. Over a third of trades courses and more than three-quarters of other skills courses had no special entry requirement.

A range of qualifications were available according to the stream undertaken. Reforms to the system of classification were preceded by changes to the structure of nomenclature. Taken together, these changes were important steps towards

Box 3. **Streams, fields of study and award structure in TAFE (1986)**

Streams

- Stream 1000 – Courses for recreational, leisure and personal enrichment
- Stream 2000 – Courses for entry to employment or further education

The stream is composed of two sub-streams:

        2100 – Basic education and employment skills

        2200 – Entry to employment or further education

- Stream 3000 – Initial vocational courses:

        3100 – Operatives (level and range of skills less than is normally required for a tradesperson, *i.e.* plant and machine operators)

        3222 – Skilled

        3300 – Trade technician/trade supervisory or equivalent

        3400 – Para-professional technician

        3500 – Para-professional higher technician

        3600 – Provides initial education and training at a higher level than paraprofessional courses and includes courses which lead to employment in vocations comparable to those entered by graduates of tertiary diploma courses

- Stream 4000 – Courses subsequent to an initial vocational course:

        4100 – Operational level

        4200 – Skilled level

        4300 – Trade technician/trade supervisory or equivalent

        4400 – Para-professional technician

        4500 – Para-professional higher technician or higher

Fields of study

Land and marine resources, animal husbandry; architecture, building; arts, humanities and social services; business, administration, economics; education; engineering, surveying; health, community services; law, legal studies; science; veterinary science, animal care; services, hospitality, transportation; multi-field education.

Award structure

- Stream 3600   Diploma
- Stream 3500/3400 Associate diploma

(continued on next page)

(continued)

- Stream 3300   Advanced certificate
- Stream 3200   Certificate
- Stream 3100/2000 Certificate
- Stream 1000   Statement of attainment
- Stream 4000   Endorsement of awards or statement of attainment

the development of a truly national structure for TAFE. The changes to the nomenclature structure were agreed in 1984 and were adopted into the new course structure. The new nomenclature provided for awards for courses assigned on the basis of their stream classification (Box 3). The traditional trade streams offered trade and post-trade certificates. In 1987, a policy change associated with the linking of TAFE and university awards was the lifting of entry-level qualifications required for technician courses from Year 10 to Year 12. This simple change gave a major further impetus to increasing Year 12 retention. At the upper level were the diploma awards for professionals. The paraprofessional stream, a relatively new stream, offered associate diplomas for the first time in 1973 and also awarded certificates and advanced certificates.

In terms of distribution of enrolments in 1986, there were 430 000 people enrolled in TAFE classes across Australia. Less than 1 per cent were enrolled in the professional stream, while the largest category was paraprofessionals with 27 per cent enrolments. Trades and related streams had a quarter of the enrolments, while just over 10 per cent were undertaking preparatory courses. Nineteen per cent of enrolments were undertaking adult education. The vast majority of enrolments were on a part-time basis. Table 2 provides data on part-time and full-time enrolments by male and female TAFE students between 1986 and 1992. The paraprofessional stream in the TAFE system, designed for technicians, semi-professional or middle-level occupations, had experienced the most rapid growth during the post-war era as a result of technological developments and the growth of community services: in 1992 it accounted for 14 per cent of enrolments in TAFE, higher technicians in particular.

Summary

Most VOTEC has been, and still is, provided primarily through publicly funded and nationally recognised TAFE colleges. In addition, a large amount of occupational training occurred non-formally or on the job within industry, but for

Table 2. **TAFE students by sex and type of enrolment, 1986-92**

	Full-time females	Full-time males	Part-time females	Part-time males	Full-time females (%)	Full-time males (%)
1986	34 930	40 162	746 486	557 133	4.47	6.72
1987	38 243	43 730	772 038	576 914	4.72	7.05
1988	45 118	47 422	793 877	596 397	5.38	7.37
1989	42 673	44 409	815 582	602 753	4.97	6.86
1990	42 159	41 565	766 034	639 568	5.22	6.10
1991	48 688	50 699	646 234	581 175	7.01	8.02
1992[1]	62 461	62 644	710 290	664 107	8.08	8.62

1.   1992 data excludes bulk enrolments.
Source: NCVER, *Selected TAFE Statistics, 1991, 1992.*

many years such training received little or no official recognition or certification. Recently, however, there has been a great push to develop structured work-based training for operatives, including in many industries not involved in the traditional apprenticeship structure. Industry has become more involved in the development and provision of training, and the number of private-sector and community education providers has expanded gradually. The proposed introduction of the new Australian Vocational Training System (AVTS) (discussed in Section 4) is intended to bring together institutional (school and TAFE) and work-based elements in a nationally recognised and certified system.

The historical development of VOTEC is linked to developments in schools and higher education, since VOTEC has often been required to fill the many education and training gaps not provided by these two sectors. Over the past 20 years, debate has focused upon three major themes:

- *The primary goals and focus of* VOTEC: two views are often placed in opposition. One view has been that it should meet the needs of industry for a skilled and flexible labour force. Another view has been that VOTEC must serve the needs of individuals seeking to fulfil personal potential and to lead constructive, productive lives. The Kangan report saw that these views are complementary, with industry benefiting from a system that valued individual clients.

- *Responsibility for funding of the* VOTEC *system*: the Commonwealth has developed an increasing role in VOTEC policy and practice through federal funding, although education and training is a state and territory responsibility under the Commonwealth constitution. This has resulted in some tensions between levels of government. Nevertheless, the degree of intergovernmental co-operation that has developed in this field in Australia is

43

very unusual in countries with a federal system, with the possible exception of Germany. Australia's progress is the more notable because the federal government lagged behind the United States and Canada in introducing substantial federal funding.

— *The assumptions and practices of* VOTEC: traditionally, there has been a clear division between school, vocational and higher education. These barriers remain strongly entrenched, despite efforts to encourage more cross-sectoral co-operation. The convergence of general and vocational education has been advocated in the Finn, Carmichael and Mayer reports in the 1990s.

VOTEC, as a sector of education, has grown in size and importance since federal, state and territory governments have seen it as playing a major role in social and economic change. Throughout the 1950s and 1960s, VOTEC attracted very little attention. It was under-valued, under-resourced and had a weak identity. In the 1970s, the situation changed as VOTEC developed into a recognised TAFE system. Training in the workplace other than through apprenticeships was largely ad hoc and firm-specific, and in many industries this continues.

In the late 1980s and early 1990s, the TAFE system once more attracted particular attention, it being seen as having a critical role in facilitating the process of micro-economic reform. The national training reform agenda, which is discussed in Section 3, is premised upon co-operation, between federal, state and territory governments and between the industrial parties (employers and unions). It is intended to develop a more diverse and responsive national vocational education and training system. The reforms focused on the implementation of a competency-based training system, the complete reform of entry-level training arrangements, and national recognition arrangements.

In 1987, the Australian Council of Trade Unions (ACTU) report, *Australia Reconstructed* (Australian Council of Trade Unions, 1987), and a federal report on *Skills for Australia* (Dawkins and Holding, 1987) both argued that the development of a highly skilled and flexible workforce, capable of working in a variety of organisational settings and with the latest technology, was the linchpin in achieving the greater productivity, efficiency and international competitiveness required in industry. The ACTU report focused on deficiencies in the national skills base, noting that international competitiveness depended upon the ability to exploit up-to-date knowledge and processes. The low proportion of young people engaged in post-compulsory education, and the growing pool of unemployed youth, were targeted as major problems to achieving these ends, although upgrading the skills of the existing workforce remains a problem without comprehensive solutions. These reports contributed to creating the environment for the national training reform agenda.

3.   THE NATIONAL TRAINING REFORM AGENDA AND THE CHANGING STRUCTURE AND PATTERNS OF PARTICIPATION IN VOTEC

Section 2 reviewed the development of policy related to VOTEC in Australia up to 1989. This section discusses the national training reform agenda and changing patterns of participation in VOTEC by young Australians in terms of progress and pathways, relating VOTEC where appropriate to general education in schools and universities.

In Section 1 it was mentioned that three critical points in time – 1989, 1992 and 2001 – have been chosen to explore changes in participation with reference to longer-trend data for major developments. In this section, participation trends over several years and the pathways and patterns of participation in 1989 will set the scene for a review of the training reform agenda. In Section 4, pathways and patterns of participation in 1992 are described, to define the context within which the AVTS was proposed in a report published in 1992. The "target scenario" for the year 2001 developed in the Finn Report illustrates the effects of participation and outcome targets recommended in that report. The 2001 "target scenario" provides a future perspective on the participation patterns for 1989 and 1992.

Participation trends: 1989

Total participation by young people in upper secondary, VOTEC and higher education in Australia has grown over the last 20 years, but the least growth has been in VOTEC. As Figure 2 shows, there has been a pronounced trend to increase apparent retention to Year 12 in public and private upper secondary schools in Australia, particularly over the last 15 years. From about 30 per cent of the cohort in 1973, apparent retention to Year 12 has increased (as a national average) to over 75 per cent. There are major variations between states and territories, with apparent retention rates of over 90 per cent in the Australian Capital Territory, while the rates in rural areas of New South Wales, Northern Territory and Tasmania are substantially below the national average. There is a notable difference in participation in remote areas, while that in non-remote rural areas is diminishing gradually. Table 3 shows that socio-economic status remain a powerful influence on Year 12 completions. Figure 3 shows that, generally, participation in TAFE by 15-19-year-olds has not grown as much in this period as apparent retention to Year 12.

While increased school retention did not advantage VOTEC, participation rates in higher education increased sharply as a result of increased Year 12 participation, with higher education being the most clearly recognised pathway. As Year 12 retention goes beyond 75 per cent on a national average basis, governments are seeking to encourage more participation in VOTEC and to avoid excessive growth in higher education delivered by universities. Wider provision of

◆ Figure 2. **Apparent retention to Year 12 by girls, boys and combined**
1970-93

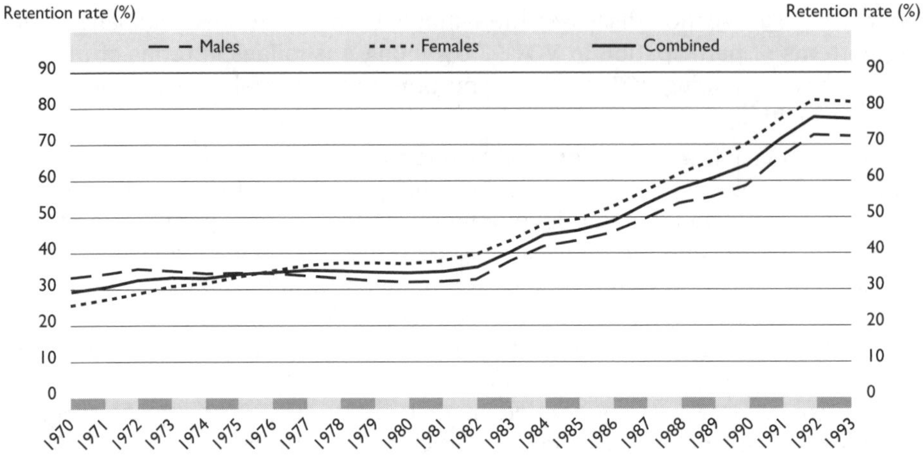

Retention rate (%)   Retention rate (%)

— — Males   ・・・・ Females   —— Combined

Source: DEET.

vocational courses in upper secondary programmes is both a direct recognition that not all of those who complete secondary education will proceed to university, and a means of preparing students for further VOTEC courses. In some states and territories this has included joint school/TAFE programmes.

The major pathways for 1988 school-leavers in 1989 are provided in Figures 4 and 5, which were projected in the Finn Report (pp. 24-25). Figure 4 reports the pathways followed in 1989 by the 62.9 per cent of 1988 school-leavers who did complete Year 12, while Figure 5 reports the pathways followed by the 37.1 per cent who did not complete Year 12.

About three-fifths of those who did complete Year 12 went on to further education, while slightly less than two-fifths did not. Most of those who went on to further education studied full-time at university, with the part-time students mostly being among the 12.1 per cent who took trade or non-trade certificate courses at TAFE. Even without further study, most of the Year 12 completers who joined the workforce in 1989 found employment.

Slightly more than two-fifths of those who did not complete Year 12 went on to further education, while slightly less than three-fifths did not, almost reversing the pattern among Year 12 completers. Moreover, the unemployment rate for

Table 3.   **Estimated Year 12 completion rates,**[1, 2]
by socio-economic status[3] **and sex**

Percentage

	1985	1987	1988	1989	1990	1991	1992
Average of three lowest socio-economic status deciles							
Males	36	43	46	47	46	56	60
Females	43	55	58	59	59	68	71
Total	39	49	52	53	53	61	65
Average of three highest socio-economic status deciles							
Males	54	63	67	67	65	75	78
Females	62	74	79	78	76	86	86
Total	58	68	73	72	70	80	82
Total							
Males	41	50	53	54	55	63	67
Females	49	61	65	66	68	75	77
Total	45	56	59	60	61	69	72

1.   Estimates only – they express the number of Year 12 completions (Year 12 certificates issued by State education
authorities) as a proportion of the estimated population that could attend Year 12 in that calendar year.
2.   ACT excluded for 1985 to 1988.
3.   The socio-economic status (SES) of students is estimated from the postcode of their home address by using an
indicator on the basis of socio-economic data obtained from the 1986 census.
Source: Australian Education Council (1993), *Statistical Annex: National report on schooling in Australia, 1992.*

those who did not complete Year 12 was four times higher, even in the relative
buoyancy of 1989 in the business cycle. Of those who did not complete Year 12
but went on to further education, most did a part-time trade or non-trade certificate course.

1989: the training reform agenda

In 1989, a report on *Improving Australia's Training System* (Dawkins, 1989*a*) was
released which strongly supported the idea of competency-based training, that
had been endorsed by a federal, state and territory report by the Department of
Labour Advisory Council. The Confederation of Australian Industry (CAI), too,
published a paper on *Australia's Vocational Education and Training System* also strongly
supporting competency-based training (CAI, 1989). Through collaboration with the
states and territories, employers and unions, the federal government embarked
on a process of reform which would bring about fundamental change to training in

47

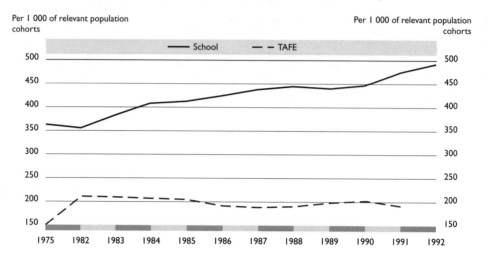

◆ Figure 3. **Full-time participation rates in schools
and total participation of 15-19 year-olds in TAFE, selected years**

Source: DEET.

the workplace, the recognition of training, and the development of skills and competencies required in the labour market.

Two special ministerial meetings held in April 1989 and November 1990 by all ministers responsible for vocational education and training, both state and federal, set the main elements of what has become the national training reform agenda. During this period, TAFE was increasingly spoken of as vocational education and training (VET), reflecting a shift towards an inclusive perspective towards public and private providers of VET. This change was formalised at a meeting of Commonwealth and State Training Advisory Committee (COSTAC) officials in February 1990. The aim of the agenda is to create a more diverse and responsive training system, while ensuring nationally consistent quality training and the recognition of skills. The proposed reforms focused on improving the quality, quantity, equity and national consistency of vocational education and training arrangements.

In November 1990, the Federal Minister for Employment, Education and Training convened a ministerial conference to consider the recommendations of a report released earlier that year by the Training Costs Review Committee, also known as the Deveson report (Deveson, 1990). The report examined training

◆ Figure 4. **Flows of school leavers who completed Year 12**

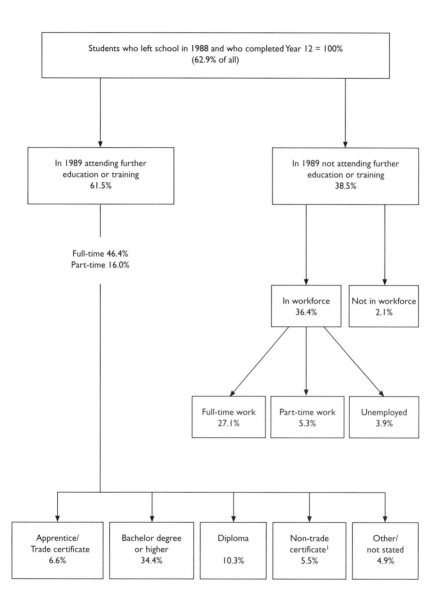

1. Includes traineeships.
Source: Finn Report (1991), based on Australian Longitudinal Survey, unpublished tables.

◆ Figure 5. **_Flows of school leavers who did not complete Year 12_**

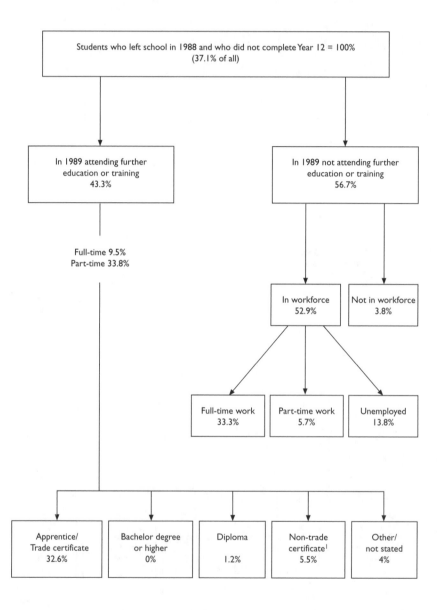

1.   Includes traineeships.
Source: Finn Report (1991), based on Australian Longitudinal Survey, unpublished tables.

wage-rates for young people and recommended a system based on competence, experience and time spent on the job.

The training reform agenda is a nationally approved programme of reform with five main themes (Lundberg, 1994a and b):

- nationally consistent competency-based training;
- national recognition of competencies, however attained;
- an open national training market;
- fair participation in vocational education and training;
- an integrated entry-level training system.

Competency-based training

All pathways in the Australian Vocational Training System (AVTS) are to involve competency-based education and training for vocational and key competencies. Competency-based training seeks to involve industry in the design, development and provision of vocational education and training so that it is adaptable and responsive to industry's needs. The heart of this approach is that training should be related to the demonstration of knowledge, skills and applications required for effective performance in the workplace. The system is therefore outcome-oriented, and importance is placed upon what people can do in the workplace rather than the time they spend in training or the amount of knowledge they acquire in formal settings.

Vocational-competency standards are developed by competency-standards bodies, many of which are part of the national network of Industry Training Advisory Bodies. However, enterprises may also submit competency standards for endorsement, and some competency-standards bodies develop cross-industry occupational or other standards. The standards for a particular industry, group or enterprise are then endorsed by the National Training Board (NTB), which also has government, employer and trade union representation. The board not only endorses the core-skill standards proposed by industry, it also provides advice and assistance to industry in identifying areas where national standards may be required. These standards are the benchmarks for curriculum development, the assessment of competency levels (including the recognition of prior learning), training delivery, course and programme accreditation, credit transfer and individual certification. Figure 6 presents this process diagrammatically.

In addition to the NTB-endorsed vocational competencies, the Finn Committee proposed, and the Mayer Committee developed, a set of generic "key competencies" which are described as being employment-related. The principles upon which Australia's key competencies are based are described in Box 4, and a list of Australia's key competencies are compared with those in New Zealand,

◆ Figure 6. ***Australia's competency-based training framework***

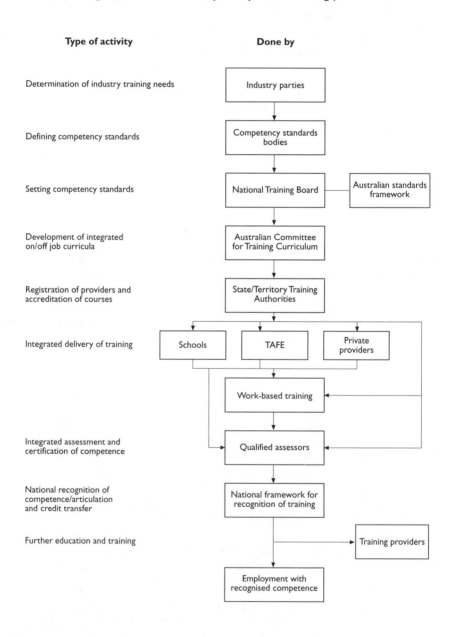

Source: Carmichael Report (1992), p. 27.

Box 4. **Australia's key competencies compared with those in the United Kingdom, United States and New Zealand**[1]

Key competencies	United Kingdom's (NCVQ) core skills	United States' (SCANS) workplace know-how	New Zealand's essential skills
• Collecting, analysing and organising information	• Communication	• Information • Foundation skills: basic skills	• Information skills
• Communicating ideas and information	• Communication • Personal skills: improving own learning and performance	• Information • Foundation skills: basic skills	• Communication skills
• Planning and organising activities	• Personal skills: improving own learning and performance	• Resources • Foundation skills: personal qualities	• Self-management skills • Work and study skills
• Working with others and in teams	• Personal skills: working with others	• Interpersonal skills	• Social skills • Work and study skills
• Using mathematical ideas and techniques	• Numeracy: application of numbers	• Foundation skills: basic skills	• Numeracy skills
• Solving problems	• Problem-solving	• Foundation skills: thinking skills	• Problem-solving and decision-making skills
• Using technology	• Information technology	• Technology • Systems	• Information skills • Communication skills
• Cultural understanding[2]	• Modern foreign language		

1. Where the UK core skills, US workplace know-how and NZ essential skills are comparable with more than one key competency, they have been repeated.
2. Cultural understanding was reinstated by ministers in July 1993.
Source: Mayer (1992), *Putting General Education to Work: The key competencies report.*

the United Kingdom and the United States. The generic competencies underpin vocationally specific competencies. The list (from the Mayer Report) has been amended to include "cultural understanding", a competency that was added by ministers in July 1993. The key-competencies development has important implications for curriculum, teaching practice, assessment and reporting in secondary schools and VOTEC. These implications were explored over three years with a Commonwealth-funded programme of pilot projects in 1993/94 to 1995/96.

The bridge between the competency requirements of work, work structures and the vocational education and training certification system is provided by the Australian Standards Framework. The standards framework is a set of eight competency levels which serve as benchmarks for the development and recognition of competency standards in relation to work across all sectors of industry. Each of the eight levels has a description attached to it (see Annex).

The National Framework for the Recognition of Training (NFROT)

Ministers agreed in November 1990 to adopt a national approach to the recognition of competencies, however they were acquired, and in March 1992 they adopted a National Framework for the Recognition of Training. NFROT includes provisions for recognition of prior learning, articulation and credit transfer, accreditation of courses, registration of private providers, and mutual recognition of credentialling of qualifications. NFROT will contribute substantially to improving the future scope for competition between TAFE and private providers through the NFROT arrangements for registration of providers and accreditation of courses. These arrangements will increase the credibility of private providers with potential users of their courses, and secure the basis for articulation and credit transfer to other public and private providers, to the benefit of those of their clientele who wish to proceed to further studies. NFROT is a structure within which it is hoped that closer co-operation will develop, but it is not working well yet. The complexity of the arrangements are proving difficult to implement in practice.

In 1994, the Ministers for Education and Training adopted the Australian Qualifications Framework. The system of qualifications covers all three sectors: school, VOTEC and universities. It will improve the development of flexible pathways by assisting people to move more easily between the education and training sectors, and between those sectors and the labour market. Currently, nine levels of qualification are offered by post-school education and training: doctoral degree, masters degree, graduate diploma, graduate certificate, bachelor degree, diploma, associate diploma, advanced certificate, and certificate.

Generally, the vocational education and training sector has offered qualifications in the last four levels, from diploma through to certificate level, and it is these qualifications that have come under close scrutiny. After much discussion it was found that there have been too few levels of qualification in vocational education and training, as the coverage by the "certificate" was found to be extremely broad. The need for at least six levels of qualification was identified and the following framework established: advanced diploma, diploma, Certificate IV, Certificate III, Certificate II, and Certificate I. Students will not have to obtain the preceding certificate/diploma in order to undertake the next level of vocational education and training qualification. Neither will it be necessary for an industry to provide a qualification at each level; rather, industries, enterprises and community groups would select qualifications at those levels appropriate to their needs.

Other training-reform themes

The adoption of an open training market as a national policy objective by a Special Ministerial Conference in November 1990 was a significant change of policy direction, since the Australian market for education and training services is not an open competitive one with full and fair competition between the providers of post-compulsory education and training services (Lundberg, 1994a and b). The implications of the decision to promote the development of a more open national training market were not clearly spelt out, but the essential concept is that Commonwealth, state and territory ministers favour the development of more competition in the provision of education and training services (Ministers of Vocational Education, Employment and Training, 1992).

One of the national goals adopted by ministers in July 1992 was to "improve access to and outcomes from vocational education and training for disadvantaged groups" (Ministers of Vocational Education, Employment and Training, 1992). This involves improvements in the rate, level, terms and outcomes of participation in education, training and employment, by categories of disadvantage, including gender, race, non-English speaking background, and disability. There are a number of issues to be addressed in this area, such as the participation of women across the full range of occupation, industry and training systems. The most common entry-level work-based training arrangement is apprenticeship, where there are relatively few females (13 per cent in 1994), with almost half of those being in the female-stereotyped occupation of hairdressing. Despite extraordinary efforts made through a variety of programmes promoting women's participation in "non-traditional" apprenticeships, the 1982 and 1989 Australian Bureau of Statistics surveys of "career paths of the trades" indicate that between 1982 and 1989, female participation in "non-traditional" apprenticeships actually declined.

Since 1990, more extensive programmes aimed at girls in upper secondary school seem to have had some success, but the results are far from seeing a change in the long-term inequity of career opportunities. Participation in technician-type courses is as heavily gender-segmented as participation in apprenticeships. As Pocock points out, the terms on which women participate in VOTEC are often disadvantageous. Difficulties in access to work-based training means that the best opportunities for women are in institution-based pathways, which have disadvantages in terms of tuition fees, earning while training, and subsequent employment and promotion prospects (Pocock, 1988).

Competency-based education and training has important equity implications at all stages. It has significant potential to improve equity outcomes, through recognition of prior learning, formal qualifications, flexible training arrangements, and the emphasis on competence achieved rather than on time in training. However, there is still the possibility for new access barriers to be erected (Davis *et al.* 1992; Poole and Nielsen, 1993). The scope for bias against disadvantaged clients of education and training was recognised by the National Training Board, and active measures were proposed to address at least some of the potential difficulties.

The themes of nationally consistent competency-based training, national recognition, an open training market and fair participation are all combined in the development of a new entry-level training system, embodied in the Australian Vocational Training System (AVTS) (see Section 4 below).

In order to control the development of a more nationally consistent and higher quality VOTEC system, the Australian National Training Authority (ANTA) was established. This is a Commonwealth statutory corporation with complementary legislation in most states and territories and is located in Brisbane with a staff of around 90. ANTA has an industry-based board of five senior representatives of both employer and employee bodies and it reports to a ministerial council made up of ministers for VOTEC in all states, territories and the Commonwealth. A key function of ANTA is the distribution of all VOTEC funds from the Commonwealth, states and territories, according to the planned delivery outlined in the profiles process.

4.   THE SYSTEM FOR THE FUTURE

This section shows how the concept of pathways defined in Section 1 has been applied in the development of the new Australian Vocational Training System (AVTS) of entry-level training. The concept of pathways is particularly useful in achieving the goals of improving international economic competitiveness through intertwining education, training and employment. This should produce a well-trained, flexible workforce in which employees, at all levels, are able to realise their full potential. The AVTS rests upon an infrastructure much of which is being developed concurrently. It includes elements such as the creation of a system of competency-based training, a framework for the recognition of prior learning, and a National Qualifications Framework (described in Section 3).

This section considers the AVTS and VOTEC pathways and patterns of participation in 1992 – the year in which the AVTS was proposed – and 2001, the year in which the targets for increased rates and levels of participation in VOTEC proposed for the AVTS are to be realised.

Participation in VOTEC: 1992

By 1992, the Australian VOTEC sector was much more complicated than it had been in 1974 or even 1989. While the TAFE colleges or institutes have traditionally provided the bulk of VOTEC in Australia, the private-provider market has been gradually increasing. This has included private-sector training providers offering accredited training to the public, and in-house training both in informal and structured settings. In addition, the less formal adult community education providers were developing a greater role in the VOTEC sector. The development of a training market which is demand-driven is a response to perceived inefficiencies of the supply approach taken in the past by the TAFE system.

In 1992, some 287 major TAFE institutions, including 135 in non-metropolitan areas, provided a full range of training encompassing preparatory, operator, trade, post-trade, technician (or paraprofessional) and, in some fields, professional levels. These institutions continued to be the major providers of the off-the-job component of entry-level training under Australia's system of apprenticeships and traineeships, with over 142 000 apprentices and trainees in training in the TAFE system in 1991/92.

Table 4 shows a pronounced increase in participation in education and training by 15-19-year-olds in Australia between 1975 and 1993. Even between 1989 and 1992 there is a 6.6 per cent increase in total participants. The dominant pattern over the period is for much less growth in VOTEC than in participation in schools and higher education. Table 5 shows that among 20-24-year-olds, there was an increase in the overall participation rate at TAFE from 5.4 per cent in 1982 to 8.9 per cent in 1992, while the increase in the participation rate in higher education over the same period was substantially greater, from 9.2 per cent to 15.6 per cent.

Table 6 presents data on the educational attainment of 15-19-year-olds, 20-24-year-olds and all Australians between 1989 and 1993.

Table 7 shows that the rate of unemployment among all persons aged 15-69 in Australia between 1989 and 1993 was strongly affected by educational achievements. Those with higher educational qualifications generally have a lower rate of unemployment. Moreover, Table 8 shows that the same pattern applied for the duration of unemployment, with those having high qualifications generally being unemployed for shorter periods of time, the notable exception being trade qualifications.

Table 4. **Participation in education and training by 15-19-year-olds**

	1975	1982	1983	1984	1985	1986	1987	1988	1989	1990	1991	1992	1993[1]	Target 2001
						Youth (thousands)								
School	447.8	453.7	484.0	510.8	548.0	563.8	613.9	626.4	616.2	606.2	643.3	639.2	637.9	726.0
Higher education	80.2	83.9	81.5	79.0	86.8	94.8	105.1	110.2	132.0	147.2	152.1	153.7	134.6	160.0
TAFE	100.3	143.1	133.6	123.0	139.8	132.3	140.6	156.7	158.0	149.0	143.9	146.5	147.7	232.0
Other	19.3	20.6	19.3	21.0	17.2	26.6	16.7	17.0	23.7	26.1	17.0	20.0	24.1	40.0
Total attending	647.7	701.3	718.4	733.8	791.8	817.5	876.3	910.3	929.9	928.6	956.3	959.4	944.3	1 158.0
Not attending	586.0	559.6	544.4	536.2	503.9	512.4	491.0	480.3	474.4	464.0	399.4	359.0	342.2	221.2
Total	1 233.7	1 260.9	1 262.8	1 270.0	1 295.7	1 329.9	1 367.3	1 390.6	1 404.3	1 392.5	1 355.7	1 318.4	1 286.5	1 379.2
						Participation rate (%)								
School	36.3	38.0	38.3	40.2	42.3	42.4	44.9	45.0	43.9	43.5	47.5	48.5	49.6	56.4
Higher education	6.5	6.7	6.5	6.2	6.7	7.1	7.7	7.9	9.4	10.6	11.2	11.7	10.5	12.4
TAFE	8.1	11.3	10.6	9.7	10.8	9.9	10.3	11.3	11.3	10.7	10.6	11.1	11.5	18.0
Other	1.6	1.6	1.5	1.7	1.3	2.0	1.2	1.2	1.7	1.9	1.3	1.5	1.9	3.1
Total	52.5	55.6	56.9	57.8	61.1	61.5	64.1	65.5	66.2	66.7	70.5	72.8	73.4	90.0

1. Data for 1993 is not strictly comparable to earlier years as it is restricted to those attending education or training for the purpose of gaining an award. Earlier years included those with an intention to undertake only partial programmes. This conceptual change most significantly affects estimates for TAFE.

Source: DEET.

Table 5. **Participation in education and training by 20-24-year-olds**

	1975	1982	1983	1984	1985	1986	1987	1988	1989	1990	1991	1992	1993[1]
Youth (thousands)													
School	5.2	6.4	10.5	5.0	5.3	5.5	3.8	6.0	4.1	4.3	7.7	7.3	7.5
Higher education	104.8	118.5	106.7	134.9	120.0	114.8	128.7	137.8	161.4	179.0	193.6	221.4	223.8
TAFE	n.a.	69.4	86.2	89.6	91.8	89.0	92.0	100.9	105.0	101.4	117.6	125.9	112.3
Other	17.8	19.0	19.2	20.7	16.7	27.6	18.6	17.0	20.9	27.2	25.1	31.1	28.6
Total attending	n.a.	213.3	222.6	250.2	233.8	236.9	243.1	261.7	291.4	311.9	344.0	385.7	372.2
Not attending	n.a.	1 076.2	1 093.0	1 069.6	1 064.0	1 064.3	1 060.6	1 042.8	1 021.2	1 020.0	1 031.5	1 035.0	1 070.1
Total	1 164.9	1 289.5	1 315.6	1 319.8	1 297.8	1 301.2	1 303.7	1 304.5	1 312.6	1 331.9	1 375.5	1 420.7	1 442.3
Participation rate (%)													
School	0.4	0.5	0.8	0.4	0.4	0.4	0.3	0.5	0.3	0.3	0.6	0.5	0.5
Higher education	9.0	9.2	8.1	10.2	9.2	8.8	9.9	10.6	12.3	13.4	14.1	15.6	15.5
TAFE	n.a.	5.4	6.6	6.6	7.1	6.8	7.1	7.7	8.0	7.6	98.5	8.9	7.8
Other	1.5	1.5	1.5	1.6	1.3	2.1	1.4	1.3	1.6	2.0	1.6	2.2	2.0
Total	n.a.	16.5	16.9	19.0	18.0	18.2	18.6	20.1	22.2	23.4	25.0	27.1	25.08

n.a.: non available.
1.   Data for 1993 is not strictly comparable to earlier years as it is restricted to those attending education or training for the purpose of gaining an award Earlier years included those with an intention to undertake only partial programmes This conceptual change most significantly affects estimates for TAFE.
Source: DEET.

Table 6. **Educational attainment of 15-19, 20-24 year-olds, and of all persons, February 1989 to February 1993 (thousands)**

	1989	1990	1991	1992	1993
	15-19 year-olds				
With post-school qualifications:	85.8	81.1	78.6	84.1	82.9
Degree	*0.4	*0.9	*0.5	*0.9	*0.7
Trade qualification	14.4	15.1	9.9	13.4	12.4
Certificate or diploma	69.8	63.1	65.9	67.3	67.1
Other	*1.2	*2.0	*2.3	*2.5	*2.7
Without post-school qualifications:[1]	734.4	741.3	687.4	643.6	614.4
Attended highest level of secondary school available	320.2	344.8	360.2	368.0	383.3
Did not attend highest level of secondary school available	412.4	396.2	325.0	275.3	231.0
Still at school	567.7	564.2	594.4	590.6	585.2
Total	1 387.7	1 386.5	1 359.7	1 318.2	1 282.5
	20-24 year-olds				
With post-school qualifications	469.9	495.7	532.6	546.8	599.2
Degree	86.4	101.5	111.7	114.4	133.0
Trade qualification	151.5	150.5	160.0	158.4	178.0
Certificate or diploma	228.7	236.0	255.0	267.6	280.0
Other	*3.4	7.7	5.9	6.4	8.2
Without post-school qualifications:[1]	820.5	815.2	814.0	844.2	823.8
Attended highest level of secondary school available	320.6	356.7	362.2	415.7	421.1
Did not attend highest level of secondary school available	496.3	450.7	448.0	427.9	399.7
Still at school	*0.3	*1.2	*3.4	*2.9	*2.1
Total	1 290.1	1 310.2	1 349.8	1 393.9	1 423.7
	All persons[2]				
With post-school qualifications:	4 852.8	4 699.0	4 896.1	5 076.5	5 322.1
Degree	957.6	987.7	1 047.2	1 139.5	1 208.3
Trade qualification	1 670.7	1 557.5	1 571.7	1 620.2	1 676.6
Certificate or diploma	2 193.2	2 089.7	2 229.2	2 272.8	2 369.5
Other	31.4	64.1	47.9	44.0	67.7
Without post-school qualifications:[1]	7 248.5	6 574.9	6 529.2	6 526.5	6 438.9
Attended highest level of secondary school available	1 465.9	1 535.7	1 607.1	1 708.7	1 813.4
Did not attend highest level of secondary school available	5 648.5	4 928.7	4 819.6	4 711.3	4 540.0
Still at school	568.1	565.3	597.8	593.4	587.4
Total	12 618.1	11 798.4	11 985.9	12 155.2	12 305.6

* Subject to sampling variability too high for most practical uses.
1. Includes persons who never attended school and those for whom secondary school status could not be determined.
2. Aged 15 to 69 years for 1990 onwards.
Source: ABS, *Labour force status and educational attainment*, Australia, Cat. No. 6235.0.

Table 7. **Educational attainment and unemployment rate, persons aged 15 to 69 February 1989 to February 1993**

	With post-school qualifications				Without post-school qualifications			Total[3]
	Degree	Trade qualification	Certificate or diploma	Total[1]	Attended highest secondary level	Did not attend highest level of secondary school	Total[2]	
Males								
1990	3.5	3.3	3.8	3.5	7.4	8.9	8.5	6.2
1991	3.7	6.6	7.3	6.2	10.4	12.9	12.1	9.4
1992	5.3	8.6	8.7	7.9	14.5	15.8	15.4	11.8
1993	5.3	9.5	10.3	8.8	15.8	17.0	16.6	12.7
Females								
1990	5.7	6.9	5.7	5.9	9.4	9.0	9.1	8.1
1991	6.6	7.2	7.7	7.5	11.3	10.3	10.6	9.6
1992	6.8	9.7	9.4	8.8	13.7	12.1	12.6	11.1
1993	7.5	11.1	10.2	9.6	13.3	11.9	12.5	11.4
Total								
1989	4.0	3.6	5.3	4.5	9.0	9.2	9.2	7.3
1990	4.3	3.6	5.0	4.4	8.3	9.0	8.8	7.0
1991	4.8	6.6	7.6	6.7	10.8	11.7	11.5	9.5
1992	5.9	8.7	9.1	8.3	14.1	14.2	14.2	11.5
1993	6.2	9.6	10.2	9.1	14.6	14.8	14.8	12.1

1. Includes those with other post-school qualifications.
2. Includes those who never attended school.
3. Includes those still at school.
Source: ABS. Labour force status and educational attainment, Australia. Cat No. 4221 0.

Table 8. **Average and median duration of unemployment, persons aged 15 to 69 February 1989 to February 1993 (weeks)**

	With post-school qualifications				Without post-school qualifications			
	Degree	Trade qualification	Certificate or diploma	Total[1]	Attended highest secondary level	Did not attend highest level of secondary school	Total[2]	Total[3]
Average duration of unemployment								
1989	23.4	63.6	31.7	39.4	23.9	59.1	50.1	44.8
1990	27.6	37.4	33.5	33.1	24.0	48.0	41.9	37.4
1991	17.9	36.0	30.0	30.2	20.7	49.7	41.7	36.3
1992	26.4	43.0	38.1	37.8	29.7	58.7	49.8	44.3
1993	37.8	51.3	43.9	46.9	34.4	66.9	56.4	51.3
Median duration of unemployment								
1989	8	19	8	9	8	18	13	11
1990	8	8	7	8	6	13	10	9
1991	8	13	11	11	9	18	13	13
1992	12	26	15	17	12	33	26	21
1993	16	26	19	22	12	34	26	24

1. Includes those with other post-school qualifications.
2. Includes those who never attended school.
3. Includes those still at school.

Source: ABS, Labour force status and educational attainment, Australia. Cat. No. 4221.0.

The Australian Vocational Training System – 1992 and beyond

Section 3 indicated that the building blocks for a new VOTEC system were progressively developed throughout the 1990s. Three major reports set the groundwork for the new system's development. The first was a report in 1991 by the Australian Education Council Review Committee on *Young People's Participation in Post-compulsory Education and Training*, otherwise known as the Finn report (Finn, 1991). This reported on goals and options for the further development of Australia's post-compulsory education and training system. The report proposed a set of employment-related key competencies and recommended the formation of a new structured entry-level training system. In Section 3, it was mentioned that the Mayer Committee expanded and developed the Finn report recommendations on key employment-related competencies, with considerably more detail on how they might be implemented. The continued development of such competencies is likely to see the ties between schools, VOTEC and industry become much closer. State and territory certificates for the completion of secondary education will be a crucial element, and students who have not completed twelve years of full-time schooling will need to develop key competencies and have them assessed.

A set of principles for a new entry-level training system was developed by the Employment and Skills Formation Council of the National Board of Employment, Education and Training in their 1992 report entitled the *Australian Vocational Certificate Training System*, better known as the Carmichael Report (Carmichael, 1992). The concept of pathways adapted from the OECD by the Finn report has been embodied within the AVTS of vocational education and training (Finn, 1991, Vol. 2, pp. 13-43). The AVTS is intended to further develop flexible pathways with a variety of exit points and nationally recognised qualifications. It would consist of flexible networks of public and private institutional providers and work-based training, applying broadly consistent principles to fit local circumstances. The principal structural features of the system were specified in the Carmichael report (Figure 7). Industry involvement is inherent to the pathways concept whenever work experience is to be integrated into the training system.

The AVTS provides a general framework which is flexible enough to incorporate the various state and territory entry-level training systems within a basically nationally consistent set of pathways. The goals of the AVTS are to:

- increase the range of vocational education and training options through flexible pathways;
- merge apprenticeship and trainees with the new system;
- extend the scope of work-based vocational training, including work-based training linked to school-based programmes;

◆ Figure 7. **Principal structural features of the AVCTS**

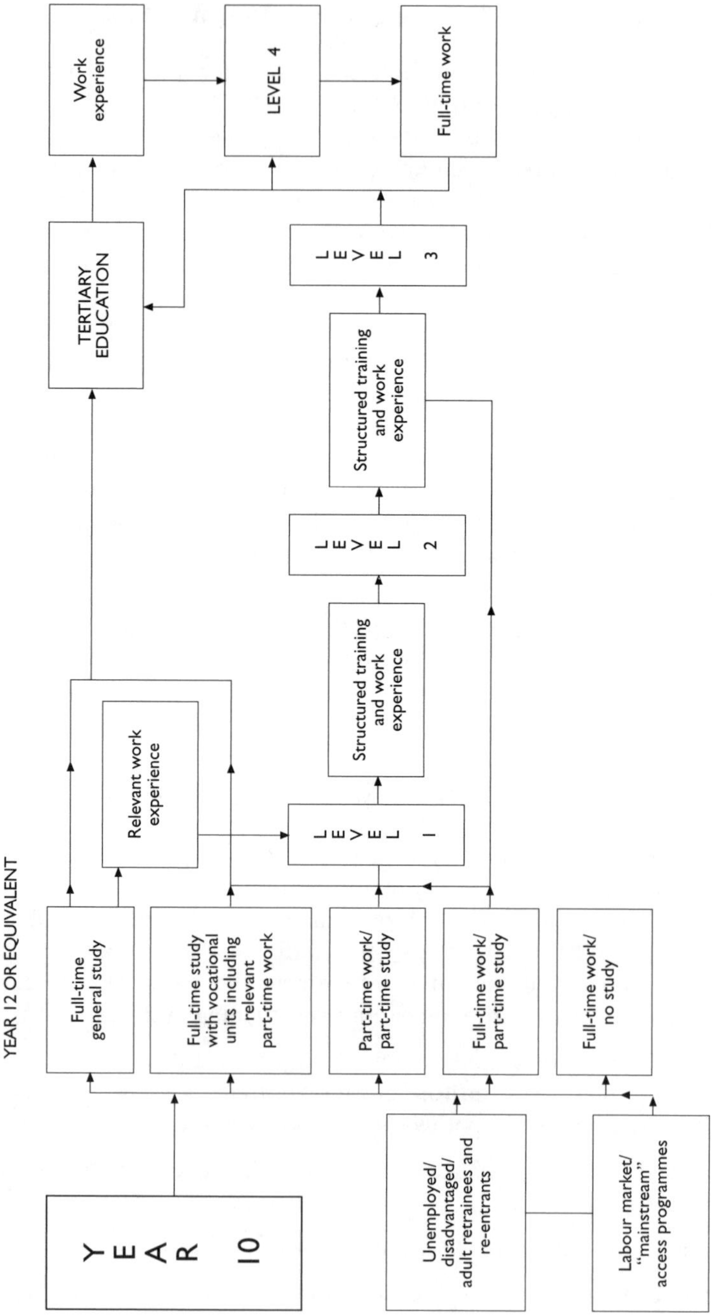

Source: Carmichael Report (1992).

- establish "networks" between public and private providers in the various sectors of education and training involving improved linkages between programmes;
- incorporate generic employment-related key competencies;
- provide for recognition of prior learning, articulation and credit transfer to higher levels of competence through all pathways;
- provide equity of access.

A Commonwealth White Paper on unemployment in 1994 announced that the Commonwealth would develop an implementation strategy for the AVTS in co-operation with the states and territories, to ensure that the new system is "owned by industry", meets industry needs, and sees governments being limited to "co-ordination, quality control and managing change" (Keating, 1994a, p. 101). An Australian Student Traineeship Foundation was established as a government-funded, "industry-driven" body to fund networks of local and regional training-brokers to assist students in upper secondary school Years 11 and 12 to combine school, work placements and off-the-job training.

The Working Nation White Paper also announced the establishment of a National Employment and Training Taskforce (NETTFORCE). This body will co-ordinate increased provision of apprenticeship and traineeships, with additional incentives being offered to employers. Training wages will apply to those involved in entry level training and to the unemployed undergoing training to re-enter the workforce. The training wage will be discounted but supplemented by Commonwealth-funded allowances. As well as income support, under a Youth Training Initiative young people will receive intensive case management and assistance with work and training placements. The Working Nation initiatives therefore complement and support the development of the AVCTS (Keating, 1994a).

An enterprise stream of training is currently under development following a proposal from the Business Council of Australia, which NETTFORCE is intended to support. Enterprise pathways would differ from the industry-endorsed pathways, in that the standards and training programmes would focus on enterprise stan-dards rather than industry objectives, although transferability and portability will remain important objectives. The enterprise would also have a role in the accredi-tation, assessment and recognition of prior learning, with appropriate quality assurance and accountability arrangements. Pilot programmes were conducted with the National Australia Bank and McDonald's Australia. In the case of McDonald's, enterprise standards have been endorsed by the National Training Board.

The Australian Traineeship System (ATS) has been extended through the introduction of the Career Start Traineeship (CST) system, which will serve as a vital bridge in the transition to the AVCTS. Formed in 1992, CST builds on the strengths of the ATS but offers additional versatility which is not found in the ATS traineeship. CST traineeships have no age-limit restrictions and are open to early school-leavers as well as mature-age workers. The CST is also competency-based, and both the length of training and the related wage increments will be determined by the aptitude of the trainee. A CST traineeship will be for a minimum period of one year, and the duration is based on the trainee's competence and/or year in which he/she left school. A trainee with a Year 10 or lower level of general education might spend as much as two years in training, with up to 50 per cent of ordinary working hours spent in off-the-job training during the first year. A trainee with Year 11 education might spend 18 months in training, with 35 per cent of time spent on off-the-job training; while a trainee with Year 12 education could expect to spend 12 months in training, with 25 per cent on off-the-job training. As with the ATS system, a number of financial incentives are available to employers and trainees.

An extensive range of pilot projects is being undertaken to test the new system. Work upon other elements which provide an infrastructure for the system is progressing concurrently. The pilot programmes are testing the viability of delivery and administrative arrangements for both institution and work-based pathways. They are also designed to promote acceptance by institutions, employers, unions, new entrants of the system, and to facilitate the transition from the present system to the new one. One hundred and thirty pilot projects have received ministerial approval, of which 68 are school and/or TAFE institution-based and 62 work-based.

The changeover to the AVTS commenced in 1995 with the Career Start Traineeships as a bridge into the new system. Existing training arrangements for the Australian Traineeship System were also converted from that time, and apprenticeships have been progressively converted so that by 1997, all traineeships are to be operating in terms of AVTS requirements.

Participation in the future scenario: 2001

The Finn report proposed a "target scenario" for pathways in the year 2001, which embodies proposals of the Employment and Skills Formation Council (ESFC) on the Australian Vocational Training System. The "target scenario" in Figure 8 is a representation from the Finn report of what the Finn Committee's recommendations (slightly less ambitious than those introduced in the AVCTS report by the ESFC) would produce by 2001 (Finn, 1991; Carmichael, 1992). It is notable that, by comparison with the 1989 cohort depicted in Section 3 in Figures 4 and 5, the proportions of "no study" are substantially smaller. The data in Table 9 draw out the implications of this scenario, in comparison with 1990

◆ Figure 8. *Target scenario–2001: simplified representation of flows*

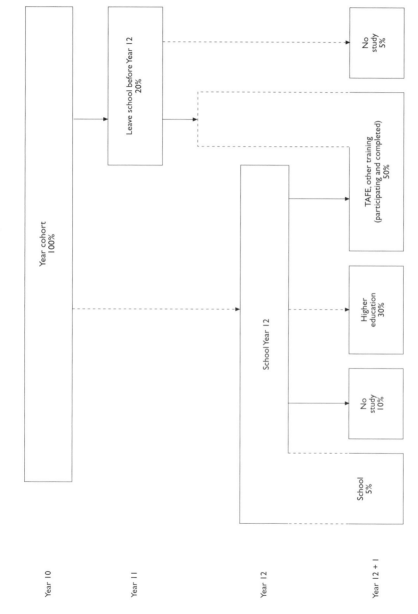

Year 10

Year 11

Year 12

Year 12 + 1

Year cohort
100%

Leave school before Year 12
20%

No
study
5%

TAFE, other training
(participating and completed)
50%

School Year 12

Higher
education
30%

No
study
10%

School
5%

Source: Finn Report (1991), based on Australian Longitudinal Survey, unpublished tables.

Table 9. **Educational participation and attainment of 19-year-olds, 1990 and target scenario**

	1990		Target 2001	
	Number (thousands)	%	Number (thousands)	%
Participating				
School	7.4	2.5	12.7	4.6
TAFE	44.9	14.9	84.3	30.5
Higher education	69.2	23.0	75.3	27.2
Other training	7.0	2.3	18.7	6.8
Attained				
TAFE	34.9	11.6	41.7	15.1
Other training	1.9	0.6	2.2	0.8
Not participating and without post-school attainment				
With Year 12	54.2	18.0	27.6	10.0
Without Year 12	81.7	27.1	13.9	5
Population				
	30.1	100	276.4	100
Percentage of 19-year-olds having attained Year 12, a vocational qualification, or still participating		72.9		95
Percentage of 19-year-olds in school or with post school participation, or attainment		54.9		85

Source: Finn (1991).

(Finn, 1991, pp. 168-171). Whereas in the 1980s the principal areas of growth in education and training were schools and universities, the "target scenario" presages substantial growth in VOTEC in Australia in the latter half of the 1990s.

Annex

AUSTRALIAN STANDARDS FRAMEWORK*

The Australian Standards Framework (ASF) is a set of eight competency levels which serve as benchmarks for the development and recognition of competency standards in relation to work across the Australian economy. The framework provides a bridge between the competency requirements of work and work structures, and the vocational education and training and certification system. This allows work, training and qualifications to be related by applying competency levels. The levels in the ASF are points in a continuum of competencies, and as such simply reflect the needs of the Australian environment.

The definition of competency levels within the framework facilitates objectivity and comparability and therefore the utility of standards within and across industries. However, the ASF is not designed nor intended to be used to determine job or occupational classifications, which remains the prerogative of the industrial parties. The allocation of jobs or classifications either within or between levels in the framework will therefore be specific to the industry or enterprise.

ROLE OF ASF

The framework serves a number of important roles in providing:

- benchmarks to enable comparisons between levels of competency in standards across industries, between industries, and between sectors within industries;
- a work-based benchmark for the alignment of vocational credentials and other forms of recognition of competency;
- a base for specifying competency levels required by the workforce, and for setting national attainment targets;
- a linkage between the requirements of work and the outcomes of education and training, and serving as a basis for relevance of training now and in the future;

---

* *Source: National Competency Standards, Policy and Guidelines*, second edition, 1992.

- a basis for promoting consistency and flexibility in the vocational education and training system;
- a basis for the recognition of prior learning;
- a basis for the recognition of competency acquired overseas.

The ASF consists of competency levels related to the characteristics of work in a general way, which can also be reflected in specific work structures, such as in industrial classifications. It is important to recognise that under a competency-based system, certification of individuals relates to the competencies required in work as specified by the relevant standard. It is not a description of the totality of competencies possessed by an individual.

ASF DESCRIPTORS

The ASF competency-level descriptors are not intended to provide descriptions of all competencies required at that level, but describe only the characteristics necessary to differentiate the level from others.

All levels relate to competent performance in work, and are not entry or training levels. Entry for individuals into the workforce may be at any level. As elsewhere in this chapter, the terms "performance in work" and "requirements of work" should be read in a broad context. That is, the ASF is not simply about the requirements of a particular job function or occupation in a particular enterprise, but more broadly about the skill requirements of work in a changing industry and enterprise context. It is expected that all levels would require individuals to have an established work orientation, but not necessarily employment experience. Competency at a particular level does not imply that the competencies at all lower levels in that industry are held, unless an industry explicitly requires this in its standards.

The main discriminating factors relating to the characteristics of work functions which are built into the descriptors in the progression from lower to higher levels are that:
- the degree of discretion, autonomy and freedom to act increases and broadens and is related to a wider span of activity;
- the range of contingencies to be dealt with and the complexity of work, as well as the extent of judgements made about it, increase and broaden;
- responsibility and accountability expand;
- the complexity, depth and/or breadth of the knowledge base required increase;
- competencies can be related to management functions and/or specialist functions.

The discriminating factors in the descriptors apply to the full expression of competency – that is, across the four components of competency: task performance, task management, contingency management, job and role environment.

Some aspects of competency, in particular motor skills and generic/key competencies such as communication and interpersonal skills, may be key discriminators of levels in particular industry standards. However, various industries combine these skills with others at particular levels in different ways, and they are therefore not generally reliable discriminators in the ASF descriptors.

The linkages between descriptors are important in establishing alignment of standards at a particular level. The critical aspect in discriminating levels may be the particular combination and inter-relationship of factors. Judgement needs to be exercised in assessing the impact of linkages between discriminating factors when determining an ASF level.

THE LEVEL DESCRIPTORS

Level 1

Work is likely to be under direct supervision with regular checking, but may take the form of less direct guidance and some autonomy where working in teams is required.

Competency at this level involves the application of knowledge and skills to a limited range of tasks and roles. There is a specified range of contexts where the choice of actions required is clear.

Competencies are normally used within established routines, methods and procedures that are predictable, and within which judgement against established criteria is also involved.

Level 2

Work is likely to be under routine supervision with intermittent checking, but may take the form of general guidance and considerable autonomy where working in teams is required. Responsibility for some roles and co-ordination within a team may be required.

Competency at this level involves the application of knowledge and skills to a range of tasks and roles. There is a defined range of contexts where the choice of actions required is usually clear, with limited complexity in the choice.

Competencies are normally used within established routines, methods and procedures, in some cases involving discretion and judgement about possible actions.

Level 3

Work is likely to be under limited supervision with checking related to overall progress, but may take the form of broad guidance and autonomy where working in teams is required. Responsibility for the work of others may be involved, and team co-ordination may be required.

Competency at this level involves the application of knowledge with depth in some areas and a broad range of skills. There is a range of tasks and roles in a variety of contexts, with some complexity in the extent and choice of actions required.

Competencies are normally used within routines, methods and procedures where some discretion and judgement is required in selection of equipment, work organisation, services, actions and achieving outcomes within time constraints.

Level 4

Work is likely to be without supervision, with general guidance on progress and outcomes sought. The work of others may be supervised or teams guided or facilitated. Responsibility for and limited organisation of the work of others may be involved.

Competency at this level involves the application of knowledge with depth in some areas and a broad range of skills. There is a wide range of tasks and roles in a variety of contexts, with complexity in the range and choice of actions required.

Competencies are normally used within routines, methods and procedures where discretion and judgement are required, for both self and others, in planning and selection of equipment, work organisation, services, actions, and achieving outcomes within time constraints.

Level 5

Work is likely to be under broad guidance. The work of others may be supervised or teams guided. Responsibility for the planning and management of the work of others may be involved.

Competency at this level involves the self-directed application of knowledge with substantial depth in some areas, and a range of technical and other skills to tasks, roles and functions in both varied and highly specific contexts.

Competencies are normally used independently and both routinely and non-routinely. Judgement is required in planning and selecting appropriate equipment, services, techniques and work organisation for self and others.

Level 6

Work is likely to be under limited guidance in line with a broad plan, budget or strategy. Responsibility and defined accountability for the management and output of the work of others and for defined functions may be involved.

Competency at this level involves the self-directed development of knowledge with substantial depth across a number of areas and/or mastery of a specialised area with a range of skills. Application is to major functions in either varied or highly specific contexts.

Competencies are normally used independently and are substantially non-routine. Significant judgement is required in planning, design, technical or supervisory functions related to products, services, operations or processes.

Level 7

Work is likely to be in accordance with a broad plan, budget or strategy. Responsibility and broad-ranging accountability for the structure, management and output of the work of others and/or functions may be involved.

Competency at this level involves the self-directed development and mastery of broad and/or specialised areas of knowledge with a range of skills. Application is to major, broad or specialised functions in highly varied and/or highly specialised contexts.

Competencies are normally used independently and are non-routine. Significant high-level judgement is required in planning, design, operational, technical and/or management functions.

Level 8

Work is likely to involve full responsibility and accountability for all aspects of the work of others and functions including planning, budgeting and strategy where required.

Competency at this level involves self-directed development and mastery or a range of knowledge and skills. Application is to major functions both broad and/or specialised within highly varied and/or highly specialised contexts.

Competencies are normally used with full independence and in contexts and combinations of great variability. The highest level of complex judgement is applied in planning, design, technical and/or management functions.

Level 8 includes all competencies that might be regarded as higher in level than those characteristics used in the descriptor to distinguish it from Level 7. There are no levels in the ASF above Level 8.

BIBLIOGRAPHY

ANDERSON, D. (1994), *Blurring the Boundaries: Public and private training colleges in the open training-market,* National Centre for Vocational Education Research (NCVER), Adelaide.

ATHANASOU, J.A., PITHERS, R.T. and CORNFORD, I.R. (1993), "The role of generic competencies in the description and classification of Australian occupations some preliminary data from the Australian Standard Classification of Occupations", in *After Competence: The future of post-compulsory education and training,* Centre for Skill Formation Research and Development International Conference, Griffith University, Brisbane, December, Vol. 1, pp. 10-19.

Australian Council of Trade Unions/Trade Development Council (1987), *Australia Reconstructed,* report of the mission to Western Europe, ACTU, Melbourne.

Australian Education Council (AEC) and Ministers of Vocational Education, Employment and Training (MOVEET) (1992), *Australian Vocational Certificate Training System: Resolutions of the Australian Education Council and Ministers for Vocational Education, Employment and Training,* Canberra, June.

BARCAN, A. (1981), *A History of Australian Education,* Oxford University Press, Melbourne.

BARNETT, K. (1993), *Swings and Roundabouts. The open training market and women's participation in TAFE, NPAWT and NCVER,* Department of Employment, Education and Training (DEET), Canberra.

BARNETT, K. (1994a), "Some can, Some can't. The impact of fees and charges on disadvantaged groups in TAFE: A discussion paper", NCVER, Adelaide.

BARNETT, K. (1994b), "Challenges and choices: A study of our providers of adult community education", NCVER, Adelaide.

BEARE, H. and MILLIKAN, R.H. (1988), *Skilling the Australian Community: Futures for public education,* Australian Teachers Union/Commission for the Future, Melbourne.

Business Council of Australia (1990), *Training Australians: A better way of working,* Melbourne.

CARMICHAEL, L. (chairman) (1992), *The Australian Vocational Certificate Training System,* Employment and Skills Formation Council, National Board of Employment Education and Training (NBEET), Canberra, March.

CASTLES, I. (1993), *Women in Australia,* Australian Bureau of Statistics, Canberra (ABS 4113.0).

Commonwealth and State Training Advisory Committee (COSTAC) (1990a), *An Implementation Strategy for Competency-based Training*, Canberra.

Commonwealth and State Training Advisory Committee (COSTAC) (1990b), *Report of the Overseas Mission to Study Developments in Vocational Education and Training*, Canberra, December.

Commonwealth Tertiary Education Commission (1986), *Review of TAFE Funding*, AGPS, Canberra, May.

Confederation of Australian Industry (CAI) (1989), *Australia's Vocational Education and Training System*, Melbourne.

Confederation of Australian Industry (CAI) (1991 and 1992), CBT – *The Australian Vocational Education and Training System*, July 1991 and January 1992, Melbourne.

DAVIS, S., DENNING, S., TRAVERS, B. and GLASBY, D. (1992), *Recognition of Prior Teaming – Implications for women*, a NPAWT project, Department of Employment, Education and Training (DEET), Canberra.

DAWE, S. (1993), *1993 National Client Follow-up Survey of Vocational Education Graduates*, NATMISS/NCVER, Adelaide, September.

DAWKINS, Hon. J.S., MP (Minister for Employment, Education and Training) and HOLDING, Hon. A.C., MP (Minister for Employment Services and Youth Affairs) (1987), *Skills for Australia*, AGPS, Canberra.

DAWKINS, Hon. J.S., MP (Minister for Employment, Education and Training) (1989a), *Improving Australia's Training System*, AGPS, Canberra, April.

DAWKINS, Hon. J.S., MP (Minister for Employment, Education and Training) (1989b), *Employment, Education and Training: Key trends and government initiatives*, Economic Planning Advisory Council, Canberra, June (EPAC Discussion Paper 89/8).

DELANEY, B. (1992), *The Gender Implications of the Finn, Carmichael and Mayer Reports*, TAFE National Staff Development Committee, VEETAC Secretariat, Canberra.

Department of Education (1976), "Transition from school to work or further study: a background paper for an OECD review of Australian education policy", Canberra.

Department of Education (1987), "Support for staying on at school: the role of student assistance in post-compulsory secondary education and TAFE", seminar paper, December, AGPS, Canberra.

Department of Employment, Education and Training (DEET) (1991a), *A New Structured Entry-level Training System for Australia*, Canberra, June.

Department of Employment, Education and Training (DEET) (1991b), *Australia's Workforce in the Year 2001*, AGPS, Canberra.

Department of Employment, Education and Training (DEET) (1992), *Essential Features of Australia's Training Systems*, AGPS, Canberra.

DEVESON, I. (chairman) (1990), *Training Costs of Award Restructuring*, report of the Training Costs Review Committee (2 vols.), AGPS, Canberra.

Employment and Skills Formation Council (ESFC) (1990), *Industry Training Advisory Bodies,* AGPS, Canberra.

Employment and Skills Formation Council (ESFC) (1993), *Raising the Standard: Middle level skills in the Australian workforce,* AGPS, Canberra, November.

FINN, B. (chairman) (1991), *Young People's Participation in Post-Compulsory Education and Training,* report of the Australian Education Council Review Committee (3 vols.), AGPS, Canberra, July.

FISHER, N. (1993), "Developing a national training market: is it a sensible strategy?", *Unicorn,* 19 (4), November, pp. 27-33.

FRASER M. (1972), *Commonwealth Financial Assistance for Technical Training Institutions,* Department of Education and Science, Canberra.

GOOZEE, G. (1993), *The Development of TAFE in Australia,* NCVER, Adelaide.

HAGER, P. (1992), "How convincing are the arguments against competency standards?", *What Future for Technical and Vocational Education and Training?,* National Centre for Vocational Education Research International Conference, Melbourne, December, NCVER, Adelaide, Vol. 1, pp. 73-87.

HAYTON, G. and LOVEDER, P. (1992), *Workplace Reform and TAFE: Four case studies,* NCVER, Adelaide.

House of Representatives Standing Committee on Employment Education and Training (1989), *The Restless Years: An inquiry into Year 12 retention rates,* Commonwealth Parliament of Australia, Canberra, October.

House of Representatives Standing Committee on Legal and Constitutional Affairs (1992), *Half Way to Equal,* Report of the inquiry into equal opportunity and equal status for women in Australia, AGPS, Canberra, April.

JACKSON, N.S. (1992), "Reforming vocational learning? Contradictions of competence", *What Future for Technical and Vocational Education and Training?,* National Centre for Vocational Education Research International Conference, Melbourne, December, NCVER, Adelaide, Vol. 2, pp. 187-200.

JOHNSTON, N. (1992), "The universities and competency-based standards", *Higher Education and the Competency Movement: Implications for tertiary education and the professions,* Centre for Continuing Education Conference, Australian National University, Canberra, June.

KANGAN, M. (chairman) (1974 and 1975), *TAFE in Australia, Report on needs in technical and further education* (2 vols.), Australian Committee on Technical and Further Education, AGPS, Canberra.

KEARNS, P., LUNDBERG, D., PAPADOPOULOS, G. and WAGNER, G. (1993), *Bridging the Tasman,* National Centre for Vocational Education Research, Adelaide, March.

KEATING, P.J., MP (1992a), *One Nation,* Canberra, February.

KEATING, P.J., MP (Minister for Employment, Education and Training, and Minister for Higher Education and Employment Services) (1992b), *Employment, Education and Training Initiatives in the February Economic Statement,* Canberra, February.

KEATING, P.J., MP (chairman) (1993), *Restoring Full Employment: A discussion paper,* Committee on Employment Opportunities, AGPS, Canberra, December.

KEATING, P.J., MP (1994a), *Working Nation: The white paper on employment and growth,* AGPS, Canberra.

KEATING, P.J., MP (1994b), *Working Nation: Policies and programs,* AGPS, Canberra.

KIRBY, P. (chairman) (1985a), *Report of the Committee of Inquiry into Labour Market Programs,* AGPS, Canberra.

KIRBY, P. (1985b), "Training for Australia's future", in *Training for Australia's Future,* Victoria Press, Melbourne.

LUNDBERG, D. (1994a), *Where are We? Reviewing the training reform agenda,* NCVER, Adelaide.

LUNDBERG, D. (1994b), *Calling the Tune: Market-responsive vocational education and training – a discussion paper,* NCVER, Adelaide.

Mayer Committee Report (chairman) (1992), *Putting General Education to Work: The key competencies report,* Melbourne.

Ministers of Vocational Education, Employment and Training (MOVEET) (1992), Common and Agreed National Goals for Vocational Education and Training, Department of Employment, Education and Training (DEET), Canberra.

MORAN, T. (1992), "The national training reform agenda: an appraisal of progress to date", keynote speech to *What Future for Technical and Vocational Education and Training?,* National Centre for Vocational Education Research International Conference, Melbourne, December.

MORAN, T. (1993), "Meeting the challenges in vocational education: ANTA and the new national priorities", *Unicorn,* 19 (4), November, pp. 9-18.

MURRAY-SMITH, S. (1971), "Technical education", in A.C. MacLaine and R. Selby-Smith (eds.), *Fundamental Issues in Australian Education,* Ian Novak, Sydney, pp. 313-353.

National Board of Employment Education and Training (NBEET) (1990), *Assistance to Disadvantaged Jobseekers,* Canberra.

National Board of Employment Education and Training (NBEET) (1991), *Social Infrastructure and Social Justice: Resources in Australia's disadvantaged schools,* Commissioned Report 9, Schools Council, Canberra, October.

National Board of Employment Education and Training (NBEET) (1992a), *Education, Training and Employment Programs, Australia, 1970-2001: Funding and participation,* Commissioned Report 11, Canberra, January.

National Board of Employment, Education and Training (NBEET) (1992b), *Post-compulsory Education and Training: Fitting the need,* Canberra, November.

National Labour Consultative Council (1987), *Labour Market Flexibility in the Australian Setting,* Canberra.

National Training Board (NTB) (1990), *Setting National Skill Standards: A discussion paper,* Canberra, July.

National Training Board (NTB) (1992), *Policy and Guidelines,* second edition, Canberra, October.

OECD (1993), *Industry Training in Australia, Sweden and the United States,* Paris.

POCOCK, B. (1987), *Man-made Skill: Women challenging the tradition in England, Sweden and Germany,* TNCRD/NCVER, Adelaide, December.

POCOCK, B. (1988), *Demanding Skill: Women and technical education in Australia,* Allen and Unwin, Sydney.

POCOCK, B. (1991), W*omen in Entry-level Training in Australia: A discussion paper,* University of Adelaide, September.

POOLE, M.E. and NIELSEN, S.W. (1993), "In the best interests of competence: ensuring the interests of women in the definition of competence", *After Competence: The future of post-compulsory education and training,* Centre for Skill Formation Research and Development International Conference, Griffith University, Brisbane, December, Vol. 2, pp. 106-114.

ROBINSON, P. (1993), *Teachers facing Change, A Small-scale Study of Teachers Working with Competency-based Training,* NCVER, Adelaide.

SCOTT, B.W. (1989), *TAFE Restructuring,* Management Review, NSW Education Portfolio, Sydney, September.

SCOTT, B.W. (1990), *TAFE's Commission for the 1990s,* Management Review, NSW Education Portfolio, Sydney, June.

TAFE National Staff Development Committee (1992), *Work-based Learning: Implications and case studies,* Melbourne.

THOMSON, P. *et al.* (1990), *Competency-based Training in TAFE,* TNRDC/NCVER, Adelaide.

THOMSON, P.P. (1992), "Assessing competence: an overview of current problems and trends in Australia", *What Future for Technical and Vocational Education and Training?,* National Centre for Vocational Education Research International Conference, Melbourne, December, Vol. 2, pp. 293-303.

TOWERS, Perrin and CRESAP Australia (1990), *Workforce 2000,* Business Council of Australia, Melbourne.

Vocational Education, Employment and Training Advisory Committee (VEETAC) (1990-1993), "Agenda papers", Canberra.

Vocational Education, Employment and Training Advisory Committee (VEETAC) (1991), "Women in entry-level training, policy review of the 1987 report", *Women in Apprenticeship,* Canberra.

Vocational Education, Employment and Training Advisory Committee (VEETAC) (1992), "Assessment of performance under competency-based training and administration of competency-based training", Consultation papers, Working Party on the Implementation of Competency based Training, Canberra.

Vocational Education, Employment and Training Advisory Committee (VEETAC) (1993*a*), *Staffing TAFE for the 21st Century – Phase 2*, Working Party on TAFE Staffing Issues, NSW Government Printer, Regents Park.

Vocational Education, Employment and Training Advisory Committee (VEETAC) (1993*b*), *A National Qualifications Framework – a paper for consultation*, Working Party on Recognition of Training, Canberra.

Western Australian Department of Employment and Training (1991), *The Western Australian New Apprenticeship Training and Assessment System (NATAS)*, Commonwealth/State Joint Project final report, Perth, April.

3

AUSTRIA

by

Lorenz Lassnig, Institut für höhere Studien, Vienna

1. INTRODUCTION

Structure of educational institutions

The Austrian education system is a comparatively clear structure of nine years of compulsory schooling (from the age of 6 to 15). The primary level features only one type of school (four years of primary school for pupils 6 to 10), whereas the lower secondary level offers two types of school (from the age of 10 to 14): four years of general secondary school or four years of academic secondary school (AHS – *Allgemeinbildende höhere Schule*, lower cycle).

The first eight years of schooling offer only general education. In the last year of compulsory schooling, however, vocational elements are offered for the first time, depending on the type of school. In Year 9 (age 14-15) several choices are available: the pre-vocational year, or the first year of an upper secondary school, be it a full-time vocational colleges, a technical college or the upper cycle of an academic secondary school (AHS, upper cycle).

The *pre-vocational year* can be regarded as an orientation year offering information on occupations and trades as well as general education (this type of school has to be attended before age 15 if none of the others are chosen).

Full-time vocational colleges offer general and vocational education up to semi-skilled or skilled worker level, depending on the duration of the course.

Technical colleges offer general education as well as technical theory and practice, with a final exam which allows graduates to be admitted to university or to start a professional or semi-professional career.

Academic secondary schools lead up to final exams entitling graduates to proceed to university.

After Year 9, the apprenticeship system is added to VOTEC; thus there are different sectors of the system: the apprenticeship system, and the VOTEC schools, as sketched above.

The *apprenticeship system* is a combination of in-company training and complementary compulsory schooling on a day- or block-release basis. These part-time vocational colleges offer additional training in the chosen occupations or trades and also some general education.

Additional courses are offered to graduates of the apprenticeship system and full-time vocational colleges in order to acquire higher-level qualifications. These courses are part of the so-called *second-chance education* which provides upgrading courses offering the same type of certification as upper secondary colleges, and a variety of courses introducing work-oriented knowledge and skills to beginners or enhancing or upgrading the knowledge and skills of graduates from VOTEC institutions.[1]

It should be emphasized that the distinction between vocational and technical colleges, and especially the naming of these programmes, is somewhat ambiguous. First, in most cases vocational and technical colleges are both parts of a combined institutional complex sharing buildings, facilities, teachers and other personnel. In institutional terms, the distinction is strongly drawn by occupational fields. Second, in Austria the distinction is labelled under the terms *Berufsbildende mittlere Schulen* ("middle vocational schools" = vocational colleges) and *Berufsbildende höhere Schulen* ("higher vocational schools" = technical colleges). The shifting refers to the hierarchical notion of "vocational" *vs.* "technical".

It may be questioned however, whether the Austrian "vocational colleges" are labelled appropriately, considering the hierarchical meaning of "vocational" in the international context. The full-time vocational colleges clearly lie somewhere between apprenticeship and technical colleges. In comparison to the apprenticeship system, the credentials of vocational colleges provide a higher degree. In comparison to technical colleges, then, these institutions provide lesser credentials – a fact true not only in terms of access to higher education but also in terms of formal qualifications required by trades and industries. The "value" of the qualifications for trades and industries is formally set by the number of entitlements to access to certain occupational categories included in the credentials of a particular study line. This system may be considered as a type of common currency of vocational credentials, with those of the apprenticeship system as the basic unit. Of course, there is a lot of informal valuation of credentials involved in labour market processes which may in certain respects be stronger than one's formal credentials.

Programmes

Programmes may be identified as the broad institutions, resulting in three main "programmes" of the VOTEC system: full-time vocational colleges, technical colleges and the apprenticeship system. As additional programmes, there is "second-chance" education and, eventually, non-university technical/vocational post-secondary courses (*Kollegs*). The main differences between these programmes are shown in Table 1.

The question remains, however, whether calling these institutions programmes is appropriate for the Austrian system. From a functional point of view, these broad institutions are abstract categories which group together very different sectoral areas. There are some 350 study lines within Austrian VOTEC at the level of upper secondary education and because of the low degree of "modularisation", it seems possible to label these courses of study as "programmes", but a meaningful overall classification at an intermediate level of aggregation is lacking. There is a well-established classification of the broad institutions on the

Table 1. **Austrian VOTEC programmes**

	Technical colleges	Full-time vocational colleges	Apprenticeship system
	Main dimensions		
Level of qualification	High	Middle	Low
Formal entitlement[1]	University, trades/industries	Trades/industries	Trades/industries
Main learning site	School-based	School-based	Work-based
Entry requirements	Prior school performance, entry exam	Prior school performance, entry exam	Compulsory school, contract for apprenticeship
Weight of general elements[2]	Approximately $2/5$	Approximately $1/3$	Approximately 4% ($1/5$ if pre-vocational year included)
	Additional dimensions		
Fields of study	65	110	170[3]
Duration	5 years (6 500-8 000 hours)	3 to 4 years (3 800-6 400 hours)[4]	2 to 4 years (5 200-9 100 hours)[5]
Certification	Yes	Yes	Yes

1.   Entitlement to trades/industries is regulated by law according to apprenticeship category, vocational and technical college certificates, and also by some university degrees.
2.   See Lassnigg (1989).
3.   Number of school curriculum subjects – there are more than 200 vocational categories.
4.   There are also schools in this sector with a one- to two-year duration, but these have been omitted because their value is rather small.
5.   Total time spent at school and on the job.
Source: Author.

Table 2. **Number of study lines available, by programme and occupational field**

	Technical colleges	Vocational colleges	Apprenticeship	Total
Agriculture, forestry, tourism	12	28	13	53
Craft, engineering, production	40	45	110	195
Business, trade, administration	1	7	11	19
Health and social welfare	–	10	6	16
Education and training	3	–	–	3
Arts and culture	9	20	30	59
Total	65	110	170	345

Note: This table does not refer to post-secondary programmes and institutions which may be seen as part of VOTEC. In the non-university sector of post-secondary education, 55 study lines may be identified: 27 located in the field of education and training, 15 in the field of technical and craft occupations, and nine in the field of health and welfare (four are distributed among the remaining categories).
Source: Author.

one hand and an unequivocal definition of the single courses of study on the other, but between these levels of aggregation several different classifications are used, which mostly are not comparable between institutional sectors. Thus the classification used for aggregation of study lines in the apprenticeship sector is completely different from that for aggregation of study lines at school.

This problem, well known within the context of the VOTEC study, was addressed in a previous research project offering an overall analysis of how the Austrian system functions (Lassnig, 1989). Despite the fact that the research described the situation before 1989, it does give a fair approximation of the present system. As an example of a meaningful classification of study at an intermediate level of aggregation, six broad occupational fields were defined and an analysis provided of the basic structures of vocational education, broken down in terms of these fields.[2]

Table 2 shows that, in each programme, the number of study lines is highest in the technical and craft occupations. This refers to the degree of specialisation within this occupational field. *Specialisation* in the Austrian context means the degree of differentiation of a broader occupational field according to specialised curricula and credentials.

Pathways

Within VOTEC

Pathways in the Austrian system of VOTEC are very much identical to the various courses of study in occupational fields. This is especially true if we refer only to the upper secondary cycle of the system where VOTEC is located. There are expected "standard careers" which are defined as completion of the chosen study line within the predetermined time-frame (normally three to five years).

In the full-time schooling sector, the specific course of study will begin in Year 9, and it is normally expected that the study line chosen will be completed after the usual number of years.

In the apprenticeship sector, the expected "standard career" is to apply for an apprenticeship in Year 10 upon completion of the pre-vocational year and then to complete apprenticeship within a contract period by passing the final examination after a given length of time.

However, there are certain exemptions to the expected "standard careers". The following factors are influential in this respect:

- *Increasing the time period because of failure at school.* Under certain conditions, a student may have to repeat a year, thus increasing the length of time in school without changing his/her formal qualification (as we will show later, this occurs rather frequently, especially in technical colleges).

- *Changing a study line within the schooling sector.* This factor is made up of at least three types of "non-standard careers": *i*) change between occupational fields, *ii*) change of level within one's occupational field either upwards, or *iii*) downwards.

  This typology can be much more complex, involving changes to higher grades or combined change and repetition, etc. Certain regulations govern these changes, in principle requiring that the whole previous curriculum of the new course of study be mastered. This system makes it relatively easy to take type *iii*) of non-standard careers and change from a higher to a lower programme within the same occupational field. This is most frequent within non-standard careers caused by the factor "change of study line"; it is to some extent an alternative to repeating a year at technical college.

- *Changing the study line after Year 9 from schooling to apprenticeship.* This is done rather frequently, especially by female students, causing declining enrolment in the pre-vocational year. Often a student tries a certain study line within the schooling sector – especially at vocational colleges – and, after failing, changes to an apprenticeship occupation.

- *Changing within apprenticeship* may also occur owing to different reasons: *i*) changing one's employer within the same study line; *ii*) changing one's study line – to facilitate such changes, "families of occupations" are defined within which certain parts of previous contracts are to be accounted for (as will be shown later, information on these processes is rather poor but nevertheless indicates a high turnover between employers within the apprenticeship system).

– *Changing from Year 8 or before directly to Year 10 apprenticeships.* This non-standard career might possibly compensate for failure during compulsory schooling, thus allowing a student to "gain" one year (or more) which had previously been "lost" because of having to repeat it.

– *Changing from schooling to apprenticeship after Year 10, especially because of failure at school.* This choice may be considered as fairly frequent; but unfortunately, there is virtually no hard evidence available about it.

– *Double apprenticeships.* A somewhat disputed new type of pathway which is pushing for standardised status, which in fact constitutes a new kind of study line.

Embedding VOTEC within the system

If the upper secondary cycle is seen within the context of those components of the system, both preceding and following it, the number of possible pathways may thus be extended.

a)   Previous career

Vocational education starts at the 9th or 10th year, but pathways may be defined as starting from the 5th year. Pupils are sorted during the lower secondary school (Years 5 to 8) according to three or four somewhat diffuse tracks which constitute the primary component in choosing a pathway through the system. Lower cycle secondary school is differentiated into two streams: the academic stream (AHS), and the general stream (Hauptschule), the latter being further differentiated according to achievement. The most important pathways combined with the institutions of lower secondary education are:

– Institution A: AHS (*Allgemeinbildende höhere Schule*) – academic stream of lower secondary school:

  • Pathway 1*a*): academic stream Years 5-8, designed for entry into higher education (enrolment in the academic stream is approximately 30 of an age cohort, with its share growing).

– Institution B: *Hauptschule* – general stream of lower secondary school, differentiated according to achievement (despite a much more complicated reality, this stream may be divided into two main categories, with a third intermediate one falling in between):

  • Pathway 1*b*): high achievement, with entry possible into higher tracks of upper secondary education; despite this path being located in another institutional context, its certificate is formally equivalent to that of the academic stream.

- Pathway 2): low achievement, designed for entry into apprenticeship (enrolment in *Hauptschule* totals approximately 70 per cent of an age cohort, with its share and numbers declining; the available information about the different categories within this stream is rather poor, but distribution of Pathways 1*b*) and 2) may be estimated at somewhat near 50:50).

At the 9th/10th year, pathways are "broken" in a somewhat complicated manner. The two main strands of VOTEC start at different grades: vocational schools in the 9th, and apprenticeship in the 10th year. The 9th year, which is the first year of vocational schooling, is also the last year of compulsory schooling (Table 3). Apprenticeship starts after compulsory schooling, but without requiring a formal certificate (only the completion of nine years' time of school is required). The 9th year of compulsory schooling may be completed either: *i*) within general compulsory school (Years 1 to 8), if one or more years have been repeated because of poor performance; *ii*) within the first year of upper secondary vocational or academic school; or *iii*) within a type of school designed specially for the completion of compulsory school by pupils who want to go further into an apprenticeship programme (pre-vocational year: *Polytechnischer Lehrgang*).

According to these mechanisms, regulation cannot exclude somebody from VOTEC – an aspect which can be considered as an essential feature of the Austrian education and training system.

Nevertheless, careers are predetermined depending on the path taken at lower secondary school. A markedly higher fraction of AHS graduates apply to higher-track programmes (academic stream or technical colleges) in Year 9 than do *Hauptschule* graduates (see below the sub-section on flows within the system).

Table 3.   **Distribution of pupils in the 9th year of their educational career**

Percentage

	1980/81	1991/92
Within compulsory school (delayed careers)	21	17
First year of upper secondary school	49	61
which included: academic track	15	22
technical colleges	14	22
vocational colleges	20	17
Pre-vocational year	30	22

Source: Author.

Box 1. **Pathways in Austrian VOTEC**

A: Without VOTEC

(A1) No *formal vocational education completed*

Not tried:

• No certificate of compulsory education, no further education

• Low achievement, polytechnic year, no further education

Drop-outs:

• Drop-outs from apprenticeship

• Drop-outs from upper secondary school

  • AHS completed, drop-outs from higher education(A2) *Eventual vocational qualifications at postsecondary level only*

• Completion of AHS from Years 5 to 12, postsecondary VOTEC

• High achievement, upper cycle AHS, postsecondary VOTEC

• Completion of AHS from Years 5 to 12, higher education completed

  • High achievement, upper cycle AHS, higher education completed**B: With VOTEC**

(A3) *Apprenticeship completed*

• Low achievement (polytechnic year possible), apprenticeship

• High achievement, polytechnic year, apprenticeship

• High achievement, first year upper secondary school, planned apprenticeship

  • High achievement, drop-out from upper secondary school, pushed into apprenticeship(A4) *Full-time vocational college*

• Planned full-time vocational college

  • Pushed into full-time vocational college [no access to other sectors, or dropping out from academic upper secondary school (AHS)](A5) *Technical college*

• Academic stream at lower secondary school (AHS), technical college completed, no further education

• High achievement in general lower secondary school, technical college completed, no further education

  • Technical college, dropping out from higher education(A6) *Double vocational education: higher VOTEC and higher education*

• Same occupational field

• Different occupational fields

b) Subsequent career

After completion of the upper secondary cycle, additional pathways are made possible by two main institutions. The first is an entitlement giving nearly equal access to university studies to graduates of technical colleges, resulting in two sorts of "double qualification": *i)* university studies in the same subject as that completed during technical college, and *ii)* university studies of subjects different from one's major at the technical college, *e.g.* a combination of engineering and business (approximately 40 per cent of all graduates of technical colleges now apply to university).

The second of these institutions are two- or three-year programmes called *Kollegs* at postsecondary level which offer the same type of certification as upper secondary technical colleges. Whereas these institutions are designed mainly for graduates of the academic stream, graduates of technical colleges can also add qualifications from fields other than those majored in at upper secondary school (approximately 10 per cent of all AHS graduates now apply to the *Kollegs*, in addition to 70 per cent starting university studies).

c) Dropping out

Some additional pathways may be defined which include dropping out at particular stages of one's educational career. A list of 20 modified pathways through the system may be identified conceptually (see Box 1).

2. QUANTITATIVE INDICATIONS AND ESTIMATES

Because there is no cohort study available in Austria, quantitative information on the distribution of the various educational pathways is difficult to obtain. Nevertheless, some rough indications or estimates can be given. Better data are available for stocks of pupils within the formal education system than are flow data within the formal system; then, it is very difficult to apply this information to age cohorts.

Quantitative information regarding the pathways outlined above will now be developed step by step.

Institutions

Tables 4 and 5 show the distribution of pupils in Years 1 to 13. An impression of the flow of a cohort through the system is given in Table 4 and the actual numbers at the different stages are presented in Table 5. The latter perspective does not give an account of a cohort, since the numbers are due to different age

Table 4.   **Absolute numbers of pupils at Years 1 to 13: Cohort 1979/80 to 1991/92**

Stocks at beginning of year, thousands

Year	Special school	Primary school							
1	1.8	98.8							
2	2.9	96.4							
3	3.5	95.4							
4	3.9	94.9							

Year	Special school	Lower secondary (General)						Lower secondary (academic)	
5	3.9	72.9						23.2	
6	3.3	73.2						22.3	
7	3.1	73.0						22.1	
8	2.9	71.6						21.2	

Year	Special school	Pre-vocational year	Vocational colleges					Technical colleges	Academic (upper)
			1 Year	2 Year	3 Year	4 Year	Total		
9	0.7	22.2	6.6	2.8	11.2	5.8	26.4	23.9	17.6

Year	Special school	Apprenticeship	1 Year	2 Year	3 Year	4 Year	Total	Technical colleges	Academic (upper)
10		51.8		2.0	8.9	4.0	14.9	20.1	16.8
11		49.7			7.3	3.4	10.7	17.3	15.5
12		47.6				2.6	2.6	16.4	14.0
13		8.7						14.4	

Source: Lassnigg (1994).

cohorts which differ in size. Overall, the absolute numbers are currently declining, indicating that age cohorts are becoming smaller.

Table 6 shows the distribution of pupils in selected years, for the cohort 1979/80-1991/92, and for the year 1990/91. Analysis of this information highlights some of the most salient features of the system, as well as some recent trends:

– The absolute numbers in Years 1 to 8 correspond roughly to the size of the age cohorts.

– About 3 per cent of all pupils are in special schools; this indicator appears to be constant.

– In Year 5 the first major selection takes place, with about one-fifth to one-fourth of an age cohort going to the academic stream. This share is currently expanding in time; but during the lower secondary cycle, there is a slight tendency to transfer to the general stream.

Table 5. **Absolute numbers of pupils at Years 1 to 13: Cross-section 1990/91**

Stocks at beginning of year, thousands

Year	Special school	Primary school							
1	1.4	90.4							
2	1.9	90.6							
3	2.1	91.5							
4	2.5	89.7							

Year	Special school	Lower secondary (General)						Lower secondary (Academic)	
5	2.7	60.6						25.3	
6	2.4	59.5						23.4	
7	2.4	59.6						22.6	
8	2.3	59.2						21.6	

Year	Special school	Pre-vocational year	Vocational colleges					Technical colleges	Academic (upper)
			1 Year	2 Year	3 Year	4 Year	Total		
9	0.6	19.5	5.1	2.3	8.2	4.3	19.9	23.8	17.0
		Apprenticeship							
10		48.3		2.0	6.6	3.3	11.9	20.5	15.7
11		46.9			6.0	3.3	0.3	17.6	15.7
12		45.8				1.9	1.9	16.5	14.0
13		8.7						14.6	

Source: Lassnigg (1994).

- From Years 8 to 9, the first important regrouping of the flows can be seen. First, the absolute number of pupils in the cohort declines at this step, owing to the direct stream of pupils who had lost time during compulsory school and had to pass to Year 10 (apprenticeship). Second, we see that the number of pupils in the general academic stream declines from Year 8 to Year 9, indicating a stream into VOTEC. Third, there is a move from the general stream in the lower secondary cycle to VOTEC, with about 25-30 per cent of an age cohort going to those technical colleges which further provide entitlements to university.

- A second regrouping takes place from Years 9 to 10. Apprenticeship recruits from the pre-vocational year; from Year 9 of the schooling sector, especially from the vocational colleges; and from Year 8, as pointed out earlier. The absolute number therefore rises from Year 9 to Year 10. There is a current tendency showing a decline in the share of vocational colleges

Table 6. **Distribution of pupils in selected years**

Percentage

				Cohort 1979/80-1991/92		
Year	Thousands	Special school	Primary school	Lower secondary (General)	Lower secondary (Academic)	
4	98.8	3.9	96.1			
5	100.0	3.9		72.9	23.2	
8	95.7	3.0		74.8	22.2	
			Apprenticeship	Pre-vocational year	Vocational colleges	Technical colleges	Academic (upper)
9	90.8	0.8		24.4	29.1	26.3	19.4
10	103.0		50.3		14.5	19.5	15.8

				Cross-section 1990/91		
			Primary school	Lower secondary (General)	Lower secondary (Academic)	
4	92.2	2.7	97.3			
5	88.6	3.0		68.4	28.6	
8	83.1	2.8		71.2	26.0	
			Apprenticeship	Pre-vocational year	Vocational colleges	Technical colleges	Academic (upper)
9	80.8	0.7		24.1	24.6	29.5	21.0
10	96.4		50.1		12.3	21.3	16.3

Source: Lassnigg (1994).

and a slight rise in apprenticeship, whereas the share of the academic stream, and especially of technical colleges, is rising.

Flows within the system

An examination of flows within the system provides some additional information:

– From the academic stream in the lower secondary cycle, 83 per cent continue their career within the schooling sector; whereas this is the case with only 50 per cent of all pupils in the general stream.

– About two-thirds of all transfers from the academic stream continue in an academic stream, whereas only one out of ten transitions from the general stream moves into the academic stream of upper secondary school.

Table 7. **Composition of flows at Years 8/9 from lower secondary
to the upper secondary institutions, 1990-91**

Percentage

		Year 9 Academic	Year 9 Technical	Year 9 Vocational	Total	Other
Year 8 academic	All academic pupils at Year 8 = 100%	53	27	3	83	17
	Flows to schools from academic = 100%	64	33	4	100	–
	All pupils at Year 8 = 100%	15	7	1	23	5
Year 8 general	All general pupils at Year 8 = 100%	5	23	22	50	50
	Flows to schools from general = 100%	10	46	44	100	–
	All pupils at Year 8 = 100 %	4	16	16	36	36

Source: Author.

– Transitions to VOTEC from the academic stream flow mostly into technical colleges, whereas transitions from the general stream flow to both technical and vocational colleges.

The composition of transitions from lower secondary to upper secondary schools shows that the decision in Year 9 has an important impact on educational career. This holds true not only for the decision to continue in school but also for the choice of schooling career. It applies especially to the general or VOTEC decision and to the level of that VOTEC decision (see Table 7).

Delayed careers during compulsory schooling

An important aspect of the Austrian system is the fact that a rather high ratio of pupils either have to repeat one or more years or have to delay their first enrolment to school because of lack of *Schulreife* (maturity to attend school). Until the 9th year, some 25 per cent of an age cohort have delayed their career; almost 20 per cent can be identified as being delayed because of failure at school. Rates of failure at school per year lie between 2 per cent and 3 per cent during primary school and the general stream of lower secondary school; in the academic stream, the failure rate rises from a level of 3-4 per cent in Years 5 and 6 to a level of 6-8 per cent in Years 7 and 8. During the lower secondary cycle, failure at school is a factor which enhances transitions from the academic to the general stream. Therefore, the total number of pupils in the general stream is rising slightly (the ratio of pupils in the academic stream who do not repeat a year in case of failure is rising from one-third in Years 5 and 6 to 40-60 per cent in Years 7 and 8, the overall ratio of outflow lying at a level of about 1 per cent in Years 5 and 6 and rising to 2-4 per cent at the higher levels).

As we have said, the accessibility of apprenticeship depends on a pupil spending the mandatory time required for compulsory school (nine years). Completion of Year 9 is not required; therefore one or more years may be "gained" in the case of delayed careers by direct transition from Year 8 to Year 10. Approximately 15 per cent of the 1979/80 beginners had experience of this path. However, it has some important implications. First, pupils do not have the incentive to gain formal credentials from compulsory schooling, being foreclosed from further possibilities. Second, if we look at the occupations or study lines within the apprenticeship system which are frequented by these pupils, we see that it is mostly the least worthwhile career opportunities which are in fact accessible to this group.

Failure and mobility at the upper secondary cycle

A distinction must be made here between the full-time schooling and apprenticeship sectors because of differences in availability of data.

Schools

As stated above, both failure and mobility rates are fairly high in upper secondary schools, especially in VOTEC. The quantitative picture is indicated by the retention rates shown in Table 8. Because of the different length of study lines in vocational colleges, it was only possible to make rough estimates. Figures indicate that the number of students in Year 11 is approximately three-quarters of those in Year 9. This estimate however, includes the mobility of successful pupils from school to apprenticeship. A recalculation can be made on the basis of failure rates and by taking into account the number of pupils who do not repeat the year failed. The average failure rate, which is about 2-3 per cent through Years 2 to 8 of compulsory school (academic stream included) increases to a rather high level of about 12-15 per cent in Years 9 and 10, then decreases step by step from Years 11 to 13 (9 to 7 to 4 per cent). An aggregated drop-out rate of about 20 per cent can be estimated, without accounting for mobility either within the school system or between school and apprenticeship.

Mobility within the school sector is substantially lower than is failure. Table 9 accounts for mobility between institutions from Year 9 onwards (mobility between Years 8 and 9 is not accounted for because of the transitional status of this step). Two types of mobility may be distinguished: *i)* mobility with failure, the year being repeated; and *ii)* mobility without failure, progressing to the next year of another institution.

Table 8. **Retention in upper secondary schools, 1987/88-1991/92**

Thousands

	Year 9		Year 10		Year 11		Year 12		Year 13	
Academic	17.6	100%	16.2	92%	15.5		14.0	80%		
Technical	23.3	100%	20.0	86%	17.3		16.3		14.4	62%
Vocational[1]	25.8	100%*	14.5	56%	10.6	41%*	(1.8)			
	16.4	100%**				65%**				
Total[2]	57.3	100%			43.4	76%				

1. Retention * is biased because of different length of study lines (one to four years); retention ** is estimated without short study lines.
2. Estimated.
Source: Author.

The number of mobile pupils in the upper secondary cycle for 1989/90 was around 4 600, of whom 3 300 (about 70 per cent) were moving within the system and 1 300 flowing into the system on non-regular paths. The average rate of mobility within the system is about 1.7 per cent, being higher in Year 9 where all institutions are involved. In Years 10 to 12, mobility concerns the technical colleges only; pupils from these institutions are changing to vocational colleges, with about two-thirds of them progressing to the next year and one-third repeating the year. In Year 9, mobility is completely connected with repetition of the year; therefore, two-thirds of overall mobility is of the repetition type. From the 3 300 changes within the system, 1 584 occur in Year 9, showing the structure indicated in Table 10.

The academic stream emerges as a loser with regard to mobility, whereas the VOTEC streams appear to be winners. The vocational colleges win more in relative terms, and the technical colleges gain more in absolute terms.

Table 9. **Mobility in Year 9, 1990**

Absolute numbers

	Academic (upper)	Technical	Vocational	Total
Academic (upper)	–	475	220	695
Technical	106	–	420	526
Vocational	19	344	–	363
Total	125	819	640	1 584

Source: Author.

Table 10. **Mobility within the upper secondary schools, 1990**

% outflow

	Year 9	Year 10	Year 11	Year 12	Average
Academic (upper)	4.0	–	–	–	1.1
Technical	2.0	3.0	5.0	1.0	2.8
Vocational	2.0	–	–	–	0.8
Average	2.5	1.4	1.9	0.6	1.7

Source: Author.

Overall, the analysis indicates that mobility within the school sector is blocked to a high degree: it frequently includes failure and repetition. After Year 9, mobility is predominantly downward, according to the hierarchy of institutions.

Apprenticeship

Failure within apprenticeship is more difficult to document. There are at least three dimensions for assessing failure: *i*) failure at part-time school and repetition of a grade analogous to failure in the school sector; *ii*) failure at the final examination; and *iii*) failure related to performance at the workplace, quitting one's apprenticeship.

Failure rates at part-time school stand at 3 per cent, low in comparison to full-time schooling. Failure at the final examination is at about 8 per cent, with the net failure rate being lower because the exam may be passed in a second attempt. The most important aspect, however – failure related to performance at work – is not documented. We know the number of apprentices who quit during a year is rather high (25-30 per cent of a beginning cohort). The reasons leading to the ending of an apprenticeship are not known. A recent study found that almost 40 per cent of beginners end their first apprenticeship before reaching the full period. The cohort drop-out rate from apprenticeship is about 20 per cent.

An important factor is mobility between the schooling and apprenticeship sectors. There is a rather strong flow from school to apprenticeship but there is virtually no mobility the other way round. This stems from the fact that knowledge acquired at school may be credited by apprenticeships, whereas knowledge acquired from apprenticeship is not credited by schools. However, there is a lack of information about the streams lying between the school sector and the apprenticeship system. In Year 10, 27 per cent of apprentices come from upper secondary schooling: in absolute terms, about 12 000 persons. As has been pointed out already, this number is partly due to the practice of "skipping" the pre-vocational year, partly reflecting a kind of dropping out of school. The actual composition is unknown. In addition, there is no information on whether there is an inflow from the school sector into higher grades of apprenticeship.

Overall, this area should be analysed in greater detail, which requires an extended database. Information available indicates a flow from school to apprenticeship, the latter system being a sort of "last chance" for drop-outs from schooling – whereas there seems to be no such final opportunity for drop-outs from apprenticeship.

3. CHANGES IN PARTICIPATION

Table 11 shows the changing participation in the VOTEC system. Whereas the number of apprentices grew by 60 per cent from 1950 to 1990, the number in VOTEC schools increased by more than 500 per cent, markedly more than pupils in academic general education. Expansion of VOTEC schools is a long-term development, but it was especially marked during the 1970s. Compared to the academic stream and to apprenticeship, different paths of development are indicated by the figures. The number of apprentices was already at a very high level in 1960, then it reached another peak in 1980 – with figures reflecting demographic development to a high extent. The academic stream expanded markedly during the 1950s and 1960s, then showed a lower expansion during the 1970s, followed by a decline during the 1980s (see Figure 1).

Within VOTEC schooling, the magnitude of vocational and technical colleges changed. During the 1950s and 1960s the vocational colleges educated a noticeably higher number of pupils than did the technical colleges. During the 1970s, the latter expanded more rapidly, reaching a size similar to that of vocational colleges. In the following decade, participation in technical colleges grew further, whereas participation in vocational colleges started to decline.

During the last decade, the demographic peak of the early 1960s had a repercussion on the VOTEC system. The years 1980-81 marked the maximum enrolment in the upper secondary cycle.

Table 11 shows that:

- in general, enrolment in apprenticeship is declining, whereas schooling has tended to reflect the demographic upturn until the early 1980s, followed by a general downturn;

- the schooling institutions leading to university access have been growing more than the lower institutions;

- within the higher stream of schooling the academic sector has been declining, whereas the technical colleges have been expanding, with the growth of the business sector being stronger than that in the engineering sector;

Table 11. **Long-term participation in VOTEC programmes**

Thousands[1]

| | Vocational colleges | | | | | | |
	Craft, engineering, production	Business	Hotel, catering, tourism	Agriculture, forestry	Social work, education, pre-school	Total	Change (%)[2]
1950	8.7	4.6	3.8	3.1	2.2	22.4	
1960	8.7	10.5	4.9	4.5	2.9	31.5	141
1970	11.8	20.2	8.7	5.5	4.9	51.1	162
1980	19.2	26.1	14.6	9.9	8.9	78.7	154
1990	20.8	12.9	11.4	10.0	10.0	65.1	83

| | Technical colleges | | | | | | |
	Craft, engineering, production	Business	Hotel, catering, tourism	Agriculture, forestry	Social work, education, pre-school[3]	Total	Change (%)[2]
1950	3.4	3.1	0.5	0.5		7.5	–
1960	10.9	7.9	1.1	1.1		21.0	280
1970	15.4	10.9	3.1	1.4		30.8	147
1980	31.3	31.1	10.7	3.0		76.1	247
1990	46.1	35.5	14.3	3.2		99.1	130

| | All programmes | | | | | |
	Total VOTEC schools (thousands)	Change (%)[2]	Academic stream years 9-12 (thousands)	Change (%)[2]	Apprentices (thousands)	Change (%)[2]
1950	29.9		13.8		92.9	
1960	52.5	176	30.3	219	141.0	152
1970	81.9	156	57.0	188	137.4	97
1980	154.8	189	75.3	132	197.0	143
1990	164.2	106	62.5	83	147.4	75

1. Schools for adults are included in the figures.
2. Number for previous decade = 100.
3. Because of various changes in this sector, no consistent figures are available.
Source: Austrian report for CEDEFOP, updated by the author.

– within the vocational colleges, the business sector has been declining, whereas the other branches have remained stable;

– within the apprenticeship system, the craft, engineering and production sector has been declining, whereas the other sectors have remained stable.

◆   Figure I.   **Upper secondary education by type of school**
1970-91

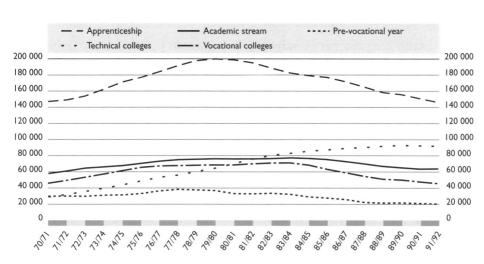

Source: Author.

Enrolment in VOTEC is very much segregated by gender:

– Vocational colleges can be considered as a female sector (with 70 per cent female enrolment), whereas apprenticeship is more markedly male (with 70 per cent male enrolment); higher-level institutions are on the average distributed equally between both sexes.

– Broken down by broad vocational fields within the different institutional contexts, the gender composition differs markedly. The craft, engineering and production sector is male-dominated (70-95 per cent), and the business sector – as well as the health and social welfare sector – is female-dominated (with figures of 70-80 per cent and about 90 per cent respectively).

4.   COMMENTS AND EVIDENCE CONCERNING THE WORKING HYPOTHESES

Educational policy issues during recent decades – a brief overview

Reforms of programmes on a broader scale which took place in Austria during the late 1960s and early 1970s included:

– shifting the end of compulsory school from the 8th to the 9th year;

– establishing the pre-vocational year;

- adding one year to the VOTEC programmes;

- broadening access to university for graduates of technical colleges;

- designing an upper secondary institution for the academic stream;

- establishing teacher education colleges at the postsecondary level;

- giving the short-term technical colleges at postsecondary level more formal status;

- establishing a comprehensive legal basis for the apprenticeship system;

- expanding the net of academic secondary schools and making the net more dense, each district to provide at least one academic secondary institution.

These changes were mostly part of a broad-scale reform of the Austrian education system which was amended in 1962. Implementation of these reforms took about ten years. The next wave of reforms started at the beginning of the 1970s, concentrating on the following issues:

- steps towards a comprehensive school at lower secondary level; large-scale experimentation with new organisational forms of the lower secondary cycle; postponement of entrance examinations to the academic stream of lower secondary education;

- broadening access to university studies; university reform trying to implement a dual-tier structure of studies, at the same time giving all higher education institutions an equal status as universities; organisational reform of universities;

- expansion of the net of VOTEC schools through a large-scale building programme aiming at the provision of facilities for one-fifth of an age cohort in VOTEC: half in vocational colleges and half in technical colleges.

This programme of educational policy was designed before the economic turbulences of the mid-1970s produced a major shift of political priorities towards labour market policies as well as action to combat the threat of rising youth unemployment. In Austria, the maximum demographic cohort reached upper secondary level at the beginning of the 1980s. At the same time, the country suffered its first major economic downturn in 1981, causing a threat of emerging youth unemployment. The consequences for educational policy took the form primarily of a shortage of vacancies in the apprenticeship sector, but there was also a move to open both the schooling sector and the university to prevent rising youth unemployment. During the mid-1980s, the apprenticeship sector was temporarily subsidised on a rather broad scale by active labour market policy measures. During this period from the second half of the 1970s until the end of the

1980s, education ranked rather low on the political agenda: emphasis shifted mainly to qualitative aspects. Nevertheless, the following changes and reforms should be mentioned:

- The general stream of lower secondary school was transformed from a dual-track organisation into a combined streaming/setting organisation, allowing pupils from high-achiever groups to progress to the programmes and institutions which provide entitlement to university access. New proposals for the reform of secondary education were formulated, aiming at different objectives. One of these was the development of stronger relations between the general lower secondary stream to academic upper-cycle general education. Another was a new programme which simultaneously tried to bring lower secondary school closer to apprenticeship and to raise the general educational basis of apprenticeship programmes.

- The curricula of VOTEC institutions were reformed, including a renaming of schools for what had been termed "female occupations".

- A comprehensive system of credits from VOTEC to apprenticeship was established.

- The upper cycle of the academic stream was reformed, including the graduation procedure.

- In the field of apprenticeship, deep and fundamental divergences remained between the interest groups involved over such broad issues as expanding part-time schooling, broadening occupational fields, creating additional learning sites and initiating mechanisms for financing and control. Despite these differences, however, some steps towards reform have taken place. Networks of enterprises may be established for the provision of additional learning sites. Part-time schooling was expanded to increase the time available for learning foreign languages and new technologies. And finally, steps were taken towards closer integration of apprenticeship and schooling.

- The most important reform in the long run, however, was the establishment of a new non-university *Fachhochschule* sector. The consequences of this reform *vis-à-vis* participation in VOTEC are not yet clear.

Most important changes which have influenced participation

The most important changes supposedly having consequences on participation in the VOTEC sector include:

Changes in programmes

- expanding the regional supply of general academic schools as well as of VOTEC schools;
- delaying the start of apprenticeship as compared to that of VOTEC;
- adding a further year to upper secondary schooling;
- broadening access to academic secondary as well as to VOTEC schools by changing selection procedures (postponing entrance examinations, providing possibilities to progress to higher levels from the general stream, etc.);
- broadening access to universities for graduates of technical colleges;
- expanding part-time schooling in the apprenticeship sector.

New programmes

- first wave of non-university institutions at postsecondary level (teacher education, education for social work);
- establishment of short-term technical colleges with a postsecondary cycle;
- establishment of "second-chance" programmes providing access to higher levels, either for pupils from vocational colleges or for those wishing to go to a technical college or university;
- establishment of new study lines on a small-scale basis within VOTEC;
- establishment of "double apprenticeships" providing simultaneous access to two vocational fields.

Disappearance of old programmes

- traditional apprenticeship study lines which are available in principle but are not actually educating any apprentices (in 1991, the number of apprentices was zero from 34 out of 230 available study lines, or about 14 per cent).

Shortages in funding

- especially during the demographic upturn, funding shortages occurred in the craft, engineering and production sectors of technical colleges;
- during more severe recessions there were frequent shortages of vacancies in the apprenticeship sector.

Over/undersupply

The issue of over/undersupply of qualifications has been heavily disputed since the late 1970s. Unfortunately, the debate has been mostly run on a rather general level and has been lacking in convincing evidence. On the one hand, there has been no objection to expanding the supply at higher levels, pointing out that during the past few years enrolment in apprenticeship has been declining, with the number of vacancies being markedly higher than that of applicants. In the long run, the threat of an undersupply of skilled workers and an oversupply of university graduates is mentioned by the advocates of this position, emphasizing especially that the majority of university graduates were educated in occupational fields close to the public sector and more or less alien from the business and enterprise sectors.

On the other hand, special attention has been drawn to the comparatively low ratio of higher education graduates in the Austrian economy, this position being underscored by the fact that economic indicators such as income, unemployment, etc., show on average better conditions for graduates from higher levels. Overall, there is agreement that the status and attractiveness of apprenticeship should be improved; particularly the aspect of further progression for graduates of the apprenticeship system to higher levels of the education system is stressed. But there is also some agreement that there is a tendency towards oversupply of university graduates in the field of humanities, especially with teachers for the higher level secondary schools. The new *Fachhochschulen* are expected to solve some of these problems.

Changing strategies by young people

- For the lower secondary cycle, young people (or their parents acting on their behalf) increasingly choose the academic stream as the privileged path to higher-level educational careers.

- For the upper secondary cycle, there is a growing propensity for graduates of technical colleges to start a university career. The vocational credentials of these programmes seem to become outweighed by the simultaneously-provided entitlement to transfer to university. It is difficult, however, to evaluate the reason. Perhaps the technical colleges are considered an alternative path to university from the start, or perhaps the changing strategies reflect declining opportunities with regard to employment.

- Young people tend increasingly to choose technical rather than vocational colleges, the latter institutions seeming to fall between technical colleges and apprenticeship.

– Access to apprenticeship increasingly takes place as an unintentional or indirect path through experience in VOTEC schools, and frequently because of failure at school.

Changing opportunities, incentives, costs and constraints (OICCs)

Because of a lack of more intensive studies in this field, the impact of changing OICCs is difficult to observe. There exist some propositions concerning OICCs which are generally assumed to be obvious, making deeper insight unnecessary. A brief general review, however, shows that many of these seemingly obvious assumptions may be misleading.

a)   Opportunities

A demographic downturn would increase opportunities for access to the more highly valued sectors, pathways or study lines. In order to retain their facilities built during the period of expansion, schools would compete for pupils and consequently lower their entrance requirements. This theory is based on some kind of "practical everyday experience" in relation to overall declining age cohorts; additionally, the "hidden assumption" that a growing share of an age cohort attending a particular programme would mean a lessening of ability may have an influence here. In fact, numbers have grown in technical colleges and academic secondary schools, whereas they have declined for apprenticeships. It was argued that, because of the oversupply of apprenticeship vacancies (up to 1992), applicants could choose among enterprises and thus drive vacancies with bad working conditions out of the market. However, there was no evidence available about the quality of apprenticeships. More detailed analysis indicated that the range of opportunities for apprenticeship graduates was narrowing, due to the competition by graduates from technical colleges.

b)   Incentives

It is widely held that the structure of educational choice in Years 8 and 9 provides strong incentives to choose a schooling pathway rather than apprenticeship. Two components are most important in this respect: first, the pre-vocational year is relatively unrewarding and lacks attractiveness in comparison to the first year of VOTEC, a notion which is reinforced by the fact that the selection procedures of enterprises offer greater rewards for VOTEC-school experience than for the pre-vocational year. Secondly, the overall more valuable credentials from vocational colleges are rewarded after three to four years, whereas the apprenticeship pathway – because it starts one year later – normally lasts four to five years. Thus, completing an apprenticeship for the best qualified occupation will consume as much time as does the choice to attend a technical college; but it is much lower in value.

For the lower secondary cycle, there are strong incentives to choose the academic stream despite the fact that the alternative general stream might possibly provide better educational conditions; the academic stream constitutes a greater probability of access to a higher-level educational career. In addition, the structure provides incentives to continue the academic stream at upper secondary level: in the case of transfer to VOTEC schools in Year 9, an entrance examination has to be passed which is not required by the academic stream.

c)   *Costs*

In terms of costs, the schooling pathways obviously cost their pupils more in terms of financial expenditure, not to speak of the risk of failure. The latter has been rising during the last decade, as is indicated by substantially increasing rates of failure, as well as higher drop-out rates.

On the other hand, apprenticeship costs comparatively little in terms of direct financial expenditure – despite the aspect of income foregone, if we take into account the productive contributions of apprentices. There is also the cost of giving up discretionary and leisure time, and in the long run, considerable financial outlay can be expected if one takes up an alternative educational career later.

d)   *Constraints*

Among the most important constraints concerning the provision of educational alternatives are not only regional supply but also the highly differentiated credentials within the hierarchy of educational levels, which make it difficult for former apprentices to resume an educational career.

5.   ELABORATION OF THE WORKING HYPOTHESES

Diversification

The Austrian system provides mixed evidence of the impact of diversification on participation in VOTEC. Traditionally, the degree of diversification has been high, as seen by the number of vocational categories represented by distinct study lines. However, the great number of such opportunities is embedded in an institutional context which is highly formalised, with the degree of institutional diversification being rather low. The development and especially implementation of new programmes is therefore difficult. If the impact of "diversification" is studied, an elaboration of what is meant by diversification would seem to be necessary. There may be several aspects of a VOTEC system, some being highly diversified and others considerably uniform.

Some empirical evidence on the development of participation in VOTEC shows firstly that despite the high number of study lines, participation tends to be concentrated in only a few categories. In the apprenticeship system in particular, the high degree of concentration is frequently put forward as a problem by those involved in policy discourse: 38 per cent of all apprentices are enrolled in only five out of about 230 study lines (Table 12).

Secondly, the increase of participation in VOTEC was mostly caused by flows into the traditional study lines. VOTEC policy, especially during the 1970s, was driven by the objective of strengthening and expanding traditional institutions.

In the apprenticeship system from 1981 to 1991, 15 new study lines emerged, with an enrolment of less than 5 000 (about 3 per cent of all apprentices in 1991). In addition, there were three pilot study lines in 1991, with an enrolment of 300. The number of former study lines from 1981 which were not followed in 1991, however, was also 15. Another type of diversification is *double apprenticeships*, where about 200 different categories can be observed, with one category dominating: cooks and waiters (46 per cent in 1981, 33 per cent in 1991). In 1981, 14 combinations of double apprenticeships had an enrolment of at least 50 apprentices; this number had increased to 19 by 1991.

In the upper secondary cycle, policy discourse in Austria has been concerned more with the objective of reducing the degree of diversification of vocational categories than with the aim of an increase in diversification. At postsecondary level, the recent development of a new legal framework of non-university institutions points in another direction. The trend towards a unified system of higher education represented by the universities, which was especially dominant during the 1970s, is no longer being followed. A new sector has been initiated, providing diversification not only in study lines but also in basic institutional aspects.

Table 12. **Concentration of apprentices in study lines, 1991**

Study lines with highest number of apprentices	Apprentices enrolled (%)		
1	11.3	30.5	13.2
1 to 3	28.1	58.7	26.7
1 to 5	37.5	67.4	38.1
1 to 10	52.8	79.6	55.6
1 to 20	69.0	89.4	70.3

Source: Author.

It may be argued that this diversification into complex pathways has contributed to the growing participation in VOTEC. The path from high achievement within the general stream of secondary education through technical colleges to employment or higher education has become an alternative to the academic stream of secondary education. However, the main aspect of this seems not to be one of diversification but rather a "double qualification" – better explained by some of the other hypotheses.

Delayed divergence

The Austrian system does not provide much evidence to support this hypothesis. The system is characterised more by early than by delayed divergence, since there is a common belief that the latter would cause an increase in general education and a lower participation in the VOTEC system.

Attention is particularly directed to the lower cycle of secondary education, where a higher degree of comprehensiveness could be perceived as a major factor to undermine the VOTEC system. Consequently, advocates of VOTEC support the strategy of strengthening tracking within the lower secondary cycle and creating stronger bonds between a "practical" track and VOTEC, especially apprenticeship.

Similar lines of argument could be heard during policy debates before the establishment of the *Fachhochschule* sector: that the creation of vocational studies as an alternative to university studies in the higher education system would weaken VOTEC at the secondary level. There are other disputes which underline the observation that, in the Austrian context, rather strong pressure exists for early divergence. The interpretation of the overall flows through the system in fact supports the hypothesis that participation in VOTEC, especially in the apprenticeship system, is to a substantial degree caused by the structural features of the system which "lock" some sectors of young people within this area.

The effects of delayed divergence on participation may be studied in the context of changes which took place during the late 1960s and early 1970s. These involved policy measures which could be classified as examples of delayed divergence include: *i)* the establishment of the pre-vocational year in 1966 which delayed the beginning of apprenticeship from Year 9 to Year 10; *ii)* the upgrading of the education of teachers in compulsory schools from secondary to postsecondary level; and *iii)* the establishment of two-year technical colleges at postsecondary level. The effects of these changes on participation have not yet been studied, but a closer look leads to the conclusion that many other aspects seem to have more impact than does delayed divergence:

– The pre-vocational year on the one hand had the effect that pupils with delayed careers had a better chance to acquire a formal certificate from compulsory school, thus increasing their overall chances for further progression in an educational career. On the other hand, delaying the beginning of apprenticeship – in combination with the possibility of spending the last year of compulsory school in the first year of upper secondary school – provided incentives to start a career within the schooling sector, and later to continue this path instead of changing to apprenticeship. Recently, this solution has come under strong criticism by the advocates of apprenticeship.

– The delayed start of teacher education was combined with the creation of a new branch of upper secondary education. The old institutions for teacher education were replaced by the upper secondary form of the academic stream. Despite some links of these institutions to the new postsecondary teacher education academies, the number of graduates from academic general education was substantially increased. Postsecondary teacher education expanded very rapidly – against general expectations in the political sphere – but in the long run, access to university was also increased.

– The two-year postsecondary technical colleges remained rather small in scale and did not transcend their marginal status of "second-chance" education, partly because of their rather demanding programme.

A new development within the education system, the establishment of *Fachhochschulen*, will provide the opportunity to study the effects of delayed divergence on participation. Two aspects will be discussed in this respect: effects on the propensity to begin a university career, and effects on the choice between either the academic stream of upper secondary education or technical college. It is too early, however, to make observations on these questions.

Flexible pathways

In principle, the Austrian education and training system is highly flexible. However, the possibilities are only partly taken advantage of. There are virtually no transitions between the different study lines within secondary education which are excluded by regulation. In general, a transition is possible if a pupil can demonstrate the knowledge required by the curricular regulations of the previous grades of the new study line. This also occurs with transitions down the hierarchical ladder within the same occupational field. If there are curricular requirements which are not part of the previously-run educational choice, these are to be met through examination. In fact, as was shown earlier in this chapter, downward flexibility is much more frequent than upward flexibility; furthermore, flexibility is often combined with failure at school.

The very openness of the apprenticeship system is an especially important feature of the system, one which causes mixed outcomes. While pupils who have failed at school are not driven out of the education system completely, selection processes and mechanisms are produced which lower the status of the apprenticeship system, putting it at the end of the hierarchical ladder.

Flexibility of transfer from VOTEC to general education is possible only at the upper rung of the system, with both technical colleges and academic secondary education providing access to university. At the lower end of the ladder, flexibility to transfer to general education is blocked to a great degree. Re-entering the schooling sector or higher education, especially from apprenticeship, is possible only at high cost. Because there are no general elements within the apprenticeship curriculum, a large amount of material has to be learned.

Transfers from general education to VOTEC do not in fact take place after Year 9 but after Years 12 or 13 because of increasing curricular requirements in VOTEC. The short-term technical colleges at postsecondary level provide the possibility for transfer from general education to VOTEC after Year 12.

Long pathways

This hypothesis is strongly supported by the Austrian system when it comes to participation in technical colleges. These colleges have offered the most expanding programmes in the upper secondary cycle during the last few decades, increasing participation in VOTEC both in absolute and relative terms. Enrolment in technical colleges continued to increase after the demographic peak of the early 1980s. In quantitative terms, the share of technical colleges within the upper secondary cycle rose from 9 per cent in 1970 to 25 per cent in 1990. This development is to a large part due to the "double qualification" credentials of technical colleges, which provide entitlement to university as well as recognised vocational credentials.

This special feature reduces the risk for young people from lower social strata of being excluded from the academic path to higher education; it is increasingly used as a pathway to higher education instead of the transfer to employment immediately after graduation. The risk is reduced firstly because an alternative credential is provided, thus reducing the necessity of going on to university. Secondly, the vocational credentials of technical colleges may be used as a basis for transition to employment in the case of dropping out from university (Table 13).

However, technical colleges in the sector of crafts, engineering and production also increase costs for students in comparison to the academic stream and other sectors of VOTEC. They impose very high demands on pupils in terms of time at school and amount of material to be learned. The rate of failure and dropping out is fairly high in this sector.

Table 13. **Transition to higher education by type of upper secondary education**

Percentage

	1975	1980	1985	1991
Academic upper secondary school	73	80	89	90
Technical: craft, engineering, and production	32	46	52	57
Technical: business and trades	37	41	46	54
Technical: agriculture and forestry	34	27	35	43
Technical: education	–	–	–	33
Total	63	67	68	71
Male	68	72	73	76
Female	56	62	68	65

Source: Author.

Exit points and segmentation

The internal logic of the Austrian system does not provide open credit points which the pupil can accumulate. Rather, it offers second-best alternatives in case of failure within the area of first choice. With the exception of drop-outs from apprenticeship, who are in fact neglected, the system does not "wipe out" pupils completely; but the system itself produces a considerable degree of individual experience with failure at school.

The "double qualification" of technical colleges may be labelled as some sort of exit point. However, if one sees it as credit earned after a comparatively long and cumulative programme, this solution seems rather a "perverse exit point" if used primarily as an expensive path to higher education rather than as VOTEC in its original sense.

Another kind of exit point is the delayed start of apprenticeship after Year 9. This solution, however, is often considered as an "anomaly" within the system, because the pre-vocational year does not provide credentials and is therefore seen as a "lost year" by many of its students. On the other hand, transfer from VOTEC to apprenticeship is recognised by an accreditation system. It can also be shown empirically that the transfer from Year 9 VOTEC schooling is valued more in terms of access to the more esteemed apprenticeships, in comparison to transfer from compulsory school or the pre-vocational year.

Overall, the Austrian system is to be characterised as a segmented system rather than a modular one, despite the fact that it provides certain mechanisms to loosen its fragmented character. These mechanisms grossly increase the hierarchical and partitioned nature of the system.

Broad occupational fields

This aspect is one of the most disputed in Austrian policy discussions. Certain critics, especially those from the unions, are opposed to the high degree of specialisation of study lines, and propose reforms which would develop more broad categories. Others, especially from the crafts industry, defend the existing structure. It is difficult to give an objective account of the relative "broadness" or "narrowness" of occupational fields. How can this aspect be measured except perhaps by looking at the number of various study lines within the different sectors of the educational system?

Evidence on this has been provided earlier in this chapter, showing that there are more numerous study lines in programmes aimed at the craft, engineering and production sectors than in programmes geared to all the other sectors, with the study lines in the craft sector more narrow than the others. However, the occupational and employment system is also structured differently in these sectors. There are more distinct occupational categories in the craft sector than in the administration sector, etc. VOTEC structure and employment structure interact in a complex manner and it is therefore difficult to find a fixed point on which to base a comparison.

One could perhaps analyse the transferability of curricula as a second way to measure the degree of specialisation. But despite attempts in this direction in a former study (Lassnig, 1989), this work has been mainly left undone; there is thus no documentation of curriculum items which would permit an analysis of this kind.

Formally recognised qualifications

In Austria, all VOTEC programmes provide formally recognised qualifications. On the one hand this is obviously a forceful incentive for participation; on the other, within this system it is relatively difficult for new study lines to emerge and to become recognised. In addition, conflicts between occupational groups may emerge because traditional groups are trying to monopolise certain occupational fields.

One coherent national system of qualifications

The different sorts of qualifications are grouped together into one system which uses the credentials of the apprenticeship system as a kind of currency. Most credentials, from vocational study lines up to university studies, are "translated" into some credits for apprenticeship. This system basically constitutes the strong hierarchical order of the system, which reflects the fact that all VOTEC programmes provide a certain number of apprenticeship qualifications. Credentials from vocational colleges are therefore more valuable than apprenticeships, with technical colleges providing additional access to university, etc.

The national system of qualifications is traditionally grounded in a system of requirements and entitlements for practising certain trades. This system has recently loosened up, to some extent owing to internalisation. Nevertheless, the national system of qualifications ties together the enterprise-based apprenticeship system with state regulations, giving apprenticeships a more formal status when compared to a more dominant private status as in many other countries. This aspect may be the most important factor influencing its high participation. On the other hand, the rather uniquely Austrian solution of tightly intertwined study lines, formal qualifications and occupational entitlements constitutes a complex system which presents strong obstacles to reform and innovation.

Work-based pathways leading into internal labour markets

Apprenticeship is work-based in two respects: first, access and selection are controlled by enterprises; and second, about four-fifths of all education time is under the control of the firm. However, this means accessibility to internal labour markets for only a certain number of all apprentices. Empirical evidence on this aspect is not very good so far, which can be assessed first by analysing employment after completion of apprenticeship. Survey studies indicate that about one-third remained with the enterprise for five years, whereas about two-thirds would have preferred to remain with the employer where they completed their apprenticeship. More recent research on the basis of social insurance records, however, indicates a much lower access to internal labour markets (Table 14).

A second method for assessing accessibility to internal labour markets in a more indirect manner takes as its starting point the renewal of the workforce from any given occupation. It may be assumed that the steady rate of renewal of a qualified workforce in an industry would generate a quota of apprentices of about 6-10 per cent of the total workforce. This quota can be obtained empirically within the industrial sector, which is formally distinct from the craft sector in Austria. However, only a small number of apprentices – less than one-fifth – are actually trained in the industrial sector. The quota of apprentices in other sectors is much higher, up to 40 per cent of the total workforce in some trades offering apprenticeships. From such a high quota, the conclusion can be derived that accessibility to internal labour markets is impossible because it would require unrealistically high rates of expansion in the workforce. One inevitably arrives at the overall conclusion that the mechanisms which tie the apprenticeship system to the employment system are much more indirect than mere access to internal labour markets, despite the fact that this hypothesis is true to some extent.

Table 14.   **Duration of employment of apprenticeship graduates in their training enterprise immediately after graduation**

Percentage

Duration of employment in the training enterprise	1981 cohort	1985 cohort
More than three years	8.8	5.3
Two to three years	5.3	10.1
One to two years	10.2	11.8
Six months to one year	15.3	14.8
One to six months	43.6	34.0
None	16.8	24.0

Source: Brandel *et al.* (1994).

Value of qualification

On average, the value of qualification differs by programmes, being highest for credentials from technical colleges and lowest for apprenticeships. There is considerable dispersion within the various educational levels and even some overlap between them, reflecting differences between occupational fields as well as the performance levels of individual enterprises, etc. In general, it may be stated that the influence of value on participation is modified by many of the intervening variables. In addition, there is next to no information on the value of the different educational levels in the labour market, owing to attempts to influence the general public in their educational choice.

6.   INTERVENING VARIABLES

Not many studies are available which analyse the effects of intervening variables on the choice of pathways through the educational system within a general and consistent framework. The overall functioning of the system is discussed rather hypothetically and without hard evidence (Posch and Altrichter, 1992; BMWF/BMUK, 1992). Much emphasis is put on the fact that the upper secondary vocational schools seem to "pull" young people out of the apprenticeship system. Another aspect which is heavily emphasized is the impact of the available supply of educational facilities, especially those available in the region of residence. This seems to be one of the most important factors influencing participation (Holzinger *et al.*, 1991). The aspects listed below are studied in more detail.

Gender

Participation in programmes and one's particular choice of pathway is strongly influenced by gender. The differences begin with VOTEC; in general education, the participation is rather even. But girls tend to choose full-time vocational colleges rather than apprenticeship, postsecondary VOTEC over university programmes, and service and administration occupations rather than crafts-, engineering-, or production-occupations. Trends show that participation in terms of level evens out, but distribution by occupational fields does not (Lassnig, 1989).

Labour market signals

There has been an ongoing discussion concerning the influence of labour market signals on the selection process. One position pointing out that young people do not sufficiently respond to labour market signals is based on the fact that, despite the existence of vacancies in the apprenticeship system, young people seem to prefer to apply for schooling tracks and higher education. Similar arguments are brought forward based on labour market indicators, especially the unemployed/vacancies relationship. However, evidence is mixed. Unemployment is higher for those who graduated from the apprenticeship system than it is for those who graduated from school. Because unemployment means other things for apprentices than it does for those who were in school, these indicators are not very helpful for any assessment of chances and opportunities.

Attitudes, expectations and values of young people

This factor is heavily emphasized by the general-public view which argues that attitudes and expectations are unrealistic and that economic needs are especially poorly taken into account. Changing values would lead young people into higher education and into fields not sought after by the economy. These choices would then lead to an oversupply of education rather than to the desired opportunities. On the other hand, the practical occupations acquired through apprenticeship, as well as the engineering- and business-oriented routes of higher education – which would provide ample opportunities – tended not to be adequately valued by young people. Significantly, there are some studies about the expectations of young women which show that they are strongly oriented towards combining employment and family. This is one of the strongest trends in the area of changing values. There are also studies about the factors which influence the attitudes, expectations and values of young people, showing the persistent high impact of the family in this regard.

Socio-economic status

In Austria, there is a well-known relationship between traditional paths to higher education and a person's socio-economic background. The development of the educational system – especially the expansion of the higher track of upper secondary vocational schools, which gives its graduates the credentials required for university entrance – increased educational opportunities for young people of lower socio-economic status, because of the labour market value of these programmes. This track lowers the risk in the academic track, and does not require application for the traditional academic track in Year 10. This track is very important, especially in rural areas. However, this trend leads to increased transitions to university from technical colleges – eventually counterproductive to the original mission of this track, which is to provide mid-level qualifications for the good of the economy.

Ethnic origin

This factor is especially significant for children of migrants, the "second generation" who are excluded from the better tracks of the system because of cultural factors and particularly because of poor opportunities to learn the common language.

Nature and functioning of guidance and orientation services

While many agree that these services should be improved, it is not clear through which strategies this might be done. Studies show that there is a demand for guidance and orientation and that the impact of existing services seems to be low, *e.g.* compared with the impact of advice from parents. There is much criticism of the quality of the advice received.

NOTES

1. This overview was prepared by Eleonora Schmid (BMUK).

2. Minimising the number of categories and simultaneously maximising information was a major concern of this study; in retrospect, a slightly higher degree of disaggregation could be judged as more appropriate, especially a separation of agriculture/forestry from tourism (despite the arguments for grouping them together).

BIBLIOGRAPHY

BMWF and BMUK (1992), "Diversification of higher education in Austria", background report submitted to the OECD, Vienna.

BRANDEL, F. et al. (1994), Aspekte der Arbeitsmarktintegration von Lehranfängern (Aspects of labour market entry of apprentices), IHS, Vienna.

HOLZINGER, E. et al. (1991), Der regionale Versorgungsbedarf an Bildungseinrichtunge (Regional needs for supply of educational facilities), ÖROK-Schriftenreihe, No. 91, Vienna.

LASSNIG, L. (1989), Ausbildungen und Berufe in Österreich (Training and vocations in Austria), IHS, Vienna.

POSCH, P. and ALTRICHTER, H. (1992), Bildung in Österreich (Education in Austria), Öst. Studien Verlag, Innsbruck.

4

DENMARK

by
Roland Osterlund, Department of Vocational Education and Training,
Ministry of Education, Copenhagen

1. INTRODUCTION

In Denmark, vocational education and training programmes are included in the formal youth education system under the Ministry of Education. Today they are a modernised and developed version of the former apprenticeship training programmes. Ninety-six per cent of a youth cohort enrol in youth education after leaving the *Folkeskole* (municipal primary and lower secondary school), and almost 60 per cent of these students enter into vocationally oriented youth education and training programmes (VOTEC).

However, many adults have not completed formal education beyond the *Folkeskole*. Moreover, Denmark has in recent years experienced substantial unemployment, which has often resulted in a strong demand for education and training. This means that a large part of the Danish workforce participates each year in adult education. And the number has been increasing throughout the last decade.

Both the formal youth education system and the adult education programmes and schemes offer a great variety and wide range of both vocational and general educational courses which can be adjusted to fit individual needs in almost every possible combination.

In relation to VOTEC, irrespective of the type of courses or schemes, there is a strong central and local co-operation between the public sector and the labour market. In recent years, strong emphasis has been placed on co-ordination and transparency of the systems, including co-ordination of the youth education programmes with the schemes for adult education and training.

2. STRUCTURE

The basic school (*Folkeskole*)

In addition to the pre-school class, the *Folkeskole* (municipal primary and lower secondary school) offers nine years of basic schooling and a 10th year. The pre-school is voluntary but must be made available by the municipality. The 10th year is also voluntary. Education is obligatory for nine years but there is no compulsory schooling. Pupils are aged between six and 17 years old (see Figure 1).

Pupils are taught as a class and remain together throughout the period of basic schooling. A little over 60 per cent of a class continues to the 10th year. Some pupils complete the last years of their basic schooling in "continuation schools" (*Efterskoler, i.e.* boarding schools).

Private, independent schools cater for 11 per cent of all pupils. They provide teaching which compares with that required in the *Folkeskole*. The public sector covers up to 80 per cent of the cost of these schools.

The basic school level is equivalent to levels 0, 1 and 2 in the ISCED classification.

Youth education

On completion of compulsory education, various types of education are open to pupils:

– general upper secondary education:

  • *gymnasium*;

  • higher preparatory examination courses;

– vocationally oriented education and training:

  • vocational education and training;

  • higher technical and higher commercial examination courses;

  • basic social and health education courses;

  • other types of vocational education programmes.

The youth education level covers level 3 in the ISCED classification.

Students are generally between 16 and 20 years old. Applicants for the general upper secondary courses and the technical and commercial examination courses must undergo an aptitude evaluation at the end of basic school. Applicants for vocational education and training must have completed basic school.

The *gymnasium* offers three years' general upper secondary education in two streams: linguistic and mathematical. Each of these streams has a core curriculum of obligatory subjects. Students must also choose from a number of optional

◆ Figure 1. **The Danish education system**

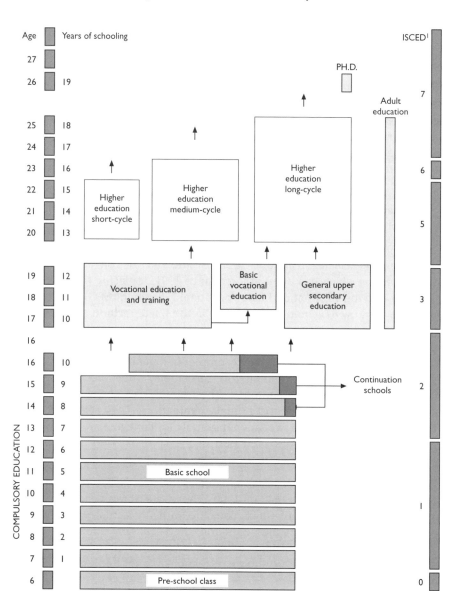

1. International Standard Classification of Education (ISCED).
Source: Author.

subjects at two levels: intermediate and high, with at least two subjects at high level. The county council establishes, runs and closes down schools, and fixes grants for operational expenses and investments. The curricula and standards are set and monitored by the Ministry of Education.

The *higher preparatory examination course* (HF) can be taken as a complete examination after a two-year course comprising a number of core subjects, three optional subjects and a major written assignment. It can also be taken following single-subject instruction. Examinations in single subjects can be grouped together for a complete higher preparatory certificate. These examinations can also be taken by individual students who have either not followed, or only partly followed, previous course instruction in the subject(s) concerned. The courses are run and monitored in the same way as the *gymnasia*.

Vocationally oriented education and training consists of a number of different programmes, of which the vocational education and training programme is the largest youth education activity.

Vocational education and training is based on the 1989 Act on Vocational Education and Training which has been in force since 1991, replacing the 1956 Apprenticeship Act and the 1977 Act on Basic Vocational Education (EFG). The courses, of which there are now 87 (compared with 300 in the past), include a number of new streams, and are organised as "sandwich" training courses, where periods of school-based education alternate with practical training in a firm. For each of the 87 courses, a committee represented by employer organisations and trade unions play a central role in determining the curriculum. They are responsible for modernising the professional content of the training part of the courses and for setting the standards for apprentices' final examinations. They also establish rules for practical in-house training. Vocational schools (or colleges) are responsible for implementation of the school-based part of the courses. They were previously called technical schools and commercial schools.

Higher technical examination and higher commercial examination courses (HTX and HHX) were instituted by an Act of 1990. These are three-years school-based courses, the last two years of which coincide with the actual upper secondary course. The first year includes elements from the vocational education and training courses – up until 1995, in fact, this first year was common to both courses. The vocational schools (colleges) are therefore responsible for implementation of the courses.

The *basic social and health education courses* (SOSU) were established in parallel to the vocational education and training courses. They likewise consist of a mixture of practical training in a workplace and of school-based education. The schools are owned by the municipalities and counties, and practical training takes place locally. It is the aim of the courses to qualify staff in the welfare, health care and nursing areas for broad-based functions.

The *other types of vocationally oriented courses* consist of a number of small programmes including agricultural education, maritime education, civil service education and some company education.

Higher education

The *short-cycle higher education courses* (one to three years' duration) are profession-oriented, aimed at specific areas of employment in trade and industry. Advanced courses of one to two years may follow some of the study programmes. The courses are offered at vocational schools, with admission requiring a vocational or upper secondary education (general or vocational) or equivalent.

The *medium-cycle higher education courses* (three to four years' duration), offered at specialised educational institutions, are varied in scope, encompassing a number of professional programmes of study. These include the university research-based bachelor's degree, which is a three-year, independent course complete in itself; and they provide a basis for vocational competence as well as for taking a master's degree. Admission to the medium-cycle programmes usually requires a successfully completed general or vocational upper secondary education or equivalent.

The *long-cycle higher education courses* (generally lasting five years after a completed general or vocational upper secondary education, *i.e.* two years after a completed bachelor's degree) are offered at universities and other higher education institutions. Here, research and teaching is conducted up to the highest scholarly level, within the faculties of social sciences, the humanities, theology, health sciences, natural sciences and engineering. Most long-cycle higher education courses consist of three-year bachelor's degree programmes, usually followed by two years for a master's degree. A general or vocational upper secondary education or equivalent is required for admission to these courses.

3. PROGRAMMES

Vocational education and training

These courses provide young people with vocational training as well as broad general qualifications.

Learning sites: As mentioned above, all but one of the 87 different courses are organised as "sandwich" training courses, including school-based learning and in-house work-based training. The distribution between school-based education and work-based training is approximately 40 to 60 per cent with some variation from course to course.

The vocational schools (colleges) are all fully privatised as non-profit organisations with a considerable capital in buildings and industrial equipment, etc. Central government pays "taximeter grants" proportional to production (*i.e.* performance pay with no ties attached) covering capital as well as running costs – in full for youth education, in part for adult. These schools have traditionally been governed by boards with equal representation of employers and employees from the geographical area concerned. The board, which is responsible to the Minister of Education for the overall management of the school, determines the annual programme of activities, and approves its budget and accounts.

The practical in-house training of students takes place in private as well as public enterprises. The training is based on a training agreement between the student and the firm, which covers all practical training and school periods of the programme, including the journeyman's test when necessary. The training is always covered by a written agreement signed by both parties (with the parents' consent in the case of a minor). It contains information on the salary to be paid by the company during the student's practical training periods and on the school periods agreed.

Assessment and certification: A student's performance is subject to continuous assessment, in the form of examinations, a teacher's assessment of the school performance, or an employer's evaluation of the practical work effort made.

Students complete their education by passing a final trade examination which varies from course to course and may take the form of a journeyman's test, a school examination or a combination of the two, the latter being the most common. The trade board decides on the specific form of the examination and conducts the journeyman's test. Upon graduation, a student receives a national skilled worker's certificate issued by the trade board. This describes the graduate's competencies and entitles him/her to unemployment benefits.

Level of education: As mentioned above, this corresponds to Level 3 of the ISCED classification.

Fields of study/training: The 87 different courses cover all major occupational fields except for those included in the few other vocationally oriented programmes in youth education or higher education programmes. Among the different specialisations, more than 250-300 occupational fields are covered.

"General" and "vocational" elements: Four different types of subject are covered by the curricula:

- Basic subjects   : One-third of the teaching hours at school;
- Area subjects   : One-third of the teaching hours at school;
- Specialised subjects : One-sixth of the teaching hours at school;
- Optional subjects   : One-sixth of the teaching hours at school.

The individual courses "stand alone"; but in fact, they often share all the basic subjects and most of the area subjects with other courses, thus ensuring flexibility and a broad perspective. In order to ensure the same flexibility and adaptability of adult education, the courses are offered in modules and as part-time education under the Act on Open Education.

Duration of courses: They normally last two to four years, with a few courses continuing for four and a half years.

Admission and entry requirements: Admission to a vocational education and training course is open to those who have completed compulsory education (normally nine years). Restricted admission has been (except for a few minor courses) abandoned, and students and employers are offered a free choice of school.

Access to further education/training: A number of courses under short-cycle higher education, including technician courses within a great variety of occupational fields and trades, are specially designed for graduates from vocational education and training courses. Students also have direct access to some medium-cycle higher education programmes. For the remaining higher education courses, graduates usually have to supplement their education within some of the academic subjects in order to be admitted. These are offered as single-subject courses from the HF, HHX or HTX courses.

In addition, a great variety of short retraining and skills-upgrading courses are offered under the programmes run by the Ministry of Labour. Almost all of them, designed for this target group, are normally offered by the same schools (colleges) as for the vocational education and training courses.

Higher commercial examination and higher technical examination courses

The higher commercial examination and higher technical examination courses (HHX and HTX) are school-based courses combining a vocational orientation with a full preparation for higher education. They are sometimes called the "business *gymnasium*" and the "technical *gymnasium*".

The HTX course was launched on an experimental basis in 1982, whereas the HHX was started back in 1888 as a private initiative. Up until the end of the 1960s, the programme was fairly small and students entered the labour market immediately upon graduation. The HHX did not qualify for admission to universities and other higher education institutions, since the general, academic part of the course was considered too weak. In 1972, however, following a revision of the content, and the introduction of more rigorous admission requirements, the programme was granted the status of a university entrance examination course.

Learning sites: As mentioned above, the first year includes elements shared with the vocational education and training courses, with the vocational schools (colleges) being responsible for the implementation of the courses.

Assessment and certification: Students' performance is subject to internal as well as external evaluation. The aim of the internal evaluation is to guide the student and teacher in the planning of further instruction.

Level of education: As mentioned above, the level is university entrance (level 3 in the ISCED classification).

Fields of study/training: Approximately two-thirds of the course consists of obligatory subjects, with the remaining third optional.

"General" and "vocational" elements: As indicated above, a substantial part of the courses consists of general, academic subjects. However, since the first year was common to the vocational education and training courses (until 1995), a significant part of the course content includes vocational elements. The courses are organised with a strong emphasis on technical (HTX) or commercial (HHX) topics which are used as points of departure for the theory, such as in the natural sciences or economics.

Admission and entry requirements: There are two ways of entering the HHX/HTX courses – either directly following the *Folkeskole* or on completion of the first year of vocational education and training. In order to be admitted, a student must be considered qualified by the vocational school.

Access to further education/training: The HHX/HTX courses qualify for admission to universities and other higher education institutions. In addition, upon completion of a practical training period in a firm, young people with an HTX examination meet the theoretical as well as vocational requirements for entry to advanced technician courses and engineering colleges. These courses are intended for graduates of vocational and technical education and training courses.

Higher education

Short-cycle higher education comprises a number of courses at middle technician level within the areas of food, construction, clothing, electronics and mechanical technology. There are, furthermore, a number of health education courses leading to a qualification as a laboratory technologist or dental technician. Maritime and home economics courses at this level include courses qualifying students as, for instance, first mates or home economics technicians. The admission requirement for some of these short-cycle higher education courses is an upper secondary school-leaving examination or a higher preparatory examination, whereas admission to other courses requires a vocational upper secondary or vocational education and training qualification.

Medium-cycle higher education: Among the range of completed courses are the diploma course in economics (HD); the degree courses in economics (HA), in applied languages, journalism, engineering (*teknikum- und akademiingeniør*), librarianship; the teacher training course for *Folkeskole* teachers; and the courses for social workers, physiotherapists and nurses.

Long-cycle higher education: Includes degree courses for lawyers, economists, doctors, dentists, veterinary surgeons and civil engineers (master's degree in engineering).

4.   PATHWAYS

As mentioned at the beginning of this chapter, a number of different types of education are open to pupils on completion of their compulsory education:

Pathways in technical education courses: At the beginning of a technical education course a student chooses between the "school route" and the "practical training route". The two pathways converge at the commencement of the "second school period". Irrespective of the choice, the duration and content of the training are the same.

Students choosing the "school route" normally enter the "first school period", lasting 20 weeks, during which time they try out work in several different trade areas and receive parallel individual and collective vocational and educational guidance. Workshop training has a central role here and is supplemented by more theoretical subjects. For students over 18 years of age, the "first school period" is optional, after which they choose their specific stream and continue with the "second school period" (also 20 weeks). A specific second school period may give access to one or more different courses, depending on the content of the school period. Students who are considered qualified may continue to the HTX course.

Students choosing the "practical training route" must enter into an agreement with a firm to start their initial training; their first school-based training coincides with the "second school period". Students from the "school route" must obtain a training agreement after completion of the "second school period". However, students who are not able to get an agreement can have their practical training at school.

Pathways in commercial and clerical education courses: The school route is organised as a combined "first and second school period" comprising 40 weeks of schooling, after which time there is a choice between a total of six different courses. Students who are considered qualified may continue to the HHX course.

The "practical training route" is based on a training agreement with a firm right from the start. During the first year of practical training, a student frequently attends school for 18 weeks in total, usually with two days at school and three days in practical in-house training. After their first year, all students receive the same training, regardless of pathway. All students from the school route must obtain a training agreement after their first year. A large number of students complete the HHX course and then continue with vocational education and training under a practical-training agreement.

Most of the graduates from vocational education and training – including those from HHX/HTX who enrol in vocational education and training – enter the labour market. Some, however, continue into higher education, generally in short-cycle programmes. Most *gymnasium*/HF and HTX/HHX graduates continue into higher education.

5. PARTICIPATION

Figures 2 and 3 illustrate the pathways between programmes in 1983 and 1993, and include figures estimating participation in them. The following conclusions may be drawn from the youth profiles of these figures:

- In 1983, 10 to 11 per cent of the cohort did not continue in youth education. In 1993 this number was below 5 per cent, with the decrease remaining very stable during this period.

- The proportion of the cohort enrolling in the *gymnasium*/HF increased during the period from 33 to 38 per cent. Up until 1992, the figure was very stable at 34 per cent.

- The proportion enrolling in vocationally oriented education at secondary level (vocational education and training and HHX/HTX) increased from 54 to 58 per cent, when, in 1992, it decreased again. The 1983 figure of 54 per cent includes 9 per cent enrolled in HHX/HTX. In 1993 this figure was 16 per cent.

- The proportion who graduated from youth education increased from 70 to 77 per cent. Owing to reduced drop-out and to a greater number of practical training places in industry, this figure is substantially higher today (1996).

- The proportion enrolling in higher education increased from 34 to 45 per cent. A stable proportion of 5 to 6 per cent of the cohort were recruited from vocational education and training and 5 per cent from the adult population.

In *short-cycle courses*, around 42 per cent of the enrolled came from the *gymnasium*/HF in 1983, 12 per cent from HHX/HTX and 35 per cent from vocational education and training. In 1993, the respective figures were 27, 21 and 42 per cent

◆ Figure 2. *Youth profile 1983*
In percentage

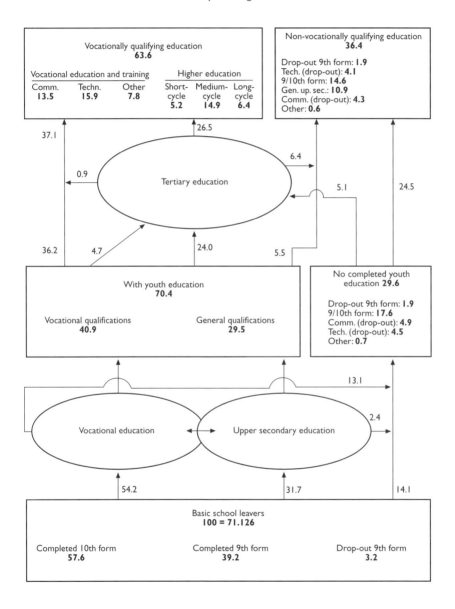

◆ Figure 3. **Youth profile 1993**

In percentage

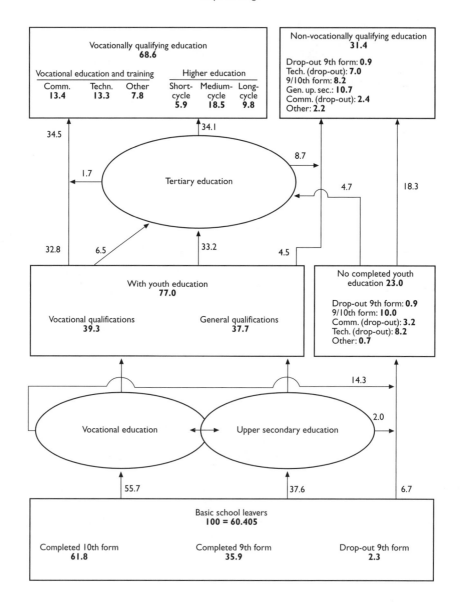

Source: Author.

respectively. The remaining were recruited from elsewhere (other higher education programmes, etc.).

In *medium-cycle non-university courses*, around 43 per cent of the students were recruited from the *gymnasium*/HF in 1983, 12 per cent from HHX/HTX, 19 per cent from vocational education and training and 5 per cent from short-cycle higher education courses. In 1993, the respective figures were 46, 13, 19 and 7 per cent.

Medium-cycle university-based courses recruited 82 per cent from the *gymnasium*/HF in 1983 and 11 per cent from HHX/HTX, whereas none were recruited from either vocational or short-cycle higher education. In 1993, the respective figures were 62, 6, 1 and 1 per cent.

In 1983, *long-cycle higher education courses* recruited 60 per cent from the *gymnasium*/HF, 3 per cent from HHX/HTX, 4 per cent from vocational education and training, 2 per cent from short-cycle higher education, 16 per cent from medium-cycle non-university-based higher education courses and 6 per cent from medium-cycle university-based higher education courses. In 1993, the respective figures were 44, 5, 2, 2, 21 and 25 per cent respectively.

5

ENGLAND, WALES AND NORTHERN IRELAND*

by
David Short, Further Education Support Unit,
the then Department for Education and Science

1. INTRODUCTION

Statutory schooling ends in the United Kingdom at age 16. The content of statutory education in England and Wales, which this section deals with, differs from that in Scotland and Northern Ireland.

"Maintained" schools in England and Wales are required to provide a broad and balanced education, involving the teaching of the national curriculum to all pupils aged 5 to 16. The national curriculum is made up of ten subjects. The core subjects are English, mathematics, science – and in Wales, Welsh. The other subjects are technology (design and technology and information technology), history, geography, music, art, physical education, and a modern foreign language.

The national curriculum is divided into four key stages according to pupils' ages: Key stage 1 (age 5 to 7); Key stage 2 (age 7 to 11); Key stage 3 (age 11 to 14); Key stage 4 (age 14 to 16).

All subjects of the national curriculum are compulsory at Key stages 1-3, except for a foreign language which becomes a requirement at the beginning of Key stage 3. At Key stage 4, pupils continue the core subjects and physical education. From September 1996 there has also been a requirement for pupils in England and Wales at Key stage 4 to study at least a short course in technology and a modern foreign language. Pupils of all ages must also study religious education, and sex education must be provided for 11- to 16-year-olds. Although

---

* This paper deals with education and training, post-16, and relates in the main to England and Wales rather than Scotland. Where references are made to the United Kingdom, it can be taken that Northern Ireland and Scotland are included. The post-16 system of education in Northern Ireland is broadly similar to that of England and Wales but differs in certain particulars which are set out in Annex 1. Unless otherwise stated, all statistics in this paper relate to England only.

careers education is not currently a legal requirement, the government considers it very important that a planned programme should be available at all maintained secondary schools. As a result, it has announced an intention to seek legislation to place this duty on schools.

There was a major review of all key stages of the national curriculum in 1994. Consequently, the statutory curriculum has been slimmed down, releasing more time for teachers to use at their discretion. Schools might choose to use this time to give more attention to the basics of literacy and numeracy, where this is appropriate, or to offer non-statutory subjects. The revision has also given schools greater freedom to choose which subjects they offer at Key stage 4, helping them to meet the needs of all their pupils aged 14-16.

The General Certificate of Secondary Education (GCSE) is the main means of assessing achievement at the end of Key stage 4. Pupils may take GCSEs in a wide range of individual subjects, including subjects outside the national curriculum. Typically, an average 16-year-old will take eight GCSEs. GCSE results are graded on a scale from A+ (which recognises outstanding achievement) to G (which is the minimum level required to obtain a GCSE certificate). Five or more GCSEs at grades A+ to C, or their equivalent, are normally required to continue into further or higher education.

Increasingly, schools may offer a range of other options alongside GCSEs, including vocational courses. Schools decide which options to offer within their timetable, taking into account pupils' needs. The Part One GNVQ, a new vocational qualification designed specifically for pupils at Key stage 4, has been piloted from September 1995.

Although most GCSE candidates are in their last year of compulsory schooling, GCSEs may be taken at any age. Many adults take GCSEs, particularly in English, Welsh, mathematics and modern foreign languages.

2. QUALIFICATION STRUCTURES

There are three main qualifications post-16 in England, Northern Ireland and Wales, and these form a qualifications framework:

– General Certificate of Education (GCE) Advanced (A-level) and Advanced Supplementary qualifications (AS);

– General National Vocational Qualifications (GNVQs);

– National Vocational Qualifications (NVQs).

The three qualifications and equivalence between them are shown diagrammatically in Figure 1.

◆ Figure 1. **Qualifications pathways post 16**

There are three qualifications pathways to higher level study and better jobs

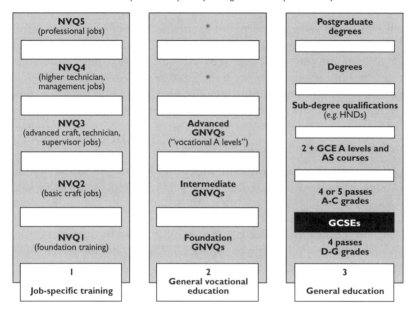

* Old-style vocational qualifications (e.g. BTECs, City and Guilds and RSAs) are being replaced by NVQs and GNVQs. Decisions are yet to be made on developing GNVQs at higher levels.
The three qualifications pathways routes are flexible. Students can choose to take various combinations – for example, an advanced GNVQ alongside a GCE "A" level – and transfer between pathways as they progress.
Source: Department for Education.

General Certificate of Education (GCE)

A-levels

GCE has traditionally been the qualification obtained by the majority of young people wishing to enter university and, as such, it serves a role similar to that of the A*bitur* in Germany or the *baccalauréat* in France. GCE is also a route to employment. Unlike the German and French qualification, GCE A-levels do not form a set course with compulsory elements; rather, a programme of GCE A-levels is a combination, selected by the student, of individual subjects. It is not uncommon for students to be able to choose their GCE A-level subjects from a selection of over 20 offered by the college or school. The majority of students who follow a

GCE A-level programme will have obtained specified grades in the General Certificate of Secondary Education (GCSE), which is taken at the end of the statutory schooling period, *i.e.* at the age of 16. The majority of full-time students take their GCE A-levels at the age of 18 after a two-year programme of study.

Unlike the final secondary school examination in some other countries, GCE A-level may be taken by part-time mode of study. Part-time students may study one GCE A-level at a time over one year, attending, for instance, evening classes in a college of further education, or build up a portfolio of GCE A-levels over an extended period. Sometimes, part-time students study one particular subject to improve their GCE A-level grade in order to enter university.

Advanced Supplementary (AS) qualifications

GCE A-levels may be combined with GCE Advanced Supplementary (AS) qualifications. These are intended to occupy half the teaching and private-study time of a GCE A-level. A student might, for instance, take two GCE A-levels and two AS qualifications instead of three GCE A-levels. As with GCE A-levels, there is no prescription on subject choice but it is intended that by a proper choice of AS subjects, a student might be able to broaden his or her overall programme with a contrasting or complementary study.

Assessment

GCE (and GCSE) examinations are administered by eight independent examining boards. Assessment is largely through externally marked final examinations. One GCE A-level subject may be examined through, for example, two examinations of up to three hours' duration. GCE A-level examinations usually test the volume of prescribed knowledge and often call for extended writing in the form of essay answers; they may require the demonstration of applied knowledge and skills through problem-solving, *i.e.* in mathematics or science; or they may entail the demonstration of creative skill through set pieces of work in subjects such as art or music.

GCE A-level and AS assessments should:

– be consistent, valid and reliable and to that end be governed by appropriate and uniformly applied procedures covering all aspects of the examination process;

– predominantly take the form of externally appraised terminal examinations;

– require that any internally judged course work be externally moderated and, in most subjects, limited to a maximum of 20 per cent of the total available marks;

– in the case of modular syllabuses, include a terminal examination and a substantial element of external estimation, both during and at the end of the course, broadly paralleling the requirements for conventional syllabuses.

GCE passes are graded, in descending order, from A to E. Normally, passes are required in three subjects in order to progress to a degree course at a university. Universities usually award places to applicants with GCE qualifications on the basis of a "points score". For instance, an applicant to University X might be required to obtain three passes at GCE A-level at grades B, B and C respectively; another way of putting this would be a "points score" of 22. The score is usually allocated on the following basis:

– GCE A-levels : A = 10, B = 8, C = 6, D = 4, E = 2;
– GCE AS-levels : A = 5, B = 4, C = 3, D = 2, E = 1.

General National Vocational Qualifications (GNVQs)

This is a new vocational qualification which was introduced on a pilot basis in five vocational areas in schools and colleges in September 1992. It was intended to have GNVQs in 14 vocational areas by 1996.

The GNVQ has three levels: Foundation, Intermediate, Advanced. The GNVQ Advanced level is equivalent to two GCE A-levels.

GNVQs are intended, largely, as a full-time course for 16-19-year-olds but may be taken by students of any age and in any mode (*i.e.* part- or full-time). The GNVQ is also an alternative qualification, to GCE A-levels, for entrance to higher education. In 1993, 83 per cent of GNVQ Advanced students were offered places at universities in the United Kingdom.

In 1995, about 160 000 young people in schools and colleges were following courses leading to GNVQs. The government's aims were that GNVQs be available in more than 1 500 schools and colleges by 1996 and that one in four 16-year-olds start GNVQ courses in 1996.

Structure

Unlike a programme of GCE A-levels which reflect the student's individual choice, a GNVQ programme constitutes a course in which all the elements (known as units) interrelate. For instance, a GNVQ Intermediate consists of nine units and a GNVQ Advanced of 15 units. There are three types of GNVQ unit: mandatory (reflecting the vocational area and core skills), optional, additional.

GNVQs, at all levels, include three core skills units comprising communication, numeracy, and information technology respectively. The development of problem-solving and personal skills is encouraged in GNVQ courses. These skills are not assessed or certified separately but they may be recorded on the student's "national record of achievement".

To add to and broaden their range of accomplishment, students may take additional units beyond the prescribed number for their course. They may, for instance, wish to take units in a foreign language or they may need to acquire additional units in mathematics in order to gain entrance to certain courses in higher education.

Assessment

Each GNVQ unit sets out in some detail the outcomes students must achieve. Assessment should cover all the outcomes specified for each unit. The evidence for appraisal in GNVQs is derived in part from projects and assignments (internal assessments) and, in part, from external tests requiring a pass mark of 70 per cent.

Assessment is based primarily on projects and assignments carried out by students, who have to produce evidence that they have covered all the requirements for each unit and maintain this in a "portfolio of evidence". Internal assessments are checked by "internal verifiers". "External verifiers" acting on behalf of the awarding body also visit centres (*i.e.* school and colleges) to scrutinise a sample of the assessments in the portfolios of evidence.

The internal assessments are complemented by externally set and marked written tests for each mandatory unit which focus on the knowledge required. Each test lasts about an hour and may be taken at different times of the year. The units can be assessed and certificated separately. Tests for the optional and additional units may be set by the institution but are subject to external verification.

Certification

A full GNVQ certificate lists the titles of all required and additional units. Units are not separately graded, but an overall grade of merit or distinction is awarded to students who have demonstrated achievement above the basic requirement. Individual units may be certificated for those who do not complete a full GNVQ.

GNVQs are administered by the National Council for Vocational Qualifications (NCVQ) which currently accredits the GNVQs awarded by three major, independent examining and/or validating bodies: the Business and Technician Education Council, the City and Guilds of London Institute, and the Royal Society of Arts Examination Board.

National Vocational Qualifications (NVQs)

NVQs are primarily, but not exclusively, intended for employees of all ages. They are based on standards of competence at work which have been defined by the employers themselves through the Industry Lead Bodies. The NCVQ requires that performance to gain an NVQ be demonstrated and assessed under conditions as close as possible to the workplace.

NVQs have been available since 1988. Previous qualifications have been reformed and new ones introduced so that, by the end of 1992, NVQs were available in over 80 per cent of occupational areas. The total number of NVQ certificates awarded by the end of 1994 was 648 950; certificates were awarded in eleven occupational areas: tending animals, plants and land (13 074); extracting and providing natural resources (4 923); constructing (46 527); engineering (61 700); manufacturing (20 030); transporting (2 229); providing goods and services (154 481); providing health, social care and protective services (55 167); providing business services (290 169); communicating (126); developing and extending knowledge and skills (524).

Structure

An NVQ is basically a statement of competence with the following components:

- a title (*e.g.* banking) which denotes the area of competence covered by the qualification;
- units of competence;
- elements of competence (sub-divisions of units reflecting tasks a person should do at work);
- performance criteria to accompany each element of competence;
- a statement which must accompany each element and specify the circumstances in which the competence must be applied (*e.g.* physical location, employment context, equipment used, etc.);
- assessment guidance;
- A-level: there are five levels, and the following definitions provide a general guide to each:
  - Level 1: competence in the performance of a range of work activities, most of which may be routine and predictable.
  - Level 2: competence in a significant range of varied work activities, performed in a variety of contexts. Some of the activities are complex or non-routine and there is some individual responsibility or autonomy.

Collaboration with others, perhaps through membership of a work group or team, may often be a requirement.

- Level 3: competence in a broad range of work activities performed in a wide variety of contexts, most of which are complex and non-routine. There is considerable responsibility and autonomy, and control or guidance of others is often required.

- Level 4: competence in a broad range of complex, technical or professional work activities performed in a wide variety of contexts and with a substantial degree of personal responsibility and autonomy. Responsibility for the work of others and the allocation of resources is often required.

- Level 5: competence which involves the application of a significant range of fundamental principles and complex techniques across a wide and often unpredictable variety of contexts. Very substantial personal autonomy and often significant responsibility for the work of others and for the allocation of substantial resources feature strongly, as do personal accountabilities for analysis and diagnosis, design, planning, execution and evaluation.

Assessment

Unlike GNVQ and GCSE/GCE results, NVQs are not graded (*i.e.* by letters or by terms such as "credit" or "distinction"). Assessment for NVQs is based on the statement of competence. Before an NVQ can be awarded, candidates must have provided evidence that they have met the performance criteria for each element of competence specified.

Access to assessment for an NVQ should be available to all who can reach the standard required. The appraisal must be independent of the mode or place of learning (*i.e.* it can be carried out anywhere – in college or in the workplace), the age of the candidate (subject to legal constraints), the time spent preparing for the NVQ (*i.e.* the candidate takes the NVQ when he or she is ready to do so – here there is no specified length of time for this).

An NVQ is an accreditation of an award made by an examining or validating body; over 100 examining/validating bodies have awards accredited as NVQs. NVQs are subject to fundamental criteria which ensure their relevance and value to employment. To be accredited as an NVQ, a qualification must be:

- based on national standards required for performance in employment, and take proper account of future needs with particular regard to technology, markets and employment patterns;

- based on assessments of the outcomes of learning, arrived at independently of any particular mode, duration or location of learning;
- awarded on the basis of valid and reliable assessments made in such a way as to ensure that performance to the national standard can be achieved at work;
- free from barriers which restrict access and progression, and available to all those who are able to reach the required standard by whatever means;
- free from overt or covert discriminatory practices with regard to gender, age, race or creed, and designed to pay due regard to the special needs of individuals.

NVQs are not subject to prescription over mode or place of delivery. That is to say, in order to obtain an NVQ, a trainee does not have to attend a particular kind of educational or training institution: there is no prescribed course content. An NVQ is a statement of competence which has been tested to prescribed standards under work-based conditions.

The combination of general and vocational education

In England and Wales the majority of school-leavers who wish to stay on in full-time education can either remain at school in a sixth-form or go to a college in the further education sector. The government is committed to the provision of choice and diversity for students and to encouraging young people to seek out the provision and institutions best suited to their aptitude and abilities.

From 1 April 1993, all colleges (including sixth-form colleges) in England and Wales came under the funding regime of a Further Education Funding Council (FEFC) for England and an FEFC for Wales. All colleges (457 in England and 28 in Wales) belong to what is called the further education (FE) sector. Colleges in the sector receive funding under a formula which recognises and rewards enrolment in a course, retention of the student during it, and achievement (*e.g.* a qualification) at the end.

The three qualifications do not always map neatly onto the institutional structures. Traditionally, school sixth-forms have concentrated on academic provision such as GCE A-level; colleges have concentrated on vocational education and training. Since the 1960s, however, colleges have offered full-time programmes for GCE A-level and, more recently, schools have introduced vocational courses into their sixth-form provision. This has led, in effect, to competition between schools and colleges for full-time students in the 16-19 age range and, more recently, for part-time students also. Furthermore, colleges are, in the main, polytechnic rather than monotechnic and offer a wide variety of courses to a diverse range of students.

Thus, England and Wales differ from many other OECD countries in having post-16 institutions which can offer a wide range of qualifications and not (except in a minority of cases) post-16 institutions specialised in particular kinds of post-16 qualifications. As a result of this flexibility in institutional arrangements, it is possible for post-16 students to follow programmes which combine study for more than one kind of qualification. Such programmes can provide a combination of general and vocational education.

It is common for post-16 full-time students to combine study for one qualification with study for another. For instance, students on a GNVQ course may combine this with study for one GCE subject. Alternatively, a student may combine a GNVQ with related NVQ units. Some students, whose main programme of study is three GCE A-level subjects, may take some NVQ units as well. All these permutations can provide students with the breadth and diversity which result from a combination of general and vocational education. This combination of general and vocational education is facilitated by the variety and diversity of qualifications on offer in most colleges in the further education sector and, increasingly, in schools. Currently, there are no official statistics available on the extent to which students combine study for more than one qualification, post-16.

Parity of esteem

The government wants equal status for academic and vocational education. A Government White Paper entitled *Education and Training for the 21st Century* (Cm 1536, May 1991) states (para. 4.2): "The Government wants to remove the remaining barriers to equal status between the so-called academic and vocational routes". This statement is fundamental to what is known in the United Kingdom as the "parity of esteem" debate, in relation to qualifications. In 1989, the Secretary of State for Education spoke of "(...) the excessive dominance of A-level (GCE) as the route into higher education". In recent years, the number of students entering universities with qualifications other than GCE A-level has steadily increased. The latest statistics on entry qualifications to higher education are shown in Table 1.

Training and Enterprise Councils

In 1988, the government issued a White Paper, *Employment for the 1990s*, which announced the establishment of local Training and Enterprise Councils (TECs) in England and Wales (and Local Enterprise Councils in Scotland — LECs). TECs were set up to encourage employers to invest in their workforce, to assess the local labour market, to identify opportunities, and to co-ordinate activities for local training, enterprise and business growth. The primary role of the TECs is to

Table 1. **Qualifications held by UK-domiciled undergraduate new entrants 1994-95**

	Age			
	Under 21	21 to 24	25 and over	Total
	Full-time			
Degree or higher level, credits from higher education institutions	600	1 635	2 439	4 674
GNVQ/GSVQ/NVQ/NSVQ 4, 5; HND/HNC certificates of education, including BTEC equivalent	4 155	4 942	3 099	12 196
Professional qualifications	96	397	1 763	2 256
GCE A-Level, AS courses and equivalents	124 000	10 149	7 439	141 588
GNVQ/GSVQ/NVQ/NSVQ 3	322	69	86	477
ONC or OND, including BTEC and SCOTVEC equivalents	14 699	4 494	2 837	22 030
GNVQ/GSVQ/NVQ/NSVQ 1, 2	104	68	154	326
GCSE O-level: SCE O-grades and standard grades	1 268	996	1 870	4 134
Other qualifications	5 429	5 272	13 804	24 505
Not known/no formal qualifications/not needed	27 380	10 022	12 777	50 179
Total	178 053	38 044	46 268	262 365
	Part-time			
Degree or higher level, credits from higher education institutions	86	2 135	11 728	13 949
GNVQ/GSVQ/NVQ/NSVQ 4, 5; HND/HNC certificates of education, including BTEC equivalent	460	2 245	8 677	11 382
Professional qualifications	102	976	8 202	9 280
GCE A-Level, AS courses and equivalents	1 269	1 973	9 238	12 480
GNVQ/GSVQ/NVQ/NSVQ 3	21	27	49	97
ONC or OND, including BTEC and SCOTVEC equivalents	1 331	1 717	4 760	7 808
GNVQ/GSVQ/NVQ/NSVQ 1, 2	18	19	113	150
GCSE O-level: SCE-O grades and standard grades	247	869	7 936	9 052
Other qualifications	394	1 271	8 193	9 858
Not known/no formal qualifications/not needed	1 616	3 995	23 544	29 155
Total	5 544	15 227	82 440	103 211

Cf. Glossary at the end of the chapter.
Source: Higher Education Statistical Agency's Student Record.

identify and meet local training needs. The TECs took over most of the functions of the Training Agency.

The 82 TECs in England and Wales are private companies. Some 1 200 top business and community leaders are actively involved. The budget for the TEC/LEC-delivered programmes in 1993-94 was £2.2 billion. They administer Youth

Training (YT) and it is normally a condition of TEC funding that the trainee takes an NVQ where this is available.

TECs are also responsible for other new initiatives such as youth credits (which will be available throughout the country from April 1995). Youth credits are a new way of helping young people to choose and buy high-quality training with employers or other providers of training such as colleges. By funding providers rather than the individual, youth credits represent a major shift in policy, since they will help young people to make informed choices about their own training and future. The Modern Apprenticeship initiative (see Annex 2) seeks to increase the number of young labour market entrants equipped with high-level craft, technical and supervisory skills. Around 40 000 young people will ultimately qualify each year at NVQ Level 3 or higher, through the workplace training route. Prototype schemes in 14 industry sectors began in September 1994, and national delivery was scheduled to commence in September 1995 along with the introduction of Accelerated Modern Apprenticeships. These have a similar rationale and provide young people who remain in education until the age of 18 with the opportunity to obtain high-level technical and supervisory skills (NVQ) at Level 3 or above. They recognise that some young people defer career choices until they have obtained higher-level qualifications such as GNVQ Advanced or GCE A-levels.

3.   PARTICIPATION AND PROGRESSION

The highest qualification held by people aged 16-59 in the United Kingdom is shown, by age and sex, in Table 2. In recent years, the staying-on rate in full-time education has steadily increased, as the statistics in Tables 3.1a to c show. The most striking feature of these statistics is the increase in full-time participation rates at ages 16, 17 and 18. The increase for 16-year-olds was from 48 per cent in 1983/84 to 72 per cent in 1993/94, but the increase for 17-year-olds is proportionately larger; it is then greater again for 18-year-olds, indicating an improvement in retention and progression over this period. The steady improvement has meant that the United Kingdom as a whole now ranks high on the international scene in respect of the proportion of 16-year-olds undertaking some form of education or training (see Figure 2).

The increase in the staying-on rate in England is attributable to a number of causes rather than one single factor. It is not uncommon for the increase to be ascribed to changes in the social-class structure of the population. For instance, higher participation is associated with the non-manual socio-economic groups which represent a gradually increasing proportion of the population as a whole. This hypothesis, however, whilst containing perhaps a measure of truth, is flawed. Changes in social-class structure are gradual and could not, by themselves,

Table 2. **Highest qualification[1] held by people aged 16-59, by age and sex, United Kingdom, 1993**

	Age groups					
	16-59	16-24	25-29	30-39	40-29	50-59
	All persons					
Numbers (thousands)	33 699	7 017	4 667	8 262	7 739	6 014
%	100	100	100	100	100	100
	Highest qualification (%)					
Degree or equivalent	11	5	14	15	13	9
Higher education below degree level	7	4	8	8	8	7
GCE A-level or broad equivalent[2]	16	23	16	15	13	11
GCSE O-level or equivalent[2]	26	37	31	26	21	17
Other qualification[3]	13	13	15	13	13	12
No qualification	27	19	17	22	32	44
	Males					
Numbers (1 000s)	16 918	3 574	2 363	4 138	3 860	2 984
%	100	100	100	100	100	100
	Highest qualification (%)					
Degree or equivalent	14	5	15	18	17	13
Higher education below degree level	6	4	7	7	7	6
GCE A-level or broad equivalent[2]	21	25	20	21	19	18
GCSE O-level or equivalent[2]	27	36	29	26	22	21
Other qualification[3]	11	11	13	10	10	10
No qualification	22	20	16	18	25	33
	Females					
Numbers (1 000s)	16 780	3 443	2 304	4 124	3 879	3 030
%	100	100	100	100	100	100
	Highest qualification (%)					
Degree or equivalent	9	4	12	13	9	5
Higher education below degree level	8	3	8	9	10	8
GCE A-level or broad equivalent[2]	11	20	13	10	7	5
GCSE O-level or equivalent[2]	26	39	32	26	19	13
Other qualification[3]	16	14	17	16	17	15
No qualification	31	19	17	26	38	54

1. More detailed information on the levels of vocational qualifications was collected in 1993, allowing a more accurate allocation of such courses to the broad equivalents of GCE A-levels and GCEs. The information published in previous volumes is not comparable at these levels with that published here.
2. From 1993, Trade apprenticeship and City and Guilds, which were previously all included with A-levels, have been split between A- and O-level equivalents.
3. Includes CSE below Grade 1, YTS certificate, RSA and other qualifications.
Source: Education Statistics for the United Kingdom, 1994.

Table 3a.   **Participation of 16-year-olds in education, England, 1983/84 to 1993/94**

Estimated population aged 16 (%)

	Academic year					
	1983/84	1989/90	1990/91	1991/92	1992/93	1993/94
	Males[1, 2]					
Level of course:						
GCE A/AS-level	21.1	27.3	29.4	31.5	32.5	33.6
Advanced GNVQ					0.1	1.6
Advanced NVQ and other equivalents	3.1	3.4	3.9	4.9	5.6	5.9
GCSE	8.8	8.8	9.7	11.2	10.1	7.4
Intermediate and Foundation GNVQ[3]					0.1	3.9
NVQ Levels 1, 2 and other courses	10.0	11.2	11.4	14.5	17.3	16.5
Institution of study:						
Maintained secondary schools:						
Grant-maintained		0.2	0.7	1.8	3.3	6.3
Other maintained secondary	18.8	20.3	21.6	23.4	23.3	20.7
Special schools	0.6	0.7	0.7	0.7	0.7	0.7
Independent schools	5.1	6.5	6.7	7.0	6.9	7.3
All schools	24.6	27.6	29.7	32.9	34.2	34.9
Sixth-form colleges	3.9	5.6	6.2	7.0	8.0	8.5
Tertiary colleges	1.3	3.7	4.1	5.3	5.2	6.0
Other FHE institutions	13.8	14.5	15.1	17.5	19.0	20.1
All FE colleges	19.0	23.7	25.3	29.8	32.2	34.7
Full-time participation[4]	43.6	51.3	55.1	62.7	66.4	69.6
Number of full-time students (1 000s)	171.2	168.4	170.9	186.3	189.7	192.4
Part-time participation	18.7	18.7	16.0	11.4	9.1	8.6
Number of part-time students (1 000s)	73.2	61.3	49.7	33.7	26.0	23.8
Total participation	62.3	70.0	71.1	74.1	75.5	78.2
Total number (1 000s)	244.4	229.7	220.6	220.0	215.7	216.2
Male population aged 16 (1 000s)	392.4	327.9	310.3	297.0	285.7	276.5
	Females[1, 2]					
Level of course:						
GCE A/AS-level	22.3	31.5	34.4	37.0	38.8	39.9
Advanced GNVQ					0.1	2.4
Advanced NVQ and other equivalents	2.1	3.9	4.7	5.7	6.6	6.4
GCSE	11.3	8.9	9.9	10.8	8.9	6.2
Intermediate and Foundation GNVQ[3]					0.2	4.8
NVQ Levels 1, 2 and other courses	16.0	14.0	14.3	16.6	18.5	15.4
Institution of study:						
Maintained secondary schools:						
Grant-maintained		0.1	0.4	1.5	3.1	6.3
Other maintained secondary	22.4	23.5	25.2	26.8	26.7	23.8
Special schools	0.5	0.5	0.5	0.5	0.5	0.5
Independent schools	4.0	5.6	5.8	6.1	6.2	6.4
All schools	26.8	29.7	32.0	34.9	36.5	37.0

Table 3a. **Participation of 16-year-olds in education, England, 1983/84 to 1993/94** *(cont.)*

Estimated population aged 16 (%)

	Academic year					
	1983/84	1989/90	1990/91	1991/92	1992/93	1993/94
	Females[1, 2]					
Sixth-form colleges	4.7	6.5	7.3	8.2	9.1	9.9
Tertiary colleges	1.9	4.9	5.3	6.4	6.2	6.9
Other FHE institutions	18.7	17.7	19.2	21.1	21.8	21.9
All FE colleges	25.3	29.2	31.8	35.8	37.1	38.7
Full-time participation[4]	52.2	58.8	63.8	70.7	73.6	75.6
Number of full-time students (1 000s)	192.6	180.8	186.2	197.4	197.8	196.5
Part-time participation	14.2	12.8	10.3	7.9	6.7	6.2
Number of part-time students (1 000s)	52.6	39.4	30.1	22.1	18.0	16.2
Total participation	66.4	71.7	74.1	78.6	80.3	81.9
Total number (1 000s)	245.2	220.3	216.3	219.5	215.9	212.6
Female population aged 16 (1 000s)	369.3	307.3	291.7	279.3	268.9	259.7
	Males and females[1, 2]					
Full-time participation[4]	47.8	55.0	59.3	66.6	69.9	72.5
Number of full-time students (1 000s)	363.8	349.2	357.1	383.7	387.5	388.9
Part-time participation	16.5	15.9	13.3	9.7	7.9	7.5
Number of part-time students (1 000s)	125.7	100.7	79.8	55.8	44.1	40.0
Total participation	64.3	70.8	72.6	76.3	77.8	80.0
Total number (1 000s)	489.6	450.0	436.9	439.5	431.6	428.9

1. Excludes students in further and higher education establishments, the Open University and employer-based Youth Training.
2. Students taking more than one course are counted only once – the highest in the sequence in the table.
3. Foundation GNVQ included in Other Courses for 1993/94; the small number of pilot GNVQ courses in 1992/93 is not shown.
4. The schools total includes special schools, not shown separately.
Source: *Statistical Bulletin – Participation in Education by 16- to 18-Year-Olds in England: 1983/84 to 1993/94,* Department for Education, 1995.

explain more than a small fraction of the observed long-run rate of increase in participation (about 1-1.5 per cent per year), let alone the much larger increases of the last few years (about 4 per cent per year since 1988).

An increasing number of young people are staying on in full-time education to take a vocational qualification. The introduction of GNVQs has proved popular.

145

Table 3b. **Participation of 17-year-olds in education, England, 1983/84 to 1993/94**

Estimated population aged 17 (%)

	Academic year					
	1983/84	1989/90	1990/91	1991/92	1992/93	1993/94
	Males[1, 2]					
Level of course:						
Higher education	0.3	0.2	0.2	0.2	0.3	0.3
GCE A/AS-level	20.0	24.3	26.4	28.9	31.0	31.9
Advanced GNVQ					0.1	1.5
Advanced NVQ and other equivalents	3.5	4.8	5.7	7.4	8.9	9.8
GCSE	1.3	1.4	1.5	1.9	1.9	1.5
Intermediate and Foundation GNVQ[3]					0.1	1.0
NVQ Levels 1, 2 and other courses	3.1	5.0	5.1	6.3	7.7	7.3
Institution of study:						
Maintained secondary schools:						
Grant-maintained		0.1	0.5	1.2	2.3	4.3
Other maintained secondary	11.9	12.7	13.2	14.0	14.3	13.0
Special schools	0.4	0.5	0.5	0.5	0.5	0.5
Independent schools	4.0	5.3	5.6	5.9	6.2	6.3
All schools	16.3	18.5	19.8	21.7	23.3	24.1
Sixth-form colleges	2.8	3.9	4.3	4.9	5.6	6.5
Tertiary colleges	0.8	2.7	3.0	3.8	4.3	4.8
Other FHE institutions	8.5	10.8	12.1	14.5	16.9	18.3
All FE colleges	12.0	17.4	19.4	23.2	26.8	29.6
Full-time participation[4, 5]	28.5	36.2	39.5	45.1	50.3	53.9
Number of full-time students (1 000s)	114.8	126.6	129.8	140.2	149.6	154.5
Part-time participation	17.4	21.1	19.7	17.2	13.3	11.3
Number of part-time students (1 000s)	69.8	73.8	64.7	53.4	39.4	32.4
Total participation	45.9	57.3	59.2	62.3	63.6	65.2
Total number (1 000s)	184.6	200.4	194.6	193.6	189.0	186.9
Male population aged 17 (1 000s)	402.2	349.8	328.9	310.5	297.1	286.9
	Females[1, 2]					
Level of course:						
Higher education	0.2	0.3	0.3	0.3	0.3	0.4
GCE A/AS-level	21.1	26.7	29.6	32.9	35.4	36.8
Advanced GNVQ					0.1	1.8
Advanced NVQ and other equivalents	2.4	4.8	5.8	7.5	8.9	10.1
GCSE	2.3	1.7	1.9	2.1	2.0	1.4
Intermediate and Foundation GNVQ[3]						1.0
NVQ Levels 1, 2 and other courses	9.0	8.4	8.5	9.6	10.8	9.3
Institution of study:						
Maintained secondary schools:						
Grant-maintained		0.1	0.3	1.0	2.1	4.4
Other maintained secondary	13.2	14.4	15.5	16.7	17.1	15.9
Special schools	0.3	0.4	0.4	0.4	0.4	0.4
Independent schools	3.0	4.3	4.8	5.1	5.4	5.6
All schools	16.5	19.3	21.0	23.2	25.0	26.2

Table 3b. **Participation of 17-year-olds in education, England, 1983/84 to 1993/94**
(cont.)

Estimated population aged 17 (%)

	Academic year					
	1983/84	1989/90	1990/91	1991/92	1992/93	1993/94
	Females[1, 2]					
Sixth-form colleges	3.3	4.7	5.1	5.9	6.8	7.7
Tertiary colleges	1.3	3.6	4.1	5.0	5.2	5.8
Other FHE institutions	14.0	14.5	15.9	18.4	20.7	21.1
All FE colleges	18.6	22.8	25.1	29.2	32.7	34.6
Full-time participation[4, 5]	35.2	42.3	46.4	52.7	58.0	61.2
Number of full-time students (1 000s)	133.9	139.3	143.3	154.5	162.3	165.0
Part-time participation	10.9	12.8	11.5	10.1	8.5	7.7
Number of part-time students (1 000s)	41.4	42.1	35.4	29.5	23.7	20.8
Total participation	46.2	55.1	57.8	62.8	66.4	68.9
Total number (1 000s)	175.4	181.4	178.7	184.0	186.0	185.8
Female population aged 17 (1 000s)	379.9	329.3	308.9	293.0	280.0	269.8
	Males and females[1, 2]					
Full-time participation[4, 5]	31.8	39.2	42.8	48.8	54.0	57.4
Number of full-time students (1 000s)	248.7	265.9	273.1	294.7	311.8	319.5
Part-time participation	14.2	17.1	15.7	13.7	10.9	9.6
Number of part-time students (1 000s)	111.2	115.9	100.1	82.9	63.1	53.2
Total participation	46.0	56.2	58.5	62.6	65.0	67.0
Total number (1 000s)	360.0	381.8	373.2	377.6	374.9	372.8

1. Excludes students in further and higher education establishments, the Open University and employer-based Youth Training.
2. Students taking more than one course are counted only once – the highest in the sequence in the table.
3. Foundation GNVQ included in Other Courses for 1993/94; the small number of pilot GNVQ courses in 1992/93 is not shown.
4. The schools total includes special schools, not shown separately.
5. Includes higher education, not shown separately.
Source: Statistical Bulletin – Participation in Education by 16- to 18-Year Olds in England: 1983/84 to 1993/94, Department for Education, 1995.

Young people see this qualification as a route to both higher education or employment.

Since 1985, the Department of Education and the Employment Department have jointly funded research into young people's early experiences of work, training and education. The research is conducted by Social and Community

Table 3c. **Participation of 18-year-olds in education, England, 1983/84 to 1993/94**

Estimated population aged 18 (%)

	Academic year					
	1983/84	1989/90	1990/91	1991/92	1992/93	1993/94
	Males[1, 2]					
Level of course:						
Higher education first degree	7.3	8.9	9.8	11.3	13.4	14.6
Higher education sub-degree	1.2	1.4	1.7	2.0	2.3	2.5
GCE A/AS-level	4.3	4.5	5.1	5.9	6.2	6.4
Advanced GNVQ						0.7
Advanced NVQ and other equivalents	2.2	3.0	3.5	4.5	5.7	6.8
GCSE	0.3	0.3	0.4	0.5	0.5	0.5
Intermediate and Foundation GNVQ[3]						0.3
NVQ Levels 1, 2 and other courses	1.5	2.3	2.5	3.2	3.9	4.0
Institution of study:						
Higher education university	7.5	9.2	10.1	11.6	13.6	14.8
Higher education FE college	1.0	1.1	1.3	1.8	2.2	2.3
Maintained secondary schools	1.4	1.1	1.2	1.5	1.7	1.9
Independent schools	0.5	0.7	0.8	0.8	0.9	1.0
Sixth-form colleges	0.7	0.9	1.0	1.3	1.5	1.7
Tertiary colleges	0.3	1.0	1.2	1.6	1.8	2.3
Other FE institutions	5.4	6.4	7.3	9.0	10.6	11.9
Full-time participation[4]	17.0	20.7	23.3	27.7	32.4	36.1
Number of full-time students (1 000s)	69.8	77.0	81.7	91.2	100.6	107.7
Part-time participation	17.3	17.9	17.3	16.8	14.5	12.1
Number of part-time students (1 000s)	71.3	66.5	60.8	55.1	45.0	36.1
Total participation	34.3	38.7	40.6	44.5	46.9	48.2
Total number (1 000s)	141.1	143.5	142.6	146.3	145.7	143.9
Male population aged 18 (1 000s)	411.8	371.1	351.0	328.9	310.7	298.3
	Females[1, 2]					
Level of course:						
Higher education first degree	6.6	8.7	9.9	11.8	14.3	15.7
Higher education sub-degree	1.1	1.3	1.5	1.7	2.2	2.3
GCE A/AS-level	3.5	4.3	5.1	6.1	6.3	6.6
Advanced GNVQ						0.6
Advanced NVQ and other equivalents	1.1	2.4	2.8	3.7	4.6	5.7
GCSE	0.4	0.4	0.4	0.5	0.5	0.4
Intermediate and Foundation GNVQ[3]						0.2
NVQ Levels 1, 2 and other courses	3.4	3.8	4.1	4.9	5.6	5.5
Institution of study:						
Higher education university	5.8	7.8	9.0	10.4	12.9	14.3
Higher education FE college	1.8	2.2	2.4	3.1	3.6	3.7
Maintained secondary schools	1.1	1.0	1.2	1.5	1.6	1.8
Independent schools	0.3	0.5	0.6	0.7	0.7	0.8
Sixth-form colleges	0.6	0.9	1.0	1.2	1.4	1.6
Tertiary colleges	0.3	1.1	1.3	1.7	1.9	2.3
Other FE institutions	6.2	7.4	8.3	10.1	11.5	12.6

Table 3c. **Participation of 18-year-olds in education, England, 1983/84 to 1993/94**
(cont.)
Estimated population aged 18 (%)

	Academic year					
	1983/84	1989/90	1990/91	1991/92	1992/93	1993/94
	Females[1, 2]					
Full-time participation[4]	16.3	21.0	24.1	28.9	33.7	37.3
Number of full-time students (1 000s)	63.4	73.9	79.9	89.7	99.1	105.0
Part-time participation	9.4	10.1	9.3	9.4	8.5	8.2
Number of part-time students (1 000s)	36.8	35.5	30.9	29.0	25.1	23.1
Total participation	25.7	31.1	33.5	38.3	42.3	45.5
Total number (1 000s)	100.2	109.4	110.7	118.8	124.2	128.1
Female population aged 18 (1 000s)	389.5	351.9	330.7	310.3	293.9	281.2
	Males and females[1, 2]					
Full-time participation[4]	16.6	20.9	23.7	28.3	33.0	36.7
Number of full-time students (1 000s)	133.2	150.9	161.6	180.9	199.7	212.7
Part-time participation	13.5	14.1	13.5	13.2	11.6	10.2
Number of part-time students (1 000s)	108.0	102.0	91.7	84.2	70.1	59.2
Total participation	30.1	35.0	37.2	41.5	44.6	46.9
Total number (1 000s)	241.2	252.9	253.3	265.1	269.8	271.9

1. Excludes students in further and higher education establishments, the Open University and employer-based Youth Training.
2. Students taking more than one course are counted only once – the highest in the sequence in the table.
3. Foundation GNVQ included in Other Courses for 1993/94; the small number of pilot GNVQ courses in 1992/93 is not shown.
4. The schools total includes special schools, not shown separately.
Source: Statistical Bulletin – Participation in Education by 16- to 18-Year Olds in England: 1983/84 to 1993/94, Department for Education, 1995.

Planning Research and is published as a Youth Cohort Study (YCS). The Department for Education arranges for schools to generate a sample that is representative of 16-17-year-olds in England and Wales. Young people are sent postal questionnaires at annual intervals – 16-17, 17-18 and 18-19 respectively. They cover a wide range of topics which include school experiences, jobs and training, as well as details of parental employment and level of education.

Consistent distinction between full- and part-time study is a problem in international comparisons – for example, Germany, France and other countries record all participants in apprenticeship programmes as being in full-time education and training. There are thus larger differences between countries in full-time

◆ Figure 2. **Full- and part-time participation in education
and training of 16- to 18-year-olds**
(1992)

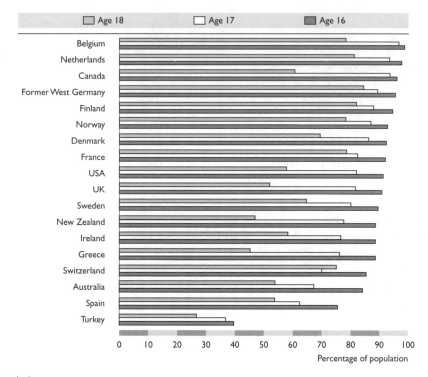

Source: Author.

participation rates than in overall rates. The United Kingdom has the lowest full-time participation rates but the highest part-time.

The Youth Cohort Study (YCS) provides information on, for instance, routes taken by various groups of young people from full-time education into the labour market, and their qualifications; on gender and differences in pay and training received; on parental occupations and parental educational levels and rate of entry into higher education. Because the main core of questions has remained largely the same from one cohort to the next, the YCS is also able to provide information on how these routes, and the numbers of young people following them, have changed over time.

YCS research indicates that the level of examination success at age 15/16 (*i.e.* in the GCSE) is a powerful determinant of whether a young person stays on in full-time education, with the level of the parents' education seen as a similar determining factor.

The effect of unemployment on the staying-on rate has been the subject of considerable research but without any conclusive result. Nonetheless, there seems no other plausible explanation for the surge in the staying-on rate in the early 1980s. Unemployment may also have contributed to the increase in the early 1990s, but it is unlikely to have been the dominant factor, given that the recent increase in the staying-on rate has been more than double that in the early 1980s. Although the rise in unemployment has been smaller, the staying-on rate increase was already well under way before the upturn in unemployment occurred.

In 1988, the government introduced the GCSE as the main examination for pupils at age 16, *i.e.* at the end of the period of statutory schooling. The GCSE replaced the General Certificate of Education at Ordinary level (GCE O-level) and the Certificate of Secondary Examination (CSE). Assessment for the GCE was mainly by externally-marked final examinations; for the GCSE, it is through a combination of externally-marked final examinations and internally-marked, externally-moderated course work. Attainment levels increased with the introduc- tion of the GCSE. It is probable that some pupils decided to stay on in full-time education because they had been motivated by their enjoyment and success in course work and their overall achievement in the GCSE. Some support for this assumption is provided by the YCS research, which shows an increase in the proportion of young people expressing positive views about their final two years of schooling since the introduction of the GCSE.

Other factors that are believed to have boosted the staying-on rate over the last five years are the withdrawal of 16-17-year-olds' eligibility for social security benefits; local management of schools, which has rendered much more visible the financial incentive to schools of encouraging their pupils to stay on after 16; and peer-group pressure, given that staying on has now become the norm.

The fall in the staying-on rate in 1983/84 (the only time this has ever hap- pened) and the absence of any recovery over the following few years are some- times ascribed to the expansion of the Youth Training Scheme, which provided an additional choice to young people who would otherwise have had to choose between staying on and unemployment.

Factors determining the level and type of course pursued by those who stay on are various, *e.g.* the choice of a Level 3 course (A/AS levels) at age 16 rather than Level 2 is governed overwhelmingly by young people's degree of GCSE success. Therefore, if the staying-on rate is rising more rapidly than GCSE attainment (as it did, for example, in the early 1980s and to a lesser extent again recently), this will increase the proportion of relatively low-qualified stayers-on, and thus reduce the proportion on Level 3 courses. There seems nevertheless to be a gradual trend towards Level 3 courses. Moreover, there is a steady trend in favour of vocational courses, even though for Level 3 at least these are still very much in the minority.

The very marked decline in part-time participation over the last few years appears to be entirely explicable in terms of a squeeze imposed by the increase in full-time participation.

4. NATIONAL TARGETS FOR EDUCATION AND TRAINING

In 1991, the Confederation of British Industry (CBI) determined some national targets for education and training which had the support of the government. These targets were then revised and set out in the government's second White Paper, *Competitiveness: Forging Ahead,* published in May 1995:

Foundation learning

- by age 19, 85 per cent of young people to achieve five GCSEs at Grade C or above, an Intermediate GNVQ or an NVQ Level 2;

- 75 per cent of young people to achieve Level 2 competence in communication, numeracy and information technology by age 19; and 35 per cent to achieve Level 3 competence in these core skills by age 21;

- by age 21, 60 per cent of young people to achieve two GCE A-levels, an Advanced GNVQ or an NVQ Level 3.

Lifetime learning

- 60 per cent of the workforce to be qualified to NVQ Level 3, Advanced GNVQ or two GCE A-levels;

- 30 per cent of the workforce to have a vocational, professional, management or academic qualification at NVQ Level 4 or above;

- 70 per cent of all organisations employing 200 or more employees, and 35 per cent of those employing 50 or more, to be recognised as Investors in People.

The progress was as follows:

Foundation Target 1

– By the autumn of 1994, 63 per cent of young people up to age 19 in Great Britain were qualified to NVQ Level 2 or equivalent.

Foundation Target 2

(No figures were available to indicate progress towards this target.)

Foundation Target 3

– By the autumn term of 1994, 41 per cent of young people up to age 21 in Great Britain were qualified to NVQ Level 3 or equivalent.

Lifetime Target 1

– By the autumn of 1994, 40 per cent of the employed workforce in Great Britain were qualified to at least NVQ Level 3 or equivalent.

Lifetime Target 2

– By the autumn term of 1994, 23 per cent of the employed workforce in Great Britain were qualified to at least NVQ Level 4 or equivalent.

Lifetime Target 3

– Progress data up to the end of February 1995 showed that the number of organisations with 200 or more employees recognised as Investors in People had reached 486, representing a 6 per cent progress. In addition to recognition, the number of organisations employing 200 workers or more who had made a commitment to work towards the Investors Standard was just over 3 440.

Annex 1

NORTHERN IRELAND'S POSITION

While the post-16 qualifications framework in Northern Ireland is the same as that for England and Wales, there are some differences in administrative structures and in funding and quality assurance arrangements.

MANAGEMENT OF FURTHER EDUCATION COLLEGES

Further education colleges in Northern Ireland offer the same range of qualifications as their counterparts in England and Wales. However, while responsibility for funding the latter was transferred to the Further Education Funding Councils in April 1993, colleges in Northern Ireland continue to be funded and managed by the five Education and Library Boards (local education authorities).

TRAINING

On the training side, Northern Ireland has no Training and Enterprise Councils (TECs). In Northern Ireland, a government agency – the Training and Employment Agency – has overall responsibility for training both the 16-19-year-old age-group and older persons. The Agency provides training directly through its network of training centres and also contracts with other bodies, such as further education colleges, for the delivery of a wide range of training programmes. The Training and Employment Agency is also responsible for the provision of careers and employment services in Northern Ireland.

QUALITY ASSURANCE

The Education and Training Inspectorate (ETI) of the Department of Education has overall responsibility for quality assurance in schools, colleges and training institutions in Northern Ireland. The ETI monitors and reports on the quality of provision and outcomes and on the standards being achieved by the students. It gives information and advice to both the Department of Education and the Training and Employment Agency.

Annex 2

MODERN APPRENTICESHIPS

In December 1993, the Secretary of State for Employment launched widespread consultations with industry on setting up the system of modern apprenticeships. The main features of these would be:

- An apprenticeship pledge, would be signed by both the apprentice and employer, setting out a statement of the training offered and the qualification aimed for.

- The apprenticeship would provide preparation for, but not a guarantee of, a job.

- Apprenticeships would vary in length according to the young person's ability but might be between two and a half years and four years.

- The government would invest £1.25 billion in credits and apprenticeships over the following three years; school leavers would receive training credits which they could cash in with employers who were able to provide the training required.

- It was expected that there would be up to about 150 000 apprentices in training at any one time.

In May 1994, the government published its first White Paper on competitiveness, entitled *Competitiveness – Helping Business To Win* (Cm 2563). In this, the government challenges industry to develop, from 1995, accelerated modern apprenticeships for 18-19-year-olds. If industry plays its part, government will provide funding of £107 million over the three years to 1997/98. This means that by the end of the century an extra 30 000 young people a year will achieve NVQs at Level 3 or higher.

GLOSSARY

CBI: Confederation of British Industry
ETI: Education and Training Inspectorate
FE: Further Education
FEFC: Further Education Funding Council
GCE: General Certificate of Education
GCSE: General Certificate of Secondary Education
GNVQ: General National Vocational Qualification
NCVQ: National Council for Vocational Qualifications
NRA: National Record of Achievement
NVQ: National Vocational Qualifications
TEC: Training and Enterprise Councils
YCS: Youth Cohort Study
YT: Youth Training

6

FRANCE

by

Claude Pair and Sylvie Lemaire,
Directorate for Evaluation and Planning (DEP), Ministry of National Education

1. THE FRENCH EDUCATIONAL SYSTEM AND ITS EVOLUTION

General structure

The general structure of the French initial training system is shown in Figure 1 (further training will not be considered in this chapter). The ages at which pupils normally reach the different levels are shown at the left; however, since grade-repeating is relatively frequent, a number of pupils fall behind. For example, 32 per cent of pupils have repeated a grade by the end of elementary school, and 43 per cent by the end of middle school, although grade-repeating has declined in recent years.

Schooling is compulsory between the ages of 6 and 16. However, nearly all pupils begin school at the age of 3, and a substantial number begin even earlier (approximately 35 per cent). Moreover, 95 per cent of pupils continue to attend school after the age of 16. In Figure 1, the participation rate at the various levels is shown by the width of corresponding rectangles. Four levels can be distinguished:

- *nursery school (école maternelle)*, which precedes compulsory education, and elementary school (*école élémentaire*), up to the age of 11;
- *middle school (collège)*, which all children are required to enter for four years of compulsory secondary education, known as the sixth, fifth, fourth and third grades (however, there are still traces of the previous arrangement, where certain students left the *collège* after the first two years – fifth form); the *collèges* also have a special education stream, attended by 3 per cent of pupils;
- *high school (lycée)*, where 90 per cent of middle-school students continue their studies in the various curricula (general, technical, vocational);
- *higher education (enseignement supérieur)*, into which 45 per cent of a given age group currently enter (this percentage is rising).

◆ Figure 1. **Structure of the French education system**

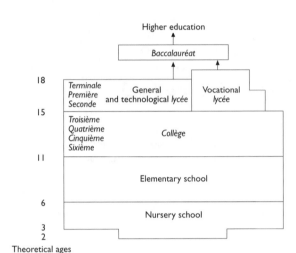

Source: Authors.

In addition, outside the education system per se, there is an *apprenticeship system* where work in a company alternates with training in an Apprentice Training Centre (*Centre de formation d'apprentis*), which is most often run by a company-related organisation. The apprentices (about 11 per cent of a given age group) generally enter the system after middle school, but apprenticeship is beginning to develop at the higher levels.

Figure 2 shows the pathways available after middle school. Students who remain in the education system enter a high school, which may be of two kinds:

– *High school for general and technical education* (*lycée d'enseignement général et technologique*), which is a single institution, entered by about 60 per cent of a given age group. After three years of study, it leads to a general or technical *baccalauréat*; there are three general streams (literary, economic and social, scientific) and two technical streams (industrial and tertiary), each of which offers several fields of specialisation; after the *baccalauréat*, the large majority of students go on to the higher education level;

– *Vocational high school* (*lycée professionnel*), entered by 30 per cent of a given age group, leading to a vocational diploma in the industrial or tertiary sector. After two years of study, there is a skilled worker's diploma, either the

◆ Figure 2. **Pathways in 1992-93**

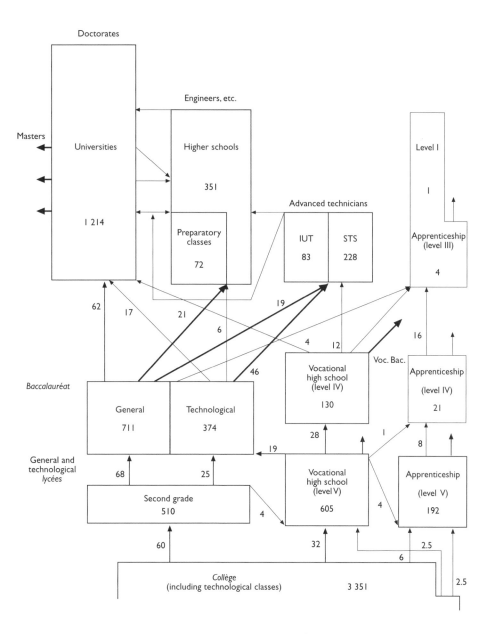

traditional Vocational Aptitude Diploma (*Certificat d'aptitude professionnelle*, or CAP) or the Vocational Studies Diploma (*Brevet d'études professionnelles*, or BEP) created in 1967. After two more years, for a large number of BEP holders, there is the vocational *baccalauréat*, which is conceived as a terminal diploma, even if the pursuit of higher education is theoretically possible.

Higher education takes three forms:

– *Universities*, which receive slightly more than half of the entrants and have open admission; in addition to the traditional general and professional streams (medicine, law, etc.), since 1970 various streams preparing students for occupations in the industrial and business sector have been established; the most recent (1991) are the Vocationally-oriented University Institutes (*Instituts universitaires professionnalisés*), which are entered one or two years after the *baccalauréat* and from which students graduate four years after the *baccalauréat*;

– *Higher schools* (*écoles supérieures* or *grandes écoles*) which prepare for various occupations (engineering, business, paramedical, architecture, education, etc.). Students are generally admitted to these schools by competitive examination; for some schools, candidates may sit for the examination immediately after the *baccalauréat*, while for others (the most prestigious schools), they must first complete a programme of preparatory classes in a *lycée*;

– *Technical higher education* (*études technologiques courtes*). These studies, lasting two years, receive about one-third of entering students and lead to an advanced technician level. Students prepare for the diploma either in a *lycée* (*Sections de techniciens supérieurs*, or Advanced Technician Sections) or in a university (*Instituts universitaires de technologie*, or University Institutes of Technology); applicants are admitted through case-by-case selection.

Apprenticeship can prepare for the same vocational and technical diplomas as full-time schooling, although in practice it mainly trains operatives and clerical employees. In addition, it prepares for the vocational diploma of master-craftsman, which was initially reserved for further training.

Transformations since the beginning of the 1980s

The changes that have taken place reflect a continuous evolution rather than a wide-ranging reform. The main features of this transformation include prolongation of studies, extension of vocational streams and postponement of choices between streams.

The two preceding decades had seen the creation of the middle school from distinct institutions. In 1975, a common core was finally imposed for the first two years (except for special education). There were still multiple options after this, however. Some students left middle school to prepare for the first vocational diploma, the CAP, in a vocational high school or an apprenticeship. Others remained in middle school, but in specific classes for students having difficulties in school who had little hope of going on to further studies; these students generally waited until they reached the age of 16, and only half entered an apprenticeship programme.

In the course of the last decade, these "orientations by failure" after the fifth grade were to decrease (from 20 per cent in 1980 to 4 per cent in 1991), and it was decided to eliminate them for 1992 in accordance with the principle that students should complete middle school before choosing an orientation. In order to permit effective instruction, however, measures were implemented to maintain certain distinctions in content during the last two years of middle school (fourth and third grades) but without compromising the pursuit of further studies. In 1984, at the same time as the new subject of technology was introduced into all middle-school classes, "technical" fourth and third-grade sections were created with a significant part of the instruction – at least ten hours a week – devoted to technical disciplines as a way of motivating students and exposing them to ideas, including general knowledge. In fact, these technical sections have often been set up in vocational high schools, where they were easier to organise, but they do not prepare for an occupation, and today they are gradually being transferred into the middle schools.

In addition, since 1992, students with learning difficulties who now remain in middle school after the fifth grade have benefited from a special support programme organised by the middle school, which enjoys a large measure of freedom in this area, permitting them to go on to a high school, usually vocational, or to an apprenticeship. There are, however, recurring discussions about the existence of this "single middle school": the 1993 round was to make it possible to re-institute pre-apprenticeship classes after the fifth grade.

The evolution of the middle school leads to that of the vocational high school. In the course of the decade, the preparation for the CAP in three years after the fifth grade attracted fewer and fewer students and almost disappeared entirely. Entry into the vocational high school has shifted towards the third grade, and the most common diploma prepared for is the BEP, taking two years, which leads to the same level of employment as the CAP (skilled worker) but is less specialised (the BEP offers some 50 specialisations as compared to 300 for the CAP) and is more oriented towards the tertiary sector. More generally, a great effort was made at national level during this period to redefine diploma content towards less specialisation and greater adaptability. In view of their common level, a link has been established between the CAP and BEP: the BEP's competencies are oriented towards a family of occupations, while the CAP is a specialisation directed more towards performances that are directly applicable to a specific occupation. Most students preparing for the BEP also obtain a CAP. In addition, since 1983, these two national diplomas can be extended by complementary education and training adapted to local employment, usually for a one-year period; the number of participants remains limited, however.

At the same time, the BEP is increasingly becoming a prerequisite for further studies. This occurs in two different ways. The first is through a "reorientation class" for the technical *baccalauréat* which permits entry into higher education, notably technical. Participation in this programme, known as the first-grade "adaptation class" (*première d'adaptation*), increased threefold between 1980 and 1986. The stagnation period that followed can be explained by the creation of the second path for the continuation of vocational education, the vocational *baccalauréat*. This diploma was to enjoy tremendous popularity, and the present trend is for BEP holders to continue their studies towards a *baccalauréat*. It can now be said that a technical and vocational stream has been created, with entries and exits occurring at various levels, including the technical fourth and third grades, preparation for the BEP, the technical and vocational *baccalauréat*, the advanced technician sections and even engineering schools. This development is the result of both the changing economy and the social demand for longer schooling, as well as organisational decisions.

Apprenticeship follows the same pattern, although in a more modest way. Until 1987, it usually led only to the CAP. Since then, it can, by law, serve as a preliminary step for any technical or vocational diploma, all the way to that of engineer. This should enable apprenticeship to go beyond the craft and small business sector, which constitutes most of its activity, in order to include the large companies and even the public administrations. This transformation has been relatively slow despite the incentives provided by successive governments; however, the situation appears to be changing more rapidly, but three quarters of apprentices are still preparing for the CAP.

For general and technical high schools, organisational changes have been less significant. In 1981, a common first year (second grade) was established for the different streams, although distinctions are still maintained through a system of options. Subsequently, until 1992, an effort was made to make these distinctions less determining for a student's future. In particular, it is now no longer indispensable to choose technical options in the second grade in order to continue towards a technological *baccalauréat*. However, for these high schools, the main change lies not in structural transformations but in a sharp increase in numbers, which modifies the student population. The same is true for higher education institutions.

◆ Figure 3. **Pathways in 1980-81**

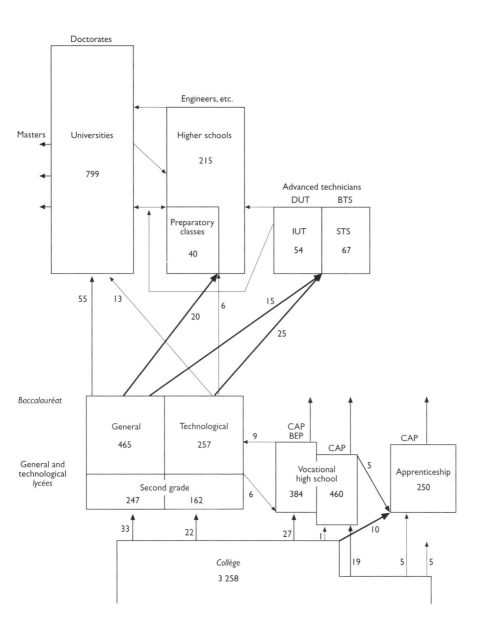

The changes introduced into the structure of the education system between 1980 and 1992 can be seen by comparing Figures 2 and 3. In addition to these changes, there has also been a major effort to bring schools closer to enterprises. Outside the education system, too, a certain number of emergency measures have been taken to aid labour market entry among the unemployed, especially unskilled workers, through various mechanisms and contracts that in principle combine training and work.

2. TRAINING "PROGRAMMES"

The various "programmes" (as defined by the OECD's VOTEC study) available after primary school are described in Table 1. We have shown the levels of training and qualification attained, which the French classification breaks down into six stages:

- Exits without a qualification, that are divided into:

  • Level VI: exits from middle school before the final year;

  • Level V bis: exits from middle school during the final year (*i.e.* the third grade) or from the vocational *lycée* before the final year;

- Level V, corresponding to the level of a skilled worker: exits from the vocational *lycée* after receiving the CAP or BEP, or exits from the general or technical *lycée* before the end of the final year;

- Level IV, corresponding to what are sometimes known as "technicians'" jobs, even though it is not always easy to identify the jobs to which this term refers: exits at the level of the *baccalauréat*, whether or not it has actually been obtained;

- Level III, for advanced technicians: exits with a first-cycle higher education diploma (two years after the *baccalauréat*);

- Level II: exits with a second-cycle higher education diploma (three or four years after the *baccalauréat*);

- Level I: exits with a higher education diploma requiring at least five years of study (engineers, physicians, etc.).

These levels are roughly comparable with the following ISCED international classification levels (in inverse order): ISCED 2 corresponds to Levels VI and V bis, ISCED 3 to Levels V and IV, ISCED 5 to Level III, ISCED 6 to Level II and ISCED 7 to Level I.

Table 1. **Programmes of the French education system**

Programme	Type of school	Diplomas awarded	Level of training	Duration	Entry level	Possible continuation	Curricula	Different streams
Middle school (lower secondary)	College	Certificate of lower secondary education	Vbis non-vocational	4 years	All children enter after elementary school (normally at age 11)	– general and technological *lycée* – vocational *lycée* – apprenticeship	General education, including technology	– general and technological 4th and 3rd grades – a special education stream
Full-time preparation for CAP	Vocational *lycée*	CAP	V	2 years (3 years if after 5th grade)	After college (formerly after 5th grade, today on an exceptional basis)	– employment – preparation for BEP – in some cases, preparation for vocational *baccalauréat*	– general and vocational – training programmes in enterprises	Industrial and tertiary specialisations
Full-time preparation for BEP	Vocational *lycée*	BEP (and CAP)	V	2 years	After college	– preparation for vocational *baccalauréat* – preparation for technological *baccalauréat* – employment	– general and vocational – training programmes in enterprises	Industrial and tertiary specialisations
Preparation for CAP in apprenticeship programme	In enterprises and Apprentice Training Centres (CFA)	CAP	V	2 years	After college (formerly after 5th grade, today on an exceptional basis)	– employment – some options for continuing vocational studies, in particular in apprenticeship programme	Work in enterprises General and vocational education in CFAs	Industrial and tertiary specialisations, especially in the fields of crafts and trade
Second grade	General and technological *lycée*	–	V, but not vocational	1 year	After college	General or technological secondary education and preparation for BEP on an exceptional basis	General fields Possible technological options	Through options

Table 1. **Programmes of the French education system** *(cont.)*

Programme	Type of school	Diplomas awarded	Level of training	Duration	Entry level	Possible continuation	Curricula	Different streams
General secondary education	General and technological *lycée*	General *baccalauréat*	IV	2 years	Second grade	Higher education	General fields	3 streams: – literary – economic and social – scientific, with options
Technological secondary education	General and technological *lycée*	Technological *baccalauréat* or Technician's Diploma for some specialisations[1]	IV	2 years	Second grade BEP (entry in first-grade "adaptation class")	Higher education, especially technological	General and technical fields	2 streams: – industrial – tertiary, with specialisations
Full-time preparation for the vocational *baccalauréat*	Vocational *lycée*	Vocational *baccalauréat*	IV	2 years	BEP	– employment – higher education on an exceptional basis	– general and vocational – training programmes in enterprises	Industrial and tertiary specialisations
Advanced Technician Sections (STS)	General and technological *lycée*	Advanced Technician's Diploma (BTS)	III	2 years	General or technological *baccalauréat*, and vocational *baccalauréat* on an exceptional basis	– employment – some options for continuing higher education to Level II	– general and vocational – training programmes in enterprises	Industrial and tertiary specialisations
University Institutes of Technology (IUTs)	Universities	University Diploma of Technology (DUT)	III	2 years	General or technological *baccalauréat*, and vocational *baccalauréat* on an exceptional basis	– employment – some options for continuing higher education to Level II	– general and vocational – training programmes in enterprises	Industrial and tertiary specialisations

Table 1. **Programmes of the French education system** (cont.)

Programme	Type of school	Diplomas awarded	Level of training	Duration	Entry level	Possible continuation	Curricula	Different streams
Other higher education programmes	– universities – preparatory classes in lycées – higher schools	– Bachelor's degree – Master's degree – Doctorate – diplomas from higher schools	II and I	3, 4, 5 years or more	General or technological baccalauréat, and vocational baccalauréat on an exceptional basis	Employment	– general and vocational training programmes in enterprises	Various specialisations
Other apprenticeship programmes (one fourth of apprentices)	In enterprises and Apprentice Training Centres	– BEP – vocational certificate – vocational baccalauréat – BTS – DUT – Engineering diploma	V IV IV III III I	Varied	Same as for full-time education	– employment – continuation of studies	Work in enterprises General and vocational education in CFAs	Industrial and tertiary specialisations Primarily vocational certificate and BEP

1. Throughout this chapter, the Technician's Diploma is considered to be equivalent to the technological baccalauréat.
Source: Authors.

3. VOCATIONAL AND TECHNOLOGICAL PATHWAYS

Vocational pathways

Students enter vocational pathways after middle school, which they now normally complete in four years, after the third grade. The largest stream in terms of numbers enrolled is the two-year programme to prepare for the BEP in a vocational *lycée*, during which pupils often prepare for the CAP at the same time. They can then begin working life, at Level V. However, the current trend is for these graduates to continue their studies, usually for a further two years, leading to the vocational *baccalauréat*, a Level IV diploma. Nevertheless, even when they leave school at this level, most of them find jobs as skilled workers, since the only advantage of a vocational *baccalauréat* rather than a BEP is that it makes it less difficult for graduates to find a job and improves their prospects for the future.

A pathway that is less common today, and one primarily chosen by pupils having difficulties in school, is to prepare for the CAP in a vocational *lycée* or an apprenticeship programme, and to enter the job market at Level V.

Technological pathways

The first year of the general and technological *lycée* (the second grade) is common to all pupils. They then have the option of a two-year programme leading to the technological *baccalauréat*. It is relatively rare for pupils to leave the education system after reaching this level, and they can continue in this pathway in the two-year programme to prepare for the Advanced Technician's Diploma (*Brevet de technicien supérieur*, or BTS) or, less frequently, for the University Diploma of Technology (*Diplôme universitaire de technologie*, or DUT). After the general *baccalauréat*, a number of students also go on to prepare for the BTS or DUT. In both cases, they generally enter the labour force at Level III.

Early streaming and crossover points

In reality, the points at which pathways diverge are less clear-cut than the preceding paragraphs might suggest. Pupils often begin to prepare for these pathways in the years before, which may even appear to be early streaming. Thus, in middle school, the fourth and third-grade technological programme leads mainly to a vocational stream, especially the BEP, while some third-grade programmes, known as the work-oriented third grade, lead to the CAP. Similarly, in the general and technological *lycée*, options chosen in the second grade prepare students for technological and especially industrial streams.

There are many crossover points between pathways, and these have increased over the past decade. The most formally organised of them is the option of preparing for the technological *baccalauréat* after completion of the vocational BEP diploma, through a specific programme known as the first-grade "adaptation class" (*première d'adaptation*).

However, there are a number of other crossover points: in the vocational stream, the possibility of preparing for a BEP after completing a CAP, which allows students to pursue their studies; the option of preparing a vocational *baccalauréat* directly after obtaining certain kinds of CAPs of a high level; the possibility of going from a *lycée* to an apprenticeship programme and, more rarely, the converse; the option of continuing to Level IV in an apprenticeship programme after receiving the CAP; the possibility of going on to higher education after the vocational *baccalauréat*, especially in the Advanced Technician Sections; and, after the DUT or BTS, the option of continuing higher education in a university or college, which is becoming increasingly prevalent.

4.   PARTICIPATION IN THE DIFFERENT PROGRAMMES

Enrolments and transition rates

We shall study the trend in numbers of students enrolled in the various programmes and the flow of students going on to another programme by comparing two reference years, 1980 and 1992. Figure 3 shows the year 1980 while Figure 2 shows 1992. The number of students in each programme is indicated, in thousands, during the school year beginning in the reference year. These figures are for metropolitan France.

The transition rates for the reference year are also shown, *i.e.* the percentage of students leaving each level who go on to other programmes (those repeating the year are not taken into account); the 100 per cent total would include the percentage of those leaving school or going on to unusual programmes not shown in the figure. However, the transition rates of students exiting middle school have been shown in terms of the full annual cohort. The transition rates to higher education cannot be calculated with complete accuracy, and some students enrol in more than one programme, which means that total enrolments are somewhat lower than the overall figures given. These show that nearly all recipients of a general *baccalauréat*, 80 per cent of those with a technological *baccalauréat* and a small number of vocational *baccalauréat* holders continue their studies, so that the continuation rate can be estimated at 45 per cent of the age group.

Although the birth rate was relatively constant during the 1960s (*i.e.* the relevant decade for Figure 3), ranging between 840 000 and 880 000 births per year, it fell rapidly after 1974, stabilising at around 750 000 births per year between 1975 and 1979, and then rising temporarily to 800 000. As a result, the data shown in the figure for 1992 reflect a situation of demographic change in which cohorts are smaller than in the figure for 1980. Nevertheless, the findings can be evaluated in terms of the share of an age group that reaches each level

Table 2. **Diplomas obtained, ISCED levels III-V**

Cohort (%)	1980-81	1992-93
Level V	80	94
comprising:		
vocational	41	38
CAP holders	28	31
BEP holders	9	21
Level IV	34	63
comprising:		
vocational	–	7
technological	12	19
baccalauréat holders,	27	55
comprising:		
vocational	–	6
technological	8	15
Level III		
technological (BTS, DUT)	4.5	12

Source: Authors.

and obtains a diploma. Table 2 presents the most significant figures at the end of each of the reference school years.

A study of cohorts

It should be borne in mind that in the preceding analysis the cohorts are of different sizes at the various levels, which, in a time of demographic change and increasing school participation, makes it difficult to compare two different levels. Consequently, it is of interest to supplement this analysis by following the progress of a cohort through the education system. The flows in terms of percentage for three cohorts are shown in Figures 4, 5 and 6:

- the cohort of the 860 000 people born in 1966 (Figure 4), whose progress essentially followed that shown in Figure 3;

- the cohort of the 870 000 people born in 1970 (Figure 5), whose progress coincided with the changes described above;

- the cohort of the 760 000 people born in 1975 (Figure 6), whose pattern of studies is shown in Figure 2; most of the members of this cohort had just finished their secondary studies, and their rates of access to higher education are estimates.

◆ Figure 4. **Cohort 1966**

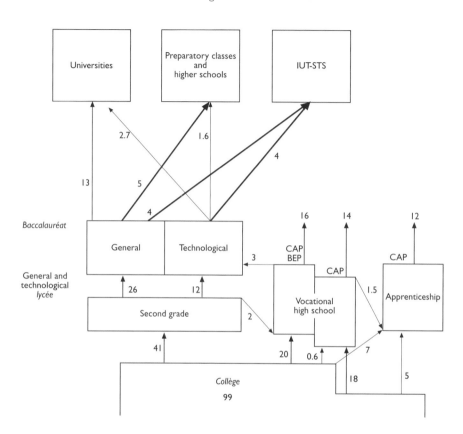

Source: Authors.

For each programme, the difference between incoming and outgoing students corresponds to drop-outs and to pupils pursuing unusual programmes of study.

Overall findings

During the period being considered, one observes a substantial growth in enrolments and a clear rise in the level of educational attainment.

◆ Figure 5. **Cohort 1970**

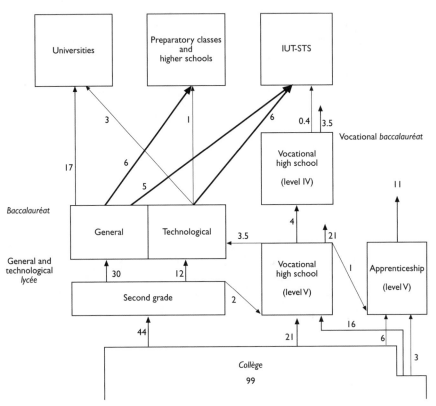

Source: Authors.

Although *lycée* enrolments rose only moderately at a rate of less than 20 per cent because of demographic decline, enrolments in higher education, which were not yet affected by this decline, grew by nearly two-thirds. The share of *baccalauréat* holders in a cohort doubled in 12 years. This growth led to the change in the pattern of exits from the education system at different levels (Figure 7).

Exits at the lowest level decreased, *i.e.* exits without a qualification (among which, exits at Level VI fell faster than those at Level V bis and exits at the lowest

◆ Figure 6. **Cohort 1975**

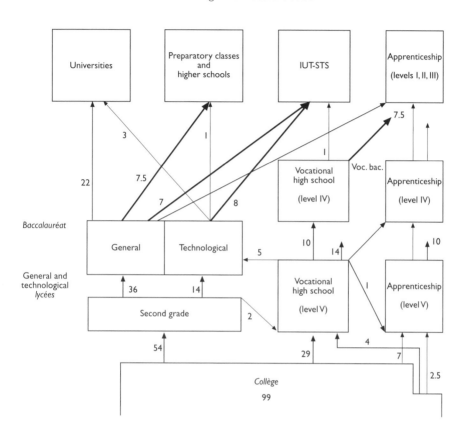

Source: Authors.

level of qualification). On the other hand, exits at the *baccalauréat* level or with a higher education diploma increased.

However, these growing enrolments did not lead to increased participation in vocational pathways, since the number of young people in vocational *lycées* and apprenticeship programmes fell during this period roughly in proportion to the drop in the population within age groups, while flows of incoming students fell even further. However, the pattern of these pathways changed. Firstly, the level of incoming students rose as students who had prepared for the CAP for three years

◆ Figure 7. **Exits from the education system by level**

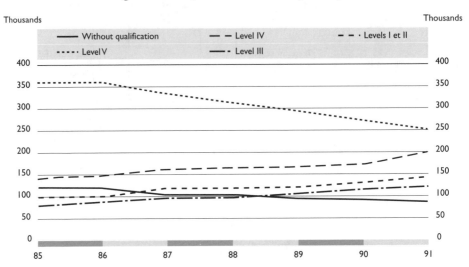

Source: Authors.

after the fifth grade were increasingly replaced by those who had prepared the BEP and CAP for two years after the third grade, which automatically led to a drop in enrolments. Moreover, these pathways were extended beyond Level V with the creation of the vocational *baccalauréat*, which partially reversed the drop in enrolments. These trends are indicated in Figure 8, which shows the change in vocational *lycée* enrolments in terms of the level of incoming students. The trend was less clear-cut for apprenticeship programmes, since although the number of apprentices dropped from 250 000 to 218 000, it fluctuated throughout the period and the rise in levels of incoming apprentices was only beginning to be felt. However, for vocational streams as a whole, even though enrolments were dropping, the proportion of students who obtained diplomas in a cohort increased.

The growth in enrolments had a greater impact on technological pathways. Enrolments in technological secondary education grew by 45 per cent; the flow of incoming students into the second grade increased at a somewhat lower rate, but was reinforced by the flow of BEP holders entering into the first-grade "adaptation class", which grew from 13 000 in 1980 to 48 000 in 1992; thus, vocational training did play a role in this growth of technological education. However, the greatest surge in enrolments was in tertiary technological training (+155 per cent), which was a higher rate of growth than in other higher education programmes. This

◆ Figure 8. **Enrolments in vocational high schools**
(not including agricultural education)

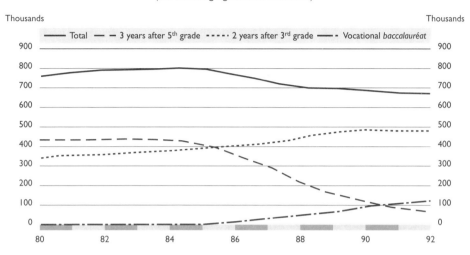

Source: Authors.

growth primarily took place in the Advanced Technician Sections (STS), in which enrolments increased by a factor of 3.4 (Figure 9). Enrolments in the University Institutes of Technology (IUT), located in universities, grew at a less impressive rate (54 per cent), no doubt because they are more costly to establish and are less widespread geographically, but they too have grown significantly since 1989.

In secondary education, the increase in the length of schooling has primarily been due to the increased length of general education, which has meant that choices are made later, especially the choice of a vocational or technological stream. Thus, in general and technological *lycées*, enrolments in the general stream increased by 53 per cent, while the share of the technological stream has dropped from 35.6 to 34.4 per cent. However, the overall share of technological and vocational *baccalauréats* increased significantly.

Breakdown by vocational sector

If we are to see the trends of technological and vocational training more clearly, we must analyse them in terms of the occupations for which they prepare students. In this way, it can be seen that during the period being considered there was a growth of the most modern specialisations, such as electronics and

◆ Figure 9. **Enrolments in Advanced Technicians Sections**

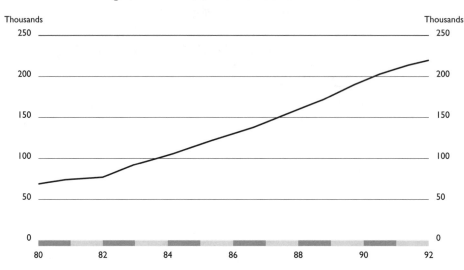

Source: Authors.

marketing techniques, at the expense of more traditional fields such as mechanical engineering, the chemical industry or secretarial work.

Nevertheless, we shall use the more traditional distinction between vocational sectors and divide them into industrial and tertiary occupations, excluding agricultural training. Table 3 shows the breakdown of enrolments in these sectors for the main vocational and technological programmes in 1980-81 and 1992-93; enrolments are given in thousands.

The tertiary sector's share increased on all fronts. However, the rise in levels of educational attainment, and especially the decrease in Level V, heightened this phenomenon, which meant that enrolments in the industrial sector, even though they rose at the higher levels, dropped overall. Furthermore, these trends coincided with employment trends.

Breakdown by gender

During recent decades, there has been increasing female participation in the labour force, which is linked to the development of the tertiary sector. It is therefore of interest to analyse enrolment trends by gender.

Table 3. **Enrolments in different sectors**

Enrolments	Industrial sector (thousands)		Tertiary sector (thousands)		Tertiary (%)	
	1980-81	1992-93	1980-81	1992-93	1980-81	1992-93
Preparing for:						
Full-time CAP-BEP	405	251	359	297	47	54
Apprenticeship CAP-BEP	175	103	66	80	27	44
Vocational *baccalauréat*	–	48		81	–	63
Technological *baccalauréat*	82	110	160	234	66	68
STS	20	55	42	155	68	74
IUT	30	40	24	43	44	52
Total	717	629	651	886	48	58

Source: Authors.

In middle school, which is compulsory, the breakdown of boys and girls is essentially the same as that of their age groups. However, there has been a slight increase in the proportion of boys, which is no doubt owing to the fact that all young people must now remain in school until the end of *collège*; since girls have a higher success rate, this meant that in the past they were less likely to drop out of school prematurely. This increase is also due to a more surprising phenomenon, which is a slight rise in the proportion of boys within age groups, no doubt the result of infant mortality trends.

The increase in the percentage of boys is more clear-cut in *lycées*, in the second grade (from 43.5 per cent in 1980 to 46 per cent in 1992) and in the programmes that follow, both general (from 41 per cent in 1980 to 44.5 in 1992) and technological (from 46.5 per cent in 1980 to 52 per cent in 1992). Here, the decisive factor is the rise in the participation rate, which makes it possible for boys to begin to catch up with girls. Nevertheless, there is a larger percentage of girls in general secondary education, and this figure increases with each additional year of schooling.

Trends are different in higher education. In universities, the percentage of young women (51 per cent in 1980, 56 per cent in 1992) is now the same as in general secondary education. In preparatory classes for the *grandes écoles*, the number of women has increased (from 30 per cent in 1980 to 37 per cent in 1992), even though men still predominate, as they do in all scientific fields. In higher schools, there are more women than men (57 per cent) because of the importance of paramedical and socially-oriented schools, and this percentage changed little between 1980 and 1992. Overall, the growth of higher education has been more favourable to women than to men (50 per cent in 1980, 54 per cent in 1992).

Table 4   **Percentage of females in main programmes**

Enrolments	Industrial sector		Tertiary sector		Overall education	
	1980-81	1992-93	1980-81	1992-93	1980-81	1992-93
Preparing for:						
Full-time CAP-BEP	15	13	85	73	48	46
Apprenticeship CAP-BEP	3	3	80	66	23	30
Vocational *baccalauréat*	–	7	–	70	–	46
Technological *baccalauréat*	15	11	76	68	53	48
STS	17	14	79	67	56	52
IUT	20	19	57	55	36	38

Source: Authors.

It could be concluded that there is a trend towards homogeneous behaviour, with a convergence of female and male participation rates in general and technological secondary education on the one hand, and in secondary and higher education on the other. However, this is only an overall effect, for the specialisations chosen remain very different, especially in vocational and technological educational, as is shown in Table 4.

There are still very few females enrolled in the industrial sector, and their share is even declining. They are still in a substantial majority in the tertiary sector, and their numbers are increasing, although the percentage of males is rising taking advantage of this sector's growth. Overall, females' share of vocational and technological education has remained substantially the same at around 44 per cent.

Breakdown by socio-professional background

The findings here are derived from a study based on a sample of some 20 000 pupils who entered middle school in 1980; thus, pupils who were progressing at the normal rate were born in 1969 and ultimately sat for the *baccalauréat* in 1987 or 1988. Table 5 shows the percentage of access to various programmes and levels in terms of the socio-professional category of the family head.

Students' social background continues to have a strong influence on the pathways chosen and the results achieved. For example, if we compare two of the most strongly contrasting cases, *i.e.* senior managers (including teachers) and workers, we see how rarely the former enter vocational pathways while the majority of the latter do, and we observe the gap between the results achieved, since the former are three times more likely to obtain the *baccalauréat* than the latter. The other categories are more similar, and some are even able to take advantage

Table 5. **Differences between pathways according to socio-professional background of the family head**

Percentage

	Entry into vocational *lycée* after 5th grade	Obtained CAP	Entry into vocational *lycée* after 3rd grade	Obtained BEP	Entry into 2nd grade	*Baccalauréat* level	Obtained *baccalauréat*
Senior managers	4	3	9	6	87	86	77
Mid-level occupations	16	9	23	15	62	63	52
Professions and self-employed	22	14	26	17	51	50	41
Clerical workers	23	14	29	19	47	49	39
Farmers	25	14	39	28	41	49	39
Manual workers	33	19	30	19	30	32	24
Total	24	14	27	17	46	48	39

Source: Authors.

179

of a vocational pathway to obtain the *baccalauréat* without attending the second grade; this possibility has considerably expanded recently (with the addition of the first-grade "adaptation class" and the preparation for the vocational *baccalauréat*, the flow in 1992 was 106 000 students, compared with only 11 000 in 1980); however, this possibility had not yet developed fully for the cohort being considered.

A similar study had been made earlier for a cohort entering middle school in 1973. If we compare the findings of the two studies, they show that schooling has grown longer for the poorest social categories, and today the *lycée* and *baccalauréat* are more open to everyone. However, the pathways followed are still different, since technological and especially vocational training tend to be more frequently chosen by young people from a less affluent background, and school-leavers without a qualification are primarily from these groups. The gaps between these two cohorts are narrowing, but only slightly.

5. LABOUR MARKET ENTRY

Any attempt to explain this subject must take into account the signals from the labour market, *i.e.* the advantages of possessing a given diploma.

Wages and working conditions

Figure 10 shows the trend of the average wage by age group in terms of the diplomas held for the year 1992.

For the 25-29 age group, wage-earners without a diploma earned on average 90 per cent of the wages of a Level V diploma holder; *baccalauréat* holders earned 1.1 times the wages of a Level V diploma holder; the ratio was 1.3 for Level III diploma holders and 1.8 for Levels and II. These gaps widen in the course of their careers. These ratios remained stable during the period, except for Levels I and II, whose advantage diminished somewhat towards the middle or end of their careers, although it increased at the time of entry into working life, since the ratio had only been 1.4 in 1976, despite the fact that the number of higher-level diploma holders increased.

The possession of a higher-level diploma also has an impact on the position held within a company. This is not surprising, but it has considerable impact right from the time employees are first hired. Thus, in the years 1989-91, holders of a *baccalauréat* or a higher diploma between the ages of 25 and 29 were 6.3 times more likely to have a managerial position or mid-level occupation than employees without the *baccalauréat*. This ratio is regressing slightly, since it was 7 during the 1984-86 period. The advantage is greatest for women (a ratio of 8.6 in 1989-91) and for individuals from a less affluent background, since for children of

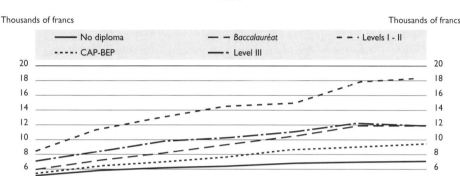

◆ Figure 10. **Average wage by age group**
1992

Thousands of francs

Thousands of francs

--- No diploma --- Baccalauréat --- Levels I - II
····· CAP-BEP --- Level III

Source: Authors.

manual or clerical workers, who with the same diploma have less chance of obtaining jobs of this kind, the *baccalauréat* increases their chances by a factor of 7.3 and even of 10 for women. Consequently, obtaining the *baccalauréat* or a higher diploma remains an investment for young people from a less affluent background.

Access to employment

During the period being considered, unemployment rose sharply for the population as a whole. The unemployment rate, which was approximately 6 per cent in 1980 (and 3 per cent in 1970), rose until 1986, fell slightly between 1986 and 1990, and then continued to climb, exceeding 10 per cent in 1992 and continuing to rise significantly since that time. Between 1982 and 1990, the number of unemployed (according to the ILO definition) increased by 22 per cent, even though the number of jobs also grew by 3 per cent. These seemingly contradictory phenomena can be explained by demographic factors and by the growth in the female participation rate (61 per cent in 1982, 73 per cent in 1990).

The trend has been the same for young people but with sharper fluctuations and a significantly higher unemployment rate than for other groups; among secondary school-leavers in 1991, 21 per cent were unemployed at the beginning of

February 1992 and only half had a job, which most often was insecure, while the remainder were in training programmes, were doing their military service or were economically non-active. Young women were more often unemployed than young men, even if the effect of military service is taken into account.

However, the unemployment rate varied considerably, depending on the diploma held. Figure 11, which concerns young people under 25, shows that the gap between unemployment rates, which was quite narrow 20 years ago, has widened at the same time as unemployment and school participation rates have increased. Thus, in 1994, there was a 14-point gap between the unemployment rate of holders of the *baccalauréat* or higher diplomas and those without diplomas; this rate was even higher for women. In particular, the situation of holders of higher education diplomas did not deteriorate significantly between 1980 and 1992, even though their numbers increased substantially.

These findings can be supplemented with an analysis of the conditions of access to employment after leaving the main educational programmes, *i.e.* the likelihood of being unemployed for a year during the initial period of working life (two years and nine months) and the probability of having direct access to a stable job. There is a strong correlation between the level of education and

◆ Figure 11. **Unemployment rates of young people under 25**

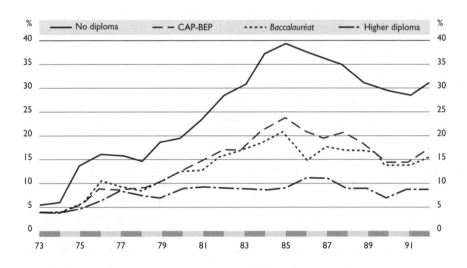

Source: Authors.

access to employment, the most favourable situation being that of graduates of engineering and business *grandes écoles* (Level I), followed by school-leavers from Levels II, III, IV, V, V bis and VI. At Levels V (CAP, BEP) and IV (*baccalauréat*), industrial training is more advantageous than tertiary training, but the opposite is true at Level III (BTS, DUT). Among all *baccalauréat* holders, those in the tertiary technological stream are in the least favourable position, coming just after holders of literary and economic *baccalauréats*; holders of general scientific *baccalauréats* have a better chance of direct access to stable employment than holders of industrial *baccalauréats*. Moreover, the problem faced by holders of the BEP or industrial *baccalauréats* is less one of labour market access than of stability of employment.

At a comparable level of diplomas, apprentices are unemployed somewhat less often during the months after leaving an apprenticeship programme, especially if they remain in the enterprise in which they were trained. For example, for 1989 school-leavers at Level V, 22.1 per cent of former apprentices were unemployed on 1 February 1990, as compared with 23.3 per cent of former vocational *lycée* students. Even more important is the fact that former apprentices are more frequently regular salaried employees, while *lycée* graduates usually have recourse to subsidised temporary first-job contracts. But the situation varies from one region to the next, and comparisons are not very meaningful, since the occupations for which apprentices and students prepare are not the same, nor is the distribution by gender; for example, young women are somewhat more frequently unemployed after completing an apprenticeship programme.

6. FACTORS FOR ANALYSIS

The actors

In secondary education, the orientation of students among the various pathways open to them at the end of each programme is a relatively complex process in which an effort is made to reconcile the wishes of students and their families with their teachers' recommendations; if an agreement cannot be reached, the decision is made by the school principal or by a board of appeal. In the case of vocational training, student choices may also be restricted by the limited number of places available. In recent years, families have been given a somewhat more important role, either through certain formal changes – such as permitting students to repeat a grade rather than being streamed into a pathway against their wishes, eliminating streaming at the end of the fifth grade or allowing the school principal to decide in the event of a disagreement – as well as through improved practices, such as better communication, greater respect for students' wishes and an increase in the number of places available when these were insufficient. As for

183

the choice of higher education streams, students are in principle free to choose their stream in universities, while this is subject to the decision of individual schools in the "selective" branches of higher education, which include technological and occupational training.

Consequently, it would be rash to assume that the various trends are primarily due to structural changes, for there are many actors whose decisions or views play a role: first and foremost, young people and their families; teachers, who play an important role in the orientation of students; public and private schools; and the public authorities, who are ultimately responsible for educational programmes, in particular the Ministry of National Education, but also other ministries and regional and local authorities, especially since the decentralisation legislation of 1983-85; employers, either directly as organisers of training through apprencticeships, or indirectly through the employment market in what they say about their needs or the influence they can exert on national and local decision-makers.

An explanation of the various trends should therefore be sought by comparing the expectations of the business world, the aspirations of young people and their families, the intentions of the authorities and the corresponding changes in the education system, and the reactions of the education system itself, especially that of teachers.

Thus, the period preceding the one we are discussing, *i.e.* the 30 years that followed the Second World War, witnessed the transformation of production techniques, the industrialisation of the country, the development of the tertiary sectory, and the expansion and diversification of jobs. Economic growth and job diversification made possible a higher standard of living, the development of female employment and unprecedented social mobility. All these factors led to increased demand for education, both on the part of individuals and certain sectors of the economy, which needed a pool of available labour that they could tap to ensure their growth and flexibility. However, at the same time some employers' manpower needs were such that they were satisfied with a poorly trained workforce in a Taylorian organisation of work, since they feared that better trained workers would not fit in well with this kind of design. The public authorities, through planning, sought to ensure that education met economic needs, while at the same time trying to promote a certain democratisation of education. This led to an increase in the resources devoted to education, made possible by the country's growing wealth, and to much broader access to secondary education, despite the resistance of certain teachers and some public opinion. However, it also resulted in an increasingly complex education system, in which the process of streaming students became much more formal and widespread.

A background of economic crisis

With the economic crisis that followed, increased competition worldwide, the resulting reorganisation of enterprises and uncertainty over the future, the vast majority of employers now say they need young people with a higher level of training. They expect all workers to take responsibility and be adaptable, which they formerly only required of managers. Nor are these merely empty words, for, as we saw in Section 5 above, all labour market indicators show that wages, working conditions and hierarchical position in the enterprise, unemployment rates and means of access to employment all point in the same direction, towards a greater preference for candidates with higher levels of training. On the other hand, the situation of young people without skills is increasingly precarious as high unemployment has become entrenched, aggravated by technological change and industrial restructuring aimed at increasing competitiveness, at a time when large generations are coming into the labour market and female activity continues to develop.

However, the precise kind of training that is desired is far from clear. What employers say they need falls into two categories: on the one hand, they emphasize the transverse skills of reasoning, ability to communicate, independence, ability to take responsibility and to work as part of a team, adaptability, creativity and even ethical standards, which are no doubt fostered by a general education; on the other hand, they wish to attract young people to vocational training, especially in the industrial sector, which can be of greater immediate use to the enterprise, and they often point out that there are unfilled job openings in this sector. This dichotomy can be interpreted as the outcome of the demand for similar general skills for all levels of staff, even though enterprises are very diverse and their organisation, although it has changed, still remains quite hierarchical. This explains why employers encourage a higher level of vocational training, but which is still oriented towards preparing pupils for jobs as skilled workers, such as the vocational *baccalauréat*. However, the real conditions of hiring favour candidates with a higher level of general education over those with vocational skills, especially in the service sector. This confusion is compounded by the fact that the most vocal business spokesmen, who are all too often the representatives of large enterprises, are not doing most of the hiring (nor, for that matter, do they send their own children to receive the training they are recommending).

Social demand

Young people and their families expect training to lead to a satisfactory career. It is by no means certain that this was the case 50 years ago, but today all opinion polls are unanimous on this point, which shows the importance that education has come to have in individuals' lives. By "satisfactory" is understood a career leading to upward social mobility (an expectation which arose during the period of economic growth and which is still strong) but also increasingly one which is sheltered from the threat of unemployment.

The signals from the labour market encourage young people to prolong their initial training. There is admittedly a possible alternative, which is to begin working earlier with the intention of resuming training later. Although this is theoretically possible, it is a path that is rarely taken and involves considerable risk. Furthermore, there is still the problem of finding a first job, which encourages students to continue their education. This effect is particularly strong in highly industrialised regions where jobs were formerly easy to find, which led to lower school participation, but which are now particularly hard hit by the crisis. Increasingly, young people only leave the education system when they are unable to continue – that is, when they fail in school.

There is much less incentive to enter vocational streams, which are less likely to lead to higher levels and which force pupils to specialise early. Uncertainty about the future and young people's general desire to keep as many options open as possible have reinforced this trend. Most importantly of all, there is a rejection of industrial jobs, since the image of this sector has become increasingly negative, not only because of traditional French attitudes but also because of the decline of industry since the economic crisis. The longer duration of schooling and better information have opened up further possibilities, but at the expense of vocational, and especially industrial, training. Nevertheless, vocational training does give students with the greatest difficulties an opportunity to obtain a qualification, but this does not really meet enterprises' needs nor does it enhance the image of this kind of training; furthermore, it is largely chosen by young men, since young women generally avoid it.

Decisions of the public authorities

The public authorities take into account both economic and social demand. From the economic standpoint, they generally express the conviction that human resources are the primary resource of a country such as France and that they hold the key to the growth which is necessary to solve the problem of employment. As a result, the public authorities strongly promote education and provide the funding necessary to meet social demand. It must be said that longer schooling also has an immediate positive effect on unemployment statistics. Furthermore, the public authorities are often concerned with making education more democratic, even though this consideration sometimes comes second to economic needs.

The measures taken to prevent pupils from dropping out during middle school have addressed two concerns. In 1989, the Guideline Act on Education solemnly reaffirmed that two goals set several years earlier by two successive ministers would be met by the year 2000:

- no students would leave school without a qualification;
- 80 per cent of a generation would reach the level of the *baccalauréat* (level IV).

In turn, these measures increased social demand for education. These steps were admittedly taken during a decentralisation of responsibilities (or rather of decreased centralisation). The regions now play a more influential role in the establishment of educational programmes in *lycées*, their goal being to attract enterprises and to gain a reputation for educational excellence; at times there are even rivalries among cities, and "local patriotism" develops. Plans established by schools are also taken into account more fully, even though, in the public education system, they do not ultimately make curriculum decisions; this is done by the rector (*recteur*), who represents the Minister of National Education within a region, whose scope for action has also increased. All these factors are directed toward the same goal of establishing a higher level of training in schools, which further stimulates the social demand for education.

Both the national and regional public authorities particularly wish to develop technical education and vocational training and apprenticeship, especially in the industrial sector. Their aim is simultaneously to improve technical skills within the country, as enterprises request, to combat unemployment among young people and to help those pupils who are having difficulty in school to succeed, for they are the ones most likely not to acquire any skills.

However, these goals are in contradiction with that of raising the level of training, since technological and especially vocational training lead to the lowest levels of skills. This has resulted in the measures described above which aim at lengthening the duration of streams, developing crossover points and reassessing curricula. They have not been entirely effective in the case of vocational training, as we have seen, but they have no doubt made it possible to prevent it from being abandoned completely as enrolments have increased, and to promote more democratic access to the *baccalauréat* and higher education, as has also been observed.

The role of teachers

Although teachers are a highly diverse group, on average they are less concerned with economic demand and the need to prepare students for an occupation. They continue to believe that schools have a key role to play in opening up individuals to the world and in contributing to a more democratic society. In their view, their primary role is to impart a general education, to foster the pupil's personal development and to form good citizens. These attitudes are naturally more characteristic of teachers in general streams, who often know little of other educational programmes or of the modern industrial workplace, yet it is precisely these teachers who essentially have responsibility for the orientation of students. As for teachers in vocational and technological streams, their main concern is to raise the level of their *lycée* by introducing vocational *baccalauréat* programmes or Advanced Technician Sections.

However, teachers' concern with the intellectual and personal development of young people is sometimes in contradiction with their behaviour when problems are encountered or their concept of the requirements of their teaching lead them to try to shed their worst pupils, who either transfer to another type of school or enter "working life" – and which used to mean they would find a job but now usually means they join the ranks of the unemployed. On the other hand, whenever possible, teachers naturally prefer that the best pupils continue to study at their school.

These two attitudes naturally establish a hierarchy of training, which favours the longer and more general training options, with general education ranking first (literary sections were formerly most prestigious but have now been overtaken by scientific sections), followed by technological education and, last of all, vocational training. Since teachers play an important role through the perceptions they instil in their pupils, the advice they give and their help in orientation, this hierarchy is deeply rooted in secondary education. Students are often not admitted to a general and especially a scientific stream because of inadequate performance, but they are never prevented from entering a vocational stream (at the end of the fifth grade or at the end of the third grade) or technological stream (at the end of the second grade). The tertiary technological stream, in particular, which competes most directly with the general streams, is the least prestigious of the pathways in general and technological *lycées*. The situation is different in higher education, where technological and vocational education, especially in STSs and IUTs, is selective – unlike in universities, which have open admission.

This hierarchy of training is all the stronger when it is reinforced by information from the labour market. It also reflects France's traditions, in which general education has always been the preferred path to social advancement.

From a convergence to divergence

In the 1980s there was a rare convergence between economic demand, which favoured a higher general level of training to overcome the crisis, and the demand of young people and their families, who desired social mobility and saw that job opportunities and initial working conditions improved with the level of training. This convergence delighted education officials and teachers, who attached great value to education's role in social integration and the promotion of the individual.

As a result, the public authorities encouraged this trend not only in words but also by their deeds. This general consensus quickly produced results which far exceeded expectations. As Table 2 shows, the targets set by the 1989 Education Act are well on their way to being reached on schedule, or at least very nearly so.

But the convergence did not extend to the streams to be emphasized. The ambivalent position of employers made it difficult for the public authorities to overcome the traditional image of vocational training's low status in the opinion of teachers and the public. It is legitimate to make one of the goals of vocational training not only to help pupils in difficulty to succeed in school but also to promote their social advancement, but this does not enhance the image of such training. It no doubt explains why the development of vocational training in secondary education has been a relative failure, even in the field of industrial technology. The goal of enabling 80 per cent of young people to attain the *baccalauréat* level has been interpreted – and criticised – as though it only concerned the general *baccalauréat*, even though this figure naturally includes the technical and vocational *baccalauréats*, which play a significant role. Young people from a less affluent background are the ones most easily persuaded to take up vocational and technological studies, which allows for more democratic access to the *baccalauréat* and higher education; however, social barriers, even if they have been partially broken down, have not been eliminated. They have taken a different form, namely the hierarchy of the various streams.

Nevertheless, vocational streams make it possible to train young people who formerly would have gone through the education system without acquiring skills; the population of these streams has changed, and a portion of their previous population is now enrolled in general or technological education. Consequently, they play an essential role in building up school enrolments, as do the technological streams. Moreover, although it is still difficult to attract students voluntarily to vocational *lycées*, the fact that these students can continue their studies after the BEP provides them with a pathway to advancement that can offset their initial disappointment, which is a clear example of the interest of segmented and flexible pathways.

However, there are two pathways which enable these students to continue their studies: the first leads to the technological *baccalauréat* and then to higher education, which means that it is unquestionably a stream leading to social advancement; the other, created in response to demand from business in 1985, leads to the vocational *baccalauréat* and then to labour market entry. Contrary to what the preceding paragraphs might suggest, the stream most frequently sought by BEP holders is currently the one that leads to a vocational *baccalauréat*. This can be explained by the tendency of students, who generally come from a less affluent background, to continue in the same training programme rather than changing schools, and by teachers' desire to keep their best students. However, students are often frustrated when, after completing the *baccalauréat*, they find it very difficult to continue their studies; this was not a very serious problem when jobs were plentiful, but currently the situation is becoming much more critical.

Somewhat similar circumstances can be observed after students complete the technological *baccalauréat*. These students usually choose the most accessible pathway for continuing their studies, rather than the longest and most prestigious one, by enrolling in an Advanced Technician Section in a *lycée*. Until now, school-leavers who have attended an STS have had relatively little difficulty in finding a job at this level, and only a small number ask to continue their studies, unlike in IUTs, but here too the situation might change rapidly if the job crisis continues.

A second divergence can have an impact on the role of industrial training, in which enrolments have often been dropping sharply. Admittedly, the share of jobs in the industrial sector has declined even as the service sector has continued to grow, but the choice of young people has been even more marked. Moreover, candidates hired in the service sector have a general education, most often of fairly advanced level. The problem is particularly serious for young women, who are reluctant to enrol in industrial training courses and concentrate on a small number of occupations, despite efforts of the public authorities to the contrary. This may explain why they have greater difficulty in finding jobs, although the few young women who do choose an industrial occupation also encounter the same problems.

These divergencies in the balance between streams may have contributed, around 1990, to the fact that there was high unemployment at the same time as unsatisfied manpower needs in some industrial fields; businesses say that this was indeed the case. In any event, medium-term forecasting is difficult and all concerned have given up attempts at long-term planning as of the 1970s. More-over, the most recent period has amply shown the futility of any kind of forecast-ing in this field.

Today, however, it would seem that the continuing crisis and rising unem-ployment have fundamentally eroded the consensus of the 1980s. Although longer schooling initially slowed down exits from the education system, which made unemployment less acute, this situation could not continue indefinitely. Later, there was a phenomenon of substitution, in which firms took advantage of the labour market conditions to hire staff with higher levels of skills, even though this meant downgrading them, at least at first. This is reflected by the gap between the curves shown in Figure 11. The first result of this development was the virtual disappearance of stable employment for the most vulnerable among young people, those who did not have a qualification, which led to a most disturbing social failure – and not just an economic one – since these young people become increasingly marginal as their numbers decline. It also led to

difficulty for those with a low level of skills, despite the effort they had invested in acquiring a qualification. Next, it led to a reduced expectation of social advancement, since young people have realised that the statistical effect which, at a given time, shows that it is beneficial to pursue a higher level of education, is subsequently eroded by the general raising of the educational level. Lastly, even those with a high educational level are no longer sheltered from unemployment. The fact is that the expectations of the 1980s have not materialised and jobs have disappeared as the level of education has risen. It is tempting to conclude that these two facts are interrelated, *i.e.* is it because of technical change and cutthroat competition that enterprises have cut back the number of jobs as qualifications have risen?

We must not paint too bleak a picture. The raising of educational levels has made firms more competitive; it has made it possible to modify the structure of employment by creating more positions of responsibility; and more than ever, education increases people's chances of finding a job. All things considered, the raising of the level of training has not produced all the results hoped for, but it has had a positive impact although it may be hidden by particularly difficult economic conditions.

Nevertheless, the fact remains that to some extent the earlier consensus was based on a misunderstanding, for although there is unquestionably economic demand for a higher level of education and training, this does not mean that the economy will absorb an unlimited supply, for it will only take on staff according to its needs. While it is an asset for young people to have the highest possible level of training, this is no guarantee of a job, since, in a difficult economic situation, those who already have jobs do everything they can to hold on to them.

It is not easy to foresee the future. The complex employment situation continues to encourage the stopgap solution of prolonging schooling and emphasizing general education over technological and vocational training. However, we cannot rule out the possibility of a drastic shift in behaviour, *i.e.* that despair would discourage young people from making any investment in education at all. Whatever the future may hold, it will be difficult to adapt training – and the education system more generally – without having a clearer vision of what the future role of work in men's and women's lives will be.

BIBLIOGRAPHY

AFFICHARD, J. *et al.* (1994), "Apprentis et élèves de lycées d'enseignement professionnel: l'insertion dans les entreprises", *Synthèse*, No. 93, CEREQ, Paris, January.

CEREQ (1990), "L'avenir du niveau V (CAP-BEP): filières de formation et d'emploi", *Études*, No. 56, Centre d'études et de recherches sur les qualifications, Paris.

CEREQ (1992), "L'insertion professionnelle des diplômés de l'enseignement supérieur", *BREF*, No. 82, Paris, December.

CEREQ (1993*a*), "L'apprentissage en 1992: une formation en cours de renouvellement", *BREF*, No. 86, Paris, April.

CEREQ (1993*b*), "La population active 1990: plus diplômée, plus tertiaire, plus féminine", *BREF*, No. 87, Paris, May.

CEREQ (1994*a*), "Bacheliers professionnels: plus nombreux dans une conjoncture plus difficile", *BREF*, No. 95, Paris, February.

CEREQ (1994*b*), "Higher education graduates: despite increasing numbers, employment prospects remain good", *Training and Employment*, No. 14, Paris.

CEREQ (1994*c*), "Emploi des femmes: une réalité de plus en plus éclatée", *BREF*, No. 104, December, Paris.

Direction de l'Évaluation et de la Prospective (1981-1994), *Notes d'information*: 81.05, 81.22, 90.25, 92.43, 93.08, 93.15, 93.23, 93.26, 93.32, 93.36, 93.38, 93.42, 93.44, 93.46, 93.50, 94.15, 94.16, ministère de l'Éducation nationale, Paris.

Direction de l'Évaluation et de la Prospective (1984-1993), *Repères et références statistiques sur l'enseignement et la formation*, ministère de l'Éducation nationale, Paris.

Direction de l'Évaluation et de la Prospective (1992), *Flux d'entrée des nouveaux bacheliers dans l'enseignement supérieur*, tableaux statistiques 6111, ministère de l'Éducation nationale, Paris, June.

Direction de l'Évaluation et de la Prospective (1992-1994), *L'état de l'école, 30 indicateurs sur le système éducatif*, No. 2, No. 3, No. 4, ministère de l'Éducation nationale, Paris, October.

Direction de l'Évaluation et de la Prospective (1994), "Scénarios de développement du système éducatif", *Éducation et Formations*, No. 39, ministère de l'Éducation nationale, Paris, November.

DUBOIS, M. (1993), "Après un DUT ou un BTS: poursuites d'études ou entrée dans la vie active", document de travail, No. 87, Centre d'études et de recherches sur les qualifications (CEREQ), Paris, September.

ELBAUM, M. and MARCHAND, O. (1993), "Emploi et chômage des jeunes dans les pays industrialisés: la spécificité française", *Premières synthèses*, ministère du Travail, de l'Emploi et de la Formation professionnelle, No. 34, October, pp. 1-34.

INSEE (1993a), *Annuaire statistique de la France*, Institut national de la statistique et des études économiques, Fontainebleau.

INSEE (1993b), "Activité professionnelle et emploi, permanences et inflexions depuis 10 ans", *Économie et statistique*, No. 261, Institut national de la statistique et des études économiques, Fontainebleau.

GRELET, Y. and VINEY, X. (1991), "Dix ans d'insertion professionnelle des jeunes à l'issue de l'enseignement technique court", *Études*, No. 58, Centre d'études et de recherches sur les qualifications (CEREQ), Paris, February.

KIRSCH, J.L. et al. (1989), "Dossier formation et emploi: niveau IV de formation et baccalauréat professionnel", *Études*, No. 49, Centre d'études et de recherches sur les qualifications (CEREQ), Paris, May.

MAGRO, R. (1994), "Le système éducatif face aux transformations de la relation formation-emploi: le cas de la filière secrétariat", *Dossiers Éducation et Formations*, No. 47, December.

OECD (1994a), "Itinéraires et participation dans l'enseignement technique et la formation professionnelle", Paris, November.

OECD (1994b), "Le nouveau rôle de l'enseignement technique et de la formation professionnelle (VOTEC): contexte, acteurs, enjeux", Paris, November.

TANGUY, L. (1991a), *L'enseignement professionnel en France: des ouvriers aux techniciens*, Presses Universitaires de France, Paris.

TANGUY, L. (1991b), *Quelle formation pour les ouvriers et les employés en France?*, La Documentation française, Paris.

VENEAU, P. (1994), "Formes d'usage des baccalauréats professionnels", *Dossiers Éducation et Formations*, No. 47, December.

ZARIFIAN, P. et al (1993), "80 pour cent d'une classe d'âge au niveau baccalauréat", *L'orientation scolaire et professionnelle*, 22, No. 2.

ZILBERMAN, S. (1990), "Les trois premières années de vie active d'une cohorte de jeunes sortis en 1986 de l'enseignement secondaire (emploi, chômage, stages)", document de travail, No. 55, Centre d'études et de recherches sur les qualifications (CEREQ), Paris, May.

7

GERMANY

by

Gernot Weißhuhn and Felix Büchel, Technical University, Berlin

I. INTRODUCTION[1]

Germany's vocational education policy activities are above all directed toward adapting the vocational training programmes to the different demands of an employment system subject to technical and structural change. Worth mentioning, for instance, are the reforms of ordinances for recognised training occupations and the introduction of new training occupations. These measures include further options after the successful conclusion of vocational training in an enterprise, such as access to *Fachhochschulen* (specialised colleges of higher education) and higher education institutions or admission to *Berufsakademien* (post-secondary vocational education institutions) (see BMBW, 1993a, pp. 3 ff). The current and quite controversial discussion on these questions is taking place against the backdrop of considerable changes in the approach of young people to general education over the last ten to twenty years. These changes are characterised by an unwaivering trend toward higher general education certificates: the data shows increased enrolment in *Gymnasien* and *Integrierten Gesamtschulen* and, at the same time, a decrease in relative attendance at *Hauptschulen*, as well as a rapidly growing proportion of school-leavers acquiring certificates for admission to *Fachhochschulen* and higher education institutions. This last trend has resulted in escalating numbers of students starting a course of study. In contrast, the number of school-leavers making the transition from lower secondary level into Dual Vocational Training has stagnated.

We must also take into account significant changes in young people's approach to education within the general education system, since this behaviour also leads to changes in transition into the vocational education system including: vocational training in recognised industrial-technical and commercial occupations – the dual system of (initial) vocational education and training –, full-time training programmes in schools such as *Berufsfachschulen* (full-time basic vocational school), *Fachschulen* (specialised technical school) and health system schools. In addition, this chapter will examine the transitions of school-leavers from general education into *Fachhochschulen* and universities, *i.e.* into the vocational education system in the wider sense. From this perspective, the term VOTEC (Vocational and Technical Education and Training) has to be interpreted in the German training system so as to include all vocational training pathways and participation in programmes. Since the enormous readjustments in the education system of the new federal *Länder* have not as of yet been completed, the present investigation is restricted to the old federal *Länder*.

The chapter is divided into three main parts:

1. a statistical account of the trends in young people's educational behaviour (participation in different forms of general education, followed by transition into the various vocational training pathways) over the past years in the old *Länder* of the Federal Republic of Germany;

2. an analysis of the socio-economic factors determining education-related choices and success in education;

3. a brief description of the objectives of vocational education policy measures during the last few years.

The first section is a synopsis of the major trends observed in the data on transitions made in the German education system over the last few years. Apart from official statistics on education, we have used those of the *Bund-Länder* Commission for Educational Planning and Research Promotion (*Bund-Länder-Kommission für Bildungsplanung und Forschungsförderung* – BLK) (see BLK, 1994) and the *Bildungsgesamtrechnung* (flows through the education and training system) prepared by the Institute for Labour Market and Occupational Research (*Institut für Arbeitsmarkt und Berufsforschung* – IAB) of the Federal Institute for Labour (*Bundesinstitut für Arbeit*) (see Tessaring *et al.*, 1993). The data covers the period from 1984 to 1991, in some cases only up to 1990, owing to a lack of current data. This time period was chosen for study because the longitudinal data on individuals' educational choices, which we evaluate in the second section, is avai-lable from 1984 onwards.[2]

Individual characteristics such as gender, nationality, and social background, carry a special meaning in terms of the distribution of educational opportunities. One goal of education policy in the past, as at present, is to reduce or, ideally, to counterbalance completely sexual and social inequalities through the school system. Nevertheless, attempts to examine the realisation of these education policy goals quickly run up against the limits of the available statistical data. Official statistics on education chiefly cover the populations of pupils and students in the individual branches of the education system but contain little data on the central flows between branches. Therefore, we have to rely on newer secondary sources although they, as a rule, do not, or only partially, allow differentiation according to gender, nationality, social background, etc. For this reason, we cannot attempt to analyse such structures in the statistical part of this chapter. The pupil and student populations are differentiated according to the occupational status of the head of family on the basis of sample censuses and other official statistics on education. However, such cross-sectional distributions as the distribution of pupils in the different types of general education according to the occupational status of the head of family can only be called upon to a limited extent as an indicator of a constant class-specific selection. (For a contrasting viewpoint, see Klemm *et al.*, 1990, pp. 91 ff.) This is due to the fact that a series of other variables have not been taken into consideration which are also a factor in the decisions made on education.

The second section, therefore, will attempt to work out the multitude of independent and intervening qualifiers which influence the behaviour of young people when making educational and vocational transitions. With the help of multivariate methods, the factors determining decisions made on vocational training are investigated on the basis of appropriate longitudinal data gathered on individual persons for the period from 1984 to 1992. Here we will distinguish the most important determinants of the behaviour that guides the demand for education and success in education. Above all, we examine the influence of variables in the social background of young people, such as family and income, the region in which they live, as well as the influence of individual factors of gender, nationality and other characteristics.

Owing to the relatively short period of time for which the longitudinal data drawn upon here was collected, the consequence of qualifiers whose influence had a delayed effect on education-related decisions can hardly be captured. Such qualifiers include, in particular, labour market indicators like the employment outlook for different qualification certificates and income levels – assuming that this information is available in valid form and that it is perceived and made use of by those responsible for decisions on education. Nevertheless, one aspect of the connections to the labour market is taken into account in the investigation when we examine the whereabouts of graduates after they have completed a vocational training programme. Here, the statistical section presents the aggregate development of transitions into various ultimate situations such as entrance into gainful employment, unemployment, or into a new training programme. By means of multivariate analysis, the second part investigates the most important transitions following the two vocational training pathways most prominent in the Federal Republic of Germany: apprenticeship training and higher education programmes. These transitions are those leading into gainful employment and they provide the most valuable indicator for the success of a vocational training programme.

The third section sketches the contents and objectives of the education policy of the federal government over the past few years. Owing to the rather static character of this policy, the description follows in concise form.

2. TRAINING PATHWAYS IN THE GERMAN EDUCATION SYSTEM

Types of training alternatives and pathways

In the German system, general education is divided into the primary level (primary and special education schools with four grade-levels, in some cases six grade-levels because of *Länder* differences resulting from education federalism) and lower secondary level (general secondary education) which includes *Hauptschulen, Realschulen, Gymnasien, Gesamtschulen* and an orientation Level II that exists independently of the other school types (see Figure 1). These are followed by upper secondary level which is composed of vocational and continuing general education pathways. The vocational education pathways include the dual system of vocational training (*i.e.* training in schools and enterprises for recognised training occupations), full-time training at *Berufsfachschulen, Fachschulen*, health system schools and *Berufsakademien.*[3] Some of these institutions, however, still award the *Realschulreife*. Continuing general education pathways are offered by *Gymnasien, Gesamtschulen, Fachoberschulen* (specialised upper secondary school) and *Fachgymnasien* with the goal of awarding a *Fachhochschulreife* (certificate granting admission to the *Fachhochschulen*) or *Hochschulreife* (*Abitur*: upper secondary leaving certificate, giving access to higher education). In addition to these alternatives, there are also other training institutions at which the *Fachhochschulreife* and *Hochschulreife* (for *Berufsoberschulen* and *Technische Oberschulen*) can be attained after completion of vocational training or sufficient prior work experience. In some cases a double qualification can be attained (*Kollegschulen* in North Rhine-Westphalia). And finally, the *Fachhochschulen, Gesamthochschulen* and universities make up the tertiary level.

Development of enrolment in general education schools

Educational choices within general education

Of main interest is the distribution of pupils within the types of schools existing in the general education system at the 7th grade level (see Table 1), since at this point in the decision-making process the choices regarding the type of school have to a great extent been finalised – aside from possible adjustments to these decisions which play a quantitatively subordinate role. Here it is evident that the influx of pupils into *Gymnasium* (1984: 28.5 per cent; 1991: 32.5 per cent) has continued to increase. The relative proportion attending *Hauptschulen*, in contrast, is decreasing, while the proportion of pupils attending *Realschulen* remains approximately constant. The proportion of pupils in *Integrierten Gesamtschulen* is climbing noticeably.

◆ Figure 1. **The German education system**

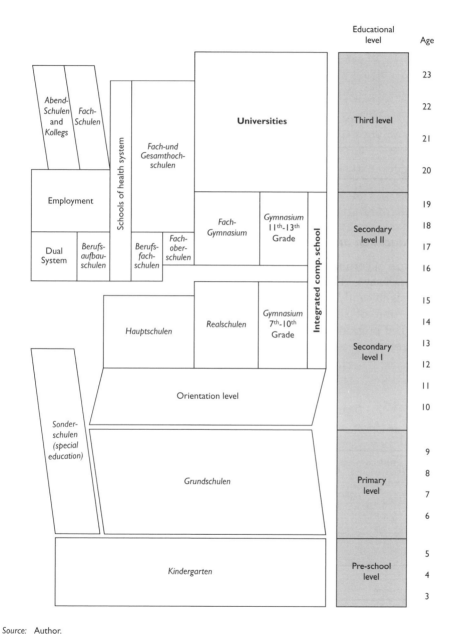

Table 1. **Enrolments in general education, lower secondary level, 7th grade**

Percentage

	Hauptschule	Realschule	Gymnasium	Integrierte Gesamtschule	Pupils	Pupils[1] (in 1 000s)
1984	38.4	28.3	28.5	4.8	100	736.5
1985	37.7	28.3	28.8	5.2	100	654.6
1986	36.9	28.4	29.9	4.8	100	606.4
1987	35.5	28.5	30.9	5.1	100	590.0
1988	34.3	28.3	31.6	5.8	100	583.7
1989	33.1	28.3	32.5	6.1	100	590.7
1990	32.7	28.0	32.6	6.7	100	602.4
1991	32.4	27.9	32.5	7.2	100	608.2

1. Does not include special education or Waldorf schools.
Source: Statistisches Bundesamt, *Series Bildung und Kultur (Fachserie 11)*, Series 1; authors' calculations.

General education and vocational school-leavers

The type of certificate is decisive for the transition into the various vocational training pathways. The proportion of school-leavers with Hochschulreife has increased significantly (from 21.0 per cent in 1984 to 26.3 per cent in 1991), while the proportion of school-leavers with a Hauptschule certificate continues to decrease. The proportion of graduates with a Realschule certificate, in contrast, has remained relatively constant over the course of time (see Table 2).

Table 2. **Distribution of pupils leaving general education according to the type of certificate**

Percentage

	Without Hauptschule certificate[1]	With Hauptschule certificate[1]	Realschule certificate or equivalent[2]	Fachhoch-schulreife	Hochschul-reife	School-leavers	School-leavers (in 1 000s)
1984	8.3	34.3	35.8	0.6	21.0	100	1 002.8
1985	7.5	33.4	36.5	0.6	22.0	100	956.6
1986	7.3	32.1	36.9	0.6	23.1	100	889.8
1987	7.1	31.6	36.5	0.6	24.2	100	835.8
1988	7.2	30.1	36.4	0.6	25.7	100	770.8
1989	7.6	29.9	35.7	0.7	26.1	100	709.4
1990	8.0	29.7	34.9	0.8	26.6	100	672.3
1991	8.2	29.8	34.9	0.8	26.3	100	655.5

1. Including special education.
2. Does not include those who have completed vocational schools *(Berufsaufbau-, Berufsfachschulen)*.
Source: *Grund- und Strukturdaten*, BMBW, 1993/94; *KMK Documentation* No. 121, 1993; authors' calculations.

Transitions of pupils leaving general education (lower secondary level) into vocational education

The following sections trace the transition of general education school-leavers and, in some cases, vocational school-leavers into subsequent vocational training pathways (vocational training in enterprises – primarily in industrial-technical and commercial occupations – full-time training programmes in schools such as Berufsfachschulen, Fachschulen and those of the health system, vocational education in Fachhochschulen for technical professions, economics and administration, as well as universities). Here we have distinguished between two types of school-leavers: pupils leaving lower secondary level and drop-outs with or without a Hauptschule or Realschule certificate, and school-leavers who have attained the Hochschulreife. This distinction was made because the qualification levels of these persons differ greatly, as do their resulting vocational education opportunities.

Transition rates of school-leavers from lower secondary level to various vocational training pathways are shown in Table 3.

The transitions from lower secondary level aim mainly for the dual system, whose proportion of participants remained at the level of 40 per cent between 1984 and 1991 with minimal fluctuations. The transitions into Berufsfachschulen (full-time schools requiring at least one year of attendance) have demonstrated an upward tendency. A large number of those who choose this type of training, however, transfer after one year to the dual system as well. The basic vocational

Table 3. **Distribution of pupils leaving general education without Abitur[1]**

Percentage

	1984	1985	1986	1987	1988	1989	1990	1991
Young people without training contract	5.1	5.7	5.7	5.9	5.6	4.8	5.1	4.1
Gymnasium, Fachoberschule, civil service career	8.2	8.5	8.7	8.7	8.9	8.8	8.7	8.6
Full-time vocational training year (Berufsgrundbildungsjahr)	10.6	10.5	9.6	9.0	8.5	7.8	7.1	6.6
Vocational preparatory year (Berufsvorbereitungsjahr)	5.1	4.8	4.1	4.0	4.4	4.6	5.2	5.4
1st year of vocational school[2]	26.8	27.9	27.9	28.9	29.8	29.8	29.7	29.6
1st year of Fachschule	3.0	3.1	3.3	3.5	3.9	3.9	4.3	4.1
Trainees in 1st year of dual system[2]	41.1	39.5	40.7	40.0	38.9	40.3	39.9	41.6
Transitions (in 1 000s)	786.3	740.4	678.4	628.2	567.8	518.8	487.8	477.8

1. Those who have successfully or unsuccessfully completed lower secondary level with or without Hauptschule or Realschule certificate.
2. 1991 preliminary result.
Source: BLK; Statistisches Bundesamt, Series Bildung und Kultur (Fachserie 11), Series 2; Grund- und Strukturdaten, BMBW, 1993/94; authors' calculations.

training year (Berufsgrundbildungsjahr, usually used to impart basic skills related to the field of work) is losing importance. A slightly downward tendency can be noted in the already low proportion of young people who have no training contract.

Transitions of general education school-leavers with Hochschulreife

The following section shows the choices made by school-leavers with the Hochschulreife when making the transition from general education into vocational training. Here we should mention that the transitions of those with Hochschulreife from vocational schools as well as those with Fachhochschulreife coming from both general education and vocational schools should also be taken into account. It becomes apparent, however, that the school-leavers from vocational schools with a Hochschulreife (general or subject-related) carry little weight with an average of approximately 20 000 persons per year and can therefore be neglected. Of great significance are the school-leavers with Fachhochschulreife from vocational schools (ca. 60-70 000 persons between 1984 and 1991). Their transitions (e.g. into Fachhochschulen or the dual system), however, cannot be captured statistically. This is why the analysis has to be limited to the tran-sitions of school-leavers from general education schools with Hochschulreife.

Data on the whereabouts of these school-leavers is equally lacking in the official statistics. They list the numbers of young people who began a course of study during each year under investigation. These, however, are cumulative figures which contain both direct transitions into Fachhochschulen and higher education institutions, as well as the transitions of students who delayed beginning a course of study after attaining their Fachhochschulreife or Hochschulreife some years before (owing to military service or completion of a training programme in the dual system, for example). Yet the focus of the present investigation is limited to the vocational training choices made by the streams of school-leavers during each of the years from 1984 to 1991. Accordingly, data must be gathered, above all, on the direct transitions into universities and dual vocational training. Data on these transitions has been collected for general education school-leavers with Hochschulreife in the comprehensive survey of the IAB (see Tessaring et al., 1993, pp. 149 ff). This data demonstrates that a large part of the school-leavers (34 to 37 per cent) first enter into military or community service in accordance with legal regulations. On the basis of this information, we exclude these transitions in the calculations presented in Table 4. It becomes evident that a growing number of the remaining school-leavers immediately enter university, while the proportion making the transition into the dual system declines. The proportion of transitions into gainful employment (as a rule, entrance into civil service career programmes) is also falling slightly. And finally, if we only take into account the distribution of direct transitions into universities and the dual system, then we see a shift toward

Table 4. **Distribution of pupils leaving general education with** *Hochschulreife,*
excluding transitions into military service

Percentage

	1984	1985	1986	1987	1988	1989	1990
University	34.9	31.9	33.6	37.6	39.9	40.2	40.8
Fachhochschule	6.3	6.3	7.0	6.8	6.7	6.4	6.6
Dual system	24.8	25.4	35.2	24.0	22.9	21.2	20.3
Berufsfach-, Fachschule, health system school	6.1	6.7	5.7	5.9	5.9	5.8	5.5
Gainful employment	10.8	11.2	10.5	9.2	8.6	11.2	11.7
Non-gainful employment	7.6	8.0	8.4	7.8	9.0	7.6	7.8
Unemployment	6.4	6.7	6.4	6.3	5.0	3.6	2.0
Other school-leavers	3.1	3.8	3.2	2.4	2.0	4.0	5.3
School leavers[1] (in 1 000s)	154.7	151.9	145.1	141.9	138.3	128.1	127.4

1. Does not include transitions into military/community service.
Source: *Grund- und Strukturdaten,* BMBW, 1993/94; *Bildungsgesamtrechnung* (flows through the education and training system) prepared by the IAB; authors' calculations.

immediate entrance into university, clearly at the expense of direct transitions into the dual system.

Development of entrance into the labour market
of those who have completed a vocational training programme

The last sections of the statistical account investigate the whereabouts of those who have completed the different vocational training pathways (dual system, B*erufsfachschulen, Fachschulen, Fachhochschulen,* higher education institutions). Of special interest in this part is the entrance of the various school-leavers and graduates into the labour market (first placement of gainful employment after completion of vocational training). It is expected that differences in entrance into the labour market will become visible here, differences which might in turn influence the training decisions of future generations.

Whereabouts of those who have completed the dual system

First we consider the whereabouts of those who have successfully or unsuccessfully completed the dual system of vocational training in schools and enterprises. Here, we can fall back on the data in the comprehensive survey on education prepared by the IAB. It should be pointed out that the number of unsuccessfully completed certificates cannot be calculated by subtracting the number of successful completions (school-leavers) from the whole because the successful completions do not include those individuals who have previously

Table 5. **Distribution of those who have completed the dual system**[1]

Percentage

	1984	1985	1986	1987	1988	1989	1990
Gainful employment[2]	76.7	76.6	76.0	74.0	74.5	73.5	78.2
Unemployment	7.5	7.9	7.0	6.8	6.4	6.1	3.8
Non-gainful employment	5.9	6.1	6.4	6.7	6.7	7.3	7.3
Fachhochschule and higher education institutions	2.0	1.8	1.8	1.7	2.3	2.3	2.5
Vocational school[3]	3.4	3.5	3.9	4.6	4.9	5.2	4.0
Fachgymnasium, Fachoberschule	4.3	3.9	4.6	5.9	4.9	5.3	4.1
School-leavers and drop-outs (in 1 000s)	598.9	638.7	684.0	684.3	649.7	617.0	557.0

1. Including drop-outs.
2. Including military/civil service.
3. *Berufsfachschulen*, health system schools, *Fachschulen*. Numbers have been rounded, which may lead to differences in sums.
Source: *Bildungsgesamtrechnung* prepared by the IAB; authors' calculations.

attained a higher level certificate (*e.g.* at *Fachschulen, Fachhochschulen*, higher education institutions) and have been classified accordingly (see Tessaring *et al.*, 1993, p. 100). However, the number of those who were definitively unable to attain a certificate (after repeated examination) is relatively low (ca. 4 to 5 per cent) (see BLK, 1987, p. 49). The relevant findings are shown in Table 5, where it is apparent that approximately 76 to 78 per cent of those who have completed the dual system have entered into gainful employment (with a slightly upward tendency until the year 1990). In contrast, the number of those who registered themselves as unemployed immediately after completing their vocational training is falling.

Whereabouts of those who have completed Berufsfachschulen, Fachschulen and health system schools

Data on the whereabouts of those who have completed *Berufsfachschulen, Fachschulen* and health system schools has been taken from the comprehensive survey on education prepared by the IAB and is shown in Table 6 (only for those who have completed *Berufsfachschule*, as this is the largest group in full-time vocational training) and Table 7. Here it is also impossible to calculate the number of unsuccessful completions, owing to the same problems present in the data on individuals who have completed the dual system.

Table 6 demonstrates that the majority of those who completed *Berufsfach-schulen* entered into the dual system (51 to 55 per cent with a slightly downward tendency) after one year of training in a *Berufsfachschule*, as a rule. Accordingly, the *Berufsfachschule* fulfils, to a large extent, a preparatory function for vocational train-

Table 6.   **Distribution of those who have completed _Berufsfachschulen_**[1]

Percentage

	1984	1985	1986	1987	1988	1989	1990
Dual system	54.8	55.8	60.2	63.6	62.6	54.9	51.2
Fachoberschule/Fachgymnasium	1.0	1.2	1.5	1.8	1.7	2.5	3.0
Fachschule[2]	18.1	17.9	15.6	14.9	15.7	15.4	17.4
Gainful employment[3]	8.3	9.2	8.9	7.8	8.0	13.9	15.9
Unemployment	7.5	6.6	5.9	5.5	4.7	4.1	3.4
Other school-leavers	10.3	9.3	7.9	6.4	7.3	9.2	9.1
School-leavers and drop-outs (in 1 000s)	224.6	216.4	208.5	200.6	187.9	181.0	167.0

1.   Including drop-outs.
2.   Including health system schools.
3.   Including military/community service.
Source: _Bildungsgesamtrechnung_ prepared by the IAB; authors' calculations.

ing in the dual system. Of further import is the transition into _Fachschulen_ (17 to 18 per cent) which provide extended vocational training (_e.g._ training for master craftspeople, technicians). Transfers into gainful employment also demonstrate an upward tendency until the year 1990, while during the same period fewer and fewer school-leavers became unemployed.

Table 7 summarises the school-leavers from _Berufsfachschulen_, _Fachschulen_ and health system schools (completion levels I). An account is given of their whereabouts to display the significant transition goals more clearly. In this instance too, we see that the majority of school-leavers under observation transfer to the dual

Table 7.   **Distribution of those who have completed _Berufsfachschulen_,
health system schools and _Fachschulen_**[1]

Percentage

	1984	1985	1986	1987	1988	1989	1990
Basic vocational training and preparatory year	3.7	3.3	3.0	2.6	2.0	3.1	2.3
Berufsfachschule, health system schools, _Fachschule_	14.7	14.4	12.4	11.7	12.3	11.9	13.4
Dual system	45.3	45.7	48.6	50.7	49.9	43.5	39.7
Gainful employment[2]	29.1	30.1	30.3	29.2	30.8	37.4	41.0
Unemployment	7.2	6.5	5.7	5.8	5.0	4.1	3.6
School-leavers and drop-outs[3] (in 1 000s)	275.3	268.0	261.2	255.5	239.2	232.8	217.6
School-leavers and drop-outs[4] (in 1 000s)	308.7	299.8	289.3	284.7	272.9	266.0	249.0

1.   Including drop-outs.
2.   Including military/community service.
3.   Does not include transitions of school-leavers and drop-outs into _Fachoberschulen/Fachgymnasien_, _Fachhochschulen_, higher education institutions, non-gainful employment, migration or mortality.
4.   All school-leavers and drop-outs.
Source: _Bildungsgesamtrechnung_ prepared by the IAB; authors' calculations.

system, with a falling tendency though (from 45.3 per cent in 1984 to 39.7 per cent in 1990). Transitions into gainful employment demonstrate a marked climb, while the proportion of those who become unemployed has declined respectively. It should be emphasised that part of the school-leavers transfer between Berufsfach-schulen, health system schools and Fachschulen (13 to 14 per cent). In addition, the numbers have been calculated for transitions into Fachoberschulen/Fachgymnasien (for purposes of attaining the Fachhochschulreife or Hochschulreife) and transitions into Fachhochschulen and higher education institutions; the same holds for transitions into unemployment as well as migration and mortality (remainder: completion levels II).

Whereabouts of graduates and drop-outs from Fachhochschulen and higher education institutions

The last section of the statistical part of our investigation shows the placement of graduates and drop-outs from Fachhochschulen and higher education institutions. We take only successful Fachhochschule graduates into account (excluding drop-outs; attendance and examinations completed in the same year; see Table 8). The placement in gainful employment lies noticeably high (over 80 per cent).

As finally we look at the whereabouts of successful graduates (attendance and examinations completed in the same year; see Table 9) from higher education institutions, we see that about 71 to 85 per cent of all graduates go into gainful employment. This percentage lies below that of Fachhochschule graduates. The rates of the starting unemployed among university graduates also turns out to be higher than those of Fachhochschule graduates; this holds in particular for the last three years under investigation (1988-90).

We conclude the description of trends in transition and completion behaviour found within the various training programmes with two remarks on one of

Table 8.   **Distribution of *Fachochschule* graduates**

Percentage

	1984	1985	1986	1987	1988	1989	1990
Gainful employment	81.7	83.0	85.8	83.4	82.2	85.8	87.5
Unemployment	12.7	10.7	9.1	11.0	10.8	7.0	6.6
Non-gainful employment	5.6	6.3	5.1	5.6	7.0	7.2	5.9
Degrees[1] (in 1 000s)	39.4	45.1	44.6	45.5	50.9	54.0	54.0
All graduates and drop-outs[2] (in 1 000s)	49.5	55.3	53.3	54.2	59.2	64.0	66.5

1.   Graduates who completed attendance and examinations in the same year.
2.   Including degrees completed in previous years; including migration and mortality.
Source: Bildungsgesamtrechnung prepared by the IAB; authors' calculations.

Table 9. **Distribution of university graduates**

Percentage

	1984	1985	1986	1987	1988	1989	1990
Gainful employment	71.3	72.5	76.8	74.5	74.9	80.9	85.4
Unemployment	14.7	13.7	13.2	14.4	14.5	8.2	7.8
Non-gainful employment	14.0	13.8	10.0	11.1	10.6	10.9	6.8
Degrees[1] (in 1 000s)	113.0	116.0	118.0	121.9	118.1	133.3	122.2
All graduates and drop-outs[2] (in 1 000s)	126.4	129.3	128.2	133.0	124.1	148.0	136.0

1. Graduates who completed attendance and examinations in the same year.
2. Including degrees completed in previous years; including migration and mortality.
Source: *Bildungsgesamtrechnung* prepared by the IAB; authors' calculations.

the most important indicators of the efficiency of training programmes, namely the starting unemployment rates specific to each training sector.

Measured against this indicator, all groups of school-leavers and graduates as well as all training pathways that were investigated show a slightly downward tendency until the year 1990. This is mostly due to the economic upswing that began around 1984 and held on until about 1991/92. At the same time, the starting unemployment rates of graduates and drop-outs from the different vocational training pathways do not differ greatly during the observed time period of 1984-90. These rates cannot be expected to exert any significant signalising influence on those who take decisions on education and, on this basis, it is not likely that future streams of admissions will be redirected within the various vocational training sectors.

3. DETERMINANTS OF EDUCATION PARTICIPATION, TRANSITION BEHAVIOUR AND ENTRANCE INTO THE LABOUR MARKET

The results shown in Section 2 provide information on the development of education participation in Germany at the highest possible level of aggregation: the summation of all education-related decisions of individual persons which were deemed relevant. The comprehensiveness of this information facilitates our objective, which is to trace the development of essential influencing factors over time in the most compact manner possible.

With regard to education policy, however, we are not only interested in the question of how education-related decisions as an aggregate change over the course of time, but also whether we can observe strongly deviating patterns of education participation within different socio-economic groups of persons. An investigation of this material is the topic of this section.

A correspondingly differentiated analysis of education-related behaviour is only limitedly or not at all possible on the basis of aggregate data available from official or semi-official statistics; disaggregate characteristics that provide information above and beyond the gender and nationality of a school participant are, as a rule, not available. Consequently, an analysis of the socio-economic determinants of individual education-related behaviour has to be based on personal data which contains information concerning the education-related decisions being studied, as well as material on factors suspected to influence these decisions. With this in mind, it becomes clear that the topic of this investigation requires high standards to be set for the database. Longitudinal information on individual persons is a must if we, as is planned in this investigation, are to carry out time-related cross-sectional analyses, such as school attendance in a certain grade-level, or analyses of transitions, such as those from general education into vocational training.

In addition to this, we aim to test not only the classic influencing factors like gender, age and nationality, but also a multitude of suspected determinants of education-related behaviour stemming from the social background, such as education level and labour market participation of the parents, household context, regional information and more. Although a great number of prior partial studies[4] have researched the connection between social background and participation in education, a thematically broad empirical study on the influence of social background on education-related decisions over several decision levels has not yet been accomplished for the federal republic, owing to the unavailability of a sufficiently extensive database.

In the meantime, however, a federal record has become available which appears to be remarkably suitable for the evaluation to which we aspire. The following section describes this record.

Database

The multivariate evaluations of this investigation are based on data of the socio-economic panel SOEP, administered by the German Institute for Economic Research (*Deutsches Institut für Wirtschaftsforschung* – DIW) in Berlin. Representative for the population living in the federal republic, this record contains diverse cross-sectional information on households and individuals. The starting sample from the year 1984 covers almost 6 000 households. Every head of household was given a questionnaire, with those household members aged 16 years or older (more than 12 000 persons) being additionally asked in a separate questionnaire about facts and opinions of various parts of their life, primarily on the topics having to do with their participation in schooling and the labour market. The common household number makes it possible to tie together information on persons and households as well as the personal data of the various household members – *e.g.* data on children with that on their parents. The households and persons in this sample were then surveyed yearly, each time with one slightly modified questionnaire; this newly gathered data can also be tied longitudinally to the fixed numbers assigned to the households and persons. The database is continually expanded to include divided households, persons new to an existing panel-household, as well as those household members who turn 17 in the survey year.[5] In the meantime, survey results are available for nine survey years ("waves"). This data from the years 1984-92 forms the basis for the present investigation.[6]

Investigative approach

The events of interest are then analysed in partial evaluations which are independent of one another. In each partial evaluation, all persons are recorded for whom the corresponding event can be observed during the evaluation period 1984-92.

The model specifications for establishing the determinants of the different events assume that influencing factors remain constant over the evaluated investigation period. Nevertheless, the time factor does not go unheeded: the time-dependent level effects in the occurrence of certain events are controlled by including the year in which the event was observed (for a more detailed description of the investigative approach, see Weißhuhn and Büchel, 1994).

Method of evaluation

The influence of the given co-variates on the investigated events is ascertained by probit analysis in all partial evaluations. This method ascertains to what extent the various values of included exogenous variables influence the probability of producing one of the different values of the endogenous variables. These probabilities, which vary according to unit of investigation, cannot, however, be directly observed. Instead, they are estimated by way of a latent variable model. The calculation of the likelihood of this type of model is described in detail in Maddala (1985, pp. 46-49) (for a more detailed description of the method of evaluation, see Weißhuhn and Büchel, 1994).

The effects exerted by the individual co-variates cannot be directly derived from the estimated parameters in a probit model. For this reason, the following outcome interpretation is limited to a discussion of the direction, strength and significance of the estimated parameters, as is generally the practice with this method of evaluation.

Model specifications and outcomes

Each of the following sub-sections presents a single self-contained analysis, independent from the other partial evaluations. The sections each include an account of the model specifications and case selection specific to the evaluation, tabular documentation of the outcomes (see annex), as well as an interpretation of the established outcomes.[7]

Type of school attended in the 7th grade-level

As for the development of educational behaviour in general education schools for the 5th, 7th and 9th grades, the multivariate analysis is limited to observing the situation in the 7th grade. At this grade, pupils have by and large committed themselves to a certain level of achievement, *i.e.* they have decided upon a specific type of school. Since the attended grade level was not explicitly surveyed in the SOEP, the age of the respondents (13 years old in the survey year) must be used for the case selection. As such, a certain lack of distinction will have to be accepted in the operationalisation caused by not including respondents who have to repeat a grade.

Respondents are categorised ordinally according to the type of school attended (*Hauptschule*, *Realschule* or *Gymnasium*), *i.e.* according to the standards of achievement set by the school. In the case of attendance at an *Integrierte Gesamtschule*, such a categorisation is not possible, owing to incomplete information on the exact type of school attended. Equally impossible is the allocation of those attending Waldorf and special education schools, who are excluded from this partial evaluation; the loss in cases numbers, however, is low. Also excluded are pupils in boarding schools and other homes, owing to the sampling concept of the SOEP. The outcomes of the model estimation is shown in Table A1 of the annex.

Girls are somewhat more strongly represented in higher-level types of schools than boys; the effect, however, is only significant at the 10 per cent level. Foreign children are distinctly underrepresented in schools with a higher requirement level than German children. Those from self-employed, white-collar and civil service households usually attend higher-level types of schools, with children of civil servants having the most favourable starting conditions. Interesting about this outcome is that children from blue-collar households at the time of attendance in the 7th grade do not differ significantly in their qualitative educational behaviour from children of households where the head is either not gainfully employed or is unemployed.

By far the greatest and, at the same time, strongest effect on pupils' participation in education is exerted by the education level of the head of household. If he or she has completed the *Abitur*, then chances increase dramatically that the child also will attend a school with a higher level of requirements as compared to children from other households.

Children also have more favourable prospects as the age difference between the child and head of household increases. We are not, however, able to determine whether this effect stems from older parents who have a higher income and more experience in life, or if it should be attributed exclusively to the parity of the children within the family context and, with it, above-average encouragement of the youngest child.

Foster children and those with other untypical familial relationships to the head of their household do not have any worse educational prospects at the time of the study than children who live with their parents. In contrast, children who are raised by single parents are disadvantaged compared to other children; the effect, however, is only significant at the 10 per cent level.

As the size of the household increases, the educational prospects of the children worsen. What is remarkable about this outcome is that this cannot be simply attributed to the fact that the number of family members tends to grow in households that have a low level of education and consequently a low income level, since these characteristics are separately controlled in the model estimation. This outcome more likely results from the fact that only-children tend to receive more intensive care and attention from their parents, which presumably manifests itself in higher expectations of the parents with respect to the child's achievement in school and work as well. As the household income increases, so too do the educational prospects of the children, as one might expect.

An interesting outcome occurs with regard to the regional distribution of educational prospects. At the federal *Land* level, no significant differences can be determined. This seems remarkable when we consider that questions on education fall under the sovereignty of the federal *Länder*. Apparently the efforts of the Standing Conference of Education Ministers (*Ständige Konferenz der Kultusminister der Länder in der Bundesrepublik Deutschland* – KMK) to equal out education opportunities nation-wide have been successful, at least in the area of general education. Yet when we observe the effect of the size of the community, it becomes evident that starting educational opportunities in cities are significantly better than elsewhere – presumably due to the better and spacially closer offerings in *Gymnasien*.

The effects of the year-variables reproduce the strong trend towards attendance at higher-level schools as documented in Table 1. The high significance level of the estimated bounds verifies the appropriateness of the chosen ordinal form of the probit model, while the likelihood-ratio statistic verifies the quality of the entire model.

Type of general education certificate

While the previous sub-section focused on the early distribution of educational prospects, here we deal with the question of which school-leaving certificates are actually realised and by which groups of persons. The quality of general education certificates determines to a great extent future opportunities in vocational education and in the labour market. A comparison of the two outcomes gives us, at the same time, information as to which groups most frequently fail in their attempts to successfully complete an appropriate school programme, *i.e.* fail to complete the certificate foreseen for the type of school they attend.

Of interest is the situation that exists when pupils leave the general education school system. Persons who attained a school certificate over the second education route are therefore excluded from this partial evaluation by way of comparison with the vocational education level. School certificates that were attained in vocational training schools such as *Berufsaufbauschulen* and *Berufsfachschulen* also go unconsidered. Since the socially formative household situation of the respondents is of such special importance in this evaluation, we also exclude a few additional school-leavers who at this early point in time already live in their own household. Finally, only registered school-leaving certificates are evaluated that correspond to one of the school types investigated in the previous sub-section, for reasons of case numbers. This implies the exclusion of a few persons who have the *Fachhochschulreife* in particular (see Table 2).

Only explicitly registered school certificates are analysed, due to some inconsistencies in the comparison of the school and work situation from the year of the survey and the year before, with a possible school certificate attained in between. The category "Departure from school without a certificate" can therefore not be evaluated, in contrast to the descriptive analysis (see Table 2).

The analysis of the determinants of the quality of an attained general education certificate is made with an ordinal probit model as well; the influences are tested of the same co-variates as in the previous sub-section.[8] The outcomes are shown in Table A2 in the annex.

Male pupils who, according to the outcomes of the previous analysis, were underrepresented in school programmes with higher standards of achievement, do not attain significantly fewer certificates as compared to female pupils. This might easily lead to the conclusion that girls in *Realschulen* and/or *Gymnasien* demonstrate an above-average drop-out rate.

The unequal prospects among young foreigners carry over into the observation of school-leaving certificates; the effect of nationality is the strongest of tested, influencing variables. Children from self-employed and white-collar households have the best prospects of achieving a higher-level certificate. Of interest with respect to the occupational position of the head of household is, additionally, that children of blue-collar workers gain even fewer school-leaving certificates than children of those who are not gainfully employed. Children of civil servants do not attain an above-average number of certificates. This outcome is surprising against the results found in the previous partial evaluation: civil servants manage to place their children in school types with higher standards of achievement to an above-average extent, yet these children later demonstrate an overproportionally high drop-out rate.

As found in the previous partial evaluation, the strong effect of the household head's education level holds here too, although slightly weakened; the influence of age difference remains as well. New, on the other hand, if only at a 10 per cent level of significance, is a worsening of prospects for children who do not grow up with their parents. It could be that the specific problems in the personality development of young people in this age group have a much more negative effect on the school behaviour than exists among those raised by their parents. Another outcome appears, however, among children who are raised by a single parent: the disadvantage regarding attendance at higher-level schools, which was established in the previous partial evaluation, does not carry over with regard to the school-leaving certificate actually attained.

The negative influence of the size of the household as well as the positive influence of household income on the education prospects are present from allocation to a certain type of school up until the concluding certificate.

The prospects of attaining a higher-level school-leaving certificate are distributed relatively evenly over all federal *Länder*; as with the allocation to one of the various types of schools, no significant differences occur. On the other hand, the "city bonus" no longer applies here: in the city it is obviously easier to enrol in a school with higher standards of achievement; the achievement standard of the certificates for which the pupils strive seem to be of the same high calibre in cities as in other places, which means that higher drop-out rates occur in the cities.

The insignificance of the year variables can be traced back to the contrary development of *Realschule* certificates and the *Abitur* which have a relatively higher value as compared to *Hauptschule* certificates (see Table 2). The significance level of the estimated bound and the likelihood-ratio statistic both speak for an adequate modulation of the situation under investigation.

Direct transitions from Hauptschule and Realschule school-leavers into the dual system

The form of vocational education most frequently chosen by young people after completion of a *Hauptschule* or a *Realschule* certificate is to enter into an apprenticeship in an enterprise within the framework of the dual system (see Table 3). In this sub-section we investigate which young people decide upon this form of training and which do not. As a criteria for their decision, we draw upon the occupational status of the respondents in the survey year in which they retrospectively registered their school-leaving certificate. This reference point in time usually exists about six months after the certificate was gained.

In addition to the exclusion of those with *Abitur*, the same selection criteria apply as in the previous section. The model specifications are slightly modified since we do not take information on the federal *Land* into account. The type of school-leaving certificate is entered into the model as an additional co-variate. The outcomes of the binary probit estimation are found in Table A3 in the annex.

Young males decide upon an apprenticeship significantly more frequently than females, with children of foreigners being strongly underrepresented. We cannot determine from this whether women and foreigners are discriminated against by employers when it comes to allocating training places, or whether these groups of persons, for social reasons, enter directly into non-gainful employment or unqualified labour where a higher income can be realised in the short term than in a training position.

A significantly higher transition rate cannot be determined for *Realschule* school-leavers than for *Hauptschule* school-leavers. This "comforting" outcome verifies that enough training places are available even for the formally weaker qualification of a *Hauptschule* school-leaver.

An interesting result is observed in the influence of the household head's social status on the education decision being investigated. Children from households with a higher education level or higher occupational prestige (self-employed, white-collar workers) are underrepresented in the dual system. We might suppose that higher qualified parents attempt to motivate their children who have completed *Hauptschule* or *Realschule* to achieve the *Abitur* after all, by attending a *Berufsfachschule* for example.

Children who do not grow up in their parents' household are strongly underrepresented in the observed transitions into the dual system. Here too we are unable to answer the question of whether discrimination takes place on the part of the employer or whether parents tend to make the special efforts necessary to procure a suitable apprenticeship position more easily for their own children than for other members of the household.

The highly significant influences of household size and income found in the previous partial evaluations no longer appear to play a role in the education-related decisions investigated here. It is evident (as in the following partial evaluations) that these influencing factors lose importance as the age of the respondent advances.

Young people who grow up in small cities enter into an apprenticeship position less than do those in more populous regions, owing to the shortage of apprenticeships in rural areas.

The control for the year of certificate completion demonstrates a strong trend toward the dual system beginning around 1987/88. This might be attributable to the improved offers in apprenticeships which followed in the wake of efforts to overcome the recession.

Direct transitions of those with Abitur *into higher education institutions*

As was done for respondents with *Hauptschule* and *Realschule* certificates, we now investigate those with the *Abitur* to determine which groups of persons choose the "classic" vocational education pathway for this school-leaving certificate. The traditional route for *Gymnasium* school-leavers is to go on to a higher education institution (see Table 4).

The case selection and establishment of the reference point in time essentially correspond to those in the previous partial evaluations. Owing to the higher average age of those with *Abitur* compared to *Hauptschule* and *Realschule* school-leavers, we also exclude those persons who did military or community service directly after completing their *Abitur*. In relation to the previous evaluations, the model specifications remain unchanged. The outcomes of this evaluation are shown in Table A4 in the annex.

A surprising outcome occurs with regard to the influence of nationality on the education-related decisions under investigation. Although foreigners were constantly underrepresented in higher qualifying education programmes in the previous partial evaluations, they now decided to enter a course of study immediately upon completion of *Gymnasium* at a frequency rate that is above average. Presumably, children of foreigners who manage to accomplish the *Abitur* – which is rather untypical, as shown below – are characterised by a single-minded determination that lasts well beyond the duration of *Gymnasium*.

The influence of the occupational position of the head of household continues to weaken. Children from white-collar households demonstrate a slightly upward trend toward choosing the most direct path to the highest vocational qualification achievable after completing the *Abitur*; no significantly conspicuous differences occur in the remaining occupational positions addressed here. However, of interest is the fact that in an arena of lessening significance – all remaining household variables tested do not exert any influence – the effect of the education level of the head of household remains unwavering: children of educated parents are significantly more successful in taking a direct path to the university.

215

Those with an *Abitur* from middle-sized cities are underrepresented in direct transitions into higher education institutions. However, this outcome should not be assessed too highly against the backdrop of a low significance level and a relatively few number of cases. The same holds for the absence of the year effect which does not correspond to the upward aggregate trend displayed in Table 4.

In conclusion, we can point out how the group compositions of *Hauptschule* and *Realschule* school-leavers as well as those of school-leavers with the *Abitur* vary widely with regard to the respondents' social background (see the column of mean values in Tables A3 and A4). In groups with a lower qualification level, the – unweighted – proportion of foreigners is approximately twice as high as compared to the group of those with the *Abitur*; the discrepancy is even greater with children of blue-collar workers. The per capita income of households in which school-leavers with the *Abitur* are raised is one and a half times as high as the households of *Hauptschule* or *Realschule* school-leavers. However, the education levels of the parents demonstrate the most distinct differences: the percentage of parents who successfully completed *Gymnasium* is five times as high in the group of school-leavers with the *Abitur* as for those who completed *Hauptschule* or *Realschule*. This outcome verifies in a particularly vivid manner the ever present influence of the parental home on the widely varying educational prospects of the children.

Transitions into gainful employment after completion of an apprenticeship

In this partial evaluation, we examine which young people are successful in entering into gainful employment immediately upon completing their apprenticeship and which are not. The entrance into gainful employment is numerically by far the most important type of transition after completion of the dual system (see Table 5). The reference category is the status of (registered) unemployment. Here again, persons who do their military or community service directly after completing their apprenticeship are excluded from the investigation. In contrast to the partial evaluation above, everyone who has successfully completed an apprenticeship, regardless of their previous schooling or vocational experience, is entered into the investigation, and not just those with *Hauptschule* or *Realschule* certificates. Analogous to the previous partial evaluations, the reference point for time of observation is the occupational status existing in the same survey year in which the school-leaving certificate was retrospectively registered for the previous year.

In contrast to the situation in the previous partial evaluations, a considerable number of respondents no longer live in their parental household at the time of observation (see above). To exclude these persons would not only greatly reduce the number of cases, it would presumably also distort the outcome since there is no way of telling whether persons who have already left home show work patterns other than those of the (until now) immobile comparative group. But to include the first group in the investigation requires leaving out those model variables which characterise the situation in the parental household. Information on the occupational status and education level of the parents is potentially available for each respondent, however, because this data exists independently of their living situation.

Age, education level and job qualification of the apprenticeship graduates are included as additional co-variates in the model. The training occupation can only be entered in a highly aggregated form into the investigation because of the number of cases. The outcomes of this partial evaluation are displayed in Table A5.

At first glance, the influence of the parental home on the transition behaviour examined again shows a continuing decrease as the respondent grows older: no significant effects are observed which result from the occupational position or education level of the parents.

Older apprenticeship graduates have more difficulty in making the transition into entry-level employment than do younger ones. This effect might be attributable to a selection effect which comes into play through the lower than average capabilities of pupils who have to repeat a grade. On the other hand, those with an *Abitur* have significantly better chances of making a smooth transition from the dual training system into the world of work than do *Hauptschule* school-leavers. This outcome is not very surprising: school-leavers with the *Abitur* not only have an advantage in terms of general education qualification but they also usually manage to procure the best apprenticeship positions which then lead to a better vocational qualification basis.

No significant differences can be determined in the transition into entry-level employment with regard to gender or nationality. This also holds, perhaps unexpectedly, for the different training occupations, although one must take the high aggregation of this influence into account when interpreting this outcome. The size of the community in which the respondent resides also demonstrates no effect.

The chances of a young person obtaining a job immediately after finishing an apprenticeship are, however, decisively determined by the regional unemployment rates. The more unfavourable the situation on the labour market, the worse the chances of employment for those entering into the workforce. This regional effects takes on by far the highest significance level of all estimated model parameters. Regardless of the regional labour market situation, the chances apprenticeship graduates have of quickly obtaining a job grew during the years

1991/1992. Here we see the positive effect on employment in the short boom period on the western German labour market resulting from unification.

Transitions into employment comparable with the training qualification after completion of an apprenticeship

The fact that we can observe the entrance into gainful employment after completion of an apprenticeship does not in itself make it possible to draw any conclusions as to whether the preceding vocational training process has led to a successful conclusion. Of decisive importance is the quality of the job performed after training has been completed, or more exactly, whether the type of employment corresponds to the content and achievement standard of the training programme. In recent times this problem of matching has gained considerable importance in public discussion about the quality of the education system. Official statistics make no contribution to this topic: they distinguish whether someone is employed or unemployed, and zones in between such as inadequate, *i.e.* underqualified, work go unheeded. Accordingly, there exists no account of this complex process in the descriptive part of the present study (Section 2). Nevertheless, at this stage we investigate which apprenticeship graduates are successful in making a direct transition into work that is on a par with their training qualifications and which persons are willing to start their career with an underqualified position.

All persons are entered in this partial evaluation whose entrance into gainful employment was observed in the evaluation of the preceding section. All employed people are asked about the requirement level of their work in the SOEP. A distinction is made between those who answered the question with "successfully completed vocational training required" and those who gave a more explicit job description. The reduction in case numbers as compared to the value "entrance into gainful employment" in the preceding evaluation results from missing values in these variables. The set of tested co-variates remains unchanged. The outcomes of this model estimation are documented in Table A6.

Only three conspicuous points can be observed. Older apprenticeship graduates not only have a worse chance of finding work directly after the training period, they are also overrepresented in unqualified jobs. Children from blue-collar households are equally overrepresented in underqualified positions, although this effect is only observed at a 10 per cent level of significance. Presumably the social climate or low household income forces them to take up work immediately after completion of vocational training, irrespective of the quality of the job offer. Trainees who finish an apprenticeship in the area of "trade" enter less frequently into underqualified work upon completion than do the comparison group which is primarily comprised of trainees in production occupations. This can be explained by the special employment situation in the area of trade which is characterised by lower paid jobs, even for trained *Warenkaufleute* (shop-keepers), and, at the same time, by a surplus of unfilled positions. In this area, trainees have no difficulty finding work on a par with their training qualification – frequently in their old training enterprise.

Transitions into gainful employment after graduation from a higher education institution

The last multivariate partial evaluation analyses the direct transition of higher education graduates into gainful employment. Taking up work is also the most frequent form of transition for higher education graduates after leaving a higher education institution (see Table 9). We now examine which graduates of higher education are successful in finding work immediately upon completion of their degree and which are not. The design of this evaluation corresponds to that which was implemented above. The reference category not only includes unemployed persons for reasons of case numbers, it also includes all non-gainfully employed. The combination of both of these categories seems legitimate for the group of higher education graduates, since we can assume that persons with the highest level of education are always potentially prepared to work. At the same time, this group is more strongly aware than others of how prospective employers regard the unemployed. As such, the question of whether unemployed higher education graduates register as unemployed or not says little about the actual search status of those concerned.

All persons are covered by the investigation who completed their degree in the year preceding the survey. Excluded from the survey are persons who went directly into military or community service. The household situation of the respondents, on the other hand, is not taken into account since the majority of higher education graduates no longer lived in their parental household at the time of the investigation (see above). Instead of the field of the training occupation, the subject of study is included in the model; again, a high aggregation of this information is necessary, owing to the number of cases. The relatively low number of cases in this partial evaluation requires an additional aggregation of various model variables for the reason that the accompanying individual values are too weakly represented (for the chosen operationalisation, see the display of outcomes). The outcomes of this partial evaluation are found in Table A7.

Once again we see a strongly levelled-out picture with regard to the opportunity distribution. The personal characteristics of age, gender and nationality do not exert any significant influence on the direct transition into gainful employment. The same is true for the social background of the respondents. In connection with the identical results on this variable complex, it can be determined that the influence of the social background on the training and labour market behaviour diminishes considerably the longer the duration of training or the older the person grows.

The subject of study chosen only influences work prospects to a certain extent at a significant level: those who have a degree in languages or cultural sciences/humanities have distinctly better chances of employment than the reference group with degrees in economic and social sciences. This outcome can be explained by the fact that students in the former group traditionally establish extremely close contact with the labour market early on in areas that are related in content to their course of study, for example in the areas of journalism and culture. Whether the job performed after the degree has been completed is actually comparable with the qualification level, *i.e.* requires a university degree, or whether a part-time job begun during the time at the university is simply "prolonged" disregarding the degree that was completed in the meantime, cannot be further analysed because of too few case numbers in the evaluated database.

Young graduates of higher education primarily find their first position in the city. Of final interest is the outcome that – in contrast to the entrance into the world of work of those who completed an apprenticeship, see above – the size of the regional unemployment figure maintains no significant influence over work prospects. This confirms the well-known fact that as the qualification level of an employee increases, so too does their willingness to relocate regionally, and in doing so are only minimally subject to regional labour market conditions as compared to persons with lower qualifications.

4. CURRENT LINES OF DEVELOPMENT IN EDUCATIONAL AND VOCATIONAL TRAINING POLICY MEASURES

Following the statistical analysis of the most significant trends in participation within different vocational training pathways, as well as the investigation of the determinants of young persons' training behaviour, we now conclude by briefly sketching the specific directions that the implemented educational and vocational training policy measures have taken during the period under review. In general, it can be determined that no profound, *i.e.* structure altering, measures have been realised in educational and vocational training policy during the last few years. Such measures might include the abolishment of the three or four-tiered system in general education or creating vocational and general education programmes of equal value, with the aim of allowing greater permeability between the various educational pathways. The main reasons for that situation lie in the very controversial views on the necessity of educational and vocational training policy strategies for structural changes[9] and in the federal structure of the German training system. It should also be pointed out, however, that education policy certainly has taken into account the distinctly changing educational desires of the population and of young people.

In the area of general education, while characterised by declining enrolment in *Hauptschulen* and increased enrolment in *Gymnasien* and *Integrierten Gesamtschulen*, the supply of teachers (pupil/teacher ratio) has been improved in all of the old federal *Länder* (see KMK, 1993, pp. 36 ff).

In dual vocational training (training in recognised training occupations), the existing structure of vocational training in schools and enterprises has not been changed. The supply and demand ratio for training places in enterprises has, however, left a situation of insufficient supply and a surplus of training places (see BMBW, 1993*a*, p. 15). This development results from the demographically determined decline in lower secondary level school-leavers (with or without *Hauptschule*, *Realschule* certificates or their equal) and from changing educational behaviour in general schooling, as well as from the stabilisation of training-place offers from enterprises, in the sense that the enterprises had not sufficiently adjusted their number of offers to the decline in demand for training places. Moreover, a series of measures were undertaken to reshape the contents of vocational training. Here focus was placed on reshaping training ordinances (*op. cit.*, pp. 83 ff) by incorporating aspects of basic vocational education. These efforts are accompanied by a series of qualification measures for certain target groups (young people without a general education certificate or training contract, those who repeatedly applied for apprenticeship positions, special education school-leavers, the handicapped and young people in danger of dropping out of training, among others). These qualification measures take the form of support for training places in enterprises at the federal and *Land* level, provision of enterprise-independent facilities to promote the disadvantaged, the guarantee of aid which accompanies training, as well as implementation of vocational preparatory educational measures with the framework of the Federal Institute for Labour.

In the area of vocational training in *Fachhochschulen* and universities, personnel resources have been expanded in the wake of the growing number of admissions of students, and yet the ratio of students to academic personnel has declined. This development has, however, taken different courses within the area of *Fachhochschulen* and universities.

The number of students in *Fachhochschulen* in Western Germany grew 4.1 per cent yearly (BMBW, 1993*b*, and authors' calculations) during the period from 1984 to 1990,[10] while the number of academic personnel grew at an average of 0.8 per cent per year. This means that the ratio of students to academic personnel has worsened at an average of 3 per cent per year. The ratio of students to professors has demonstrated a parallel development.

The number of students at universities grew by an average of 2.9 per cent yearly between 1984 and 1990, while the figure for academic personnel increased by a yearly average of 0.8 per cent, so that the ratio of students to academic personnel fell at a yearly average of 2.1 per cent. The number of professors dropped at a yearly average of 1.3 per cent, with the ratio of students to professors at universities declining at a yearly average of 4.2 per cent. When evaluating these developments, we must take into account among other things, however, that the mean duration of study at *Fachhochschulen* and universities increased during the period. (The mean length of time for a course of study at a university increased from 12 semesters in 1984 to 12.8 in 1991; at *Fachhochschulen* from 7.8 to 8.4 semesters during the same period) (see Statistisches Bundesamt, 1989 and 1993).

This development exists in a series of study programmes that have a high and permanent overload of students (ratio of those actually studying to the capacity), an overload not visible in the average values for all study programmes given above. In the last few years this has led to a concentration of education policy discussions in the area of higher education, aroused above all by fears that higher education programmes might suffer a loss in quality since the general shortage in funding of the public budget. Spending for higher education was also cut in the wake of the competition for funding which existed within the federal budget, between the federal and *Land* budgets and within the *Land* budgets. Some examples are the freezing of higher education construction funding, for which the federal government is responsible, and the deceleration of increases in higher education spending within the individual *Land* budgets.

In several *Länder*, additional savings are to be made in higher education spending through the reform of study programmes (mainly by tightening the time schedule). This is joined by considerations for restructuring funding within higher education spending, which means intensified expansion of *Fachhochschulen* at the expense of universities. This educational policy discussion between the federal government, *Länder* and special-interest groups reached its preliminary high point in November 1993 during a debate on principles of education and research policy with the Federal Chancellor ("Education Summit Meeting"). However, the discussion continues as a result of the strongly diverging views that have appeared to date among the educational policy institutions concerned.

NOTES

1. We would like to thank Suzanne Sanabria Albrecht, Berlin, for translation assistance. We would also like to thank Dr. Klaus Schweikert from the Federal Institute for Vocational Education and Training Affairs (Bundesinstitut für Berufsbildung – BIBB), Berlin, for his valuable support from the start of the project up through publication. An extended version of this text (including a glossary) has been published in both German and English (see Weißhuhn and Büchel, 1994).

2. For an exact description of the database, see Section 3.

3. Do not have state recognition at the present time.

4. For an up-to-date overview of literature, see e.g. Müller and Haun (1994).

5. For a more specific description see Weißhuhn and Büchel (1994). For details on the design of the survey, see Projektgruppe Panel (1993).

6. The authors would like to thank Dr. Rainer Pischner and Joachim Frick, German Institute for Economic Research (Deutsches Institut für Wirtschaftsforschung – DIW), Berlin, for copying individual variables from the gross inventory of the SOEP which were not available in the evaluated public-use file.

7. At this stage, we should point out that a comparison of the unweighted mean values of the exogenous variables and the distribution of the endogenous variables in the multivariate analyses with descriptive findings displayed in Section 2 has little meaning, owing to the over-proportional representation of the foreign population in the sample.

8. The recoding of the year dummies is undertaken owing to the low number of cases for the year 1984.

9. See, for example, the different positions in BMBW (1993a), pp. 3ff.

10. 1991 and the following years are omitted because delimitation problems occurred when East Berlin was added to Berlin in the wake of unification.

Annex

OUTCOMES OF MULTIVARIATE EVALUATIONS OF SECTION 3

Table A1. **Determinants of the distribution of pupils in general education: 7th grade (Western Germany, 1984-92, ordinal probit)**

Co-variates	Coefficient	Chi²	Mean
(Constant)	−1.1408**	14.4093	−
Male	−0.1241◊	3.3337	(0.492)
Foreigner	−0.2830**	10.3794	(0.417)
Head of household:			
− blue-collar worker	−0.0015	0.0001	(0.517)
− self-employed person	0.5427**	10.4016	(0.075)
− white-collar worker	0.5982**	19.4341	(0.213)
− civil servant	0.8006**	20.5593	(0.086)
− with *Abitur*	1.0925**	42.5110	(0.075)
− age difference relative to child	0.0109*	3.9391	(30.264)
No son/daughter	−0.2547	1.4332	(0.030)
Raised by a single parent	−0.2572◊	3.1475	(0.075)
Size of household	−0.1448**	21.4631	(4.558)
Household income per capita (deflated ÷ 100)	0.0282**	10.430	(8.046)
Federal *Land*:			
− Berlin	0.2189	1.2343	(0.034)
− Schleswig-Holstein	0.0066	0.0011	(0.035)
− Hamburg/Bremen	0.2597	1.4578	(0.025)
− Lower Saxony	0.0356	0.0692	(0.085)
− Hesse	0.0720	0.3197	(0.097)
− Rhineland-Palatinate/Saarland	0.1197	0.5357	(0.052)
− Baden-Württemberg	0.1669	2.5676	(0.212)
− Bavaria	0.1280	1.3619	(0.185)
Size of community:			
− > 500 000 inhabitants	0.2552*	5.7565	(0.470)
− 20 000 to 100 000 inhabitants	0.1169	0.6999	(0.100)
− < 20 000 inhabitants	0.0041	0.0013	(0.277)
Years:			
− 1985/86	0.2275*	4.3319	(0.259)
− 1987/88	0.3025**	7.0975	(0.219)
− 1989/90	0.4246**	12.7844	(0.183)
− 1991/92	0.3056**	6.5043	(0.171)
(Estimated level of significance)	0.8519**	21.6925	−

n = 1 300
Log likelihood = −1 154.45
Likelihood-ratio statistic = 413.18**
Dependent variable (unweighted case numbers):
  0 = *Hauptschule* (n = 636)
  1 = *Realschule* (n = 331)
  2 = *Gymnasium* (n = 333)

Levels of significance:
  ** (p < 0.01), * (p < 0.05), ◊ (p < 0.10)
Does not include pupils from other schools.
Reference categories:
  − Head of household: not gainfully employed/unemployed
  − Federal *Land*: North Rhine-Westphalia
  − Size of community: 100 000 to 500 000 inhabitants
  − Year: 1984

Source: Authors' evaluation of the Socio-economic Panel (SOEP).

Table A2. **Determinants of the distribution of pupils leaving general education according to the type of certificate (Western Germany, 1984-92, ordinal probit)**

Co-variates	Coefficient	Chi^2	Mean
(Constant)	−0.9659**	7.6825	–
Male	−0.0331	0.1834	(0.555)
Foreigner	−0.5375**	26.6114	(0.314)
Head of household:			
– blue-collar worker	−0.2544*	3.8844	(0.430)
– self-employed person	0.3335◊	3.4841	(0.077)
– white-collar worker	0.3176*	5.4422	(0.264)
– civil servant	0.2651	2.0811	(0.089)
– with *Abitur*	0.7286**	17.7512	(0.075)
– age difference relative to child	0.0174**	6.8544	(30.112)
No son/daughter	−0.4322◊	2.8940	(0.024)
Raised by a single parent	−0.0246	0.0304	(0.106)
Size of household	−0.1169**	10.4059	(4.250)
Household income per capita (deflated ÷ 100)	0.0302**	11.1558	(9.672)
Federal *Land*:			
– Berlin	−0.1046	0.2691	(0.040)
– Schleswig-Holstein	−0.1677	0.3962	(0.023)
– Hamburg/Bremen	−0.0822	0.1104	(0.025)
– Lower Saxony	0.0901	0.4424	(0.125)
– Hesse	−0.1794	1.5745	(0.099)
– Rhineland-Palatinate/Saarland	−0.0502	0.0858	(0.067)
– Baden-Württemberg	−0.1888	2.5359	(0.190)
– Bavaria	−0.2009	2.3196	(0.131)
Size of community:			
– > 500 000 inhabitants	−0.0158	0.0175	(0.485)
– 20 000 to 100 000 inhabitants	−0.2272	2.0576	(0.102)
– < 20 000 inhabitants	−0.2084	2.6639	(0.262)
Year:			
– 1987/88	−0.0694	0.4961	(0.277)
– 1989/90	0.0414	0.1550	(0.215)
– 1991/92	0.0664	0.3282	(0.171)
(Estimated level of significance)	1.3683**	537.9255	–

n = 947
Log likelihood = –861.28
Likelihood-ratio statistic = 297.02**
Dependent variable (unweighted case numbers):
  0 = *Hauptschulabschluss (Hauptschule* certificate):
    n = 345
  1 = *Realschulabschluss* (*Mittlere Reife*) (*Realschule* certificate): n = 393
  2 = *Hochschulreife* (*Gymnasium* certificate): n = 209

Levels of significance:
  ** (p < 0.01), * (p < 0.05), ◊ (p < 0.10)
Does not include school-leavers without a certificate; does not include school-leavers with: other certificate, own household, certificate attained over the second education route, certificate attained after *Fachoberschule* or *Berufsfachschule*.
Reference categories:
  – Head of household: not gainfully employed/ unemployed
  – Federal *Land*: North Rhine-Westphalia
  – Size of community: 100 000 to 500 000 inhabitants
  – Years: 1984/86

Source: Authors' evaluation of the Socio-economic Panel (SOEP).

Table A3. **Determinants of the probability that an apprenticeship starts directly upon completion of *Hauptschule* or *Realschule* (Western Germany, 1984-92, binary probit)**

Co-variates	Coefficient	Chi^2	Mean
(Constant)	−0.4184	0.9992	–
Male	0.3655**	14.0526	(0.533)
Foreigner	−0.4970**	15.7954	(0.374)
Realschule certificate (*Mittlere Reife*)	0.0520	0.2476	(0.532)
Head of household:			
– blue-collar worker	−0.0106	0.0046	(0.509)
– self-employed person	−0.4223◊	3.0938	(0.067)
– white-collar worker	−0.4137*	5.3461	(0.217)
– civil servant	0.1149	0.2072	(0.065)
– with *Abitur*	−0.5993*	4.1465	(0.034)
– age difference relative to child	0.0037	0.2113	(29.835)
No son/daughter	−1.0129**	7.7831	(0.027)
Raised by a single parent	−0.1767	0.8894	(0.094)
Size of household	−0.0026	0.0042	(4.377)
Household income per capita (deflated ÷ 100)	0.0182	1.5964	(8.724)
Size of community:			
– > 500 000 inhabitants	−0.0573	0.1625	(0.484)
– 20 000 to 100 000 inhabitants	−0.0114	0.0034	(0.104)
– < 20 000 inhabitants	−0.3069◊	3.6875	(0.265)
Years:			
– 1987/88	0.2980*	5.7587	(0.277)
– 1989/90	0.2973*	4.9160	(0.213)
– 1991/92	0.3561*	6.3212	(0.181)

n = 741
Log likelihood = −474.82
Likelihood-ratio statistic = 61.52**
Dependent variable (unweighted case numbers):
 – 0 = no transition into apprenticeship: n = 425
 – 1 = transition into apprenticeship: n = 316
Reference point in time: wave in which the school-leaving certificate was retrospectively registered

Levels of significance:
 ** (p < 0.01), * (p < 0.05), ◊ (p < 0.10)
Does not include school-leavers with: own household, certificate attained over the second education route, certificate attained after *Fachoberschule* or *Berufsfachschule*.
Reference categories:
 – School-leaving certificates: *Hauptschule* certificate
 – Head of household: not gainfully employed/unemployed
 – Size of community: 100 000 to 500 000 inhabitants
 – Years: 1984/86

Source: Authors' evaluation of the Socio-economic Panel (SOEP).

Table A4. **Determinants of the probability that a course of study at a higher education institution starts directly upon completion of the *Abitur* (Western Germany, 1984-92, binary probit)**

Co-variates	Coefficient	Chi²	Mean
(Constant)	−0.9420	0.6672	–
Male	0.1141	0.2459	(0.454)
Foreigner	0.7512*	4.0959	(0.190)
Head of household:			
– blue-collar worker	−0.4021	0.8846	(0.218)
– self-employed person	0.8882	2.7694	(0.115)
– white-collar worker	0.0489◊	0.0138	(0.356)
– civil servant	0.1106	0.0445	(0.138)
– with *Abitur*	0.8240*	6.3744	(0.178)
– age difference relative to child	−0.0014	0.0045	31.218)
No son/daughter	−0.0363	0.0024	(0.023)
Raised by a single parent	0.0430	0.0111	(0.138)
Size of household	0.0645	0.2529	(3.891)
Household income per capita (deflated ÷ 100)	−0.0055	0.3642	13.017)
Size of community:			
– > 500 000 inhabitants	−0.0435	0.0159	(0.523)
– 20 000 to 100 000 inhabitants	−1.0905◊	2.8823	(0.092)
– < 20 000 inhabitants	−0.3634	0.9033	(0.241)
Years:			
– 1987/88	−0.1504	0.2421	(0.259)
– 1989/90	0.1818	0.3505	(0.195)
– 1991/92	−0.0719	0.0439	(0.207)

n = 174
Log likelihood = −90.54
Likelihood-ratio statistic = 29.40*
Dependent variable (unweighted case numbers):
 – 0 = not admitted to a university programme:
  n = 123
 – 1 = admitted to a university programme: n = 51
Reference point in time: wave in which the school-leaving certificate was retrospectively registered

Levels of significance:
 * ($p < 0.05$), ◊ ($p < 0.10$)
Does not include school-leavers with: own household, certificate attained during second-education track, transition into military/community service.
Reference categories:
 – Head of household: not gainfully employed/unemployed
 – Size of community: 100 000 to 500 000 inhabitants
 – Years: 1984/86
Source: Authors' evaluation of the Socio-economic Panel (SOEP).

Table A5. **Determinants of the probability that employment comparable to the training qualification is found directly after completion of an apprenticeship (Western Germany, 1984-92, binary probit)**

Co-variates	Coefficient	Chi^2	Mean
(Constant)	2.5248**	6.9146	–
Age	–0.1013*	6.2170	(21.200)
Male	0.1218	0.2240	(0.600)
Foreigner	–0.3113	1.5501	(0.197)
Training occupation in area of:			
– trade	1.0573*	4.5362	(0.115)
– banking/insurance	0.1538	0.0792	(0.043)
– Elect. data processing office/administration	0.4371	2.0380	(0.187)
– health/gastronomy/cleaning	–0.1408	0.1387	(0.082)
Mittlere Reife	0.2218	0.9993	(0.387)
Abitur	0.1829	0.2759	(0.134)
Father or mother:			
– blue-collar worker	–0.5999◊	3.7896	(0.449)
– self-employed person	0.0479	0.0098	(0.085)
– white-collar worker	–0.0412	0.0130	(0.243)
– civil servant	–0.4089	0.9241	(0.079)
Size of community:			
– > 500 000 inhabitants	0.2535	1.0189	(0.393)
– 20 000 to 100 000 inhabitants	0.7028	2.3252	(0.092)
– < 20 000 inhabitants	0.1281	0.2274	(0.305)
Regional unemployment rate	–0.0036	0.0077	(7.922)
Years:			
– 1987/88	0.2554	1.0918	(0.236)
– 1989/90	0.7356**	8.5540	(0.325)
– 1991/92	1.2199**	12.8382	(0.210)

n = 305
Log likelihood = –119.27
Likelihood-ratio statistic = 52.32**
Dependent variable (unweighted case numbers):
 – 0 = work not comparable (= underqualified) to training qualification: n = 56
 – 1 = work comparable to training qualification: n = 249
Reference point in time: wave in which apprenticeship certificate was retrospectively registered
Source: Authors' evaluation of the Socio-economic Panel (SOEP).

Levels of significance:
 ** (p < 0.01), * (p < 0.05), ◊ (p < 0.10)
Reference categories:
 – Training occupation in area of: production/ technology/mining/agriculture, other, unknown
 – School-leaving certificate: *Hauptschule* certificate
 – Father/mother: not gainfully employed/unemployed
 – Size of community: 100 000 to 500 000 inhabitants
 – Years: 1984/86

Table A6. **Determinants of the probability that a respondent takes up gainful employment directly after completing an apprenticeship (Western Germany, 1984-92, binary probit)**

Co-variates	Coefficient	Chi^2	Mean
(Constant)	3.8588**	18.9929	–
Age	–0.0816*	5.6473	(21.347)
Male	–0.1876	0.5703	(0.602)
Foreigner	–0.3143	1.7876	(0.213)
Training occupation in area of:			
– trade	–0.2702	0.8212	(0.114)
– banking/insurance	0.0496	0.0069	(0.042)
– Elect. data processing office/administration	–0.0355	0.0142	(0.178)
– health/gastronomy/cleaning	–0.2999	0.7895	(0.105)
Mittlere Reife	0.1372	0.4336	(0.385)
Abitur	0.8308*	4.8131	(0.136)
Father or mother:			
– blue-collar worker	0.0991	0.1558	(0.446)
– self-employed person	0.2493	0.3385	(0.092)
– white-collar worker	0.0071	0.0005	(0.220)
– civil servant	–0.1513	0.1605	(0.079)
– with *Abitur*	–0.5206	1.0140	(0.026)
Size of community:			
– > 500 000 inhabitants	0.2215	0.9109	(0.374)
– 20 000 to 100 000 inhabitants	–0.1825	0.3571	(0.101)
– < 20 000 inhabitants	0.4295	2.6007	(0.327)
Regional unemployment rate	–0.1143**	10.0288	(8.029)
Years:			
– 1987/88	–0.0533	0.0569	(0.248)
– 1989/90	0.0070	0.0009	(0.279)
– 1991/92	0.7837*	3.9949	(0.187)

n = 455
Log likelihood = –128.43
Likelihood-ratio statistic = 45.51**
Dependent variable (unweighted case numbers):
 – 0 = registered as unemployed: n = 47
 – 1 = placement in gainful employment: n = 408
Reference point in time: wave in which apprenticeship certificate was retrospectively registered

Levels of significance:
 ** (p < 0.01), * (p < 0.05)
Does not include graduates who transferred into military or community service
Reference categories:
 – Training occupation in area of: production/ technology/mining/agriculture, other, unknown
 – School-leaving certificate: *Hauptschule* certificate
 – Father/mother: not gainfully employed/unemployed
 – Size of community: 100 000 to 500 000 inhabitants
 – Years: 1984/86

Source: Authors' evaluation of the Socio-economic Panel (SOEP).

Table A7. **Determinants of the probability that a respondent takes up gainful employment directly after completing a university degree (Western Germany, 1984-92, binary probit)**

Co-variates	Coefficient	Chi^2	Mean
(Constant)	4.5296	0.5673	–
Age	–0.0101	0.0620	(29.043)
Male	0.0956	0.0998	(0.621)
Foreigner	–0.7317	2.2085	(0.078)
Programme of study:			
– language/culture	1.3820*	5.4146	(0.112)
– mathematics/natural sciences	0.1147	0.1009	(0.181)
– human medicine/veterinary medicine	0.2539	0.3713	(0.121)
– engineering/agriculture/forestry	0.3088	0.5713	(0.138)
With additional vocational qualification	0.4901	1.4044	(0.164)
Father/mother:			
– self-employed/white-collar/civil servant	–0.3327	0.8125	(0.793)
– with *Abitur*	–0.1568	0.2854	(0.345)
Size of community:			
– > 500 000 inhabitants	0.8524**	9.4373	(0.638)
Regional unemployment rate	–0.0507	0.6196	(8.629)
Year	–0.0447	0.4754	(87.845)

n = 116
Log likelihood = –65.65
Likelihood-ratio statistic = 20.560
Dependent variable (unweighted case numbers):
 – 0 = registered as unemployed/not gainfully employed: n = 42
 – 1 = placement in gainful employment: n = 74
Reference point in time: wave in which degree was retrospectively registered
Source: Authors' evaluation of the Socio-economic Panel (SOEP).

Levels of significance:
 ** (p < 0.01), * (p < 0.05)
Does not include graduates who transferred into military or community service
Reference categories:
 – Programme of study: economics and social sciences, other, unknown

GLOSSARY

Abitur	(See *Gymnasium*)
Arbeitslosigkeit/Arbeitslos-Meldung beim Arbeitsamt	Unemployment/registered as unemployed at the employment exchange. All persons are considered unemployed who have no or only minimal gainful employment and, at the same time, are looking for work. In most cases, but not all, those concerned are also registered as unemployed at the employment exchange. An individual is "registered as unemployed" at the employment exchange when he/she has become unemployed and subsequently registers him/herself as unemployed at the employment exchange. Merely a visit to the employment exchange or job centre does not qualify.
Berufsakademie (also *Fachakademie*)	Institution for vocational education that requires at least a *Realschule* certificate or its equivalent and provides full-time, two- or three-year training programmes. These institutions aim at imparting scientifically-based, while at the same time practical, vocational training.
Berufsaufbauschule	A school for young people who are or have been in a vocational training programme or are working. Schooling is begun after an individual has attended a vocational school for at least six months, in which case attendance runs parallel to vocational school. This school can also be attended after compulsory vocational school has been completed. It is usually organised according to subject; full-time schooling lasts one to one-and-a-half year, while part-time schools take three to three-and-a-half years.

Upon successful completion, a *Fachschulreife* is awarded, which is equal to a *Realschule* certificate.

Berufsfachschule

A full-time school lasting at least one year that can be attended, usually on a voluntary basis, after completion of full-time compulsory school in order to prepare for an occupation or full vocational training. Pupils have no prior practical vocational training. *Berufsfachschulen* are to be distinguished from *Fachschulen*.

Berufsgrundbildungsjahr

Basic vocational training year.
This is usually attended prior to vocational training in an enterprise (apprenticeship) and, as a rule, takes the form of full-time vocational schooling.
Successful completion of the basic vocational training year leads, in most instances, to the year being counted towards a subsequent vocational training programme, as long as this falls within the respective field of work for which the young person was prepared.

Berufsschule

Vocational school.
An institution existing within the framework of general compulsory school. As a rule, it is attended by young people after they have completed full-time compulsory school until 18 years of age, or until completion of a practical vocational training programme.
The part-time form of vocational school is attended by trainees.

Berufsvorbereitungsjahr
(*Berufsbefähigendes Jahr*)

Vocational preparatory year.
For those young people who, after completing general compulsory school, neither enter into a training relationship (apprenticeship) nor into continuing general or vocational full-time school and also do not begin a basic vocational training year.

Betriebliche Ausbildung
(*Duales System*)

Vocational training in an enterprise (dual system).
"Apprenticeship": vocational training in a training enterprise with concurrent attendance at a (part-time) vocational school.

	Certificates: skilled worker (in industry), skilled white-collar worker (*e.g.* businessman in industry), journeyman in trade. In special cases, the trainee may be released from compulsory vocational school.
BLK (*Bund-Länder Kommission für Bildungsplanung und Forschungsförderung*)	Joint Federal and *Länder* Commission for Educational Planning and Research Promotion (only authorised to make recommendations).
Duales System	Dual system. (See *Betriebliche Ausbildung*.)
Fachakademie	(See *Berufsakademie*.)
Fachgymnasium	(See *Gymnasium*.)
Fachhochschule	Subject-related or specialised institution of higher education requiring a general certificate granting admission to institutions of higher education (*Abitur* or *Hochschulreife*) or a specialised certificate (*Fachhochschulreife*).
Fachhochschulreife	(See also *Fachhochschule*.) The *Fachhochschulreife* can be attained at the following schools: *Berufsfachschulen, Fachoberschulen, Fachgymnasien, Kollegschulen* and *Fachschulen*. It grants admission to *Fachhochschulen*.
Fachoberschule	An institution which awards the *Fachhochschulreife* after two years. Admission to this type of school requires a *Realschule* certificate or its equivalent. Successful completion grants admission to a course of study at a *Fachhochschule*.
Fachschule	Attendance is permitted after completion of a vocational training programme and practical work experience or when evidence of talent in a specialised area is shown. This type of school imparts extensive specialised further educational training in an occupation. Full-time attendance lasts between six months and three years.

	Fachschulen include all schools for master craftspeople, all technical schools, *Berufsakademien* and *Berufsfachakademien*.
Gesamtschule	(See *Integrierte Gesamtschule*.)
Grundschule	Primary school: 1st through 4th-, 5th- or 6th-grade level.
Gymnasium	5th-, 6th- or 7th- through 13th-grade level. Secondary school within general education that usually directly follows primary school. In addition, there are *Progymnasien* (5th- to 10th-grade level) and *Aufbaugymnasien* (11th- to 13th-grade level). Some of the *Aufbaugymnasien* start as early as the 8th- or 9th-grade level. A certificate of completion (*Hochschulreife* or *Abitur*) attained at a *Gymnasium* grants admission to a course of study at an institute of higher education. *Fachgymnasien* also belong to *Gymnasien*.
Hauptschule	5th- or 7th- through 9th- or 10th-grade level. Imparts a general education as a basis for practical vocational training, and prepares individuals for attending vocational school. Formerly called *Volksschule*.
Hochschule	(See *Universität*.)
Hochschulreife	(See *Gymnasium*.)
IAB (*Institut für Arbeitsmarkt- und Berufsforschung*)	Institute for Labour Market and Occupational Research. A research centre of the Federal Institute for Labour (*Bundesinstitut für Arbeit*).
Integrierte Gesamtschule	General education school in which pupils are collectively taught without being assigned to a particular type of school and yet are still able to attain one of the various certificates awarded in the structured school system (*Hauptschule*, *Realschule*, *Gymnasium*).
KMK (*Ständige Konferenz der Kultusminister der Länder in der Bundesrepublik Deutschland*)	Standing Conference of Education Ministers for the *Länder* of the Federal Republic of Germany. A central co-ordinating organ for education policy.
Mittlere Reife	(See *Realschule*.)

Realschule	5th-, 6th- or 7th- through 10th-grade level. Secondary school within general education requiring four to six years of attendance at primary school. Attendance lasts from four to six years. Successful completion of the *Realschule* generally provides access to upper-level non-academic occupations of all kinds. A *Realschule* certificate grants admission to *Fachoberschulen* and is therefore also referred to as *Fachoberschulreife*. Certificate: *Mittlere Reife*, or intermediate certificate.
Schulartunabhängige Orientierungsstufe	Orientation level existing independently of all other school types. A combination of the 5th and 6th grades, which falls under secondary general education.
Schule des Gesundheitswesens	Health system school. Imparts training for non-academic occupations in the health system (*e.g.* nurse, children's nurse, midwife, masseuse, occupational therapist, medical baths attendant). Pre-nursing schools are also included within health system schools that, as a rule, exist as independent facilities of health institutions or as part of establishments for social nursing or social education.
Sekundarstufe I	Lower secondary level. Encompasses 5th- through 9th- or 10th-grade levels.
Sekundarstufe II	Upper secondary level. Encompasses all education pathways (both general and vocational) that follow lower secondary level.
Sonderschule	Special education school. Full-time compulsory school which promotes and looks after physically, mentally or emotionally disabled or socially disadvantaged children who cannot be taught, or at least not with sufficient success, in normal schools. *Realschule* and *Gymnasium* special education schools also come under this heading.

237

Universität/Hochschule	University institution of higher education. Education institution that requires a general or specialised Abitur for admission and leads to a degree in higher education after several years of study. Volkshochschulen do not fall under this heading since their curricula come under further and continuing education.
Waldorfschule	Waldorf school. Independent (not state-run) school that bases its different schooling programmes on the educational theories of Rudolph Steiner.

Source: Infratest Sozialforschung (1992); authors' supplements.

BIBLIOGRAPHY

Bundesminister für Bildung und Wissenschaft (BMBW) (1993a), *Berufsbildungsbericht, Series Grundlagen und Perspektiven für Bildung und Wissenschaft*, No. 34, Bonn.

Bundesminister für Bildung und Wissenschaft (BMBW) (1993b), *Grund- und Strukturdaten*, Bonn.

Bund-Länder-Kommission für Bildungsplanung und Forschungsförderung (BLK) (1987), *Künftige Perspektiven von Aolventen der beruflichen Bildung im Beschäftigungssystem, Series Materialien zur Bildungsplanung*, No. 15, Bonn.

Bund-Länder-Kommission für Bildungsplanung und Forschungsförderung (BLK) (1994), *Beschäftigungsperspektiven der Absolventen des Bildungssystems*, Bonn.

Infratest Sozialforschung (1992), *Das Sozio-ökonomische Panel, Welle 9 (West). Anlagenband zum Methodenbericht*, Munich.

KLEMM, K. et al. (1990), *Bildungsgesamtplan '90*, Weinheim and Munich.

Kultusministerkonferenz (KMK) (1993), *Schüler, Klassen, Lehrer und Absolventen der Schulen 1982 bis 1991*, Documentation No. 121, Bonn.

MADDALA, G.S. (1985), *Limited-Dependent and Qualitative Variables in Econometrics*, Cambridge.

MÜLLER, W. and HAUN, D. (1994), "Bildungsungleichheit im sozialen Wandel", *Kölner Zeitschrift für Soziologie und Sozialpsychologie*, Vol. 46, No. 1.

Projektgruppe Panel (1993), "Das Sozio-ökonomische Panel (SOEP) nach zehn Jahren", *Vierteljahrshefte zur Wirtschaftsforschung*, Vol. 62, No. 1/2.

Statistisches Bundesamt (1989, 1993), *Bildung im Zahlenspiegel*, Wiesbaden.

TESSARING, M. et al. (1993), *Bestand und Bewegung im Bildungs- und Beschäftigungssystem der Bundesrepublik Deutschland, Series Beiträge zur Arbeitsmarkt-und Berufsforschung*, No. 170, Nuremberg (supplemented for 1989 and 1990 by the IAB in May 1993, "Übergänge zwischen Bildung, Ausbildung und Beschäftigung", mimeo, Nuremberg).

WEIßHUHN, G. and BÜCHEL, F. (1994), *Bildungswege und Berufseintritt im Wandel* (Changing pathways and outcomes of the German education system), Bertelsmann, Gütersloh.

8

ITALY

by

Marinella Giovine, Institute for the Development of Vocational Training (ISFOL), Milan

1. STRUCTURE OF THE EDUCATION SYSTEM

In Italy, there is a limited range of options open to young people when they finish their compulsory education at 14 years. The options are:

- to go on to upper secondary school to study for a diploma leading to further education;
- to join a vocational training course on a regional authority training scheme (course length varies from 500 to 2 400 hours);
- to take up an apprenticeship, lasting on average two years;
- to take up a job under different types of employment contract, particularly employment-training contracts.

Upper secondary school

There are four different pathways through upper secondary school, generally lasting five years (see Figure 1). Pupils are free to choose which routes to take and which schools to attend, provided they hold the middle school (lower secondary cycle) leaving certificate. There are no constraints at all on choice, not even in the form of guidance counselling. These pathways correspond to different types of education and training:

- a general, comprehensive education in the humanities and sciences at *licei* (*liceo classico*, *liceo scientifico* and *liceo linguistico*) and at the *istituto magistrale* and *scuola magistrale* (teacher training colleges for primary and infant school teachers respectively);
- an education in the arts at arts schools (*licei artistici*) and arts institutes (*istituti d'arte*);
- technical education and training at technical institutes (*istituti tecnici*);

◆ Figure I. *Structure of the education system*

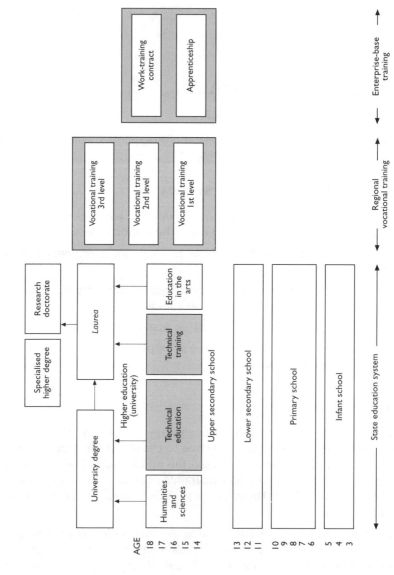

Source: CEDEFOP.

– vocational education and training at vocational institutes (*istituti professionali*).

All four pathways lead to a diploma (*diploma di maturità*) qualifying students to go on to higher education. The various streams and specialised branches of the technical and vocational institutes also equip students to enter the job market. The vocational institutes prepare skilled blue- and white-collar staff, whilst the technical institutes train technicians.

The vocational institutes originally offered two- or three-year courses without the option of remaining in education afterwards. Courses were subsequently extended by two years so that students could study for the *maturità* diploma and then go on to higher education. The vocational content of the course is concentrated in the first three years, with a certificate attesting to a student's skills. During the last two of these three years the teaching is less applied, in order to prepare students for the *maturità* diploma.

The technical institutes offer courses that teach the subjects leading to the qualification (electrical engineer, surveyor, accountant, etc.) over the full five years, covering them in greater depth in the last two years. There is no intermediate point of departure from these courses.

Higher education

In Italy, virtually all higher education is provided in the universities. University teaching is faculty-based and this includes courses for engineers, agronomists, architects and doctors. Senior technical staff are therefore educated at university.

The value of the *maturità* diploma as a university entrance qualification varies according to the duration of the secondary education. After five years, a student can choose any type of higher education, but the choice is limited after the four-year cycle. For instance, a diploma from a primary school teacher training college only qualifies pupils for teacher training faculties; the diploma from the arts *liceo* qualifies pupils for the architecture faculty. However, a four-year cycle can also be extended by a one-year preparatory course to qualify pupils for all faculties. Three-year cycles, such as at infant school teacher training colleges, do not qualify pupils for university entrance. A system of selective entrance may also operate in some faculties in large towns and when there are limited job opportunities in the professions being studied for (particularly medicine and architecture).

A *laurea* degree is awarded at the end of higher education, lasting from four to six years, depending on the faculty. The *laurea* qualifies students to go on to a second level and a two-year specialised higher degree or a three-year research doctorate.

Short higher education courses are a very recent phenomenon in Italy. The three-year university degree, or *diploma universitario*, was not introduced until 1990. This degree is designed to enable students either to enter the job market armed with occupational skills or to continue studying at university. It is still too soon to be able to assess the choices graduates make in respect of further education and how successful they are in finding employment.

Regional vocational training schemes

Vocational training courses run by regional authorities are essentially aimed at two types of young people: those who only have the middle school leaving certificate marking the end of compulsory education and/or who have dropped out of secondary school, and those who have a secondary school diploma but are not going on to university.

Several countries are currently in the process of devolving to the regions responsibility for vocational training – in particular, alternating classroom/workplace training. Italy is therefore interesting, in that the regional authorities have been largely responsible for vocational training for the last 25 years.

The strength of this system is that regional authorities are well placed to plan training on the basis of courses (generally three-year courses) tailored to the specific requirements of employers and job seekers in each geographic area. This is a distinct advantage over the state education system where teaching methods and curricula hardly ever change and where the system is the same throughout the country despite the huge regional differences that exist, particularly between north and south.

However, diversity is also a weakness. Training seems to be better organised and more effective in those regions which are the most developed economically and socially. This all serves to highlight the disparities between regions, especially for the least skilled and those who have problems finding a job. This is the case despite the fact that the authorities in the less developed regions have greater financial resources. State action would be needed to try to address these disparities, but this appears to pose many institutional and administrative problems.

Apprenticeship and other job training initiatives

The duration of apprenticeship contracts varies according to the apprentice's age and the firm's business. The apprentice may have to take special tests at the end of his/her contract to obtain certification of his/her occupational skills.

Apprenticeships follow a different pattern in Italy than in most other countries, in that the employer is fully responsible for the training. Training is acquired on the job, without any skills training plan nor any control. It therefore cannot really be termed "alternating training". Further, to reform the apprenticeship system would be difficult, since it is hard to change the practices of employers who are able to use young people as cheap labour without any real commitment to skills training. However, the advantage of apprenticeships is that they are a good way into employment for young people.

The same applies to job training contracts and other workplace situations: they too are considered as potential ways of acquiring a recognised qualification – any worker can in fact ask the employment office to assess and certify his/her occupational skills. But the certificate issued is of no value for returning to the formal education system.

Pathways for young people

The education system is designed to allow pupils to move from one level to another. Hence, in the vocational and technical streams, both at secondary level and at higher level, the process of practical learning is always paired with a process of "general" learning, particularly in scientific and technical subjects. This structure provokes conflicting reactions between those who consider that it is not providing the skills firms need and those who believe that it is the best way to ensure that skills are not overspecialised or geared to transient labour needs.

However, the Italian system is also characterised by:

– a limited choice of school/training/job curricula and pathways;
– long curricula, with few intermediate exit points;
– compartmentalisation between streams, preventing pupils from transferring from one to the other.

There is therefore a kind of main route through the system for young people coming to the end of their compulsory education, *i.e.* to continue their studies at secondary school. This takes five years, with no intermediate exit points other than to a vocational institute. There is virtually no possibility of switching streams in secondary education – a serious matter, given that the choice is made at the age of 14.

Drop-out rates are high because of the essentially academic approach taken to teaching in all the streams. This approach does not really meet the needs and expectations of the different populations in upper secondary schools, nor even the technical or vocational colleges.

The regional vocational training courses are generally filled by relatively disadvantaged youngsters looking to acquire short-term skills. The teaching methods differ from those used in schools, where these young people failed to succeed. Following one of these courses is generally considered as an alternative to school. However, the certificate obtained does not have the same value as a school certificate and cannot be used as a passport back to the school system.

Apprenticeships attract a fairly mixed population. The young apprentice is in a fortunate position compared with other youngsters of the same age looking for jobs, since he/she is in regular employment, earning a decent wage and has the possibility of gaining solid occupational skills. However, as with young people on regional authority training courses, apprentices have also left the school system, and the qualification that they gain does not allow them back into it.

2. PARTICIPATION IN VOCATIONAL AND TECHNICAL STREAMS

Figure 2 shows the main flows within the education system, including departures, through dropping out (AB) or after gaining a certificate, into vocational training and the job market: regional authority vocational training (FP), apprenticeship (APP) and other "non-training" activities (AANF) which include job training contracts and other workplace situations. The *licei* in this figure include primary school teacher training colleges and the arts *licei*.

Trends in participation in state education

In the 1991-92 academic year, a total of 2 858 000 pupils were enrolled in upper secondary schools. 1 828 000 of these, virtually 60 per cent, were enrolled at technical or vocational schools. In the technical (and vocational) schools, pupils are almost evenly split between those following courses geared to the agricultural and industrial sectors and those aimed at the tertiary sector.

Seventy per cent of pupils who are awarded the secondary school leaving diploma go on to university. Of the first-year enrolments, approximately 18 per cent are in the "technical" faculties (engineers, agronomists, architects, etc.), 12 per cent in the scientific faculties, 3 per cent in the medical faculties, whilst the economics and law group account for 45 per cent. Most of the rest are in arts courses. The faculties currently offering the best employment prospects are the engineering, law and economics faculties.

Over the last decade, *i.e.* on the basis of information available between 1982-83 and 1991-92 (see Tables 1 and 2), there have been no major changes in the pattern of enrolment in secondary education streams, in spite of the following developments:

- the student population in upper secondary education rose considerably (almost 400 000 additional pupils, an increase of 16 per cent);
- significant changes occurred in the job market, such as a 5 per cent rise in unemployment, a 12 per cent labour market shift to the tertiary sector, and a growing number of women in employment.

◆ Figure 2. **Flows¹ in the education system**

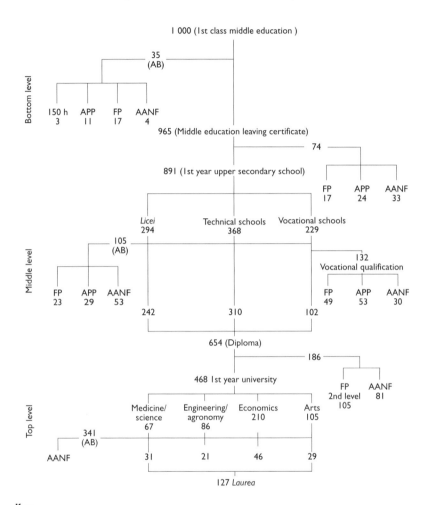

Key:
AB: Drop-outs
APP: Apprenticeship
FP: Vocational training
AANF: Other non-training activities
Licei: Classical, modern, language, arts, primary school teacher training colleges
Vocational schools: Vocational institutes, art institutes, infant school teacher training colleges

1.   The method used to calculate flows is the hypothetical cohort method, based on data for the 1991-92 academic year. The
     method is based on the application, at all levels of the education system, of transition rates for the year in question.
Source: CENSIS data processing and estimates, using ISTAT and Ministry of Employment statistics.

Table 1. **Secondary education, 1982-83 and 1991-92**
Total enrolment by type of school

Number and percentage

	1982-83	1991-92
Vocational schools	473 859 (19.2)	541 899 (18.9)
Technical schools	1 101 032 (44.6)	1 285 731 (45.0)
Licei	596 551 (24.1)	747 868 (26.2)
Others	298 594 (12.1)	282 723 (9.9)
Total	2 470 036 (100)	2 858 221 (100)

Source: Author.

There was a drop in participation, albeit a small one, in secondary school vocational and technical streams. This can be seen in particular by comparing the 1982-83 and 1991-92 figures for first-year secondary education enrolments. During this period, the number of pupils entering technical schools as a percentage of total secondary school entrants remained unchanged, whilst the number of new entrants into vocational schools dropped by nearly 2 per cent.

Table 2. **Secondary education, 1982-83 and 1991-92**
First-year enrolment, by type of school and by sex

Number and percentage

	1982-83		
	Boys	Girls	Total
Vocational schools	87 982 (25.4)	82 319 (23.8)	170 301 (24.6)
Technical schools	184 771 (53.3)	110 856 (32.1)	295 627 (42.7)
Licei	62 496 (18.0)	70 318 (20.4)	132 814 (19.2)
Others	11 537 (3.3)	81 680 (23.7)	93 217 (13.5)
Total	346 786 (100)	345 173 (100)	691 959 (100)
	1991-92		
Vocational schools	91 477 (24.5)	74 017 (21.0)	165 464 (22.8)
Technical schools	192 596 (51.6)	117 522 (33.4)	310 118 (42.8)
Licei	76 904 (20.6)	94 578 (26.8)	171 482 (23.6)
Others	12 532 (3.3)	66 083 (18.8)	78 615 (10.8)
Total	373 479 (100)	352 200 (100)	725 679 (100)

Source: Author.

In contrast, the number of students entering *licei* (humanities and sciences) rose by over 4 per cent. One particular reason for this was that *licei* were taking in pupils who would traditionally have entered primary school teacher training colleges, whose role has gradually diminished.

During the period in question, there was no apparent change in enrolment patterns for the different types of school, not even among the female population, even though major qualitative and quantitative changes had occurred over this ten-year period in female participation in employment.

Female participation in vocational schools dropped more than did male participation. The ratio of females in technical schools increased slightly, but virtually only in those geared towards the tertiary sector. There was a 6 per cent rise in female pupils in the *licei*, but this can be almost entirely attributed to the decline in teacher training colleges with their traditional predominance of female students.

These data show that, in Italy, economic and social changes have very little impact on the educational choices of young people, or – to be more precise – of parents, given that these choices are made (and are virtually irreversible) at 14 years of age, at the end of compulsory education.

Having said that, the 1980s were a decade of profound structural changes in production, a time when the growth in new technologies became apparent to all. There has also been a great deal of media attention, sometimes too much, on the emergence of new professions in the sectors affected by the change. But none of this has influenced the choice of education streams. This type of decision is influenced by other factors (see below).

Characteristics of stream participants

The information available on the characteristics of pupils in different educational streams in Italy is unfortunately incomplete. The only source other than the small amount of data obtainable from national statistics is information from a few surveys of diploma holders. These surveys concentrate mostly on specific geographical areas. The particular ones that will be considered are (see bibliography):

- the *Entrata nella vita attiva* (EVA: entry into the labour market) survey, conducted by ISFOL in 1987;
- the *Indagine sui percorsi scuola occupazione* (IPSO: survey on schoolwork pathways), conducted by IRSPEL on diploma holders from schools in the Latium region (which includes Rome);
- the 1989 survey by the job market observatory for the Lombardy region (which includes Milan) on *Ingresso e permanenza nel mercato del lavoro dei qualifi-*

cati diplomati e laureati (entry to and employment in the job market of skilled young people, school diploma holders and university graduates);

- the survey *Diplomati delle superiori; scelte di studio e di lavoro* (education and employment choices for higher education graduates), carried out in 1992 in the province of Trento by the job market observatory.

Some information confirming certain characteristics of young people who are attending or who had attended the different types of secondary school can also be obtained from surveys into different aspects of young people's lives, including the survey on young people with job training contracts in their first jobs and the various IARD surveys (particularly IARD, 1993).

National statistical sources (ISTAT, 1993) show that underachievement varies considerably, depending on type of school. During the academic year 1991-92, 8 per cent of pupils who enrolled at upper secondary school were repeaters. And whilst the figure was 4 per cent in *licei*, it was as high as 9.7 per cent in vocational schools and 9.9 per cent in technical schools.

The number of pupils staying on at secondary school beyond the school-leaving age is high (see Figure 2). However, radical selection is practised in the first two years of this level of education. Repeater rates are also higher then than they are in the three years after.

There are considerable differences between education streams. Repeaters represent 5.6 per cent of pupils enrolled in the first year of *licei* and 13.2 and 14.4 per cent of first-year enrolments in vocational and technical schools, respectively.

The fact that teaching is more intensive in vocational and technical schools than in *licei* (more subjects and teaching hours per week) has only a slight impact on these differences. The main factors influencing student performances throughout the secondary school cycle, and particularly in the first two years, are achievement in compulsory education and family background. These two factors are also closely linked.

The IPSO survey figures show that 1.2 per cent of *liceo* diploma holders, 4 per cent of technical school and 8 per cent of vocational school diploma holders had repeated at least one year during their compulsory education. The EVA survey reveals that top marks were obtained in the middle school leaving certificate (end of compulsory education) by 93 per cent of *liceo* humanities diploma holders, 67 per cent of *liceo* science diploma holders, 42.8 per cent of technical school diploma holders and 19.9 per cent of vocational school diploma holders. A similar survey conducted at a later date in the province of Trento revealed that top marks were obtained in the middle school leaving certificate by 74 per cent of *liceo* diploma holders, 48 per cent of technical school diploma holders and only 26 per cent of vocational school diploma holders.

As regards the differences between education stream participants according to socio-economic background:

- The Lombardy survey showed that, of the pupils who had been awarded technical or vocational diplomas, 69.3 per cent had parents whose average educational attainment was lower than the diploma, 45.1 per cent had parents with an average educational attainment equivalent to the diploma and 14 per cent parents with an average educational attainment equivalent to the *laurea* (degree awarded after higher education);

- The results of the IPSO survey showed that 57 per cent of vocational school diploma holders, 45 per cent of diploma holders from industry-oriented technical schools, 33 per cent from tertiary-oriented technical schools and 14 per cent from *licei* had parents with low educational attainment.

Other surveys have also shown that young people attending tertiary-oriented technical schools are in a middle position between those who choose *licei* and those who choose technical or vocational schools in terms of educational attainment and social and family background.

The same correlations between type of diploma obtained and family background are observed looking at the socio-professional class of the parents of young diploma holders.

Factors in choice of stream

The data all point to the fact that, at the end of compulsory education, the children of parents who are economically disadvantaged and did not do well at school themselves choose technical or vocational schools (or leave school altogether), while the children of parents who are better off materially and did well at school opt for the *licei* or, albeit to a lesser degree, tertiary-oriented technical schools.

However, it would be wrong to believe that a humble social background and poor educational achievement are inextricably linked to low job expectations and employment of the kind previously classed as "manual", particularly in industry and the skilled trades.

At the end of compulsory education, young people (or rather their parents) decide above all how long they want to stay on at school, even though it is clear that this choice will essentially determine the young person's future rung on the employment ladder. In other words, the choice of school made at 14 years old is based on whether or not it is intended, or likely, that the child will continue in education after his/her diploma. This effectively means that the decision is whether to study for a further five or ten years, since there are virtually no intermediate exits in Italy other than by dropping out. The learning abilities displayed by the young person in the previous cycle, as well as the parents' ambitions and financial resources, will clearly be decisive factors in a choice such as this.

Those who, at 14 years of age, already plan to go on to university, need to choose a path that offers a comprehensive education to prepare them for any higher education stream. On the other hand, the logical choice for those who do not intend to go on to university is an educational stream that can give them as full a technical or vocational qualification as possible after five years.

Another factor that attracts the most disadvantaged young people to vocational schools is that they offer a certificate at the end of the third school year. However, the value of this certificate on the job market has declined over the years (it was always fairly low), owing to the fact that the curriculum in the first few years in vocational schools has become more general in content, geared towards staying on at school.

Information confirming the link between the type of secondary school attended and the working or non-working status after acquisition of a diploma can be drawn from numerous surveys looking at young people for a certain time after obtaining their diplomas (a time varying from survey to survey).

The EVA survey revealed that over 90 per cent of *liceo* diploma holders, almost 25 per cent of technical school diploma holders and under 16 per cent of vocational school diploma holders were still students three years after receiving their diplomas. The results of the IPSO survey on diploma holders from schools in the Latium region four years after the end of their secondary studies confirm the EVA data: 65 per cent of *liceo* diploma holders, almost 20 per cent of tertiary-oriented technical school diploma holders, a little over 10 per cent of diploma holders from other technical schools and just 7 per cent of diploma holders from vocational schools were still students. In Lombardy, almost 94 per cent of *liceo* diploma holders and 21 per cent of technical or vocational school diploma holders were still students three years later. The numbers were 73 and 20 per cent respectively in the province of Trento four years after obtaining the diploma.

There is therefore very little variation between geographical areas and between survey periods. The lower figures recorded in the Latium region can be explained by the narrow definition of student status (most worker students were excluded and often classed as workers).

There is no doubt that young people's failure at secondary school – which, as we have seen, occurs more frequently in the vocational and technical streams – also conditions the subsequent choice of whether or not to stay in education after the diploma. In most cases, though, the decision to opt for short or long studies is taken when moving from compulsory to secondary education.

It is worth making a few observations at this stage about going on to university and the "type" of university studies that young people choose according to the type of certificate obtained (in Italy, students can, in principle, enter any faculty from any secondary school). Certain false ideas encourage young people to make wrong choices through lack of information, one commonly heard idea being that *licei* provide the most thorough and comprehensive preparation for university, as demonstrated by the high number of *liceo* diploma holders in all university faculties and by the fact that *liceo* diploma holders outperform those with technical or vocational school diplomas.

There is no denying that students from *licei* outnumber all others in university faculties. However, as we have seen, this is due to the fact that they are far more likely to continue in education. *Liceo* diploma holders do best at university, where drop-out rates are high (65 per cent). It is worth repeating a point already made: these are students who had already demonstrated the best learning abilities at the end of compulsory education.

It is equally true that vocational and technical school diploma holders are more likely to be able to find a job if they leave school, since they have a basic training which is worth more on the job market than that of their *liceo* counterparts. It is rare for vocational school diploma holders (who are the ones most vulnerable when they leave school and often the most disadvantaged in terms of socio-economic background) to go on to university.

Among those who do continue studying after obtaining a technical diploma, there is a tendency to choose the engineering faculty or, in the case of those whose training was geared towards the tertiary sector, economics. By the same token, whilst being well represented in all faculties, *liceo* diploma holders tend to prefer the law, political science, humanities and the arts.

It is also true that, as far as the standing of professions and subjects is concerned, perceptions change when moving from school to university. Vocational and technical secondary schools are considered less prestigious than *licei*, but the same does not apply when technical and scientific faculties are compared with the humanities or social sciences. Quite the reverse, in fact: medicine, architecture and engineering, which lead to a profession, are seen as particularly prestigious faculties.

A final observation is that the distribution of school population between technical or scientific and comprehensive schools is similar in all areas of the country, despite the wide differences that exist between north and south in employment and unemployment rates, per capita income, the structure of the production system, etc.

This also shows that geographical variables have relatively little impact on education choices compared to variables related to the socio-economic status of young people and their families. In the south of the country, the relatively lower standard of living of families (which ought to encourage youngsters to enrol for technical or vocational courses) is offset by a tradition that attaches greater prestige to the humanities than to technical or scientific subjects. What is more, the propensity to embark on long courses is accentuated by the difficulties in finding a job, which are greater for young people in the south than for those in the north.

Participation in regional authority vocational training initiatives

The regional authorities have been given responsibility for promoting training initiatives, aimed particularly at employment and tailored to suit the specific local requirements of job supply and demand. Their training schemes cater for fewer students than the state secondary school courses, even though the numbers are continuing to rise: in 1992, there were 270 000 on these schemes, some of whom were adult workers, mostly from firms in the course of restructuring.

However, most of those on regional schemes are young people, particularly those (approximately 130 000 in 1992) with at most the middle school leaving certificate, and who, on leaving compulsory education or failing at upper secondary level, are attracted to relatively short training courses in order to get a qualification that might lead to a job.

The family backgrounds and educational attainment of this group are extremely modest, even more so than those on state school vocational training courses. The scheme therefore attracts a lot of young people who, after finishing compulsory education, do not want to, or cannot, for a variety of reasons, undertake a course of study lasting more than one or two years.

Job opportunities, however, are not good. One or two years after obtaining the certificate, only an average of 30 per cent have a job and rarely one that matches the type of training received. It is difficult to assess to what extent these results might be due to failings on the part of the regional authorities (for instance, in matching training provision to job market requirements) or to the personal inadequacies of those concerned (which can be only partly remedied by training). For young people between the ages of 15 and 18, the regional authority training scheme backs up the state school system by providing additional training and delaying entry onto the job market, as do many schemes launched in member states of the European Union.

The courses designed for those who already have an upper secondary school diploma play a positive role as a bridge between school and the job market. They are, in this case, an effective means of equipping the young person with the skills which the production system requires. Vocational training can in this way be a (short) alternative to university.

3. PROSPECTS FOR CHANGE

It would not be altogether correct to say that Italy needs more places on vocational and technical courses. An increase of this kind would be especially inappropriate in the case of industrial vocational training. Employment in industry is obviously dropping and there is no clear evidence that the innovations now spreading to all sectors of production will require better occupational skills. The picture is somewhat different for education geared towards the tertiary sector, since the service sector is currently growing and using medium- or high-level occupational skills on a far greater scale than the industrial sector.

On the basis of the arguments developed above, it is vital to reverse the current tendency at secondary school level to rate vocational and technical education or training lower than general education. Action needs to be taken to influence educational choices after compulsory education and to improve the way the training provision is organised, in order to combat the Italian education system, which in principle allows young people to select the type of school that best suits them, but in reality imposes a considerable degree of selection, while not allowing schools to play their proper role in encouraging social mobility.

Extending compulsory education to the age of 16 would go some way towards allowing young people to make choices conditioned a little less by family background and a little more by their actual personal aspirations. This will naturally only be possible if the additional two years fit in with current compulsory education. Clearly, if the extension represents the first two years of an educational stream selected at 14 years of age as it is now, then this goal will be achieved.

Educational provision should also enable vocational and technical and general streams to co-exist within the same structure. Another improvement would be to organise education on a modular basis so that young people can modify, at least partially, their original choices. There are a variety of experiments in hand which demonstrate the validity of these proposals. Young people are being allowed to stay on after the end of compulsory education for a standard two-year period and to decide at the age of 16 between several different options within the same structure.

Less effective, although perhaps of interest from other angles, are experimental measures aimed at supporting young people at vocational schools. Whilst these initiatives do help to lower drop-out and failure rates, they have no effect on the socio-economic make-up of the population entering this type of education. What is generally needed, in fact, is to improve the image of vocational and technical education so that it also attracts young people who intend to continue studying after obtaining their diploma.

In the regional authority vocational training scheme, there are many possibilities for reform. Since it attracts a population that is particularly disadvantaged and excluded from all other forms of training, it would seem inappropriate (and contrary to the provisions of the constitution conferring special powers on the regional authorities) to bring any form of vocational and technical education back into the state education system. On the contrary, it is better to reduce the Italian training monolith by offering young people a variety of different pathways. To achieve this aim, it would be a good idea also to redefine apprenticeship and work-training contracts to enable young people to gain occupational skills through diversified training provision.

All these different pathways should be brought under the umbrella of a standard system of certification and credits so that young people are not blocked in one path and can, at least to some extent, alter their first choice of training stream. There is virtually no standardisation in the certificates currently issued by state schools, by the regional training system and by alternating training schemes, and it is therefore not possible to switch from one system to another.

Whilst it is not claimed that formal certificates are recognised to any great extent in Italy for employment or contractual classification purposes, certificates, and particularly diplomas, do without doubt attract people to training through their value as a status symbol. Obtaining them, even by different routes, helps break down the social immobility which, as we saw above, characterises the Italian training system.

It is widely held that if guidance counselling were improved, more young people might be encouraged to enrol for vocational and technical training. Guidance counselling is clearly still very inadequate and needs to be more widely available, especially to allow young people to make better-informed choices at the end of compulsory education. However, such counselling cannot significantly influence attitudes which, as stated above, are strongly linked to socio-economic variables. Moreover, guidance counselling is only meaningful if the training provision really does offer a wide range of choice.

Even more important than guidance counselling is the need for a better balance within compulsory education between the arts and humanities and science and technology. A major reform of compulsory education in the 1970s introduced highly career-oriented subjects and activities into the curriculum (technology courses, scientific observation, etc.). This was almost a revolution in Italy, since these subjects replaced arts subjects such as Latin. Despite this, scientific and technical subjects are still underrated in compulsory education, leading to a form of discrimination between pupils. The most gifted (who will be the ones to go on to a *liceo* and hence long education) are still thought to be those with the greatest facility of expression in Italian, an ability which is obviously closely linked to family sociocultural level. Scientific and technical education therefore needs to play a more important role in compulsory education, particularly through heavy investment in teacher training.

Wider and better participation in vocational and technical education and training in the future will thus require:

- institutional engineering, to link the different training systems, particularly for certification;
- a major national and regional teacher training programme, covering all levels in the education system;
- development of guidance counselling and the-right-to-education initiatives in order to encourage young people coming from vocational and technical secondary schools to go on to higher education.

BIBLIOGRAPHY

CENSIS (1993), *Rapporto sulla situazione sociale del paese 1993*, F. Angeli, Milan.

IARD (1993), *Giovani anni '90*, Il Mulino, Bologna.

IRSPEL (1993), *La condizione giovanile nel Lazio*, F. Angeli, Milan.

ISFOL (1988), *Il lavoro dei giovani*, F. Angeli, Milan.

ISFOL (1989), *Percorsi giovanili di studio e lavoro*, F. Angeli, Milan.

ISTAT, *Statistiche dell'istruzione*, statistical data (covering a number of years).

Lombardy Region – Job market observatory (1989), *Ingresso e permanenza nel mercato del lavoro dei qualificati, diplomati, e laureati nell'anno scolastico 1984-85*, Milan.

Province of Trento, Job centre (1993), *Diplomati delle superiori, scelte di studio e lavoro*, Trento.

9

THE NETHERLANDS

by

Elly de Bruijn and Eva Voncken,
Kohnstamm Institute for Research in Education, Amsterdam

I. INTRODUCTION[1]

Changing patterns

In the Netherlands over the past two decades, several reforms have been implemented in vocational and technical education and training. Indicators of changing participation patterns over the past 15 years include:

- a decline in the number of students entering the pre-vocational stream in favour of the number of students entering the general stream in the first stage of secondary education;

- a "jump" in enrolment in vocational and technical education programmes at intermediate level in the upper secondary education, which students enter at the age of roughly 15 or 16;

- more students tending to choose a combined pathway of general and vocational and technical education: they start upper secondary school with general education and complete their studies with vocational and technical education and training.

This chapter aims both at documenting and clarifying pathways in the Netherlands: changes in the supply of vocational and technical education and training and in the actual routes that young people follow through the system. The period covered is from 1975 until 1992 (Figure 1).

Scope of the study: pathways to and through vocational education

Admission to vocational and technical education and training generally occurs after eleven years of compulsory full-time education (seven years of primary education starting at the age of five, and four years of secondary education).

◆ Figure I. **Structure of Dutch education system[1] and number of students, full-time and part-time**
(Total = 3.3 million students)[2]

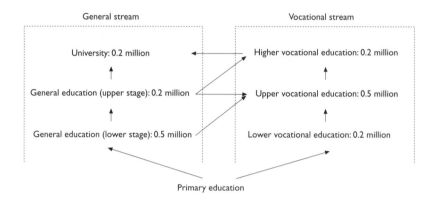

1. This scheme is based on the situation before 1993.
2. 110 000 pupils in special education not included.
Source: Authors.

Until August 1993, after primary schooling – at the age of 12 – pupils were allocated to four secondary education programmes: LBO (lower vocational education, duration four years), MAVO (lower general education, duration four years), HAVO (general education, duration five years) and VWO (pre-university education, duration six years) (Figure 2).

LBO is a preparatory branch of vocational education at lower level, a combination of general and pre-vocational education. The curriculum and the qualification level provided by these four programmes differed, although many schools organised a transition period, in which the curriculum was almost the same for all students of LBO/MAVO, MAVO/HAVO/VWO and HAVO/VWO. Selection and allocation have been based chiefly on pupils' learning abilities and on the outcomes of ability tests (in theoretical subjects). These programmes are described in Section 2, as are the programmes at upper level. Vocational education[2] at upper level consists of three different main streams:

– upper secondary vocational full-time education (MBO, consisting of long and short courses);

– the apprenticeship system (LLW); the off-the-job part of training is provided by BBO schools (day-release courses);

◆ Figure 2. **Diagram of the Dutch education system**

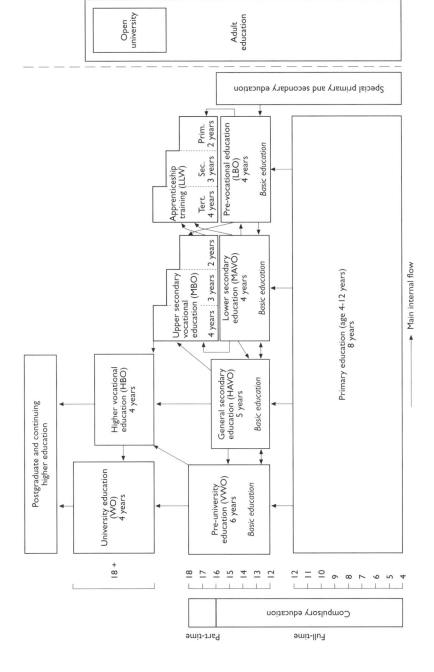

- higher vocational education at tertiary level (HBO, a programme at the same level as university but with a somewhat lower status).

This study focuses on upper secondary vocational education, which most students enter at the age of approximately 16. Considering the moment pathways start to differ, we also include:

- the allocation of pupils after primary schooling to lower stage: general education on the one hand (MAVO, HAVO, VWO) and pre-vocational education on the other hand (LBO);
- the relation with general education in terms of:
  - transition from initial programmes to vocational education (with a diploma of a general education programme);
  - transition from general to vocational education during programmes (without a diploma of a general education programme);
- vocational programmes at tertiary level (HBO), which in this study are perceived as the final programmes of pathways, either following after general education or as part of a vocational pathway.

Policy and reforms concerning VOTEC: visible in participation patterns?

Effects of policy measures are of course difficult to identify. Different developments, which may occur at the same time, are very likely to interrelate with policy measures taken. Moreover, many policy measures are in reality measures taken to reinforce changes already taking place. In this sub-section we refer only to major reforms which are likely to be reflected in participation patterns:

- implementation of the Secondary Education Act (1968), aimed at harmonisation of the lower stage of secondary education; according to the Secondary Education Act, all students should have the opportunity to receive both general and vocational education; general education was meant to precede vocational education and training;
- extensions of full-time and part-time compulsory education and training in the 1970s and 1980s;
- the transformation of lower secondary vocational education into pre-vocational education, which eventually led to a change of name in 1992: LBO became VBO;
- the introduction of short full-time MBO in 1979 (KMBO, duration two years), as well as up-grading and orientation courses, in response to the "gap" in the provision of educational programmes for drop-outs from lower secondary education, full-time upper vocational and technical education and

apprenticeship. In 1991, KMBO was integrated with regular MBO colleges, which until then only provided full-time courses lasting three or four years.

Focusing on the seventies and eighties implies that recent reforms, intended to harmonise the different modes of vocational training and enhance coherence of the rather fragmented system of VOTEC, will not be discussed here (see OECD, 1994).

Another important reform, not yet reflected in the figures on participation patterns, is the introduction of basic education (*Basisvorming*). In August 1993 a common curriculum was introduced within the first three years of lower secondary education: "basic education", which consists of a compulsory core curriculum covering 15 subject areas[3] clustered in teaching areas. The Ministry of Education and Science sets the core targets for each of the 15 subjects which schools are obliged to test. Students have to finish the core programme of basic education within a minimum of two years and a maximum of four. After two years of basic education, students are advised on the types of further education and training available.

The implementation of basic education implies that pathways start to differ after completion of basic education. However, combined pathways are possible at an earlier stage: combining basic education with (the upper years of) VBO, combining basic education with MAVO, HAVO or VWO. At which stage pathways will actually start to differ, is not yet clear. This might vary between schools, groups of students, etc. Pupils leaving primary schools nowadays are still advised to enter one of the four above-mentioned programmes at lower secondary level. Moreover, this advice is based on the same criteria as before.

Content of the study

Section 2 consists of a description of programmes in lower secondary (general and vocational), upper secondary vocational and higher vocational education. Patterns of participation and transition figures within lower secondary education and upper secondary education are presented. Finally the destination of the outflow from upper secondary education is described. In the third section the qualification level obtained before entering the labour market as well as the differences in labour market value of several programmes are reflected on. The fourth section describes the formal provision of pathways and indications of the actual tracks young people follow from the moment they enter secondary education till the moment they enter the labour market. In Section 5 some conclusions are drawn on changed patterns of participation over the years.

2. PROGRAMMES, PARTICIPATION AND TRANSITIONS

In this section, lower secondary education (first stage) and upper secondary education (second stage) are described. Students attend lower secondary education from age 12 to 16. Upper secondary education is entered by students aged 16, who in most cases have not yet completed the twelfth year of (part-time) compulsory schooling. In respect to each stage we first describe programmes and participation rates and finally statistics concerning transitions.

Lower secondary education: the general stream is favoured above the pre-vocational stream

Programmes

- *General education.* Lower secondary education covers MAVO and the first three years of HAVO and VWO. The upper classes of HAVO and VWO are part of upper secondary education. Many schools have transition periods of one or two years, consisting of a core curriculum for either MAVO/HAVO/VWO or LBO/MAVO. Counselling and orienting activities concerning further education and/or work are included in most schools for MAVO, HAVO and VWO.

  - MAVO: *lower secondary general education.* MAVO consists of four years of full-time education in which students take general subjects such as language, mathematics, physics, biology, etc. In the 1970s and beginning of the 1980s, a three-year programme existed as well. Examination after three years led to a MAVO C diploma, examination after four years to a MAVO D diploma. Many graduates from the three-year programme stayed on to obtain the D diploma. In the eighties this three-year programme was discontinued. A MAVO diploma offers access to Year 4 of HAVO (further general education) or full-time vocational education (MBO) or apprenticeship training.

  - HAVO: *general secondary education.* HAVO is a five-year full-time course in which 12-17-year-old students take general subjects. They enter the first year of HAVO after primary education or they enter Year 2 or 3 after a transition period. A HAVO diploma offers access to Year 5 of pre-university education (VWO) or the first year of higher vocational education (HBO). Transition from Year 3 (with certificate) to MBO or apprenticeship is possible.

  - VWO: *pre-university education.* VWO is a six-year full-time course preparing 12-18-year-old students for entrance to university or higher vocational education (HBO). VWO includes *athenaeum, gymnasium* and *lycée.* At *gymnasien,* students are also educated in classical languages; at the *athenaeum* and *lycée* this is optional. Students enter the first year after primary education or they enter Year 2 or 3 after a transitional period. Graduates from HAVO are allowed to enter the fifth year of VWO. A

VWO diploma offers access to HBO or university. Transition from Year 3 (with certificate) to MBO or apprenticeship is possible.

- *Pre-vocational education*: LBO (*called* VBO *since* 1992). LBO is a full-time course of four years, consisting of a combination of general and pre-vocational subjects. The content of the vocationally oriented subjects is still quite general and introductory. Students are not supposed to enter the labour market without further vocational training. LBO includes several programmes oriented towards distinct occupational fields, *i.e.* commercial, technical, home economics, agricultural and trade. Some schools organise a short practical training period in which students are able to get acquainted with the type of work in the occupational field of their choice.

For the technical, home economics and agricultural fields there is also an individualised programme tailored to students with more limited learning abilities: IBO. This programme includes fewer general subjects and the content of the programme is more practical. Admission to IBO is on the basis of a psychological report.

The LBO examination includes six subjects, two to four of which are vocationally oriented, and is set on three levels: B, C and D. D level is only possible for the general subjects (the fourth – lowest – level is the A level of the IBO). Diplomas at C and D level are comparable to the MAVO diploma. A diploma with at least three subjects at C level gives access to MBO and apprenticeship training (in the same occupational field as the examination subjects). A diploma with less/different subjects at C level offers access to upgrading and bridging courses within MBO and the apprenticeship system and to short vocational courses within MBO. LBO offers the opportunity to stay on an extra year after examination in order to prepare for a further examination (in some or all subjects) at a higher level of study and examination in additional subjects.

Experiments with modularisation and certification in the upper classes of LBO are aimed at crediting LBO graduates for prior learning, with respect to vocational subjects within MBO and the apprenticeship system.

Participation rates of 12-15-year-olds

Almost 100 per cent of the age group is enrolled in full-time education; less than 1 per cent do not follow any education (*i.e.* the 15-year-olds). Participation in general education at the first stage has increased over the years, whereas participation of lower vocational education has as a result decreased. Over two-thirds of each year group – except for 12-year-olds who still attend primary school – are involved in general education, whereas 25-30 per cent are involved in lower vocational education. A minor percentage of 12-15-year-olds attend special education for students with learning difficulties. Boys seem to attend special education more often than do girls. Overall, more boys than girls are enrolled in lower pre-vocational education. In deciding between MAVO and LBO, girls choose MAVO, which offers them better prospects than LBO; boys opt for the technical courses within LBO, which offer them the same or even better prospects than MAVO.

Transition from primary schooling to lower secondary education

Figure 3 shows the destination of pupils leaving primary school. Most pupils enter general education programmes – up to 73 per cent in 1992. The number entering special education has been slightly increasing over the years. For the most part it concerns pupils who were sent to special education at an early age. Various reasons explain the increase in participation in special education, *e.g.* features of the population, teaching methods at primary school, and the organisation of schools and central policy. It is speculated that nowadays primary schools advise pupils with learning and/or behaviour problems (and their parents) to enter schools for special education at an earlier stage, because staff are more capable of detecting problems/learning disabilities, and/or because staff are more aware of the opportunities special education can offer pupils with problems. Also,

◆ Figure 3. **Destination of pupils leaving primary school**
1975-1992

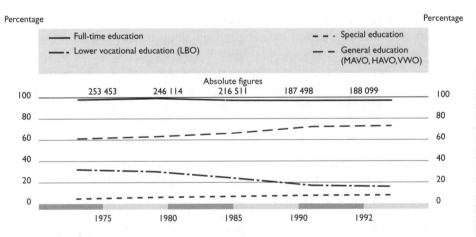

Note: Pupils not attending full-time education may attend part-time education (if they completed compulsory education or for special reasons), they may attend special classes for foreigners or other special provisions.
Source: Authors.

the pupil population of primary schools has become more heterogeneous. Recently, experiments have been implemented in which primary schools and those for special education co-operate to offer pupils support to keep them within primary school.

The outflow from lower secondary education

The outflow from programmes within lower secondary education can be divided into four groups of students: *i*) graduates from MAVO; *ii*) school-leavers of general educational programmes without a diploma – drop-outs from either Years 1 to 4 of MAVO or Years 1 to 3 of HAVO/VWO; *iii*) graduates from LBO; and *iv*) drop-outs from LBO.

Over the years, the proportion of qualified and unqualified outflow from the various programmes at lower stage has been relatively stable. Each year about 13 per cent of the total number of students enrolled in general education, graduate; about 82 per cent proceed with general education; and 5 per cent drop out from general education.

The total number of students in LBO has declined since the end of the 1970s to 220 000. The qualified outflow from LBO increased during this period from 12 per cent to about 28 per cent in 1992; the unqualified outflow remains stable at about 6 per cent, whereas the number of students proceeding with lower secondary vocational education has decreased to about 65 per cent in 1992. The drop-outs from general education outnumber those from vocational education. However, nearly all drop-outs from general education programmes continue with another programme, whereas this percentage is less for vocational courses. The proportion of graduates is higher in LBO than in general education, for the obvious reason that HAVO/VWO examinations take place only after five or six years and that the major part of HAVO/VWO students proceed with HAVO/VWO.

Upper secondary education: MBO and apprenticeship show an upward tendency

Programmes

As at the lower secondary level, there are two main streams within upper secondary education: general education programmes – the upper years of HAVO (Years 4 and 5) and VWO (Years 4-6), as described above – and upper secondary vocational and technical education at intermediate level.

This second stream covers a number of different programmes. The two main types of programmes are (full-time) MBO programmes[4] and those within apprenticeship training. Programmes within the apprenticeship system have been modular for several years already, also allowing for some flexibility. In the case of MBO, modular programmes are more recent and flexibility has not been achieved straight away (de Bruijn, 1992 and 1993). All programmes within upper vocational education and training are accessible only for students who have completed full-time compulsory education, while most programmes have additional entry requirements. Upper secondary vocational education and training includes the following programmes:

a) *Full-time vocational and technical education*

   − *Transition programmes* (duration maximum one year). These orienting and upgrading programmes are intended for students who, at the end of full-time compulsory education, do not have an (appropriate) diploma or certificate from lower secondary education, or have not yet chosen a particular occupational field. The full-time transition programmes include short practical training periods for orientation. They allow for tailoring to individual needs such as upgrading with respect to specific subjects, or orienting activities in a range of occupational fields. The programmes are modular and allow students to meet the entry requirements of the vocational programmes.

   − *Two-year vocational modular programmes.* The two-year full-time vocational courses consist of theory and practice at school, alternated with practical training periods at the workplace. Each course is modular, including theoretical learning, experimenting with practical skills, application of theory and practical skills at work placements, and reflecting on as well as assimilating these work experiences. One goal of this programme is not to make a traditional separation between "general" and "vocational" elements. Most (more "general") learning targets are therefore specified in terms of their meaning for the occupational field or job.

The short courses cover almost all occupational fields: the technical sector, agriculture, administration, trade, commercial services, social services and health care. The majority of the short courses focus on the technical sector, although nearly half of the short MBO population is enrolled in courses on administration and commercial services. There are no specific entry requirements except to have completed full-time compulsory education, although students without an appropriate LBO or MAVO diploma start with or follow alongside a transition programme. The vocational courses qualify students for operating at assistant level and are the full-time equivalent of the elementary courses within apprenticeship training. Successful completion allows students to enter the long full-time courses. If proceeding with a course within the same occupational field, students are allowed to skip some parts of the first two years of the long courses. Graduates are also allowed to enter advanced courses within the apprenticeship system in the same occupational field.

- *Three-year full-time vocational courses*. These programmes are mainly school-based. All courses include short practical training periods at the workplace, varying from once a year (*e.g.* within health care) to one short period during the whole course (*e.g.* administration courses). The three-year courses cover occupational fields within administration, social services and health care.

The major part of the course is oriented towards theory and practice of the occupational field the course qualifies one for. General subjects take some 10 per cent of the total amount of time and are covered in the first half of the programme. The courses are modular in a thematic sense – as is the case with the short courses –, integrating the different subjects and specifying most learning targets to "operations" within the occupational field. Entry requirements are a MAVO or LBO diploma with examination of relevant subjects, or a certificate stating transition to HAVO 4 or VWO 4. The courses qualify students for jobs at middle-management level, although most graduates start with craft jobs. They are allowed to enter higher vocational education in the same occupational field or to take advanced courses (tertiary level) within the apprenticeship system.

- *Four-year full-time vocational courses*. The four-year courses are the equivalent of the three-year full-time courses, covering occupational fields within the technical sector, agriculture, trade and catering/tourism. However, they include a full year of training on the job (either the third or fourth year), mostly offered at two or three different placements. Sometimes short orienting periods of training on the job are included as well. Some schools split up the full training year into shorter periods and offer a four-year alternated programme, for instance in agriculture and catering/tourism. The technical sector mostly provides a traditional programme of three years at school and one year training on the job. Some four-year courses are modular, integrating the various "general" and "vocational" subjects and learning targets.

Entry requirements are specified in the same way as for the three-year courses. Students receive a certificate if they pass the three years at school and a diploma if they complete the practical training year as well. Here also, the diploma qualifies them for jobs in middle management, though most graduates start with craft jobs too. Likewise, the certificate allows students to enter higher vocational education HBO in the same occupational field, and the diploma also gives graduates access to advanced courses (at tertiary level) within the apprenticeship system.

b) *Part-time vocational training*

- *Apprenticeship training.* The provision of courses within apprenticeship training includes transition programmes, elementary and advanced courses. Some programmes strongly resemble their equivalent in full-time education. Colleges that offer both modes of training integrate these programmes to a transition stage, allocating students to the adequate or preferred level, sector and mode of training. Other programmes (particularly those focusing on upgrading) take the form of a pre-programme as part of the elementary course.

The elementary courses vary from one to three years – depending on the particular occupational field and on the diplomas/qualifications already obtained – and qualify students for starting jobs at craft level. Entry requirements are an LBO C, a MAVO diploma or a certificate showing transition to either HAVO 4 or VWO 4. The diploma of the elementary courses allows trainees to enter the advanced courses.

The advanced courses (one to four years) qualify for jobs at both craft and executive level. Within some occupational fields, advanced courses are set at two different levels (also at tertiary level). Entry requirements are a diploma of the elementary courses or a certificate proving transition to MBO Year 3. Diplomas or certificates must relate to the same occupational field. Additional entry requirements for advanced courses at tertiary level are a diploma of advanced courses or an MBO diploma of long courses in the same occupational field. A diploma from the advanced courses (even at tertiary level) does not give access to higher education as do the full-time MBO courses. Further training is, however, possible within adult education, specific training courses, and s o on. Entrance to HBO is possible by passing an entrance examination.

The elementary and advanced courses are provided by 31 branch-specific national bodies which are responsible for the on-the-job part of the training. They also formulate attainment targets and course outlines – in the end set by the Ministry of Education and Science – and develop curriculum documents and teaching materials. Schools/colleges are responsible for the off-the-job part of the training (one day a week) and most of the transition programmes. Most courses are modular, integrating on- and off-the-job training. The off-the-job part of the training of, in particular, the elementary courses includes a limited general programme (social studies, language, physical education). The on-the-job part may have different formats: *a)* working/learning in one firm; *b)* working/learning in two or more firms; *c)* some of the on-the-job-part is done at a special training place, organised by several firms or established by a large firm; or *d)* combinations of *a*) and *c*) or *b*) and *c*). Trainees obtain a diploma only if they have attended both the on- and off-the-job parts of the training (including examination).

- *Day-release courses and non formal education.* Day-release courses (BBO) comprise various programmes, the major part concerning off-the-job training of apprentices and the transition programmes. Both types of programme can also be attended by youngsters who are not apprentices but are either employed or unemployed and who either want to or must (if they have not completed part-time compulsory education) enter a specific course for reskilling or upgrading or for other reasons. Without the on-the-job part of training, participation and examination of BBO does not offer a formal qualification.

Participation rates of 16-20-year-olds

At the age of 15/16, students have to attend another year of schooling for at least two days a week. After this year they are allowed to leave the education system. This might cause students to leave upper secondary education before completing a course. However, although dropping out of educational programmes at upper secondary level is more common than at lower secondary level, there is no evidence that large numbers of students/trainees leave programmes the moment they complete compulsory education. On the contrary, students/trainees tend to stay on.

Participation rates of 16-20-year-olds increased over the years, in particular in full-time education. Consequently, the number of students not participating in full- or part-time education has dropped. In 1979, 88 per cent of all 16-year-olds participated in full-time education, in 1990 this further increased to 93 per cent. The increase is shown most among the 16+, *e.g.* about half of all students aged 19 still participated in full-time education in 1990, whereas ten years earlier only about 30 per cent participated. Women leave (full-time) education at an earlier age than men, though this difference diminished over the years for the 16-18-year-olds.

One explanation for this difference is that full-time vocational programmes within MBO in administration, trade and social services (which are traditionally attended by women) are three-year courses, whereas the technical courses (traditionally attended by men) take four years. Also, there are less female than male repeaters. Women also hardly attend part-time education: technical courses make up the bulk of provision within apprenticeship training. Participation in part-time education is stable among the 16+: about 15 per cent of males and about 8 per cent of females are in part-time education.

Figure 4 shows the distribution of students over the various full-time education programmes within upper secondary education. At the age of 16 most students attend general education, both upper (HAVO/VWO) and lower secondary general education (MAVO; Years 1-3 of HAVO/VWO). Most students from 17 years up attend upper secondary education. Within post-compulsory education, vocational and technical education is favoured above general education.

Conclusions on participation of students aged 12-20

- At the age of 15 most students still attend programmes at lower secondary level, mainly general education. Over the years, the number of students (particularly girls) attending general education has increased at the cost of enrolment in vocational education at lower secondary level. This tendency is even stronger for the younger age group.

- At the age of 17 most students attend programmes at upper secondary level, the minority of whom attend general education. At upper secondary level, general education is not favoured above vocational education. However, the composition of the group of students in the upper years of HAVO and VWO programmes has changed over the years: the majority of students attending the upper years of HAVO/VWO have already been directed to HAVO/VWO programmes at lower secondary level (in Year 2 or 3 of lower secondary education), whereas in earlier days MAVO graduates tended to make up the biggest part of the upper classes of HAVO/VWO. Almost one-third of all 17-year-olds participate in MBO courses.

- The change at lower secondary level is not seen much at the upper secondary level as far as enrolment in general education is concerned. The former LBO students nowadays enter MAVO programmes, but at the upper secondary level enter vocational education again; former MAVO students already enter HAVO/VWO at lower secondary level and stay on at upper secondary level.

- The increased participation rates of the 16-20-year-olds are explained mainly by increased participation in upper secondary vocational education at intermediate level, in particular full-time MBO (see below). More graduates and drop-outs of programmes at lower secondary level who, in earlier years, left the education system, now proceed with education programmes, in particular vocational education. More graduates and drop-outs from upper secondary general education (in particular HAVO), who before left the education system, proceed with vocational and technical education as well. So among the increased number of students entering general education at the lower secondary level there seems to be a group of students who later on (have to) transfer to vocational education after all.

◆ Figure 4. **Participation of 16-20 year-olds in educational programmes[1]**

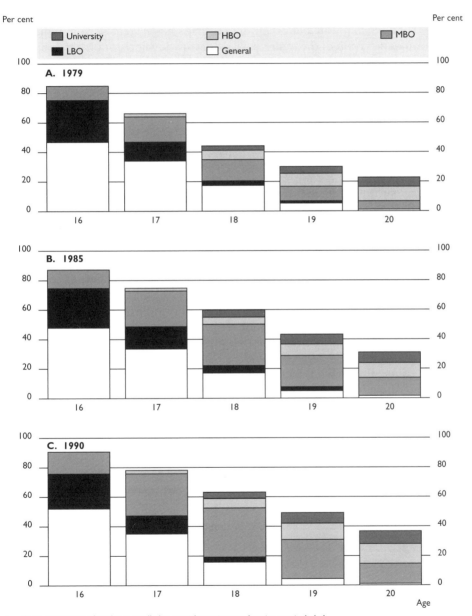

1. Small proportion of students enrolled in special or primary education not included.
Source: Authors.

Participation in vocational education at intermediate level

a)   Full-time vocational education: MBO

Over the years, participation in MBO courses has increased very rapidly. As was shown earlier, one of the main reasons for this development is that participation rates of youngsters of 16 years and older, in particular women, have in general increased considerably. This expanded participation (whether of drop-outs or graduates) can almost directly be translated in increased enrolment in MBO and is not accounted for by any growth in the total population (Table 1).

The increase in the number of MBO students is concentrated in the economics/administration sector. Enrolment in studies in social services and health care has relatively decreased (although it remained stable in absolute figures between 1970 and 1991). Participation rates for MBO are still increasing. In contrast to predictions for the 1990s that the total number of MBO students would descend because the relevant age group is in decline, it has recently turned out that the absolute decrease is much smaller than had been expected and that relatively the increase is continuing.

Increased participation rates and a preference for vocational and technical education is not a typical Dutch development. In all OECD countries, participation rates for this age group have increased, the explanation being today's more complex society, technological changes, and more complicated and sophisticated ways of labour organisation which call for broader, more specialised or higher qualifications. Also, the improved opportunities for all to attend education, and the increased welfare in general, could account for this. The greater participation in MBO courses may be typical of the Dutch situation and is related to the structure of the education system and the programmes provided. Although participation in higher education at tertiary level (*i.e.* higher vocational education, HBO and university) has grown as well (for HBO this may at least partially be caused by

Table 1.   **The increase in MBO participation**

	1970	1975	1980	1985	1987	1989	1991
Total population of 16-18 age group	670 000	711 000	760 000	739 000	737 000	664 000	588 000
MBO students: absolute figures	77 000	103 000	158 000	274 000	295 000	294 000	284 000
% of total age group	12	15	21	37	40	44	48
MBO graduates	24 000	32 000	35 000	51 000	56 000	59 000	57 000

Source: Authors.

increased MBO participation), the increase with regard to MBO seems to be rather spectacular. Moreover, participation in general education at upper secondary level remains relatively stable.

MBO has a rather unique position in the education system. Since the mid-1980s, MBO graduates have had a strong labour market position and good career prospects. They are qualified in two ways: for skilled work at intermediate level which is characterised as "clean work", and executive work with some organisational tasks and responsibilities. Although further education after MBO is not a major option, MBO offers clear opportunities to proceed with higher education (HBO), and some 10-30 per cent of the MBO graduates actually do so.

b)   Part-time education: apprenticeship training[5]

About 10-15 per cent of the 16-20-year-olds (mostly male) attend part-time education, which in most cases means apprenticeship training. After a sharp decline in the mid-1970s and the beginning of the 1980s (when there was a recession), a successful campaign to double the number of apprentice places was started in 1983. Compared to 1982, in 1987 twice as many new apprentices started with an elementary course, despite the fact that the qualified and unqualified outflow of LBO and MAVO (the traditional "sources" of the elementary courses) in absolute figures had been decreasing. At the end of the 1980s and beginning of the 1990s, apprenticeship training as a whole involved nearly half as many students as full-time MBO.

In Table 2, enrolment of apprentices during 1968-1990 is shown, based on a ministerial report (Ganga, 1992). It concerns apprentices who have an "agreement" or contract with an employer to follow apprentice training. Differences between several sources on participation figures are due to different perspectives and administrative difficulties. The figures shown are rather low.

Proportionately the number of trainees within the advanced courses increased much more than within the elementary courses: in absolute figures the number was multiplied by five, whereas the figure within elementary courses rose by 40 per cent. This indicates that more trainees (and employers) find further training necessary. The major part of these new trainees are qualified and unqualified LBO and MAVO school-leavers (who at a later point decided to continue training), drop-outs and a small number of graduates from full-time MBO and general education.

Women now participate more often in apprenticeship training than they did 20-25 years ago. Also, older employees (re-)enter apprentice training, elementary as well as advanced courses, more often. Since 1986 it has been possible to enter apprenticeship training even if an employee is over 27 years old. This also

Table 2. **Apprentices with an "agreement" and number of female apprentices**

	Elementary courses	(%)	Advanced training	(%)	Total	Index 1968 = 100	Participation of women	% of women in the total
1968	58 676	85	10 106	15	68 692	100	4 779	7
1970	61 593	85	10 512	15	72 105	105	6 230	9
1972	57 393	81	13 650	19	71 043	103	8 011	11
1974	53 649	79	14 343	21	67 992	99	11 144	16
1976	40 263	74	14 379	26	54 642	80	9 664	18
1978	50 574	79	13 243	21	63 817	93	10 563	17
1980	58 425	79	15 916	21	74 341	108	12 393	17
1982	43 443	70	18 253	30	61 696	90	11 832	19
1983	41 926	71	17 235	29	59 161	86	13 190	22
1985	56 023	76	17 911	24	73 934	108	17 422	24
1986	70 577	74	24 189	26	94 766	138	21 778	23
1987	75 799	72	29 741	28	105 540	154	24 499	23
1988	75 783	69	34 309	31	110 092	160	27 220	25
1989	77 936	66	40 584	34	118 520	173	29 802	25
1990	82 421	65	44 967	35	127 388	185	32 556	26

Source: Ganga (1992).

explains why, despite the increase in apprenticeship courses, enrolment in part-time education for the 16-20-year-olds has hardly increased.

Transition from lower to upper secondary education

Four groups of outflow from lower secondary education have been outlined. Changes in the destination of these four groups are now discussed.

– The most important change in the destination of MAVO graduates is a decrease in students proceeding with general education and an increase in graduates entering MBO: in only 15 years this last percentage for both boys and girls nearly doubled (from 38 per cent to 74 per cent in 1992), whereas the proportion proceeding with general education decreased from 31 to 18 per cent. The most recent popular destination for both boys and girls within MBO are courses on administration and commercial services. Amongst boys, technical courses are also popular, while girls prefer social services and health care (a manifest example of gender-segregation).

– In 1992, LBO graduates entered MBO more frequently than in 1975 (24 per cent in 1975 to 49 per cent in 1992). In contrast with MAVO graduates, the increase in LBO graduates entering MBO is partly accounted for by the increased participation in short MBO courses (in particular, girls). The short courses do, at least partially, attract LBO graduates who do not enter part-time training or apprenticeship training or long full-time courses. There-fore, the increase in graduates entering MBO has a different background for MAVO graduates than for (female) LBO graduates. Day-release courses have been the second most popular option over the years.

- The majority of drop-outs from lower secondary general education proceed with LBO and recently also short MBO. This situation has been quite stable over the years.

- The majority of drop-outs from LBO proceed with day-release courses and short MBO. Over the years, the destination of drop-outs from LBO has changed considerably (the relative number of drop-outs from LBO being quite stable at 5-7 per cent). There seem to be no persisting tendencies. In the 1970s, almost half of all drop-outs withdrew from the education system. Since then, the number leaving the system has fluctuated: in the mid-1980s it was at its lowest – 10 per cent – while in 1992 it was 40 per cent. The number of drop-outs entering apprenticeship training, day-release courses or non-formal education fluctuates severely, probably in reaction to the labour market prospects for this group with the lowest qualification level, and to experiments and projects within non-formal education. In the mid-1980s, apprenticeship took up over half of the drop-outs. From then on it has been more or less stable at 30 per cent. Short MBO seems to be an attractive programme, in particular for girls. From the moment it was introduced, the number of drop-outs entering short MBO rose to somewhat less than 20 per cent. There was a steady increase to 7 per cent in 1992 of drop-outs entering special education. The number entering general educa-tion (MAVO) declined steadily.

Qualification of students enrolled in vocational and technical education and training

The previous section focused on the transition from lower to upper secon-dary education. Here, figures on the qualification level of students within voca-tional and technical education and training at intermediate level are presented.

a) Apprenticeship

Table 3 shows that over two-thirds of the trainees were previously enrolled in LBO, mainly in technical courses. The number of MAVO graduates and of trainees from general education (mostly drop-outs) or courses within secondary vocational education is, however, increasing steadily.

The qualified outflow from elementary courses decreased from 15 837 in 1976 to 14 151 in 1985 and increased to 22 260 in 1991 (van der Velden and Lodder,

Table 3. **Apprenticeship: qualification of trainees enrolled in elementary courses**

	LBO	MAVO	Other[1]	Total (100%)
1972	92	4	4	56 157
1975	89	7	4	41 165
1978	86	9	5	54 134
1981	84	12	5	52 875
1984	79	13	7	49 543
1987	75	14	12	86 791
1989	67	13	20	93 629
1991	68	13	20	101 670

1. Includes trainees from general education (in particular, HAVO drop-outs, but also graduates); from MBO, either drop-outs from three- to four-year MBO courses or graduates from short MBO courses; trainees from other elementary courses, mostly unqualified.
Source: Authors.

1993). Although in the 1980s the number of trainees who completed the courses doubled, the success rate of courses within apprenticeship training seems to be rather low: overall only 50 per cent;[6] 20 per cent of the trainees who enter the courses drop out before finishing, mainly in the second year; some 30 per cent do not pass the exam. The success rate of the (elementary and advanced) courses varies between the national bodies, from 30 to 77 per cent. The success rate of the advanced courses is higher than that of the elementary. Explanations for this low success rate are various and are related to:

- the culture and tradition of the branch of industry or company as to the necessity and facilities for training – some branches and companies do not stimulate employees to participate in training programmes or to finish the course by taking an exam;
- (omissions in) regulations about recognition of diplomas obtained within the apprenticeship system being reflected in wages, promotion, etc.;
- in small- and medium-sized companies, "agreements" for apprenticeship training being broken more often than in large firms;
- the quality and procedure of training being controlled by different branches and companies;
- the way in which courses are organised by the national bodies of apprenticeship training – for instance, guidance, examination structure, co-operation between school and company, etc.;
- the content of courses and the methods of teaching/training.

As to the qualification of trainees enrolled in advanced courses within apprenticeship, about 22 per cent were previously enrolled in LBO (mostly technical courses) and about 10 per cent in MAVO; 3 per cent in HAVO, 6 per cent in MBO and over half of the trainees are graduates from elementary courses.

The majority of courses within the apprenticeship training are technical. That is the reason why most apprentices have a diploma from LBO technical courses and why 90 per cent of the trainees are male. In 1988, female apprentices represented only 6 per cent of the total number of those enrolled in technical courses, and in 1991 the percentage was still only 7.5.

b)   MBO (*full-time*)

The qualifications of students entering MBO are presented in Table 4. Approximately 50 per cent of those entering MBO had obtained a MAVO diploma at the end of the previous school-year, and one-third an LBO diploma. These percentages have not changed very much over the years. For girls, though, there seems to be a shift: in the 1970s, with the exception of 1975, the number of female

Table 4.   **Qualification of students entering MBO**

	1975	1980	1985	1990	1992
Total number	41 991	70 627	107 163	97 879	97 380
	Of which in the previous school-year (%): **Lower general secondary education**				
Without diploma	2	2	3	3	3
With MAVO diploma	61	49	46	44	41
	Upper general secondary education Upper years of HAVO/VWO				
Without diploma	3	3.0	3	3	4
With HAVO diploma	2	5.0	8	9	10
With VWO diploma	1	0.3	1	1	1
	Lower vocational education (LBO)				
	25	38	37	36	33
	No full-time education				
	5	3	3	5	6

Source: Authors.

students entering was approximately 30 000, with some 45 per cent coming from MAVO and 40 per cent from LBO.

The most remarkable changes in qualifications of students entering the various sectors within MBO are:

- *technical sector*: during the period 1980-1992 the percentage of male students entering technical MBO courses with a MAVO diploma dropped from 54 to 37 per cent; the number with an LBO qualification also dropped (33 per cent in 1980, 36 per cent in 1990 and 31 per cent in 1992); the figure for male students coming from HAVO/VWO and from outside (either part-time education/apprentice training or re-entering the education system) increased;

- *social services and health care*: the number of female students with a MAVO diploma rose from 38 per cent in 1980 to 47 per cent in 1990 and dropped to 44 per cent in 1992; the figure for those with an LBO diploma dropped from 53 to 41 per cent in 1990 and to 32 per cent in 1992;

- *administration/trade*: of the male students entering, the number with a MAVO diploma dropped from 64 per cent in 1980 to 48 per cent in 1992; those coming from HAVO/VWO and from outside the system increased in number; female students also showed more or less the same changes.

Interestingly, the percentage of students who entered MBO and were not enrolled in any education programme in the previous year has increased slightly over the years. In apprenticeship this tendency is even stronger. This indicates that adults re-enter education programmes, both full- and part-time, more frequently than before. This trend also shows that traditional statistics (which focus on transitions within full-time education) are less adequate to represent the actual qualification level of either those entering courses or the outflow from the education system at a given moment.

Changes over the years in the qualifications of students entering short MBO are given in Table 5 – from the second year, short MBO exists (1980) up to 1992. Although these short courses do not have entry requirements, over half of the students entering short MBO obtained a diploma, generally from LBO. At first glance it seems that short MBO attracts a different target group than was intended. However, graduates from LBO (or MAVO) may have a diploma at a non-adequate level or may have done examinations in subjects other than those required within MBO or apprenticeship training; or graduates may prefer a period of orientation before choosing a specific course. Both these objectives were formulated at the start as appropriate for short MBO.

The success rate of the MBO courses is relatively low, although not as bad as in the apprenticeship system. Dropping out in MBO courses is estimated between 30 and 35 per cent of the total number of students entering long MBO (Janssen,

Table 5. **Qualification of students entering short MBO courses**[1]

	1980	1985	1990	1992
Total (absolute)	2 927	14 019	17 627	21 011
	Of which in the previous school-year (%): **Lower secondary general education** MAVO or HAVO/VWO Years 1-3			
Without diploma	8	6	9	11
With MAVO diploma	13	14	12	13
	Upper secondary general education HAVO/VWO Years 4-6			
	2	1	2	1
	Lower vocational education (LBO)			
Without diploma	14	12	17	11
With diploma	58	57	44	43
	Other full-time education			
In particular, drop-outs, MBO long courses; and a minor % special education	–	8	9	12
	No full-time education			
	6	3	7	9

1.   Either transition programmes for orienting and/or upgrading and short two-year courses.
Source: Authors.

1990). Figures on the success rate of short MBO courses are not available.[7] A report by the inspectorate for vocational and technical education and adult education and training (1991/1992) gives a percentage of 35 of the total population enrolled in full-time transitional programmes who within one year proceed to a qualifying programme. The success rate of short vocational courses is estimated at 60 per cent (*i.e.* 40 per cent dropping out).

Outflow from upper secondary education to labour market or tertiary education

Students and trainees leaving upper secondary education either enter the labour market or follow educational programmes at tertiary level. A third option is part-time education. Moreover, a considerable number of students and trainees re-enter full- or part-time educational programmes after one or more years. Only

31 per cent of those who entered regular part-time education had been involved in full-time education during the previous year.

Programmes at tertiary level

Higher education covers higher vocational education (non-university) and university. Both programmes represent the final stages within the hierarchy of the education system. However, a difference in social status exists: university is still regarded as a somewhat "higher qualification level" than higher vocational education. Several programmes within HBO and university have a part-time variant.

a) *Higher vocational education* (HBO)

HBO consists of full-time, three- to four-year courses at a highly specialised and professional level covering all occupational fields. Entry requirements are a HAVO diploma, an MBO diploma from the long courses (in the same occupational field) or – in the case of the four-year MBO courses that include a one-year practical training period – MBO certificates (without the one-year practical training). Some HBO colleges have developed special – shorter – programmes for MBO graduates.

HBO programmes include theoretical education combined with practical training and on-the-job experience in the form of work placements. The knowledge level is comparable to that of university programmes although presentation is oriented rather towards practical application than research.

An HBO diploma gives access to university (short two-year programmes are developed for HBO graduates). However, to compete with universities, some HBO colleges (in joint operation with British universities) recently developed additional one-year master courses to allow HBO graduates to obtain a masters degree.

b) *University*

The first stage comprises four-year full-time courses. Those who have completed the course successfully receive a title ("Dr."). The second stage – with a very limited capacity – lasts either four years in which students work on their thesis, or two years for a first degree teaching qualification. This separation of university courses at a first and second stage was implemented in the mid-1980s to replace the five to six-year programmes. Graduates from VWO and HBO are allowed to enter university programmes.

Destination of the outflow from upper secondary education[8]

In this section we will focus on the outflow from MBO and the upper years of HAVO/VWO, divided into four groups of students: *i*) graduates from HAVO and VWO (65 000 in 1992); *ii*) drop-outs from Years 4-5 of HAVO and Years 4-6 of VWO (14 000 in 1992); *iii*) graduates from MBO; and finally, *iv*) drop-outs from MBO. An important difference between *ii*) and *iv*) is that *ii*) may not have a diploma at all.

- *Graduates from general education* (HAVO/VWO). Over the years, the proportion of graduates who have not entered further education and training has declined. In 1992 only 9 per cent (mostly girls) left the education system (19 per cent in 1975). The percentage of graduates proceeding to long or short MBO (HAVO graduates) has increased from 2 per cent in 1975 to 15 per cent; for university, from 17 to 30 per cent (VWO graduates). The increase in HAVO graduates entering MBO is a little surprising, because HBO is the next stage for HAVO graduates. If only HAVO graduates are considered, this tendency is even more evident: in 1975, 3 per cent of all HAVO graduates proceeded to MBO, 52 per cent to HBO; in 1992, 33 per cent proceeded to MBO, 50 per cent to HBO. The increase in the number of HAVO graduates who enter MBO instead of leaving the education system may be the combined effect of the tendency to choose vocational education after general education and the reorganisation of HBO in the 1980s; MBO graduates have a strong labour market position and the MBO programme seems to be perceived by HAVO graduates as less difficult than HBO.

- *Drop-outs from Years 4-5 of HAVO and Years 4-6 of VWO.* Over the years, both participation in part-time education and in MBO has increased; consequently, the number of drop-outs leaving the education system has decreased. Still half of all drop-outs left the educational system in 1992. Those who proceed with MBO programmes are not always unsuccessful students of HAVO/VWO: completion of at least the first three years of HAVO or VWO gives access to long MBO courses and HAVO/MBO courses. Thus, the increase in participation of MBO might have the same explanation as with graduates: the tendency to choose vocational education after a period of general education. A new phenomenon are drop-outs (16 per cent) from HAVO and VWO who re-enter VWO/HAVO on a part-time basis. Apparently, drop-outs prefer to try and obtain a HAVO or VWO diploma but do not like to proceed with youth education nor "discover" adult education.

- MBO *(full-time) outflow.* Most graduates and drop-outs from long courses within MBO leave the education system, although they may re-enter (another programme) again later. However, an increasing proportion of all graduates directly enter HBO, as is shown in Table 6.

The qualified and unqualified outflow from the various sectors within MBO is discussed here in more detail:

- *Qualified outflow from technical courses* (ca. 13 500 in 1992). The majority of graduates leave the education system. This applies to 1975 (81 per cent) as well as 1992 (68 per cent). A considerable proportion enter HBO (19 per cent, full- and part-time), usually in the same sector. In 1992, 8 per cent entered another MBO course within the same sector. Few graduates enter day-release courses/apprenticeship training. It seems that MBO and apprenticeship training (both elementary and advanced courses) are not sequential programmes. MBO graduates who receive further training do so on the job or within the company or follow special courses offered by regular colleges or private institutions.

- *Unqualified outflow from technical courses* (ca. 12 350). MBO students who have successfully completed the three school-based years of technical courses receive a certificate to enter HBO. This explains the relatively high percentage (16 per cent in 1975; 20 per cent in 1992) of unqualified students entering HBO. The majority of the drop-outs leave the education system (78 per cent in 1975, 57 per cent in 1992). In recent years a proportion of the unqualified outflow (12 per cent in 1992) entered day-release courses/ apprenticeship or other part-time education. This may be the effect of the efforts as from 1983 to strengthen the apprenticeship system.

- *Graduates from courses in administration/trade/commercial services* (ca. 18 700). Over the years, the number of graduates from this sector who proceed with further education has increased, in particular among male graduates. The proportion of graduates leaving education declined from 91 per cent in 1975 to 65 per cent in 1992. Almost all graduates who proceed with further

Table 6. **Destination of qualifed outflow from long MBO courses**

	1980	1985	1990	1992
Total (absolute)	37 810	61 641	59 168	51 408
	Of which in the next school-year (%):			
MBO	4	7	9	13
HBO	8	7	19	26
BBO	0	3	7	4
Other part-time education	9	5	3	1
No education	80	77	62	56

Source: Authors.

training enter HBO economics. Male graduates proceed with HBO much more often than do females. In recent years this difference has been almost 20 per cent. There is a rather strong distinction between the sexes, in that male students attend the more "high-status" courses in MBO preparing for calculating and management, whereas females focus on their traditional occupations of secretary/administration.

- *Unqualified outflow from* MBO *courses on administration/commercial services/trade* (ca. 14 900). Many drop-outs from long courses within MBO administration/ commercial services leave the education system. In 1975 this happened with almost all drop-outs but decreased to 73 per cent in 1992. Drop-outs proceeding with further education do so mainly in part-time education.

- *Graduates from courses in health care and social services* (ca. 14 475). Male graduates tend to proceed with further education, whereas females leave the education system. In 1992 almost half of all male graduates proceeded with further education, while 29 per cent of females did so. Male students seem to orient themselves more to the perspective of "high-status" courses than female students do. In comparison with the other MBO sectors, an interesting tendency occurred in the mid-1980s: a shift in percentages from "proceeding with another MBO course in the same sector" to "proceeding with HBO". In recent years more female graduates have proceeded with HBO; in 1992 the proportion of female graduates who proceeded with HBO almost equalled that of males. In-service training for health care (which could be defined as between MBO and HBO qualification levels) is not included in the definition of either full- or part-time education. However, it is well known that many (female) HAVO and MBO graduates (from long courses in health care) proceed with this type of training.

- *Unqualified outflow from* MBO *courses in health care and social services* (ca. 9 050). In-service training might well explain the relatively high number of drop-outs from courses in social services and health care who leave the education system. Only very recently have day-release courses become an attractive alternative for about 10 per cent of drop-outs. In 1975 almost all left the education system; in the 1990s this declined to 81 per cent.

- *Graduates and drop-outs from short and long agricultural courses* (ca. 4 900 and 1 250 respectively). The agricultural sector includes two-, three- and four-year full-time MBO courses. Thus, the outflow from agricultural courses consists of graduates or drop-outs from short and long courses. Most graduates and drop-outs from agricultural courses leave the education system (over 90 per cent in the 1970s, almost 80 per cent in the 1980s). Graduates who continue their training do so in HBO (same sector) or MBO (same sector). The same applies (to a lesser degree) for drop-outs. In-company training and training provided by private, commercial institutions is attended by many graduates, but this is not included in the statistics.

- *Outflow from short* MBO (ca. 7 500). Until 1990, more (male) school-leavers from short MBO entered day-release courses (in particular the apprenticeship system), with a minor percentage entering long MBO courses. Since that date, these percentages have been reversed: more school-leavers from short MBO courses, in particular women, have proceeded with long courses (over 25 per cent), and the proportion opting for an apprenticeship is still decreasing. The proportion leaving the education system declined from 88 per cent in 1975 to 63 per cent in 1992. However, it is uncertain whether this development will persist; it may be a short-term effect of the merger between short and long MBO institutions, whereas before 1990 many short MBO schools worked together with BBO schools. In future years, schools for off-the-job training of apprenticeships and MBO colleges will merge and transform into broadly based regional colleges for vocational education and training. These mergers may result in more equal proportions of long (full-time) MBO courses and apprenticeship training.

Entry into HBO

Over the years, the number of HAVO graduates entering HBO have been dropping in favour of MBO graduates, since the former are inclined to opt for long courses within MBO. Another important aspect is that 35 to 40 per cent of the students entering HBO had not been enrolled in full-time education the previous year. They may have come from part-time education, in particular from adult general education (HAVO/VWO) or part-time MBO. Possibly, the majority are re-entering full-time education after having left it for one or more years (Table 7).

Table 7. **Qualification of students entering HBO**

Full-time

	1975	1980	1985	1990	1992
Absolute figures (100%)	39 464	41 010	43 894	59 198	62 966
	Of which in the previous school-year (%)				
(diploma) MAVO	5	2	0.2	0	0
(diploma) HAVO	44	43	35	24	23
(diploma) VWO	10	18	20	15	12
(diploma) MBO long	6	10	13	22	26
HBO diploma	–	–	–	–	2
University[1]	–	–	–	–	7
No full-time education[1]	37	28	32	38	30

1. The majority are students without a university diploma who transfer to HBO.
Source: Authors.

3. TRANSITION TO THE LABOUR MARKET

In this section, figures are given on the qualification level of students and trainees leaving the education system and entering the labour market. Information on activities of school-leavers of all levels, one year after leaving school, is described. Finally, some reflections on the labour market value of educational programmes are presented, in particular with respect to short MBO, apprenticeship and long MBO.

Qualification level of outflow from education, available for the labour market

Most graduates and drop-outs from educational programmes who do not proceed with further training enter the labour market. Over the years, both age and qualification level of students entering the labour market have increased. In 1968 the age of school-leavers was much lower than in 1990: in 1968, 27 per cent of school-leavers were under 16, whereas in 1990 this was 0 per cent. In 1968, 18 per cent of the school-leavers were over 20 years old; in 1990 this percentage was 53. Furthermore, in 1968 one-third of school-leavers had a HAVO/VWO, MBO, HBO or university diploma, whereas in 1990 this was over two-thirds. The economic recession at the beginning of the 1980s and the high rate of youth unemployment may be additional reasons for the change in duration of education and in qualification levels obtained, students perhaps staying on and trying to achieve the highest possible qualification.

In 1984, youth and school-leavers unemployment reached record highs. Since 1991/1992, a minor economic recession has been developing. From 1992 onwards, unemployment figures have been rising again, initially with the unemployment figures of school-leavers.

Unemployment figures for young women are even worse than for young men, in general and in particular for school-leavers. The existing strong gender segregation with respect to vocational training courses – for occupational field rather than level – has been described earlier in this chapter. But if female school-leavers/graduates of MAVO/HAVO/VWO have less chance of facing long-term unemployment than males, those who have no diploma or only a MAVO diploma often enter dead-end, low qualified jobs, such as working in shops or in the catering or commercial services. After some years they are replaced by a new generation of young and cheap employees. Those HAVO/VWO graduates who enter the labour market without additional qualifications often enter jobs where they are obliged to participate in company- or branch-specific training, and thus they acquire a vocational qualification after all.

Labour market value of educational programmes

The recession at the beginning of the 1980s had negative consequences for graduates of all types of education, including vocational education at intermediate level. However, during the 1980s, prospects for graduates of vocational and technical education and training at intermediate level improved significantly.

Information[9] on the labour market position of various educational programmes in which occupational fields are distinguished is only available for recent years. Since the end of the 1980s, a large sample of school-leavers (graduates and to a lesser extent drop-outs) from secondary education have been questioned each year about their activities one year after leaving school. In Table 8 the available statistical figures of this yearly survey are presented.

Youngsters tend to proceed more and more with (full-time) education and training; hardly any from general education leave the system. School-leavers from short MBO (with the exception of those in transitional and orienting programmes) are the ones who proceed least of all with further education, their proportion being even smaller than that of long MBO. Some overall tendencies have been observed:

- The labour market value of general education (either at lower or upper level) was declining steadily during the 1980s. In fact, in the long term and with respect to the quality of job and career prospects, additional vocational education seems to be necessary.

- Drop-outs from LBO and short full-time courses within MBO who do not proceed with education or training are in the most vulnerable positions on the labour market.

- LBO graduates have a vulnerable position in the labour market, although the prospects for LBO technical-course students seem to have improved – but only if graduates enter additional vocational training. Graduates from short MBO seem to have even worse prospects than do LBO graduates.

- Vocational education at intermediate level (full-time and apprenticeship training) and HBO offer the best prospects of finding a job. In 1991 the labour market position and prospects of HBO technical-course and MBO economics/administration students were the best.

- Male students/graduates in general seem to enter the more high-status courses and jobs with good prospects, whereas females generally enter those with lesser prospects, causing women to run a higher risk of (long-term) unemployment and to have lower wages and fewer career prospects than most men. There is a clear situation of gender segregation according to occupational field, which works out very negatively for women.

Table 8. **Activities of school-leavers one year later**

Percentage

	Full-time education	Paid job	Apprentice/ in service	Unemployed	Military service	Other	Total (100%)
	LBO Graduates (all courses)						
1990	51	16	26	2	–	4	5 394
1991	58	12	26	1	2	1	8 621
1992	62	8	25	1	2	0	5 025
	Drop-outs (all courses)						
1990	25	32	24	6	–	13	365
1991	37	25	28	5	3	2	462
1992	44	26	21	4	2	4	197
	Short MBO Graduates (all courses)						
1991	20	41	21	5	12	1	1 442
1992	28	36	20	6	8	2	1 419
	Drop-outs (all courses)						
1990[1]	26	47	8	6	7	6	208
1991	22	41	16	6	14	2	311
1992	36	28	16	14	5	3	264
	Long MBO Graduates (all courses)						
1991	34	46	5	2	12	1	9 127
1992	38	42	6	3	11	1	6 018
	Drop-outs (all courses)						
1988[2]	21	45	21	5	–	8	1 568
1990[3]	37	41	7	3	8	7	1 345
1991	41	33	15	3	6	2	3 343
1992	45	28	16	3	5	3	2 059
	General education Graduates (all programmes)						
1991	88	6	4	1	1	1	19 265
1992	90	4	4	0	0	1	11 179
	Drop-outs (all programmmes)						
1991	76	13	7	1	2	2	737
1992	83	7	5	2	1	1	444

1. Administration only.
2. Social services.
3. Administration.
Source: Authors.

Differences in the labour market value of long MBO, short MBO and apprenticeship training

A representation of the qualifications of students who leave full-time education tends to underestimate the actual qualification level of the work force (Meesters, 1992). This is not only caused by the tendency to (re-)enter regular part- or full-time education but also by the widespread participation in other training schemes, whether in-company or by private institutions. In recent years the tendency and the necessity to participate in further (part-time, specific) training has grown tremendously (Tijdens, 1994). However, this increased participation in further training courses (upgrading and re-skilling) and the upgrading of qualifications does not – or to a much lesser extent – include those with the lowest qualification level (Onstenk *et al.*, 1992).

Since the 1980s, several studies have been carried out to investigate the labour market position and prospects of the various vocational programmes at intermediate level (Geurts and Hövels, 1983; Imhoff *et al.*, 1985; Diederen, 1987; Hoeben, 1992). Some results from studies comparing short MBO to elementary courses within apprenticeship training show that:

- Graduates from apprenticeship training are less likely to lose their jobs than graduates from short MBO. However, if former apprentices become unemployed they do not find jobs more quickly than graduates from short MBO.

- Graduates from short MBO have lower wages and a lower job level than graduates from apprenticeship training.

Of course, these conclusions must be taken in the context of the economic recession at the beginning of the 1980s, short MBO being a new programme relatively unknown to employers. The apprenticeship system was under pressure. Owing to a shortage of places, only the "best" (with a diploma at the highest level of LBO) were allowed to enter, leaving the remaining students to enter the short MBO. During the 1980s the capacity of apprenticeship training was expanded, allowing more school-leavers from lower secondary education to enter.

Results from studies comparing long MBO to advanced courses in apprenticeship training show that:

- Both types of graduate find employment easily after graduation. The job (level and occupational field) of graduates from apprenticeship training links up better with the course than does the job of MBO graduates, who often start with jobs at a lower level; this may be due to the fact that the latter are new in the labour market.

- The mobility during the working career of MBO graduates is higher; furthermore, their position (level) moves to a higher level more quickly. However, because they start at lower positions, eventually (after seven years) there are few differences in the position of MBO graduates and graduated apprentices: the former move from craft jobs to middle management, the latter to executive jobs involving some management tasks. Moreover, the position of graduated apprentices is better than the position of MBO graduates, owing to the fact that they are older and have a longer work experience.

These results refer to the early and mid-1980s as well, a period of economic recession which had severe effects on entrants in the labour market.

One of the most important conclusions of these studies is that the various courses are oriented towards different segments of the labour market because of the nature of the courses themselves and the training regulations. Full-time MBO courses focus on broader occupational fields than do apprenticeship courses. Since the major part of training takes place at the workplace, apprenticeship courses also stress "technical" skills more than full-time courses. Moreover, small- and medium-sized firms and manufacturing companies more often opt for apprentices, whereas large firms choose MBO graduates, especially from the long courses.

Full-time MBO and apprenticeship training seem to be two rather separate educational pathways to professional competence. Transition[10] from one to the other does not occur much; in particular, transition from apprenticeship training to full-time MBO does not occur. Transition from full-time MBO – in particular, drop-outs from the long courses and leavers from the short MBO courses – is seen more frequently.

4. PROVIDED PATHWAYS VERSUS ACTUAL TRACKS

In the previous sections we described some of the actual tracks that young people follow from the moment they start with vocational education (or with secondary education) until the time they enter the labour market. Here, we will try to sketch the formal provision of pathways and the actual tracks young people follow, as shown through flow data provided by cohort studies. However, it will still be only fragmented information, since relevant studies are not available.

Provision of pathways: three options in the Netherlands

In Dutch secondary education three main types of pathways can be observed:

1. *vocational*: LBO → MBO/apprenticeship training → HBO;
2. *general educational*: MAVO → university; HAVO → VWO → university; MAVO → HAVO → VWO → university;

3. *combined*: from general to vocational education, *e.g.* from MAVO to MBO or the apprenticeship system; from HAVO to HBO.

This chapter focuses on 1 and 3. Within each type of pathway specific lanes are provided, *e.g* drop-outs who are without an LBO diploma, but have completed full-time compulsory education, are allowed to enter transition programmes. Afterwards, they are offered the same options as students with an LBO diploma. Within the combined pathways it is possible for LBO graduates to enter MAVO and afterwards to continue the general education programme; or, if a student has successfully completed three years of HAVO/VWO, to have the same options as MAVO graduates. Comparing the "merits" of vocational pathways and combined pathways, one observes that:

– General education (at age 12) offers students more options for further study than does starting with pre-vocational education.

– Combined pathways of general and vocational education are mostly shorter than vocational pathways.

– Vocational pathways have limited access to general pathways, with the exception of the lower secondary stage (from LBO to MAVO). In nearly all cases, general pathways lead to vocational programmes (with the exception of a general educational pathway – Type 2 above). During the 1980s this notion of completing educational pathways with a vocational qualification became very strong amongst policy makers as well as with parents and students.

Figure 5 shows these various options. In general, LBO graduates with a diploma at A- or B-level first enter transitional programmes, either part- or full-time. LBO graduates with a diploma at C-level are allowed to enter MBO or apprenticeship training directly, at least within the same occupational field. They may also enter transitional programmes first (whether for orientation or for further upgrading). In general, most transitions within vocational education and training are only allowed between courses within the same occupational field; if not, a transitional programme is required.

Actual tracks chosen

The ideal source to demonstrate (changing) patterns of participation would consist of flow data on the basis of cohort studies following students through the education system and beyond. In the Netherlands, four nation-wide cohort studies were conducted by the Central Bureau of Statistics (1964/65, 1977, 1983 and 1989). However, they focus exclusively on full-time education, and vocational

◆ Figure 5. ***Various options of pathways***

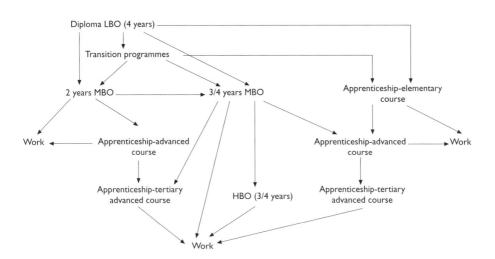

Source: Authors.

education at intermediate level is poorly represented. Some indications from the secondary education results of these cohort studies are that:

- Nearly half of the students do not follow the formal pathways as designed: 21 per cent drop out, 12 per cent obtain a diploma through an indirect track, and some 15 per cent either drop out from MBO or HBO or obtain a diploma from MBO, HBO or university through an indirect track. This percentage increases further if we take as a criterium the current government policy, which states that every school-leaver should have at least a vocational qualification at elementary level in the apprenticeship system. This criterium indicates that graduates from (at least) LBO and MAVO should pursue further (vocational) education or training. At least a proportion of those who obtained a secondary education diploma through a direct way (32 per cent of the cohort) will not do so. There are strong indications that the majority of students/trainees do not follow pathways as they are formally designed in the Dutch, rather "streamed", system of education and training.
- Between 1977 and 1983, the drop-out rate from the first school years within lower secondary education, as well as that from the upper years of secondary education, decreased.

– More graduates proceed with further education: 30 per cent of those with an LBO diploma are still enrolled in full-time education (in particular MBO); 65 per cent of those with a MAVO diploma are still enrolled in full-time education (in particular MBO); 64 per cent of those with a HAVO diploma are still enrolled in full-time education (in particular HBO); and finally, 82 per cent of those with a VWO diploma are still enrolled in full-time education (either HBO or university).

– The proportion with an MBO, HBO or university qualification probably rises by 5-10 per cent (it is, however, too soon to compare).

The longer tracks through the education system are not always the free choice of students: segregation according to gender, socio-economic and ethnic background still exists and is present even as early as in the pre-school period. Given this segregation, some tracks may suit certain groups better than others. Whereas girls fail in technical courses at LBO level (for instance, in a male-dominated culture at school), they may be "strong" and "old" enough to succeed at MBO level if they have been successful in general education. Whereas some children from "lower-class" parents or migrant children fail if they enter *Gymnasium* (in another place/street than the school of all their friends), they may succeed by starting with a transitional period in general education followed by HAVO and HBO, and then enter university after all.

Moreover, a long track in which sequential programmes are taken step by step from "low-level" to "high-level" programmes, in which every programme is successfully passed, may have a positive connotation for individuals and their families and friends. A track in which youngsters immediately aim at the "highest" level programme and fail, resulting in transition to a "lower-level" programme (or to dropping out), often has more negative connotations and the final qualification may be "lower" than the tracks chosen by more "careful" youngsters. Thus, the logic behind the various tracks that are different from formal pathways might be more rational than they may seem at first glance.

Put bluntly, the formal provision of educational pathways seems to be based on "chameleon-like" youngsters, who are thought to fit into the programme they are advised to enter at the end of primary school on the basis of the ability-test results. In other words, the basic assumption of the education system appears to be that students differ only in ability, with the educational conditions of programmes and pathways, the content, organisation, ways of teaching and learning, and competencies of teachers, bearing no influence. In reality, individuals differ in many respects, and educational programmes and pathways very often disregard these differences or may even be counterproductive in some cases.

5.   CONCLUSION

The statistics and results from research presented in this chapter are not fully adequate and complete, in particular with respect to the actual tracks youngsters follow through vocational education and training. Nevertheless, some conclusions can be drawn:

- Within a rather short period of time, participation rates in education of youngsters of 16-18 years old have risen tremendously: nearly all 16-year-olds participate in either full- or part-time secondary education. In 1979, 34 per cent of all men aged 18 and 55 per cent of women aged 18 did not attend regular education, whereas in 1990 these percentages decreased respectively to 19 and 27 per cent.

- At lower secondary level most students attend general education, at upper secondary level, a majority attend vocational education. The increased participation rates of the 16+ group is nearly entirely due to greater enrolment in vocational education and training at intermediate level.

- Most young people start with general education and transfer to vocational as the final stage of their way through the education system. The combined tracks of general and vocational education are much more frequent now than they were before.

- The qualification level of school-leavers has risen rather spectacularly: in 1968 one-third had a HAVO/VWO, MBO, HBO or university diploma, whereas in 1990 this was over two-thirds. Furthermore, the proportion of youngsters who obtain a vocational qualification after lower secondary or upper secondary general education has been growing very fast over the last 15 years.

- Dutch provision of educational programmes and pathways is rather hierarchical and streamed, with fairly rigid lines of progression. However, the majority of youngsters do not follow these "prescribed" pathways. They tend to choose their own tracks through the system. Although these are very often not completely voluntary because of segregation according to gender, socio-economic or ethnic background, it would seem to be unrealistic to design an education system with rather streamed lines of progression for youngsters to follow as such.

- This deviation from designed educational pathways not only goes for vertical progression but also for horizontal transitions (either from full- to part-time or vice versa or from one occupational field/course to another). With respect to VOTEC, the educational tracks youngsters take are not characterised by entering one particular stream (relating to a certain occupational field or mode of training) and progressing only within this one. Students transfer from full- to part-time education or from one course to another, even crossing occupational boundaries. The design of the Dutch system of vocational education and training, however, is based on the assumption that young people will stay in their "stream". This causes many difficulties for those who want to transfer from one stream to another, sometimes having to start all over again. Furthermore, the horizontal and vertical segregation of Dutch vocational and technical education does not take account of the dynamics of current occupational practice, economy and society.

– Even in the transition from education to work, in mobility and progression during working life, youngsters and adults do not follow streamed and rigid tracks. They cross occupational boundaries several times during their working lives, both horizontally and vertically. Educational as well as occupational pathways can be very irregular.

6.   RECOMMENDATIONS TO POLICY MAKERS

Creating institutional versatility, which implies youngsters being able to take any course in any educational institution, and flexibility of educational programmes, which implies credit for prior learning and qualifications, appears to be a requirement for training and education for the 16+ age group. In fact, institutional versatility and flexible educational programmes, geared to individual needs and characteristics, are necessary conditions also for lower secondary education (for the 12-16-year-olds) if the aim is to provide the best opportunities for all youngsters to obtain a qualification that offers the prospect of work and participation in society. The present harmonisation of upper secondary vocational education and training and adult education should therefore be more rigorously pursued by removing all obstacles to transfer and crossing of existing boundaries.

NOTES

1. This summary is based on an extensive country study, *Changing Pathways and Participation in Vocational and Technical Education and Training in the Netherlands* by E. de Bruijn, undertaken for the Ministry of Education and Science. It is available in English from the SCO-Kohnstamm Institute for Educational Research, Amsterdam, Publication No. 393, May 1995, 162 pages (Tel. 31 20 5550 300).

2. In the Netherlands the term "vocational education" is used for all types of vocational education, regardless of level; technical education does not refer to an advanced level of vocational education but refers to vocational programmes that prepare for jobs in industry (*i.e.* metal industry, building, etc.). For comparison with other countries, pre-vocational education (IBO), short MBO courses and the elementary courses within the apprenticeship system and non-formal education could be defined as "vocational education"; higher vocational education (HBO) could be defined as "technical education"; the advanced courses within the apprenticeship system and the long MBO courses are a mix of "vocational" and "technical" education.

3. Dutch, English, French or German, mathematics, physics and chemistry, history, geography, biology, information technology, economy, technology, home economics and care, arts, physical education.

4. Since August 1993, full-time courses have revised their attainment targets and course outlines, the major change being that courses are divided into blocks (modules) more or less integrating several subjects, that allow for certification.

5. With respect to part-time education, exact figures are less detailed as in the case of full-time MBO. Part-time education includes general education (MAVO, HAVO, VWO) for adults (16+); part-time MBO, HBO or university for adults (18+); day-release courses and non-formal education, in particular the off-the-job part of apprenticeship training. In 1990 about 340 000 students participated in regular part-time education, the majority of whom were involved in day-release courses (especially male) or VWO/HAVO/MAVO (especially female).

6. The majority of apprentices already have a diploma and at least half of them no longer attend an educational body. Some figures for comparison: the success rate of (full-time) MBO is 60 to 65 per cent; the success rate of part-time MBO is 20 per cent for courses in the technical sector and 50 per cent for courses in economics/administration/commercial services.

7. Short-MBO graduates receive a certificate for the programme units completed. The statistics make no differentiation between certificates and diplomas.

8. The outflow from the apprenticeship system and other part-time programmes is not included because of the quality of available statistics, and – more importantly – because the majority of those involved in part-time education are adults (only 5 to 10 per cent of the 16-18-year-olds attend part-time education). Nearly all trainees who leave day-release courses leave education completely.

9. See the report mentioned in Note 1 for detailed information on each of the educational programmes distinguished.

10. If transition from one pathway to another occurs, it often implies that already obtained qualifications and competencies are hardly recognised, and consequently trainees/students have to start all over again. To a lesser extent this also goes for transition from the short MBO courses to long MBO; graduates from these short courses often do not get credit for prior learning, or they are allowed to skip only a few elements of the long MBO courses.

GLOSSARY

BBO	Off-the-job part of apprenticeship training (day-release courses)
HAVO	Upper general secondary education (5 years)
HBO	Higher vocational education (tertiary level)
LBO	Lower secondary vocational education (4 years)
MAVO	Lower secondary general education (4 years)
MBO	Upper secondary vocational full-time education (long and short courses, the latter formerly known as KMBO)
VWO	Pre-university education (6 years)

BIBLIOGRAPHY

BRUIJN, E. de (1992), *Modularisation in Dutch Vocational Education and Training* (SCO-rapport 302), SCO-Kohnstamm Institute for Educational Research, University of Amsterdam.

BRUIJN, E. de (1993), "Equivalence of general and vocational education in the Netherlands", in S. Manning (ed.), *Equivalence of General and Vocational Education. 5 Country Studies*, WIFO, Berlin.

BRUIJN, E. de and HOWIESON, C. (1995), "Modular vocational education and training in Scotland and the Netherlands: Between specificity and coherence", in *Comparative Education*, Vol. 31, No. 1, pp. 83-100.

Centraal Orgaan Regionale Organen (CORO) (1988-1992), *Statistische jaargegevens van de regionale organen voor het leerlingwezen over de jaren 1987-1991* (Statistical Details of the Regional Bodies for Apprenticeship Training for the Years 1987-1991), CORO, Houten.

Central Bureau of Statistics (CBS), *Overgangen binnen het onderwijs en intrede in de maatschappij: onderwijsmatrices 1975, 1980, 1985, 1990, 1991 en 1992* (Transitions within Education and Entrance to Society: Educational matrices), SDU, The Hague.

Central Bureau of Statistics (CBS), *Schoolloopbanen en herkomst van leerlingen in het voorgezet onderwijs. Deel 4: cohort 1977, schoolloopbanen en bereikte onderwijsniveaus: stand na 12 jaar* (Educational Careers and Achieved Qualifications of the 1977 Cohort after 12 Years), SDU, The Hague.

Central Bureau of Statistics (CBS), "Onderwijs en arbeid 1992" (Education and work 1992), in *Mededelingen CBS*, No. 7936, SDU, The Hague.

DIEDEREN, J. (1987), *Beroepsloopbaan na KMBO of BBO* (Working Career after KMBO or BBO), ITS, University of Nijmegen.

DIEDEREN, H.M.N. (1993), *Schoolloopbanen en herkomst van leerlingen bij het voortgezet onderwijs. Deel 2: cohort 1982, schoolloopbanen en bereikte onderwijsniveaus: stand na 7 jaar* (Educational Careers and Achieved Qualifications of the 1982 Cohort after 7 Years), CBS, Voorburg/Heerlen.

GANGA, V. (1992), *Deelname, uitval en rendement van het leerlingwezen* (Participation, Drop-out and Success Rate of Apprenticeship Training), Ministry for Education and Sciences, Directie BVE, Zoetermeer.

GEURTS, J. and HÖVELS, B. (1983), *Het kort-MBO tussen aanbod en vraag. Een onderzoek naar de kwantitatieve aansluitingsproblematiek van schoolverlaters van LBO en MAVO* (Short MBO between Supply and Demand), ITS, University of Nijmegen.

HOEBEN, W.Th.J.G. (1992), *Beroepsonderwijs en arbeidsmarkt* (Vocational Education and the Labour Market), RION, University of Groningen.

IMHOFF, E. van, KUIJPER, H.A.M., HAEN, M.M.C.M. and RITZEN, J.M.M. (1985), *Het School – en Beroepsloopbaanonderzoek KMBO BBO* (A Study on the Educational and Working Careers of Short MBO Students and Apprentices), SVO-reeks, Swets and Zeitlinger B.V., Lisse.

JANSSEN, A.T.H. (1990), *Het interne rendement van het middelbaar beroepsonderwijs: een literatuurstudie* (The Internal Results of Upper Secondary Vocational Education: A literature study), Ministry of Education and Science, Zoetermeer.

MEESTERS, M.J. (1992), *Loopbanen in het onderwijs en op de arbeidsmarkt. Verticale en horizontale differentiatie in het voortgezet onderwijs: oorzaken en gevolgen voor de arbeidsmarktpositie van Nederlandse jongeren* (Educational Careers and Labour Market Positions), ITS, University of Nijmegen.

OECD (1992), *High-Quality Education and Training for All,* Paris.

OECD (1993), *Education in OECD Countries. 1988-1989/1989-1990: A compendium of statistical information,* Paris.

OECD (1994), *Vocational Training in the Netherlands: Reform and innovation,* Ministerie van Onderwijs en Wetenschappen and OECD, Paris.

ONSTENK, J., FELIX, C. and GIJTENBEEK, J. (1992), *Scholing lager opgeleide werknemers* (Training of Semi-skilled Workers), A and O Adviescentrum Opleidingsvraagstukken, Bunnik.

TIJDENS, K. (1994), *Arbeid en zorg: maatschapp* (Labour and Care: A partnership), Organisatie voor Strategisch Arbeidsmarktonderzoek (OSA), The Hague.

VELDEN, R. van der and LODDER, B. (1993), *Alternative Routes from Vocational Education to the Labour Market. Labour market effects of full-time vs. dualized vocational education,* ROA, University of Limburg, Maastricht.

QUEBEC

by

Lili Paillé, Ministry of Education

I. THE EDUCATION SYSTEM

The education system in Quebec offers a wide variety of educational programmes and services, from kindergarten to university.

Primary and secondary education

Primary education usually lasts six years and secondary education five years. Children enter primary class I at six years old, the cut-off point being I October of the school year in progress. Kindergarten is not compulsory for 5-year-olds, but almost all children of that age attend. The year of the pupil's 16th birthday is the final year of compulsory school attendance.

The language of instruction of primary and secondary education is French or English. Most pupils who are taught in English are from families where a parent was educated in English at primary level. Public education is administered by school boards, made up of representatives elected by those served by the board. These boards are responsible for appointing the staff needed for the provision of educational services. In 1992-93, 84 per cent of the school boards' income was provided by the Government of Quebec, with local taxation accounting for a further 11 per cent and other sources the remaining 5 per cent. Four per cent of primary and 15 per cent of secondary pupils are educated at private schools. Approximately 53 per cent of the income of subsidised private schools are provided by the State. Primary and secondary education is also offered by a number of state schools outside the network, which are dependent upon the Government of Quebec or the Canadian Government.

Secondary education diplomas are awarded by the Minister of Education to pupils who meet the required standard set by him. The secondary school leaving diploma gives access to college education, whilst the secondary school vocational diploma usually leads to the job market but also gives access to college education. Harmonisation of the educational services offered to young people with those of adults is a feature of Quebec's education system. The qualifications which may be obtained in adult education are of comparable value to those obtained by young people.

College education

College education lasts two years for students on pre-university courses and three years for those receiving technical training, essentially geared to access to the job market.

A student may study in the language of instruction of his choice. Public college education is provided by CEGEPs (*collèges d'enseignement général et profession-nel* – general and vocational colleges), run by councils made up of representatives of different interest groups, including members of the community, parents, students, staff and administrators of the college. In 1992-93, 88 per cent of CEGEPs' income was provided by the Government of Quebec. Twelve per cent of college students attended private institutions, which received 65 per cent of their income from the State. College education is also provided by a number of schools which are not dependent upon the Ministry of Education but on other ministries or bodies.

The diploma of collegial studies is awarded to students by the Minister of Education on the recommendation of the college they have attended. Qualifications are also gained for following short programmes, *i.e.* certificate of collegial studies, diploma of advanced college studies, and attestation of collegial studies, which are issued by the colleges themselves. As from the autumn of 1994, however, two diplomas only will be awarded for college study: a state diploma, *i.e.* the diploma of collegial studies, and an institution diploma, *i.e.* the attestation of collegial studies.

University education

Quebec has both English- and French-language universities, and a student is free to choose where to study. University education is divided into three study cycles, the first leading to a bachelor's degree, the second to a master's and the third to a doctorate. Universities also award certificates, diplomas and attestations which recognise the successful completion of short programmes. In 1992-93, 61 per cent of university expenditure were financed by the Government of Quebec.

The Ministry of Education

The role of the Ministry of Education varies according to the type of education. At primary, secondary and college levels it lays down a regulatory framework for teaching methods, employment relations, and funding. At university level it ensures the advancement of teaching and research by providing the necessary resources for institutions to operate and develop, whilst respecting their autonomy and promoting consultation between partners [see Ministry of Education (MEQ), *Education indicators*, 1994, pp. 12-13)].

2.   VOCATIONAL TRAINING IN SECONDARY EDUCATION

Vocational training in secondary education is administered by 97 school boards, in 183 *points de service*, and also by a number of private schools.

Features of vocational training in secondary education

Reform of vocational training has been under way since 1987-88. Under the old system the short programme was offered to 3rd and 4th grade secondary pupils and the long programme to 4th and 5th grade secondary pupils.

The new system also has two vocational streams but in both cases the pupil must have a more comprehensive basic education and be 16 years of age. Any pupil who has obtained a secondary school leaving diploma or credits at secondary 4th grade in his mother tongue, a second language, mathematics, and moral or religious education may enrol in the one- or two-year study programmes leading to the secondary school vocational diploma (DEP). Any pupil who has obtained credits at secondary 3rd grade in his mother tongue, a second language and mathematics may enrol in the study programme leading to the secondary school vocational certificate (CEP) after two years' full-time training. Pupils having obtained the DEP or CEP may then specialise if they so wish and study for an attestation of vocational specialisation (ASP).

In addition, assessment of prior learning has been established for adults as a new form of access to vocational training. General education is tested and other specific factors assessed.

Training sectors

The vocational training courses offered cover 23 sectors. A hundred twenty-two study programmes lead to the DEP, including 37 in English; 54 study programmes lead to the CEP, of which 12 are in English; and 50 lead to the ASP, with 11 in English. The sectors include:

01   administration, commerce and secretarial studies
02   agricultural techniques

03	food, hotel management and catering
04	applied arts
05	wood and allied materials
06	applied chemistry and the environment
07	construction
08	technical drawing
09	electrical engineering
10	motor-driven equipment
11	mechanical engineering
12	forestry, timber and paper
13	printing/publishing
14	industrial maintenance
15	construction engineering
16	metallurgy
17	fishery
18	textile production and the clothing trade
19	health and social services
20	civil defence
21	beauty therapy
22	transport
23	civil engineering and mining.

Courses also exist for which a school transcript, a recognition of achievement or a statement of marks are awarded, but which do not lead to the CEP, DEP or ASP. This category includes training courses in health and safety on building sites, courses relating to sites, equipment and organisations for construction workers, and refresher courses for staff in the Quebec municipal fire department. Usually funded by companies, these courses are not recognised by the Ministry of Education and consequently are not accounted for in the statistics.

School/industry relations

Since the beginning of the reforms instituted, collaboration has existed between school and industry for revisions of programme content, participation in co-operative education committees, donation of equipment, and financing of teaching materials. This collaboration has been broadened to include the management of educational institutions, the award of scholarships, and participation in the Canadian Skills Competitions. The accent is now on developing alternating classroom/workplace training, longer periods of work experience, and arrangements for partnerships of all kinds.

Enrolment in vocational training

Enrolment trends

Over a six-year period, enrolment in vocational training financed by the Ministry of Education and calculated on the basis of full-time equivalents fell by 19.4 per cent, from 38 845 to 31 300. The significant drop in the student sector (73.5 per cent) was partially offset by a rise of 99.6 per cent in adult enrolment. In 1991-92, only 15.7 per cent of enrolment for the DEP, CEP and ASP were in the student sector (Table 1).

Breakdown by training sector

Administration, commerce and secretarial studies alone account for almost one-third (32.6 per cent) of total enrolment and are dominated by women (85 per cent). Health and social services is another popular sector also mainly made up of women.

The most popular choice for men is motor-driven equipment and electrical engineering, where they account for 96.6 per cent and 95 per cent of enrolment respectively.

The three sectors which are least popular are applied chemistry and the environment (115 entrants), civil engineering and mining (191) and transport (195) (see Table 2).

Adult enrolment

Enrolment in the adult sector rose from 101 786 in 1980-81 to 236 164 in 1991-92.[1] At that time this represented 2.7 per cent of the population aged between 15 and 49. The share of adults per year enrolled in some form of continuing education keeps growing.

The profile of adult enrolment in the school boards network is as diverse as the training needs the sector has to meet. Adults enrolling in these programmes include 16-year-olds, the middle-aged, people who have lost their jobs, others who have no work experience, those who have little formal education, university graduates, recipients of welfare or unemployment benefit, and people who have just settled in Canada.

Between 1980-81 and 1991-92 the number of men enrolling tripled, compared with a rise of almost 80 per cent in the number of women, who were in the majority until 1985-86 in both types of training, and continued to be so in general education until 1990-91 (Table 3).

During this time, vocational training grew rapidly in the adult sector, with enrolment up 300 per cent in ten years. Once again the breakdown by sex was

Table 1. **Enrolment in vocational training, student and adult sector, financed by the Department of Education only,[1] from 1985-86 to 1991-92**

Streams	Sector	Type of enrolments	1985-1986	1986-1987	1987-1988	1988-1989	1989-1990	1990-1991	1991-1992
DEP, CEP, ASP, programmes (short and long programmes)	Student	Enrolment at 30 September	49 935	40 755	25 929	17 738	14 450	13 012	7 782
		Enrolment from 1 July to 30 June	–	–	–	–	–	13 886	8 922
		ETP in vocational training	32 252	26 699	18 917	14 608	12 195	10 850	7 062
	Adult	Enrolment from 1 July to 30 June	n.a.	n.a.	n.a.	43 870	29 688	33 879	40 436
		ETP in vocational training	n.a.	n.a.	n.a.	15 555	14 989	15 875	24 238
	Both sectors	Enrolment[2]	n.a.	n.a.	n.a.	61 608	44 138	47 765	49 358
		ETP in vocational training	n.a.	n.a.	n.a.	30 163	27 184	26 725	31 300
Other programmes	Adult	Enrolment from 1 July to 30 June	n.a.	n.a.	n.a.	22 284	29 792	28 954	18 952
		ETP in vocational training	n.a.	n.a.	n.a.	898	1 193	707	n.d.
All programmes	Student	Enrolment at 30 September	49 935	40 755	25 929	17 738	14 450	13 012	7 782
		Enrolment from 1 July to 30 June	–	–	–	–	–	13 886	8 922
		ETP in vocational training	32 252	26 699	18 917	14 608	12 195	10 850	7 062
	Adult	Enrolment from 1 July to 30 June	n.a.	51 140	80 941	66 154	59 480	62 198[3]	58 577[3]
		ETP in vocational training	n.a.	12 146	12 856	16 453	16 182	16 582	24 238
	Both sectors	Enrolment[2]	n.a.	91 895	106 870	83 892	73 930	76 084	67 499
		ETP in vocational training	n.a.	38 845	31 773	31 061	28 377	27 432	31 300

ETP = Full-time equivalent.
n.a. = Not available.
1. Excluding persons enrolled exclusively on programmes which are not officially recognised. Enrolment is calculated as full-time equivalent, with the number of hours spent by all students in vocational training being divided by 900. From 1985-86 to 1989-90, ETPs were calculated on the basis of enrolment, whilst from 1990-91 onwards they were calculated on the basis of the number of hours of recognised courses. In 1990-91 and 1991-92 persons enrolled in both sectors were recorded in the student sector.
2. From 1985-86 to 1989-90 the figure given is the sum of enrolment in the student sector at 30 September and the adult sector from 1 July to 30 June. In 1990-91 and 1991-92 the figure is the sum of enrolment in the student sector and the adult sector from 1 July to 30 September.
3. It is possible to enrol in more than one stream during the school year. Consequently, the sum of enrolment in the different streams is higher than the total given.
Source: Statistiques de l'Éducation. February 1994, Table 2.6.3, pp. 55-56.

QUEBEC

Table 2. **Enrolment in basic vocational training (CEP, DEP, ASP) in the 23 training sectors, by sex and age, 1992-93[1]**

	Enrolment Total	Women	Men	< 20	20-24	25-29	30 et +
01 Administration, commerce and secretarial studies	19 988	17 027	2 961	4 447	3 121	2 327	10 093
02 Agricultural techniques	1 278	674	604	306	172	151	649
03 Food, hotel management and catering	2 650	1 126	1 524	689	411	383	1 167
04 Applied arts	851	693	158	278	170	111	292
05 Wood and allied materials	324	34	290	59	50	37	178
06 Applied chemistry and environment	115	14	101	48	30	18	19
07 Construction	1 844	55	1 789	619	362	257	606
08 Technical drawing	2 079	453	1 626	648	498	270	663
09 Electrical engineering	5 742	279	5 463	2 382	1 360	647	1 353
10 Motor-driven equipment	5 716	193	5 523	2 846	1 360	591	919
11 Mechanical engineering	2 697	200	2 497	926	545	377	849
12 Forestry, timber and paper	854	81	773	410	178	73	193
13 Printing/publishing	1 228	523	705	553	260	118	297
14 Industrial maintenance	1 652	59	1 593	332	393	260	667
15 Construction engineering	1 450	11	1 439	484	424	190	352
16 Metallurgy	2 891	126	2 765	629	697	550	1 015
17 Fishery							
18 Textile production and clothing trade	340	297	43	90	62	42	146
19 Health and social services	4 779	4 066	713	1 025	835	554	2 365
20 Civil defence	422	10	412	106	267	43	6
21 Beauty therapy	3 976	3 864	112	1 914	787	396	879
22 Transport	195	10	185	25	57	27	86
23 Civil engineering and mining	191	2	189	63	49	26	53
Total for CEP, DEP and ASP[2]	61 262	29 797	31 465	18 879	12 088	7 448	22 847

1. Data at 29 September 1993.
2. Enrolment is recorded whenever entrants register for different programmes and/or under different school boards.
Source: Author.

reversed: from two-thirds in 1980-81 the proportion of women fell from the next year onwards to only 38 per cent of enrolment in vocational training in 1991-92. However, women are still concentrated in general education, where growth was less rapid than in vocational training over the 1980s as a whole.

The most notable trend in the adult sector is the rise in the number of men enrolling in vocational training (from 8 630 in 1980-81 to 60 985 in 1991-92).

309

Table 3. **Full-time and part-time enrolment in the adult sector, public and private networks, by type of training and sex, 1980-81 to 1991-92**

	1980-1981	1985-1986	1989-1990	1990-1991	1991-1992[1]
Total	**101 786**	**162 410**	**212 725**	**229 481**	**236 164**
Men	42 961	77 507	117 189	127 625	131 127
Women	58 825	84 903	95 536	101 856	105 037
General education	**76 807**	**104 625**	**104 867**	**125 114**	**138 024**
Men	34 331	45 654	46 633	59 599	70 142
Women	42 476	58 971	58 234	65 515	67 882
Vocational training	**24 979**	**57 785**	**107 858**	**104 367**	**98 140**
Men	8 630	31 853	70 556	68 026	60 985
Women	16 349	25 932	37 302	36 341	37 155

1.   Provisional date.
Source: Ministère de l'Éducation du Québec – MEQ (1993), *Indicateurs sur la situation de l'enseignement primaire et secondaire*, pp. 48-49 (Department of Education of Quebec, *Indicators on primary and secondary education*).

Age (see Table 4)

Access

Access to vocational training programmes by those aged under 20 fell rapidly in the mid-1980s (see Table 5). It dropped from 33 per cent in 1984-85 to less than 15 per cent in the space of four years, *i.e.* until just before the reform of vocational education was implemented, a process which began in 1987-88. In fact, the level of access was down only for those who did not have the secondary school leaving diploma. For those who had, the trend was in the opposite direction, with access tripling between 1984-85 (2.4 per cent) and 1991-92 (7.2 per cent).

The reform of vocational training aimed to improve entrants' general education before their admission to the new streams. This was achieved overall in 1990-91, when the majority of new entrants obtained the secondary school leaving diploma (8.0 per cent, against 7.5 per cent without this qualification). Young women reached this threshold in 1989-90 and men in 1991-92.

In addition, the short vocational stream was replaced by general education. Most of those who a few years ago would have taken short vocational programmes are now on special pathways and, more precisely, in programmes for integration into society and employment, which come under general education. Overall, the situation has been more or less stable since 1988-89, for new enrolment both with and without the diploma.

Traditionally, vocational training programmes attract more boys than girls. Thus, in 1991-92, 14 per cent of boys chose this stream compared with 10.5 per

Table 4. **Average age of persons obtaining a vocational training qualification[1]
in the student and adult sectors, public and private networks,
by stream and sex, in 1991-92 (age at 1 June)**

	Men	Women	Men and women
Student sector	22.2	22.3	22.3
Vocational stream (short programme)	29.5	29.5	29.5
Vocational stream (long programme)	30.4	30.6	30.5
DEP	20.0	20.1	20.1
CEP		22.0	23.0
ASP		19.9	20.9
Adult sector	27.6	30.9	29.0
Vocational studies without DES	32.0	34.9	32.7
DEP	27.4	29.9	28.6
CEP		30.0	34.2
ASP		24.8	29.8
Both sectors	25.5	27.4	26.4
Vocational stream (short programme)	29.5	29.5	29.5
Vocational studies without DES	32.0	34.9	32.7
Vocational stream (long programme)	30.4	30.6	30.5
DEP	24.4	25.9	25.2
CEP		28.9	32.9
ASP		23.7	27.4

1. Any person who has obtained more than one qualification during the school year is recorded in each of the streams concerned.
   DEP = Diplôme d'études professionnelles (secondary school vocational diploma).
   CEP = Certificat d'études professionnelles (secondary school vocational certificate).
   ASP = Attestation de spécialisation professionnelle (attestation of vocational specialisation).
   DES = Diplôme d'études secondaires (secondary school leaving diploma).
Source: MEQ (1994), *Statistiques de l'Éducation*, Table 3.2.4 (Education Statistics Bulletin, Department of Education of Quebec).

cent of girls. The situation is the same regardless of whether entrants have the diploma, and it is the converse of what is happening in general education, which attracts more young women. Some of the young men leaving general education earlier than women then enrol in vocational training.

Persons obtaining secondary level qualifications

Student sector

The number of persons obtaining secondary level qualifications in the student sector[2] in 1991-92 stood at 68 630 (see Table 6), 8.9 per cent up on the previous year. The increase in the number of students obtaining qualification since 1989-90 is primarily due to demographic trends.

Table 5. **Entrants into vocational training aged under 20, student and adult sectors, with or without secondary school leaving diploma, 1984-85 to 1991-92**

	1984-1985	1986-1987	1989-1990	1990-1991	1991-1992
All entrants					
Short vocational programme	9.0	7.3	–	–	–
Other programmes	24.2	19.9	15.0	15.5	12.5
without DES	21.8	13.1	7.7	7.5	5.3
with DES	2.4	6.8	7.3	8.0	7.2
All programmes	33.2	27.2	15.0	15.5	12.5
Boys					
Short vocational programme	12.4	9.9	–	–	–
Other programmes	22.4	20.6	18.5	18.7	14.6
without DES	20.5	13.8	10.4	10.3	7.1
with DES	1.9	6.8	8.1	8.4	7.5
All programmes	34.8	30.5	18.5	18.7	14.6
Girls					
Short vocational programme	5.4	4.7	–	–	–
Other programmes	26.2	19.1	11.2	12.1	10.5
without DES	23.2	12.3	4.8	4.5	3.4
with DES	3.0	6.8	6.4	7.6	7.1
All programmes	31.6	23.8	11.2	12.1	10.5

Source: Ministère de l'Éducation du Québec – MEQ (1993), *Indicateurs sur la situation de l'enseignement primaire et secondaire*, pp. 46-47 (Department of Education of Quebec, *Indicators on primary and secondary education*).

Table 6. **Award of secondary level qualifications, student sector, by network and type of training, 1975-76 to 1991-92**

	1975-1976	1985-1986	1989-1990	1990-1991	1991-1992[1]
School boards	63 047	66 097	50 028	52 304	56 395
General	47 341	49 905	42 807	46 227	51 293
Vocational	15 706	16 192	7 221	6 077	5 102
Private schools[2]	10 604	12 581	11 503	11 902	12 235
General	8 828	10 943	11 135	11 450	11 951
Vocational	1 776	1 638	368	452	284
Total	73 651	78 678	61 531	64 206	68 630
General	56 169	60 848	53 942	57 677	63 244
Vocational	17 482	17 830	7 589	6 529	5 386

1. Provisional data.
2. Including state schools depending on a department other than the Department of Education.
Source: Ministère de l'Éducation du Québec – MEQ (1993), *Indicateurs sur la situation de l'enseignement primaire et secondaire*, pp. 58-59 (Department of Education of Quebec, *Indicators on primary and secondary education*).

Similarly, the 30 per cent drop between 1981-82 and 1988-89 took place against the backdrop of a declining student population in Quebec, caused essentially by demographic factors. There are also other contributing elements, such as the increase in the number of students leaving school without obtaining qualification since 1986-87 and, more recently, the transfer of part of the student population to the adult sector.

In the early 1980s more than 68 per cent of students obtaining qualifications were enrolled in the general education programme, this proportion growing to 92 per cent in 1991-92. The increase, which took place at the expense of vocational training, was due to certain structural changes, however, such as the abolition of short vocational training courses and the fact that vocational training was increasingly attached to the adult sector.

Vocational training was much in vogue between 1975 and 1982, but the number of students obtaining a vocational training qualification then fell by 82 per cent, whilst in general education the figure rose by 3 per cent.

Adult sector

In 1991-92 over 31 000 Quebecois obtained the secondary school leaving diploma in the adult sector (see also note 2) a rise of over 300 per cent on 1982-83. During this period, growth stopped in 1988-89 only and then accelerated again (Table 7).

Table 7.   **Award of secondary level qualifications, adult sector, by network and type of training, 1975-76 to 1991-92**

	1975-1976	1985-1986	1989-1990	1990-1991	1991-1992[1]
Schools boards	4 776	9 693	14 942	19 588	31 187[2]
General	3 285	6 788	9 413	11 015	20 169
Vocational	1 491	2 905	5 529	8 573	11 018
Private schools[3]	85	391	289	221	137
General	57	21	16	19	47
Vocational	28	370	273	202	90
Total	4 861	10 084	15 231	19 809	31 324
General	3 342	6 809	9 429	11 034	20 216
Vocational	1 519	3 275	5 802	8 775	11 108

1.   Provisional data.
2.   Following revision of all students records, 7 218 DES were awarded to persons who had not been enrolled at school for a certain period of time, all aged over 30.
3.   Including state schools depending on a department other than the Department of Education.
Source: Ministère de l'Éducation du Québec – MEQ (1993), *Indicateurs sur la situation de l'enseignement primaire et secondaire*, pp. 60-61 (Department of Education of Quebec, *Indicators on primary and secondary education*).

Continuing education offers programmes leading to two types of schooling certificate. We will consider here firstly adults obtaining 5th grade secondary diplomas in general education, and secondly those obtaining a diploma with vocational mention.[3] These qualifications recognise complete programmes and are thus comparable to the qualifications awarded in the student sector.

In the early 1990s, approximately 65 per cent of persons obtaining secondary level qualifications in the adult sector were enrolled in general training, compared to 67.5 per cent in 1985-86. Vocational training grew the more rapidly over that period, its relative share up from 33 per cent to 36 per cent. The figure would actually be 46 per cent if the late addition of 7 218 secondary school leaving diplomas were ignored.

After obtaining the qualification (see Table 8)

3. TECHNICAL EDUCATION IN COLLEGES

In 1990, the college network numbered 46 CEGEPs, 25 subsidised private colleges, 29 authorised private colleges and 11 government schools. The 46 CEGEPs offer a range of pre-university and technical programmes. Private colleges and government schools usually provide a narrower range of programmes, some offering only pre-university or technical programmes.

Technical education programmes

At college level, technical education has co-existed with pre-university programmes since the CEGEPs were set up in 1967. The technical study programmes provided by CEGEPs, private colleges and government schools are established or approved by the minister and divided into 4 different types according to the qualification they lead to (see box):

– diploma of collegial studies (DEC): state programmes giving initial training;

– certificate of collegial studies (CEC): state programmes intended for adults;

– diploma of advanced college studies (DPEC): state programmes intended for adults who have already had specialist training;

– attestation of collegial studies (AEC): institutional programmes which must be approved by the minister, intended for adults.

In addition to these four types of study programme, colleges also offer tailor-made training. These activities do not necessarily lead to a qualification and are intended to provide professional development or refresher training within firms.

Table 8. **Situation of holders of secondary level qualifications, by training sector and type of qualification, 1974-75 to 1991-92**

10 months after award of the qualification

	1974-1975		1979-1980		1984-1985		1989-1990		1991-1992[1]	
	M	W	M	W	M	W	M	W	M	W
Secondary school leaving diploma (general education)										
Number of holders					23 945	27 808	24 814	29 810		
In employment	35.2	32.3	18.2	18.5	12.8	9.1	8.7	5.4		
Looking for employment	6.4	4.6	4.8	4.3	4.2	4.4	3.4	2.7		
Studying	56.3	60.4	72.1	72.7	82.3	85.2	87.5	91.3		
Non-active	2.0	2.6	4.6	4.3	0.7	1.3	0.4	0.6		
Long vocational programme										
Number of holders					3 442	6 848				
In employment	75.8	80.5	67.5	67.9	60.8	58.9				
Looking for employment	9.9	8.2	17.9	15.2	23.5	23.8				
Studying	12.9	8.5	10.7	11.5	13.7	15.2				
Non-active	1.1	2.6	3.8	5.2	2.0	2.1				
Short vocational programme										
Number of holders					1 363	558				
In employment	77.2	72.7	62.0	55.5	49.3	45.7				
Looking for employment	15.5	10.5	26.0	32.4	42.2	43.4				
Studying	7.1	15.5	3.9	3.9	6.2	6.7				
Non-active	0.0	1.1	7.9	10.0	2.3	4.3				
Supplementary vocational programmes										
Number of holders					1 089	88.0				
In employment			73.7	60.1	69.2	71.0				
Looking for employment			17.3	16.1	22.2	19.9				
Studying			6.3	9.1	7.6	9.1				
Non-active			2.2	6.5	1.0	0.0				
Secondary school vocational diploma										
Number of holders							2 613	3 043	5 275	4 936
In employment							56.6	69.9	45.7	52.9
Looking for employment							20.6	16.1	20.3	20.0
Studying							21.1	11.1	17.3	9.7
Non-active							1.8	2.8	16.7	17.5

Table 8. **Situation of holders of secondary level qualifications, by training sector and type of qualification, 1974-75 to 1991-92** *(cont.)*

10 months after award of the qualification

	1974-1975		1979-1980		1984-1985		1989-1990		1991-1992[1]	
	M	W	M	W	M	W	M	W	M	W
Attestation of vocational specialisation										
Number of holders							595	154	1 050	339
In employment							72.6	70.2	60.2	55.1
Looking for employment							15.2	18.1	17.4	18.7
Studying							11.6	11.7	11.0	8.6
Non-active							0.6	0.0	11.4	17.5
Secondary school vocational certificate										
Number of holders							306	194	1 464	1 290
In employment							52.6	57.1	37.5	50.8
Looking for employment							21.1	23.2	28.0	21.8
Studying							24.1	17.5	11.8	9.8
Non-active							2.2	2.2	22.6	17.6

1. In 1991-92, the Relance survey included adults as well as students.
Source: Paul Corbeil (1982), *Relance: finissants du secondaire*, ministère de l'Éducation du Québec (Relance survey of secondary school leavers);
P. Michel (1987), *Relance au secondaire, promotion 1984-1985*, ministère de l'Éducation du Québec;
P. Michel (1992), *Relance au secondaire, promotion 1989-1990*, ministère de l'Éducation du Québec;
N. Dion and P. Michel (1994), *Relance au secondaire, production synthèse, promotion 1991-1992*, ministère de l'Éducation du Québec.

Period of study covered by programmes

Diploma of collegial studies:	Three years
Certificate of collegial studies:	Two years
Diploma of advanced college studies:	One year
Attestation of collegial studies:	Half-year or longer

Entrance requirements

DEC: Secondary school leaving diploma in general education (DES), or vocational diploma (DEP), or other education considered sufficient.

CEC: Secondary school leaving diploma in general education (DES), or vocational diploma (DEP), or other education considered sufficient, with a study break of at least two consecutive semesters or one school year.

DPEC: Diploma of collegial studies in vocational training (DEC), or certificate of collegial studies (CEC), or other education considered equivalent.

AEC: Secondary school leaving diploma in general education (DES), or vocational diploma (DEP), or other education considered sufficient.

Programme content:
balance between general education and specialist training

DEC: Depending on the programme, between 30 and 45 per cent (but most often around one-third) of the programme consist of general education, which is compulsory and the same for everybody; and the remainder, between 55 and 70 per cent (most often around two-thirds) consist of specialist training.

CEC: The entire programme consists of specialist training.

DPEC: The entire programme consists of specialist training.

AEC: There is no strict rule providing for the breakdown of the programme between general education and specialist training. Most often, the greater part of the programme consists of specialist training.

As a general rule, students in initial training enrol in a DEC programme, whereas most adults, having already been out of the school system, return to school to take a CEC, DPEC, or AEC programme, non-programme studies or tailor-made in-house training.

The college network offers a total of 133 different programmes leading to the DEC, which are divided into pre-university training (seven programmes) and technical training (126 programmes). For technical training, in addition to the programmes leading to the DEC, 82 programmes lead to the certificate of collegial

Table 9. **College technical training programmes by family**[1]

	DEC	CEC	DPEC	AEC
Biological technology	40	6	13	31
Physics technology	45	39	5	61
Human technology	9	8	4	34
Business administration	8	18	0	46
Arts technology	24	11	2	40
Total	126	82	24	212

1. The figures given are valid as at 14 April 1992. The number of programmes changes constantly, with new ones being added and others withdrawn, particularly as far as the AEC is concerned.
Source: MESS, DGEC (1992), Service du développement des programmes, Fichier des programmes (Programme development service, programme catalogue).

studies (CEC), 24 to the diploma of advanced college studies (DPEC) and some 212 to the attestation of collegial studies (AEC). These programmes are grouped into five families (see Table 9).

Enrolment in technical training

Type of programme and programme organisation

a) *Mainstream education*

In the early 1980s, the breakdown between pre-university and technical training was roughly 50-50, but a difference between the two became apparent afterwards. In 1991 some 12 000 fewer students enrolled in technical training than in pre-university training (Table 10).

However, enrolment in technical training has risen continuously. In recent years, technical training has also accounted for a growing proportion of the student population in mainstream education, but it has not yet regained the level of the early 1980s (Table 11).

In the early 1980s there were already more female than male students in technical training. The difference then widened and in 1989, young women accounted for 58 per cent of enrolment and young men 42 per cent. Since then, the proportion of young men has grown parallel to the rise in total enrolment in technical training.

Table 10. **Enrolment by type of programme and programme organisation, mainstream education, 1980-91**

	Full-time					Part-time				
	1980[1]	1985	1989	1990	1991	1980	1985	1989	1990	1991
	Number									
Pre-university DEC	67 258	81 182	80 896	79 997	82 461	1 571	2 328	2 154	2 237	2 425
Technical DEC	66 804	75 315	65 772	66 827	70 966	1 032	1 800	1 635	1 747	1 747
AEC, CEC, DPEC	261	1 439	2 121	2 340	2 560	63	132	14	19	16
Non-programme	917	1 251	1 285	1 619	2 230	162	514	373	409	456
Total	135 240	159 187	150 074	150 783	158 217	2 828	4 774	4 176	4 412	4 644
	Percentage									
Pre-university DEC	49.7	51.0	53.9	53.1	52.1	55.6	48.8	51.6	50.7	52.2
Technical DEC	49.4	47.3	43.8	44.3	44.9	36.5	37.7	39.2	39.6	37.6
AEC, CEC, DPEC	0.2	0.9	1.4	1.6	1.6	2.2	2.8	0.3	0.4	0.3
Non-programme	0.7	0.8	0.9	1.1	1.4	5.7	10.8	8.9	9.3	9.8
Total	100.0	100.0	100.0	100.0	100.0	100.0	100.0	100.0	100.0	100.0

1. Autumn term.
Source: MESS (1993), *Regard sur l'enseignement collégial*. (Report on college education), Sheet 2, p. 19, Table 1.

Table 11.   **Enrolment in technical DECs by sex, mainstream education, 1980-91**

	1980	1985	1989	1990	1991
	Enrolment				
Men	31 575	35 026	28 320	29 173	31 797
Women	36 261	42 089	39 087	39 401	40 916
Total	67 836	77 115	67 407	68 574	72 713
	Percentage				
Men	46.5	45.4	42.0	42.5	43.7
Women	53.5	54.6	58.0	57.5	56.3

Source: MESS, DGEC, SIGDEC catalogue.

b)   *Adult education*

With regard to programme organisation, the situation in adult education is the opposite to that which happens in the mainstream. The majority of those enrolled in adult education study part-time, take short programmes, and in particular follow non-programme studies. These short programmes, AEC, CEC, DPEC and a large proportion of non-programme studies are in technical training (Table 12).

The programme family

Despite falling steadily since the mid-1980s, business administration is still the most popular programme family in technical training. However, since the early 1980s there has been a considerable rise in the number of mainstream students enrolling in human technology (Table 13), although this is not the case in adult education (Table 14). Physics technology seems to be regaining its relative share of enrolment as far as mainstream students are concerned, yet it had been falling up until the end of the 1980s. Mainstream enrolment in biological technology programmes is relatively stable, whilst it has grown substantially in adult education.

A comparison of the breakdown between boys and girls by programme family shows that, in technical training, choices differ according to gender. Greater numbers of girls than boys choose biological, human, administrative and art technology; and a very high percentage of boys prefer physics technology, where, despite their growing number, girls are still not well represented (Table 15).

Table 12. **Enrolment by type of programme and programme organisation, adult education, 1980-91**

	Full-time					Part-time				
	1980[1]	1985	1989	1990	1991	1980	1985	1989	1990	1991
	Enrolment									
Pre-university DEC	4 765	903	422	728	761	6 553	10 210	7 474	8 003	7 172
Technical DEC	2 005	1 196	695	605	602	6 478	7 468	6 447	6 674	5 754
AEC, CEC, DPEC	3 347	4 625	5 849	6 877	8 848	9 080	11 911	12 598	12 980	12 365
Non-programme	9 037	2 397	2 051	1 851	2 317	22 519	37 396	42 887	43 790	43 390
Total	19 154	9 121	9 017	10 061	12 528	44 630	66 985	69 406	71 447	68 681
	Percentage									
Pre-university DEC	24.9	9.9	4.7	7.2	6.1	14.7	15.2	10.8	11.2	10.4
Technical DEC	10.5	13.1	7.7	6.0	4.8	14.5	11.1	9.3	9.3	8.4
AEC, CEC, DPEC	17.5	50.7	64.9	68.4	70.6	20.3	17.8	18.2	18.2	18.0
Non-programme	47.2	26.3	22.7	18.4	18.5	50.5	55.8	61.8	61.3	63.2
Total	100.0	100.0	100.0	100.0	100.0	100.0	100.0	100.0	100.0	100.0

1. Autumn term.
Source: MESS (1993), *Regard sur l'enseignement collégial*, (Report on college education), Sheet 16, p. 47, Table 1.

Table 13. **Enrolment in technical DECs by category of programme, mainstream education, 1980-91**

	1980	1985	1989	1990	1991
	Enrolment				
Biological technology	13 140	14 587	14 369	14 199	14 946
Physics technology	16 708	18 167	14 275	15 084	16 776
Human technology	8 397	8 802	10 039	10 563	11 275
Business administration	25 592	29 864	22 450	22 328	23 082
Arts technology	3 999	5 695	6 274	6 400	6 634
Total	67 836	77 115	67 407	68 574	72 713
	Percentage				
Biological technology	19.4	18.9	21.3	20.7	20.6
Physics technology	24.6	23.6	21.2	22.0	23.1
Human technology	12.4	11.4	14.9	15.4	15.5
Business administration	37.7	38.7	33.3	32.6	31.7
Arts technology	5.9	7.4	9.3	9.3	9.1
Total	100.0	100.0	100.0	100.0	100.0

Source: MESS (1993), *Regard sur l'enseignement collégial*, (Report on college education), Sheet 5, p. 25, Table 2.

Table 14. **Enrolment in technical DECs by category of programme, adult education 1980-91**

	1980	1985	1989	1990	1991
	Enrolment				
Biological technology	278	774	771	728	599
Physics technology	1 628	782	776	935	786
Human technology	1 370	721	494	574	514
Business administration	4 960	5 562	4 792	4 769	4 214
Arts technology	247	825	309	273	243
Total	8 483	8 664	7 142	7 279	6 356
	Percentage				
Biological technology	3.3	8.9	10.8	10.0	9.4
Physics technology	19.2	9.0	10.9	12.8	12.4
Human technology	16.1	8.3	6.9	7.9	8.1
Business administration	58.5	64.2	67.1	65.5	66.3
Arts technology	2.9	9.5	4.3	3.8	3.8
Total	100.0	100.0	100.0	100.0	100.0

Source: MESS (1993), *Regard sur l'enseignement collégial,* (Report on college education), Sheet 18, p. 51, Table 2.

Age

The proportions in the age groups of 23 to 29 and 30 years and over increased strongly between 1980 and 1991, both for women as well as men. In 1991 three times more people aged 23 and over underwent technical training than in 1980. There has also been an increase in the proportions of these age groups in pre-university training, although it is only slight compared with the increase seen in the technical training sector (Table 16).

The participation rate represents the proportion of the Quebecois population of a specific age group attending college for pre-university or technical training. Participation rates for college study increased between 1980 and 1990 in the 15-19-year-old age group in particular: out of every 100 young people aged 17 or 18, 30 were attending college in 1980. Ten years later this figure had risen to 42, with just over 28 choosing pre-university training and 13 technical training. The increase in participation is almost entirely accounted for by pre-university training which increased its lead over technical training, at least in the second half of the 1980s (Table 17).

Table 15. **Enrolment in technical DECs by sex and category of programme, mainstream education, 1980-91**

	Women					Men				
	1980[1]	1985	1989	1990	1991	1980	1985	1989	1990	1991
	Enrolment					Enrolment				
Biological technology	9 853	10 726	10 947	10 740	11 302	3 287	3 861	3 422	3 459	3 644
Physics technology	1 395	2 010	1 983	2 117	2 373	15 313	16 157	12 292	12 967	14 403
Human technology	5 555	6 085	7 119	7 438	7 965	2 842	2 717	2 920	3 125	3 310
Business administration	16 827	19 308	14 509	14 462	14 512	8 765	10 556	7 941	7 866	8 570
Arts technology	2 631	3 960	4 529	4 644	4 764	1 368	1 735	1 745	1 756	1 870
Total	36 261	42 089	39 087	39 401	40 916	31 575	35 026	28 320	29 173	31 797
	Percentage					Percentage				
Biological technology	27.2	25.5	28.0	27.3	27.6	10.4	11.0	12.1	11.9	11.5
Physics technology	3.8	4.8	5.1	5.4	5.8	48.5	46.1	43.4	44.4	45.3
Human technology	15.3	14.5	18.2	18.9	19.5	9.0	7.8	10.3	10.7	10.4
Business administration	46.4	45.9	37.1	36.7	35.5	27.8	30.1	28.0	27.0	27.0
Arts technology	7.3	9.4	11.6	11.8	11.6	4.3	5.0	6.2	6.0	5.9
Total	100.0	100.0	100.0	100.0	100.0	100.0	100.0	100.0	100.0	100.0

1. Autumn term.
Source: MESS (1993). Regard sur l'enseignement collégial. Sheet 7, p. 29, Table 1.

Table 16. **Age structure by sex and type of DEC, 1980 and 1991**

	Women		Men	
	1980	1991	1980	1991
	Enrolment			
Pre-university DEC	32 525	46 149	36 304	38 737
	Percentage			
Total	100.0	100.0	100.0	100.0
below 22	96.5	95.0	97.5	95.7
23-29	1.7	2.2	2.2	3.2
30+	1.8	2.7	0.3	1.2
Technical DEC – number	36 261	40 916	31 575	31 797
	Percentage			
Total	100.0	100.0	100.0	100.0
Below 22	92.6	76.9	92.8	80.0
23-29	4.4	12.4	6.3	14.4
30+	2.9	10.7	0.9	5.6

Source: MESS (1993), *Regard sur l'enseignement collégial,* (Report on college education), Sheet 8, p. 31, Table 3.

Table 17. **Participation by type of training and age group, 1980-90**

Percentage

	1980[1]	1985	1988	1989	1990
Pre-university					
15-19 years	9.6	14.2	15.9	16.1	15.8
20-29 years	0.4	0.7	0.7	0.7	0.7
17-18 years	16.7	25.0	27.5	28.3	28.5
Technical					
15-19 years	8.0	9.8	8.9	8.6	8.7
20-29 years	1.2	2.0	2.1	2.1	2.2
17-18 years	13.1	15.0	13.2	13.0	13.5
Total					
15-19 years	17.6	24.0	24.8	24.7	24.5
20-29 years	1.6	2.7	2.8	2.8	2.9
17-18 years	29.8	40.1	40.7	41.3	42.0

1.   Autumn term.
Source: MESS (1993), *Regard sur l'enseignement collégial,* (Report on college education), Sheet 13, p. 41, Table 1.

Relative share of new entrants in first-year enrolment

Applications for admission to certain college programmes are increasingly being received from people who have already attended college, a trend apparent since the early 1980s. In the autumn of 1990, only one first-year entrant in two was enrolling in a college technical programme for the first time. The others might be trainees changing programme, adults, people returning to study, migrants or repeaters. A growing number of people, therefore, who are already at college or have attended college before, are competing with secondary school students to get into a technical programme, an indication of the extent of reorientation. The greatest numbers of first-year entrants who have already attended college are currently in biological and physics technology (Table 18).

Educational pathways

Programmes chosen by new entrants

New entrants' preference for pre-university training became more marked as the decade progressed. The number of new entrants to this type of training increased by 17.1 per cent between 1980 and 1991, whereas over the same period the figure for the technical DEC fell by 18.7 per cent, in all technical programme families except human and arts technology (Table 19).

Table 18. **New entrants to colleges as a percentage of total first-year enrolment in technical training programmes, 1980-90**

Percentage

	1980[1]	1983	1986	1987	1988	1989	1990
Biological technology	59.9	49.9	45.8	40.8	42.0	40.4	37.6
Physics technology	63.5	62.7	56.4	51.3	51.5	48.7	48.3
Human technology	68.6	59.9	62.8	57.2	53.5	53.4	55.6
Business administration	75.2	66.0	63.2	57.6	60.5	58.3	56.6
Arts technology	62.0	53.1	55.0	56.5	59.0	56.2	58.8
Total	67.9	61.2	57.6	52.6	53.4	51.4	50.6

1. Autumn term.

Source: Isabelle Falardeau (1992), *Les changements de programme au collégial* (Programme changes at college), MESS, DGEC, September, p. 105.

Table 19. **Programmes chosen by new entrants to college, 1980-91**

Programme family	1980[1]		1986		1989		1990		1991		Difference 1980-91 (%)
	Number	%	Number	%	Number	%	Number	%	Number	%	
Pre-university DEC											
Natural sciences	11 124	22.6	13 573	25.0	11 236	23.4	11 354	23.3	11 556	22.8	3.9
Humanities	14 816	30.1	18 350	33.8	19 163	39.9	18 916	38.7	19 324	38.2	30.4
Arts	1 855	3.8	1 613	3.0	1 639	3.4	1 749	3.6	2 061	4.1	11.1
Literature	1 875	3.8	1 808	3.3	1 470	3.1	1 577	3.2	1 793	3.5	-4.4
Sub-total	29 670	60.3	35 344	65.1	33 508	69.8	33 596	68.8	34 734	68.7	17.1
Technical DEC											
Biological technology	2 887	5.9	2 934	5.4	2 370	4.9	2 283	4.7	2 432	4.8	-15.8
Physics technology	4 514	9.2	4 042	7.4	2 751	5.7	3 252	6.7	3 426	6.8	-24.1
Human technology	2 334	4.7	2 277	4.2	2 269	4.7	2 426	5.0	2 422	4.8	3.8
Business administration	8 596	17.5	8 267	15.2	5 603	11.7	5 710	11.7	6 014	11.9	-30.0
Arts technology	1 167	2.4	1 414	2.6	1 511	3.1	1 560	3.2	1 556	3.1	33.3
Sub-total	19 498	39.7	18 934	34.9	14 504	30.2	15 231	31.2	15 850	31.3	-18.7
Total	49 168	100.0	54 278	100.0	48 012	100.0	48 827	100.0	50 584	100.0	2.9

1. Autumn term.
Source: MESS (1993), *Regard sur l'enseignement collégial*, (Report on college education), Sheet 10, p. 35, Table 1.

Changes of programme

In pre-university training, out of every 100 new entrants in the autumn of 1980:

- 72 obtained diplomas, of which:
  - 51 did not change programme
  - 21 changed programme

- 28 did not obtain diplomas, of which:
  - 14 did not change programme
  - 14 changed programme

In technical training, out of every 100 new entrants in the autumn of 1980:

- 63 obtained diplomas, of which:
  - 43 did not change programme
  - 20 changed programme

- 37 did not obtain diplomas, of which:
  - 17 did not change programme
  - 20 changed programme.

For the 1980 cohort as a whole, out of every ten persons obtaining a diploma, three had changed programme. For technical training, the number of students obtaining a diploma in the initial programme is slightly lower. The most programme changes after initial enrolment take place in the physics and arts technology families. The highest proportion of students obtaining a diploma in the initial programme is in the biological technology family (Table 20).

Persistence in programmes and obtaining of diplomas

In the autumn term following the first year, on average 80 per cent of first-year entrants re-enrol at college; the other 20 per cent are temporarily absent (they will enrol in a college programme in a subsequent semester) or permanently absent. After two years, re-enrolment falls to an average of 69 per cent, with absenteeism reaching 29 per cent. After three years, on average 30 per cent of students have obtained a diploma, 33 per cent are still studying and 37 per cent are absent (Table 21).

After that period, the proportion of students obtaining diplomas continues to rise, re-enrolment continues to fall, and absenteeism increases slightly. After eleven years the proportions are 64, 2 and 34 per cent respectively for the 1980 cohort.

Table 20. **Mainstream students of the 1980 cohort obtaining the DEC,
by whether or not they changed programme and by category of programme
at first-year enrolment, for the whole college network**

	Percentage of students obtaining a diploma		Total	
	without change of programme	with change of programme	%	Number
Pre-university training	70.5	29.5	100.0	21 383
Natural sciences	65.0	35.0	100.0	9 235
Humanities	76.9	23.1	100.0	10 012
Arts	59.9	40.1	100.0	1 033
Literature	67.9	32.1	100.0	1 103
Technical training	68.2	31.8	100.0	12 366
Biological technology	76.6	23.4	100.0	2 214
Physics technology	63.5	36.5	100.0	2 951
Human technology	72.0	28.0	100.0	1 543
Business administration	66.4	33.6	100.0	5 048
Arts technology	65.1	34.9	100.0	610
Total	69.6	30.4	100.0	33 739

Source: Isabelle Falardeau (1992), *Les changements de programme au collégial*, MESS, DGEC, September, p. 89.

Table 21. **Persistance of new entrants to DEC technical programmes, 1980-89**

Percentage

		1980[1]	1983	1986	1987	1988	1989
Number of years spent[2]							
1 year	Re-enrolment	80.6	81.2	76.5	78.9	79.6	80.6
	Persons obtaining diploma	0.0	0.0	0.0	0.0	0.0	0.0
	Absent[3]	19.4	18.8	23.5	21.1	20.4	19.4
	Total	100.0	100.0	100.0	100.0	100.0	100.0
2 years	Re-enrolment	71.1	69.4	65.5	67.6	69.4	72.2
	Persons obtaining diploma	3.1	2.9	1.7	2.1	1.9	1.7
	Absent	25.8	27.7	32.8	30.3	28.7	26.1
	Total	100.0	100.0	100.0	100.0	100.0	100.0
3 years	Re-enrolment	30.9	33.5	33.0	33.3	34.8	
	Persons obtaining diploma	36.3	30.5	25.1	28.4	27.8	
	Absent	32.8	36.0	41.9	38.3	37.4	
	Total	100.0	100.0	100.0	100.0	100.0	
4 years	Re-enrolment	12.4	13.6	14.8	15.2		
	Persons obtaining diploma	52.9	46.6	40.4	43.3		
	Absent	34.7	39.8	44.8	41.5		
	Total	100.0	100.0	100.0	100.0		

1. Autumn cohort.
2. The proportions of students re-enrolling, obtaining a diploma or absent are calculated in the autumn term following the period in question.
3. Absent temporarily or permanently.

Source: MESS (1993), *Regard sur l'enseignement collégial*, (Report on college education), Sheet 43, p. 105, Table 1.

Regardless of the year of observation and the type of training, the proportion of the 1980 cohort obtaining diplomas is higher than that of subsequent cohorts. For pre-university training the rate of diplomas granted is always noticeably higher than for technical training (Table 22).

Table 22. **Cumulative rate of granting of diplomas to new entrants to DEC programmes, by type of training, mainstream education, 1980-89[1]**

Percentage

	Pre-university training					
	1980[2]	1983	1986	1987	1988	1989
Number of years passed						
2 years	38.0	33.1	30.7	34.2	33.9	33.9
3 years	56.6	53.8	52.9	56.6	54.9	
4 years	64.5	62.1	61.0	64.3		
5 years	68.5	66.0	64.7			
6 years	70.3	67.7				
7 years	71.1	68.7				
8 years	71.6	69.2				
9 years	71.9					
10 years	72.2					
11 years	72.3					
New enrolment	29 670	31 020	35 344	33 180	33 682	33 508

	Technical training				
	1980[2]	1983	1986	1987	1988
Number of years passed					
3 years	36.3	30.5	25.1	28.4	27.8
4 years	52.9	46.6	40.4	43.3	
5 years	58.6	52.6	46.0		
6 years	60.8	54.9			
7 years	62.0	56.1			
8 years	62.6	56.9			
9 years	63.1				
10 years	63.4				
11 years	63.7				
New enrolment	19 498	20 450	18 934	15 894	15 317

1. Provisional data for the latest year of observation of each cohort.
2. Autumn cohort.
Source: MESS (1993), *Regard sur l'enseignement collégial*, (Report on college education), Sheet 39, p. 97, Table 1; and Sheet 46, p. 111, Table 1.

After obtaining the diploma

Study at university

The main objective of pre-university training is to prepare students for university and the vast majority of those obtaining this qualification do win a place there. As far as technical training is concerned, students aged 24 and under who have obtained the diploma are more inclined to opt for the labour market, the logical follow-up to that training. However, during periods of recession, when the employment rate falls, more of them go on to university. Thus, in 1990, the rate of university entry of these students reached record levels of 19.4 per cent. Generally speaking, more men than women choose to go on to university, women being more likely to enter the labour market earlier (Table 23).

Entering the labour market

Trends in access to the labour market by students with the DEC are not unrelated to the economic climate. Of those undergoing technical training, a higher proportion of women than men enter the labour market. For the last nine years, the difference has usually been nine percentage points (Table 24).

Table 23. **Holders of the DEC (aged 24 years and under) entering university, 1982-83 to 1990-91**

Percentage

	1982-83[1]	1983-84	1984-85	1985-86	1986-87	1987-88	1988-89	1989-90	1990-91
	Pre-university training								
Women	84.3	85.1	88.3	82.9	83.9	71.4	82.1	87.4	85.8
Men	87.7	86.3	84.5	83.3	84.4	75.0	78.9	86.7	86.0
Women and men	86.0	85.7	86.5	83.1	84.1	73.1	80.7	87.1	85.9
Number	18 411	13 856	20 490	20 762	20 518	20 725	21 567	20 615	21 023
	Technical training								
Women	14.4	15.2	15.4	11.6	12.5	11.3	12.4	14.9	18.4
Men	21.9	21.9	20.7	19.8	17.3	15.1	17.2	20.8	21.0
Women and men	17.4	17.6	17.5	14.9	14.3	12.7	14.2	17.1	19.4
Number	10 949	9 220	12 671	11 778	10 549	9 879	10 193	10 183	9 752

1. Year diploma obtained.
Source: MESS (1993), *Regard sur l'enseignement collégial*, (Report on college education), Sheet 48, p. 117, Table 1.

Table 24. **Holders of the DEC (aged 24 and under) in employment ten months after obtaining the diploma, by type of training and gender, 1982-83 to 1990-91**

Percentage

	1982-83[1]	1983-84	1984-85	1985-86	1986-87	1987-88	1988-89	1989-90	1990-91
	Pre-university training								
Women	8.2	10.0	7.2	10.7	9.2	11.1	11.7	8.2	8.7
Men	6.7	9.0	8.5	9.7	8.6	9.1	14.1	8.3	9.1
Women and men	7.4	9.0	7.8	10.2	9.0	10.3	12.8	8.2	8.9
	Technical training								
Women	69.9	69.8	71.1	75.1	78.3	78.6	81.0	73.1	69.9
Men	60.2	57.6	61.0	64.5	70.8	69.8	74.6	63.4	62.5
Women and men	66.2	65.4	67.2	70.9	75.5	75.2	78.6	69.4	67.0

1. Year diploma obtained.
Source: MESS (1993), *Regard sur l'enseignement collégial,* (Report on college education), Sheet 49, p. 119, Table 1.

Table 25. **Unemployment rate of holders of the DEC (aged 24 years and under) ten months after obtaining the diploma, by type of training and gender, compared with Québécois aged 20-24 years as a whole, 1982-83 to 1990-91**

Percentage

	1982-83[1]	1983-84	1984-85	1985-86	1986-87	1987-88	1988-89	1989-90	1990-91
	Women								
Technical	15.2	14.5	12.8	11.2	7.1	6.2	5.1	10.0	10.6
Pre-university	33.9	22.4	18.6	15.2	21.6	13.8	13.1	15.3	16.0
Young Québécois	15.6	15.4	18.1	12.0	12.5	10.6	12.1	15.1	13.5
	Men								
Technical	20.1	22.2	19.5	14.5	10.8	10.4	7.4	15.4	16.2
Pre-university	27.8	29.7	29.3	17.3	16.7	7.3	10.0	21.7	15.4
Young Québécois	23.9	23.8	23.0	21.9	16.6	14.7	13.3	25.9	24.1
	Women and men								
Technical	17.0	17.1	15.3	12.5	8.4	7.8	6.0	11.9	12.7
Pre-university	31.3	25.7	24.5	16.1	19.3	11.3	11.6	18.2	15.7
Young Québécois	19.9	19.9	20.7	17.2	14.6	12.8	12.7	20.5	19.1

1. Year diploma obtained.
Source: MESS (1993), *Regard sur l'enseignement collégial,* (Report on college education), Sheet 50, p. 121, Table 1.

Table 26. **Principal data from the RELANCE survey for holders of the technical DEC of all ages, by category of programme: in employment, seeking employment, studying or inactive, 1987-88 to 1991-92**

	1987-1988			1988-1989			1989-1990			1990-1991			1991-1992		
	W	M	Total	W	M	Total	W	M	Total	W	M	Total	W	M	Total
Biological technology															
Number of respondents	1 294	351	1 645	1 509	326	1 835						1 929	1 751	443	2 194
Number of holders of the diploma	2 647	820	3 467	3 012	779	3 791	2 905	704	3 609	2 445	681	3 126	2 517	651	3 168
In employment (%)	85.5	70.1	82.2	89.6	79.8	87.8	84.2	74.6	82.3	80.3	75.5	79.2	78.4	77.0	78.1
Looking for employment (%)	4.2	14.8	6.5	2.1	11.3	3.8	4.9	11.9	6.3	5.6	11.5	6.9	6.3	11.7	7.4
Studying (%)	9.2	12.8	10.0	6.9	7.1	6.9	9.7	12.5	10.3	12.9	11.9	12.7	13.4	9.9	12.7
Non-active (%)	1.1	2.3	1.3	1.4	1.8	1.5	1.1	1.0	1.1	1.2	1.2	1.2	1.9	1.4	1.8
Physical technology															
Number of respondents	179	1 029	1 208	195	1 126	1 321						1 638	253	1 377	1 630
Number of holders of the diploma	313	2 072	2 385	302	1 980	2 282	344	2 141	2 485	359	1 919	2 278	347	1 945	2 292
In employment	76.0	77.6	77.4	79.5	78.4	78.6	67.7	65.3	65.6	66.3	61.2	62.0	60.5	59.2	59.4
Looking for employment	7.3	7.0	7.0	6.2	5.5	5.6	13.1	14.0	13.9	12.0	14.1	13.8	17.0	15.5	15.7
Studying	14.5	15.0	14.9	12.8	15.9	15.4	18.3	19.8	19.6	20.3	23.1	22.7	20.9	24.5	23.9
Non-active	2.2	0.4	0.7	1.5	0.2	0.4	0.9	0.9	0.9	1.4	1.6	1.5	1.6	0.9	1.0
Human technology															
Number of respondents	583	153	736	617	133	750						1 109	842	196	1 038
Number of holders of the diploma	1 149	314	1 463	1 124	260	1 384	1 308	443	1 751	1 183	429	1 612	1 263	307	1 570
In employment	71.5	78.4	73.0	78.0	72.9	77.1	71.1	77.7	72.8	68.4	75.5	70.3	71.7	76.5	72.6
Looking for employment	8.7	9.1	8.8	6.0	6.0	6.0	10.1	8.6	9.7	10.7	12.4	11.1	8.3	15.3	9.6
Studying	18.4	11.8	17.0	13.8	20.3	14.9	16.4	12.2	15.4	18.4	12.1	16.7	18.5	7.7	16.5
Non-active	1.4	0.7	1.2	2.3	0.8	2.0	2.4	1.6	2.2	2.5	0.0	1.9	1.4	0.5	1.3
Business administration															
Number of respondents	1 483	644	2 127	1 616	663	2 279						2 546	1 713	670	2 383
Number of holders of the diploma	2 800	1 270	4 070	2 906	1 309	4 215	2 748	1 362	4 110	2 662	1 133	3 795	2 346	947	3 293
In employment	77.1	60.1	71.9	76.1	68.6	73.9	67.9	56.2	64.0	65.5	54.6	62.3	66.1	54.3	62.8
Looking for employment	5.0	6.8	5.6	6.3	3.9	5.6	10.7	12.4	11.3	10.8	10.1	10.6	11.4	10.6	11.2

Table 26. **Principal data from the RELANCE survey for holders of the technical DEC of all ages, by category of programme: in employment, seeking employment, studying or inactive, 1987-88 to 1991-92** (cont.)

	1987-1988			1988-1989			1989-1990			1990-1991			1991-1992		
	W	M	Total	W	M	Total	W	M	Total	W	M	Total	W	M	Total
Studying	16.4	32.8	21.3	17.1	27.1	20.1	19.1	31.4	23.2	22.0	35.0	25.9	20.2	34.5	24.2
Non-active	1.5	0.3	1.2	0.4	0.3	0.4	2.2	0.0	1.5	1.7	0.4	1.3	2.3	0.6	1.8
Arts technology															
Number of respondents	252	115	367	228	98	326						724			608
Number of holders of the diploma	497	200	697	580	198	778	575	211	786	694	215	909	638	221	859
In employment	73.4	68.7	71.9	75.0	74.5	74.8	64.9	70.1	66.3	62.8	65.6	63.5	64.1	59.1	62.8
Looking for employment	10.3	9.5	10.1	7.9	9.2	8.3	13.6	9.5	12.5	12.1	9.8	11.6	13.4	14.9	13.8
Studying	14.3	20.9	16.4	14.5	16.3	15.0	19.3	20.4	19.6	22.2	24.7	22.8	20.9	23.4	21.5
Non-active	2.0	0.9	1.6	2.6	0.0	1.8	2.3	0.0	1.7	2.9	0.0	2.2	1.5	2.6	1.8
Total															
Number of respondents	3 831	2 346	6 177	4 165	2 346	6 511						7 932	5 013	2 840	7 853
Number of holders of the diploma	7 409	4 675	12 084	7 924	4 526	12 450	7 880	4 860	12 740	7 342	4 375	11 717	7 111	4 071	11 182
In employment	78.6	71.4	75.9	81.4	75.4	79.2	74.2	65.5	70.9	70.7	63.3	67.9	70.9	62.0	67.7
Looking for employment	5.8	8.3	6.8	4.8	6.1	5.3	8.8	12.6	10.2	9.2	12.3	10.4	9.6	13.7	11.1
Studying	14.1	19.6	16.1	12.6	18.1	14.6	15.2	21.3	17.5	18.3	23.4	20.2	17.6	23.3	19.7
Non-active	1.5	0.7	1.2	1.2	0.5	1.0	1.8	0.7	1.4	1.8	1.0	1.5	1.9	1.0	1.6

Source: MESS et MEQ, *La relance au collégial*. Situation au 31 mars 1989 (1990, 1991, 1992) des diplômés de 1987-1988 (88-89, 89-90, 90-91) de l'enseignement collégial: formations préuniversitaire et technique (MESS/Department of Education of Quebec, *Relance survey of college education*, situation at 31 March 1989 (1990, 1991, 1992) of holders of DECs from 1987-88 (88-89, 89-90, 90-91): pre-university and technical training).

The unemployment rate of holders of the diploma and young Quebecois generally has fluctuated considerably, again owing primarily to the economic climate. Holders of technical training diplomas do, however, fare better than those with pre-university diplomas and Quebecois aged from 20 to 24 as a whole. Generally, the unemployment rate for female holders of the diploma is lower than for their male counterparts, and they obtain part-time work in greater numbers than do men (Tables 25 and 26).

NOTES

1. Adults enrolled on one or more courses which allow credits to be accumulated for the award of a diploma.

2. Students having obtained a diploma of general education and a vocational mention in the same year are counted in general education only in that year. Those having obtained several vocational qualifications in the same year are also counted only once. However, a student may be counted more than once if he/she obtains two separate qualifications in the course of different years.

3. This mention indicates that the person concerned has completed a programme of vocational training, whether or not he/she has obtained all the credits required to attain the secondary school leaving diploma.

SWITZERLAND

by
Anna Borkowsky, Swiss Federal Statistical Office
and Philipp Gonon, University of Bern

1. INTRODUCTION

In most OECD countries we can observe endeavours to strengthen the "attractiveness" of vocational education. In Switzerland, the policy is to maintain a strong division between vocational and academic tracks. Even new reforms do not challenge this two-pathway model but try to enlarge and upgrade access for apprentices to higher education by the creation of polytechnics or *Fachhochschulen*. A brief history and a description of the pathways and programmes of upper secondary education follows, showing that reforms of the educational system as a whole are on the political agenda.

History of the system

It was the Swiss *Gewerbeverband* (an association of small firms of the arts and crafts sector) that became aware, in the 1880s, that its members were no longer competitive. The rising Swiss industry with low-skilled work on the one hand and the products of countries such as France, Austria and Germany on the other, were much more successful, even in Switzerland itself. The restriction of free trade was one solution debated, but this idea was supported only by a minority of policy makers. After considerable discussion, it was decided to further the arts and crafts trade by strengthening the development of educational institutions for vocational needs. In 1884, therefore, an act was passed which allowed the federal authorities to fund vocational *Fortbildungsschulen* (further-education schools) and other institutions such as *Lehrwerkstätten* (in-house workshops). The standards of apprenticeships and the assessment of tutors were regulated by the *Gewerbeverband* itself.

In 1930, however, the first legislation at national level was introduced – the *Bundesgesetz für berufliche Ausbildung* – defining the occupations in the arts and crafts and in industry which are regulated and monitored by federal authorities. Industrialists' and workers' associations began to show interest in vocational education needs, and it became compulsory (because of pressure from the workers' associations) for every apprentice to attend school courses for one day. The "take-off" of the predominant dual system in Switzerland and its commanding role over most young people's lives after compulsory school occurred after the Second World War. Later, in 1963 the legislation was reformed slightly. The most recent federal reform regulating education in a large number of occupations was passed in 1978: the *Berufsbildungsgesetz* (BBG).

Vocational training distribution

The take-off of vocational education after the Second World War is shown in Figure 1. Fifty per cent of the generation between 1932 and 1941 who were at the beginning of an upper secondary education completed a vocational education. This proportion rose by ten points for the next two ten-year cohorts (1942-1951 and 1952-1961) and has increased slowly from 67 to 73 per cent for younger cohorts. First men, and only later women, profited from this development. There were also differences between language regions from the beginning, the German-

◆ Figure 1. **Upper secondary vocational education, by language region, gender and age**

Labour force surveys, 1991 to 1993

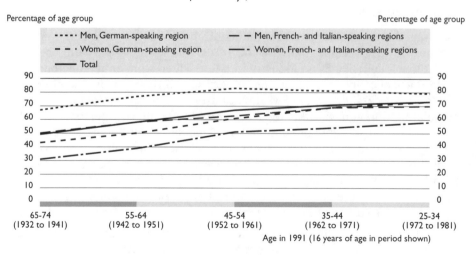

Source: Swiss Federal Statistical Office.

speaking region favouring vocational education more than the French- and Italian-speaking regions.

Firms employing apprentices

In 1985, one-third of all enterprises in the secondary and tertiary sectors of the economy with more than one employee had at least one apprentice. Participation of companies in vocational education depends on their size: while less than half of small enterprises have apprentices, the percentage rises to 95 per cent among the largest firms (Figure 2). Seven per cent of all employees in the secondary and tertiary sectors of the economy are apprentices.

Why do enterprises participate in vocational education? Data on costs and benefits of vocational education at company level are scarce. On the cost side for a firm is that of in-house training, the contribution to the expense of introductory courses and apprentices' wages (which are low in Switzerland compared to those in Germany and Austria). On the benefit side, the apprentices work productively although to an extent which varies greatly between occupations. Estimates indicate that having apprentices does at least not lead to economic loss. In the longer run, participation of an enterprise in vocational education assures the continued

◆ Figure 2. **Enterprises with apprentices, by size of enterprise, industrial and tertiary sectors**

1985

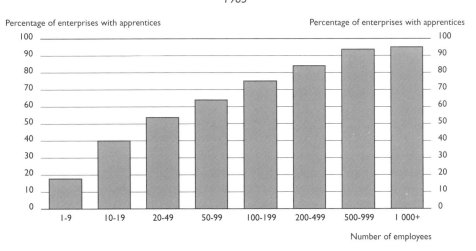

supply of a skilled labour force. However, the functioning of the system could be threatened, if there are too many "free-loading" companies which do not participate in vocational education.

The scheme of apprenticeships within an enterprise is sometimes criticised for not being systematically enough organised, owing to its direct link with the current production of the firm. However, the system involves a strong school element, and introductory courses help to form common basis for all apprentices, independently of their enterprise. Another solution to the problem of increasingly specialised production and the broader training requirements for apprentices is an exchange scheme between companies. The recent years have also seen a determined effort to raise the level of didactic competence of vocational-training tutors.

2. PROGRAMMES AND PATHWAYS

Programmes

Vocational education in Switzerland begins after completion of compulsory schooling, usually at the age of 15 or 16, i.e. nine years of primary and lower secondary education. It then continues to higher non-university education. Table 1 shows the programmes at upper secondary and tertiary levels, which are also the building blocks of pathways through the system. The most important will be described in detail.

Table 1. **Programmes at the upper secondary and tertiary levels of education**

	Upper secondary education	Tertiary education
General education	Schools preparing for university entrance certificate (maturité) Intermediate diploma school Other general education schools	University[1]
Vocational education	Berufsmittelschule and maturité professionnelle[2] Vocational schools Apprenticeship Basic vocational education[1] Teacher training[1]	Polytechnics or Fachhochschulen[2] Higher vocational schools Technical schools Preparation for professional examinations Other tertiary vocational education Teacher training[1]

1. Programmes excluded from the present study, even though a strong element of vocational training is involved.
2. Programmes instituted by current or future reforms: the maturité professionnelle in 1993, and the law upgrading certain higher professional schools to Fachhochschulen planned for 1995 or 1996.
Source: Authors.

The Swiss system is basically built up by the two distinct pathways of general and vocational education, which traditionally have few meeting points. The recent reforms of vocational education now include more general education within vocational education but do not aim at making the whole system more permeable.

Upper secondary general education

a)   Schools preparing for university entrance certificate

The Swiss *Matura/maturité* is one of the most valued certificates at upper secondary level. Its broad requirements in general knowledge give access to all universities and faculties (*allgemeine Hochschulreife*). The education is exclusively school-based. A recent reform of the certificate includes the elimination of the differentiation of types of *maturité* (or at least the reduction in the number of types), the restriction to twelve years of the maximal duration of schooling for attaining the certificate, and the reduction from eleven to nine of the minimal number of subjects included in the final examination. The reform will, however, only slightly "modernise" this traditional and, in most cantons, very elitist institution. The entry requirements in most cantons include a minimum average in marks and the successful passing of an entry examination.

b)   Intermediate-diploma schools

Intermediate-diploma schools have a specific profile just "below" that of *Gymnasia*, providing a two- to three-year course with a diploma in general knowledge (especially languages and similar subjects such as those offered in a *Gymnasium*). They are full-time schools, often linked to a traditional *Gymnasium*, very often the organisational descendants of former "higher girls' schools", and until now not very clearly situated along either the vocational or general education pathways. Most of the pupils in this programme are females, who will gain access to education in occupations such as teaching, nursery-school teaching and health care. With the introduction of the *maturité professionnelle* (see below), a new role for these schools as a parallel pathway to higher education is foreseen.

Upper secondary vocational education

a)   Apprenticeship

Apprenticeship is the predominant form of vocational education throughout Switzerland. It usually involves three learning sites: the factory or workplace for three or four days, the vocational school for one to two days a week, and introductory courses (a full-time schedule of about twelve weeks) either in a special centre or in a school, or in a factory with a specific workshop (see below). The

Swiss system is therefore often called a "tri-" system (as an extension of the dual), since an apprenticeship is considered as full-time education.

Apprenticeships last from one to four years, with the majority continuing for three to four years (see below). The certificate gained gives a solid basis for finding a qualified position in industry and trade. It is also the foundation for further education and training within one's firm, or a first step towards higher professional education. Until recently, an apprenticeship was the point of departure for a long career within a company.

b) Vocational schools

Most full-time vocational schools offer certificates equivalent to those acquired in apprenticeships in comparable occupations.

Commercial and other full-time schools. Commercial schools provide a full-time course for the business sector. Some are linked to a *Gymnasium* with an economic focus, others are private schools with specific programmes. The normal duration is two to three years. Some courses can be followed even when one has a job. There are other schools for qualification in health care, teaching, social work and music education.

Apprentice workshops (ateliers d'apprentissage/öffentliche Lehrwerkstätten). This kind of vocational education was developed in the 19th century, mainly in towns such as Zürich, Winterthur, Bern, and the French part of Switzerland. As in France, Belgium, or smaller regions like Baden and Württemberg, such institutions aimed at educating an élite of workers. Up until today, these full-time vocational schools with workshops have been of considerable relevance to occupations in the clock and watchmaking and metallurgical industries and in dressmaking.

c) Berufsmittelschulen and maturité professionnelle/Berufsmatura

Since the 1970s, *Berufsmittelschulen* (higher vocational schools) have offered supplementary general education for apprentices. In 1993 a new programme, *maturité professionnelle (Berufsmatura)* was introduced, based on a reform of the *Verordnung* (ordinance) of the *Berufsmittelschulen.*[1]

The aim was to ensure access to higher education through a newly defined curriculum. In addition to traditional apprenticeship, young people could obtain a certificate, the *Fachhochschulreife*, equivalent to the entrance certificate for higher vocational schools.[2] Four types of *maturité professionnelle* were planned: a technical, commercial, artistic *Berufsmatura* and one for trade *(gewerbliche Berufsmatura)*. In 1994, the first technical and commercial courses were offered.

The creation of the *maturité professionnelle* upgraded the already existing *Berufsmittelschulen*, which work under the same roof as the traditional vocational schools of the apprenticeship system, with apprentices taking supplementary courses for a second day each week. *Maturité professionnelle* students in a four-year apprenticeship follow an in-house course of 4 500 lessons (in addition to their normal work), 1 440 school lessons in vocational subjects and 1 440 in general subjects. The latter include the mother tongue, foreign languages, mathematics, natural science and more vocationally oriented courses in, for instance, computing, physics, ecology or economics. *Maturité professionnelle* students have 600 to 1 000 more lessons in general subjects than do "normal" apprentices with the same occupation.

The organisation of supplementary courses is very open, and different solutions are possible at local level. It is even feasible to acquire the necessary general subjects in a one-year course after a three-year apprenticeship, but the entry requirements for this are not yet clearly regulated. The stated aim of policy makers is to have 10-15 per cent of an age group in this programme. The success of the measures, however, depends upon the progress of the ongoing reform of higher vocational institutions.

Tertiary education

a)   Universities

In 1994 the Swiss university system included seven major cantonal universities, two federal polytechnic schools (ETH) and one *Handelshochschule*, a university specialising in economics and business administration for *Matura* or *maturité* students (*allgemeine Hochschulreife*). Only a small number of pupils (compared with other countries – about 7 per cent of a cohort) follow this path.

b)   Polytechnics or Fachhochschulen (Hautes écoles spécialisées)

In 1996 a new law was to be passed, upgrading to *Fachhochschulen* some higher engineering schools and the higher business and administration schools. Other schools in the higher vocational sector would also like to be upgraded, but the requirements for changing a higher education institution into a *Fachhochschule* have not yet been clearly spelled out for all schools, and the total number will probably be limited to ten or 15. A crucial point for an upgrading is the establishment of a three-year programme. The pathway designed to lead to this new kind of higher education is the *maturité professionnelle*. It is, however, not impossible for *Gymnasium* graduates to have access to such schools, provided they are able to complement their studies with practical work.

c)   Higher professional schools

The most important in number are the higher technical (engineering) and the higher business and administration schools. Other higher professional schools

341

include colleges for agricultural engineering, domestic science, industrial design, social work and education. These schools generally offer three-year full-time courses and require a three- or four-year apprenticeship as a condition for entry.

d)   Technical schools

At a middle level are two-year full-time courses in schools for technicians, for business, tourism and health care. The entry requirement here is a completed three- or four-year apprenticeship.

e)   Preparation for professional examinations

Special part-time courses lasting from a few months to some years are offered by various institutions including professional associations, vocational schools and private market-oriented schools, for the preparation of Masters' or trade examinations (Berufsprüfungen and Höhere Fachprüfungen).

f)   Other tertiary vocational education

Aside from the comparatively well-regulated sector described so far, a plethora of vocational courses at tertiary level exist, all requiring a completed upper secondary education and leading to a specific occupation. The diversity of form, content, duration and intensity of these courses makes it difficult to identify boundaries between vocational education at tertiary level and continuing education and training. Many of these institutions are only slightly state-controlled and regulated, which is part of the explicit policy of subsidiarity for the further education and training sector, i.e. the State is active only when the free market no longer delivers sufficiently.

Pathway studies

The Swiss educational system is very fragmented because of the federal structure of its 26 cantons. Pathway studies are therefore restricted to cantons, regions or even smaller units. A general description of pathways drawn from case studies reveals that:

– There is a rigid division between the general and vocational education pathways.

– There exists a wide variety of pathways besides the two basic tracks either through the general education system via a grammar school up to university level or through vocational education which includes tertiary education. Other tracks might involve some general education.

- Many pathways include time spent out of the education system – at varying points of the track. Some programmes in tertiary vocational education demand occupational experience as an entry requirement – not all "interruptions" of education are therefore ruptures of an educational career. Data shows that these interruptions create the difficult problem of how to relate the number of students leaving the system in a given year to those who enter the system again some years later.

- Pathways are classed in hierarchical order, within the vocational education system as well, showing that pupils with a good scholastic achievement have a better chance of securing the more desirable training places. Pathways and programmes can therefore be ranked according to the scholastic history of incoming students, which thus reflects the attraction of the various pathways and programmes.

- The hierarchy of occupations and hence that of vocational programmes seems to depend largely on widespread perceptions by the young, who have an unclear idea of the "hard facts" of an occupation. Any attempt, therefore, at an explanation of a student's choice of programme when all the hard facts are not known to him is subject to caution.

- There seems to be a trend towards pathways in which vocational education at the upper secondary level is followed only after completing or attending a general education programme at the same level. This trend will be examined below.

Dimensions of programmes

The OECD guidelines for the preparation of the country reports in this volume mention several dimensions of vocational education programmes. The way in which each dimension was treated in turn will now be discussed.

Certification or qualification offered

The system of apprenticeship in Switzerland aims at offering a certificate. Certain short-time vocational certificates can be acquired in two years, but many occupations require attendance of a three-year course, and other certificates are obtainable only after four years. The certificate shows the results of an examination in practical work, theoretical knowledge linked to the occupation, and general knowledge. The actual form of certification for each occupation is the same for the whole country.

Level of education

Vocational education is available at upper secondary and at tertiary levels. But much continuing education is also undertaken to achieve an occupational goal. This section will be limited to the upper secondary and tertiary levels, but it should first be mentioned that in the classification of the Swiss education system every form of tertiary education has an entry requirement of a completed upper secondary education of at least two years. Thus, even though some vocational education programmes are only for students of at least 18 years old (programmes for nursing, for instance), they are not considered to be tertiary education if their entry requirements do not formally specify a completed upper secondary education.

Degree of "modularisation"

Until recently, there has been no modularisation of apprenticeships apart from a few exceptions such as staggered programmes. The notion of B*eruf* (occupation) with its given set of qualifications is obviously opposed to a modular concept. On the other hand, there have been recent discussions on the issue of modularisation for tertiary education after an apprenticeship. A study group was asked to design a modular framework as an alternative to technical schools, higher vocational certificates (Höhere Fachprüfungen, Berufsprüfungen) and other forms of continuing education.

Learning sites

Article 7 of the B*erufsbildungsgesetz* (BBG) law defines learning sites as:

– vocational schools;
– in-house training;
– introductory courses for the training of basic skills.

The teaching of certain occupations (some commercial trades, graphics and the arts) is done only in schools. A special case are the workshops run by the state, a form of learning which has its origins in France (*ateliers d'apprentissage*), where the whole apprenticeship (theoretical and practical learning) takes place inside such an institution.

Vocational education for the majority of students means apprenticeship training: in 1993, 86 per cent of those in vocational education chose this form.[3] The remainder attended a vocational school with no in-house training: 12 per cent a full-time vocational school and 2 per cent a part-time school.

An enterprise trains an apprentice in practical knowledge and working techniques based on a curriculum and model training programmes defined by federal vocational regulations. Apprentices work under the guidance of a vocational tutor. The most important part of their practical training involves participation in the daily business of the enterprise. They are sometimes involved in a conflict between the goals of production and those of their training.

Not all apprentices encounter this situation. Two extreme cases would be:

– a crafts apprentice working together with a master and being instructed in tasks of increasing difficulty;

– industrial apprentices spending up to 40 per cent of their time in special workshops or training centres, where they work under the guidance of full-time instructors.

One indication of which of these types of apprenticeship prevails is the size of the enterprise. It is reasonable to assume that the crafts type of apprenticeship predominates in the smaller enterprise, while most of the larger enterprises implement the industrial model. This may become less true as the trend towards small firms in the modern sectors of the economy (electronics, software development, etc.) continues. One-third of apprentices hold a contract with a small firm of less than ten persons. A quarter work in large enterprises, while the remaining are employed by medium-size firms (Figure 3). There is at present no data systematically linking the size of an enterprise with other factors.

◆ Figure 3. **Percentage of apprenticeships by size of enterprise, industrial and tertiary sectors**

1985

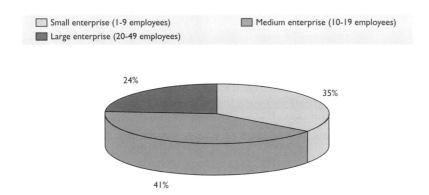

☐ Small enterprise (1-9 employees)   ☐ Medium enterprise (10-19 employees)
▪ Large enterprise (20-49 employees)

24%

35%

41%

Source: Swiss Federal Statistical Office.

At tertiary level, the favourite learning site is the school – the formal link between an enterprise-based learning site and school learning which characterises the apprenticeship system disappears. The link between practice and theory is established by requiring practical experience before certain certificates can be acquired or quite often by part-time education. In 1993, 42 per cent of tertiary vocational education students were full-time, with the remaining majority of 58 per cent part-time. The relationship between full- and part-time studies for higher vocational schools and polytechnics is somewhat different: 73 per cent of students are full-time and 27 per cent part-time.

Fields of study

Vocational education programmes at the upper secondary level are reglemented for more than 400 different occupations, thus allowing the system a flexible response to technological and organisational changes. The drawback of this great number of occupations is the implicit focus on specialisation at a time when the labour market demands young people with multiple skills. Of course, the number of students learning a given occupation varies greatly: in 1992, for example, 13 100 new students took up the largest occupation, that of commercial employee, whereas in piano-making less than ten new apprentices began their training.

Since the duration of programmes tends to vary according to field of study, Table 2 compares the number of new entrants to give an idea of the relative size of the fields of study. Around 60 per cent of all new entrants follow training in only three fields: business administration and office work, metal-working and crafts related to machinery, and health care. This is true of both sexes, even though the internal distribution is quite different.

General and vocational elements of programmes

The topics taught in-house and during introductory courses are usually related to the firm's business, but the lessons given in vocational schools are decided by federal regulation for each occupation. The proportions of vocational and general elements depend on a clear-cut distinction between them, which is to some degree lacking. Knowledge of foreign languages, for instance, is part of the job description of many occupations such as office workers and laboratory technicians, but the learning of foreign languages could with equal justification be defined as an element in the acquisition of general knowledge.

Another example are mathematics and natural sciences which form part of the curriculum for technical branches and are generally counted among the vocational subjects. Judging by yet other examples, at least one-third of lessons in general subjects are mother tongue, civics, law and economics, and sport. If all

Table 2. **New entrants into upper secondary vocational education,
by field of study and gender, 1992**

	Absolute			%		
	Total	Women	Men	Total	Women	Men
Total	60 906	27 506	33 400	100.0	100.0	100.0
Office	17 091	10 857	6 234	28.1	39.5	18.7
Metal-working/machines	11 703	156	11 547	19.2	0.6	34.6
Health care	6 186	5 613	573	10.2	20.4	1.7
Selling	5 332	3 867	1 465	8.8	14.1	4.4
Draughting, technical occupations	4 039	945	3 094	6.6	3.4	9.3
Wood, cork	2 145	82	2 063	3.5	0.3	6.2
Hotel and restaurant trade, domestic science	1 813	873	940	3.0	3.2	2.8
Cosmetics, hairdressing, beauty care	1 642	1 557	85	2.7	5.7	0.3
Food, beverages	1 256	408	848	2.1	1.5	2.5
Horticulture	1 254	775	479	2.1	2.8	1.4
Construction, building trades	1 249	9	1 240	2.1	0.0	3.7
Painting	971	201	770	1.6	0.7	2.3
Agriculture	914	26	888	1.5	0.1	2.7
Graphics industry	886	378	508	1.5	1.4	1.5
Transport	713	278	435	1.2	1.0	1.3
Other fields	3 712	1 481	2 231	6.1	5.4	6.7

Source: Authors.

foreign languages, mathematics and science lessons are considered general subjects, then specific vocational elements may account for as little as one-third of vocational school lessons. These compulsory lessons may be supplemented by optional courses.

Duration of education/training

There are three elements in the reglemented vocational training at upper secondary level which may vary: the total number of years of training, the amount of schooling, and the length of the introductory courses. All three taken together might give an indication of the amount of reglemented learning. What cannot be measured with these three indicators is the amount of learning the students themselves add by homework, by following supplementary courses at vocational schools, and by receiving formal in-house education. For these additional factors there are no statistical or other systematic data.

The length of programmes in vocational education varies between one and four years.[4] Of all students in vocational education, 37 per cent are involved in the longest programmes, another 47 per cent follow three-year programmes, and the remaining receive a short training (Table 3).

Table 3. **Upper secondary vocational education: length of programme, by gender, 1992**

	Absolute			%		
	Total	Women	Men	Total	Women	Men
1 year	8 700	5 432	3 268	4.4	6.7	2.8
2 years	20 314	14 988	5 326	10.3	18.4	4.6
3 years	92 225	49 884	42 341	46.7	61.2	36.5
4 years	73 730	9 765	63 965	37.3	12.0	55.1
Undefined	2 603	1 444	1 159	1.3	1.8	1.0
Total	197 572	81 513	116 059	100.0	100.0	100.0

Source: Authors.

The total number of prescribed lessons in vocational schools for an apprenticeship varies considerably. While it is not surprising that the longer courses involve more lessons, the number in three-year courses varies between 960 and 1 800 lessons, and those for four-year courses between 1 040 and 2 240. Introductory courses vary between zero lessons for certain occupations and more than 700 for a small number of others.[5] There is some tendency towards a correlation between the two factors, the longer introductory courses often being combined with a lower number of regular lessons. The highest number of lessons are typically found in the more prestigious industrial occupations.

By adding the two kinds of lessons together, the weight of school in the total educational experience is perceived. One-fifth of new apprentices begin their training with a low school content of less than 900 compulsory lessons,[6] another fifth will have between 900 and 1 350 lessons, one-third up to 1 800 lessons, and the final quarter more than 1 800 lessons (Figure 4). It is not surprising that there are pronounced gender differences in the total number of lessons, given the differences in fields of study and duration of apprenticeships. Further, women are overrepresented in the occupations where data is at present still lacking.

Entry requirements

The formal entry requirements for upper secondary vocational education are to be 15 years of age and to hold an apprenticeship contract (for apprenticeships) or to have passed an entrance examination (for full-time vocational schools). The requirements for tertiary vocational education include successful completion of an upper secondary education – frequently in a related field of study, usually proof of occupational experience in an associated area, and often the passing of a

◆ Figure 4. **Entrants into vocational education, by number of lessons
in school and by gender**
1992-93

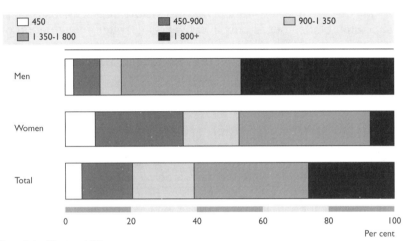

Source: Swiss Federal Statistical Office.

complicated admission procedure. Some of the more prestigious institutions of
higher vocational education have a strictly closed-admission policy: the higher
schools of music, those for applied arts, and the higher vocational schools of
business administration, for instance.

The overall effect of entry requirements (the apprenticeship contract, admission procedures) results in an element of selectivity being introduced. The selection by entrance examination and by employers (in the case of apprenticeships)
works in favour of students leaving the streams with "wider demands" at lower
secondary level – they have a greater chance of ending up in the more desirable
vocational education programmes (see Section 4).

Entitlement/access to tertiary education and training

As for conditions of entry, formal requirements are the same for those who
have completed upper secondary vocational programmes. However, openings are
much more developed in the fields of business administration and in core industrial occupations than in selling or the textile industry.

3. EFFECTS OF SIGNIFICANT REFORMS

It is not easy to define which reforms are "significant". The demographic development, for example, without being a reform, causes side-effects, and many reforms can be "significant" without having visible repercussions. In general, larger structural reforms began only a few years ago, after a long period of "soft" reforms at cantonal or local level, based on local or institutional experiences (such as new learning materials, reforms in teacher training programmes, new subjects such as ecology and computing). The most important features of the framework to which reforms have to refer are outlined below.

Reforms introduced by the legislation of 1978

The role of vocational education in the whole Swiss educational context is now discussed, beginning with the last federal reform act (the 1978 BBG – Berufsbildungsgesetz) and the 1979 decree (BBV – Berufsbildungsverordnung). This legislation regulates most occupational and vocational education at national level and provides a framework which has to be introduced by special law at cantonal level. Excluded from this regulation, however, are academic occupations, occupations in health care, education, the arts and agriculture.

The BBG ensures a continuity with the laws of 1930 and 1963. One of its main aims was to enhance the quality of apprenticeship, to guarantee its "attractiveness" in relation to general education (grammar schools, for example). In-house training came under pressure and became the main field for reforms. New measures included:

- the introduction of a programme for tutors or in-house trainers to obtain the necessary pedagogical knowledge and skills;

- the obligatory designing of a module of introductory courses to provide basic arts and crafts skills;

- the introduction of higher vocational certificates.

Other important reforms were the stricter pedagogical requirements for teachers in vocational schools, the establishing of special courses for apprentices with higher intellectual capacities, and the contrary – courses for young people with specific difficulties. These reforms are stipulated in various articles of the BBG law:

- Article 7 concerns the different forms of apprenticeship and the establishment of introductory courses and full-time schools (ateliers d'apprentissage/ Lehrwerkstätten and commercial schools).

- Article 8 regulates the minimum length of an apprenticeship to two years.

- Articles 10/11 stipulate that a *Lehrmeister* (apprentice master) must follow a special pedagogical course to enable him/her to teach young people.
- Article 16 regulates the introductory courses, which in 1995 had not yet been introduced everywhere.
- Article 35 obliges teachers to follow further education courses to improve their knowledge and skills.
- Article 36 establishes the Swiss Institute for Vocational Education as an institution for training teachers and for providing research and documentation.
- Article 51 establishes vocational examinations: the *Berufsprüfung* for qualification to higher positions in the occupational hierarchy; and the *Höhere Fachprüfung*, a certificate enabling the following of a trade, and at the same time the requirement for the position of *Lehrmeister* in many occupations.
- Article 58 establishes the technical schools.
- Article 59 regulates the higher vocational schools (for engineers, business administration, domestic science and other fields).

The BBV decree regulates certain special details and ensures implementation of the new legislation. It establishes:

- the *Berufsmittelschulen* (higher vocational schools) for students with a greater general knowledge;
- model curricula for in-house training (*Modellehrgänge*);
- optional courses (*Freifächer*);
- regulations for apprentices with special needs (*Stützkurse* and *Anlehre*).

Thus, the new legislation offers the possibility of a differentiation of vocational courses at various levels. There was, however, originally considerable opposition from the unions, who feared that the system would become too selective. But in fact, this differentiation has been quite minimal: only 1 per cent of apprentices take the *Anlehre* course with its lower requirements, and the *Berufsmittelschulen* on the other hand are attended by only 4 per cent.

Recent trends

Recent trends in reform include the revision of general education in vocational schools, and – most important – the introduction of the *Berufsmatura* (*maturité professionnelle*). This new programme in turn depends on the reform of the higher vocational institutions (higher commercial schools, schools of engineering) which should be transformed into polytechnics at a higher level comparable to the German *Fachhochschulen*.

A new legislation was initiated in 1994: the *Botschaft* (a kind of White Paper) of the *Bundesrat* (executive power of the federal authority), which was published in May 1994 and discussed in parliament in 1994 and 1995. The legislation was a pre-condition for the introduction of the *Fachhochschulen*, which are based on the entry requirement of the *Berufsmatura*. Most of the existing higher vocational schools (higher engineering schools and higher administration schools) will have to change their profile then in order to qualify as higher education institutions. However, some critical points are still undecided. Which schools will be able to be upgraded and which will remain at their present level? What is happening with other schools in fields such as music, the arts, social work, health care and languages, which are presently regulated by each canton and therefore not subject to federal reform? What will be the future role of the cantons and of the federal authorities? How will the financing be divided between the cantons and the Confederation? And last but not least, how will the traditional universities react: will there be a new discussion about funding, and how will the division of research fields between universities and the *Fachhochschulen* be established?

Effects on participation

To describe effects is not as simple as it looks. The aim of the legislation is to provide a framework for the many and quite different actors involved. The VOTEC area is, however, the only one which is clearly legislated by the federal authorities. The implementation, on the other hand, is assured by the cantons and the professional associations. Quite different and totally dependent on the traditions of the local, cantonal or industrial area are the specific solutions for the organisation of vocational schools. Thus, for example, in the French part of Switzerland a school-based vocational education is much more popular and more frequented than in the German part.

In order to identify the effects of reforms, one must link them to case studies. However, not all effects are due to legislated reforms. If, for instance, banks decided to reduce the number of their commercial apprentices, that decision would have a big impact on the whole system. Technological change too has its effect on the redefinition and revision of the reglementation of occupations.

Demographic changes, *i.e.* the drastic decrease in the number of 16-year-olds, had to be met with measures to increase the attractiveness of vocational education, such as improving the school curriculum, creating new occupations, developing new strategies of public relations, etc. A still unmet challenge is the integration of young immigrants.

The introduction of the *Berufsmatura* is an attempt to reach those who until now have preferred to choose a school-based track which allows them to continue with their studies. Whether this will work or not is dependent not only on political consensus but particularly on the higher vocational schools: whether they have the will and the means to absorb those with supplementary qualifications. Of course, the legislation itself is one point of reference and its actual application in various sectors another: *Vollzugsdefizit* (non-application) of the legislation sees many implementations delayed or not yet carried out for any clear reason.

In general, there was a rise in the number of young people who chose a vocational course up until 1988. Since then, a decrease has been noticeable. The recent reforms, by designing new pathways, can thus be seen to be in relation to such a change. On the other hand, there is the danger that strengthening of the school-based part of the dual system will lead to a demotivation of entrepreneurs to offer apprenticeships. Only the coming years will show what the effects on participation will be.

4. PATTERNS OF PARTICIPATION IN PROGRAMMES AND PATHWAYS

The data on participation in programmes and pathways at national level is uneven: while participation data is complete from the 1977 school year onwards, there is no systematic follow-through of pathways. Participation in pathways will therefore have to be estimated using stock data and data on the transition between two school years. Description of the patterns of participation will include consideration of the following aspects:

- upper secondary vocational in comparison with upper secondary general education;
- fields of study, learning sites, length of programmes;
- the transition from lower secondary to upper secondary education;
- pathways through upper secondary education;
- access to higher vocational education.

The years since 1977 – participation in programmes

Participation in upper secondary education

The educational experience of the 15-20-year-olds serves as an example of the rise in educational participation since 1980. Among the 15-year-olds, the majority are still in compulsory school, since upper secondary education generally starts at age 16 and lasts until 18 or 19. In 1993, at least four-fifths of the cohort were still in education up to the age of 18. Between 19 and 20, the participation rate drops sharply down to one quarter. From 1980 to 1993, the overall participation for each age group had risen considerably – by an average of 7 percentage points for ages 16-18, but the pattern of participation by age had stayed the same (Figure 5).

◆ Figure 5. **Participation of 15-21-year-olds**
in secondary education
1980, 1985, 1990, 1993

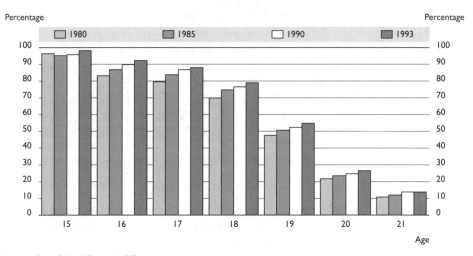

Source: Swiss Federal Statistical Office.

While the participation in upper secondary education had risen considerably, the estimated figure for the overall rate of entry into upper secondary education[7] had increased only from 90 per cent of the generation in 1980 to 92 per cent in 1993 (Table 4). This slight overall rise contrasts with a small decrease in the male entry rate and an increase of 7 percentage points for females. For males of both language regions, the difference between 1980 and 1993 is quite small, while both female groups show the same increase. The pattern of rising participation in upper secondary education shown in Table 4 is therefore mostly due to the increase in female participation.

Upper secondary education: general vs. vocational education

Three different aspects of the "competition" between general and vocational education will now be discussed:

– vocational education among entrants to upper secondary education;
– all vocational education entered by the cohort;
– vocational education in the completion rate of upper secondary education.

Table 4. **Participants in upper secondary education,
by gender and language region, 1980, 1985, 1990, 1993**

Percentage

	1980	1985	1990	1993
All	90	94	94	92
Men	96	99	95	94
Women	84	90	92	91
Men in German-speaking cantons	96	97	94	94
Men in French- and Italian-speaking cantons	94	100	98	96
Women in German-speaking cantons	83	88	96	90
Women in French- and Italian-speaking cantons	90	98	97	97

Source: Authors.

The shift in relative weight of general and vocational upper secondary education takes place against the background of a general rise in participation in upper secondary education.

a)   General vs. vocational education: all entries, 1977-1993

Figure 6 shows the evolution of entries in upper secondary education from 1977 to 1993. The main developments, the increase in entries until 1984 and their subsequent fall, are due to demographic factors: the size of the relevant cohort has also changed considerably. What is interesting is the fairly sharp rise in number of students entering general education in the last three years, while the decrease in entries in vocational education has not been halted. These figures would argue for a shift towards general education.

b)   Vocational education entered by the cohort

The data on all entries includes a number of double entries to different programmes of upper secondary education. In 1993, an estimated 80 per cent of the cohort had entered a vocational programme and 32 per cent a general programme – including double entries.[8] In 1980,[9] the overall participation in vocational education had been higher – 84 per cent of the cohort had participated, whereas in general education the figure had been much lower (23 per cent). The intervening years had seen a gradual increase in the rate of participation in general education, and an increase in vocational education until 1985, followed by a decrease up until 1993 (Figure 7). Obviously, the numbers displayed in Figure 4 include double counting (see below).

◆ Figure 6. **Number of entrants into upper secondary education,**
by programme and gender
1977-93

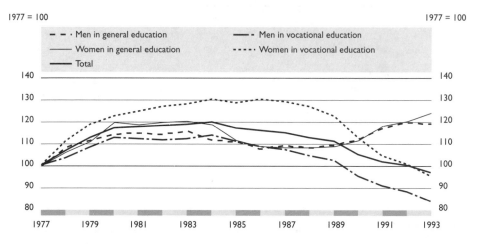

Source: Swiss Federal Statistical Office.

◆ Figure 7. **Entry rate in upper secondary education,**
by programme
1980, 1985, 1990, 1993

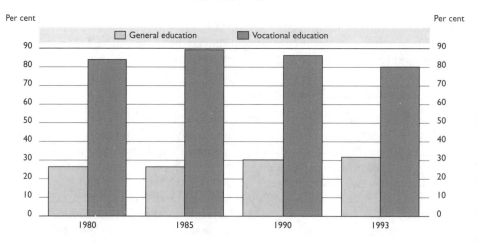

Source: Swiss Federal Statistical Office.

For all gender and language groups, preference for a general education in the most exacting programme, namely the schools preparing for the university entrance exam, is increasing (Table 5). All language and gender groups had followed the same pattern of increase in vocational education until 1985, after which there was a decrease. Despite small shifts in the relative importance of the various programmes, what is most striking are the constant patterns: the majority of all groups enter vocational education at one time or another; males attend vocational education more frequently than females, and both genders of the

Table 5. **Entry rate in upper secondary education,
by programme, gender and language region, 1980, 1985, 1990, 1993**

Percentage

	1980	1985	1990	1993
All				
Schools preparing for university	16	17	20	22
Other general education	7	8	8	10
Vocational education	84	89	86	80
Men				
Schools preparing for university	16	16	19	20
Other general education	4	5	6	7
Vocational education	87	92	86	82
Women				
Schools preparing for university	17	18	22	24
Other general education	9	10	10	13
Vocational education	80	87	86	78
Men in German-speaking cantons				
Schools preparing for university	14	13	16	17
Other general education	3	3	3	5
Vocational education	91	94	89	85
Men in French- or Italian-speaking cantons				
Schools preparing for university	22	23	26	28
Other general education	9	10	11	13
Vocational education	76	85	79	76
Women in German-speaking cantons				
Schools preparing for university	15	15	19	22
Other general education	9	10	10	13
Vocational education	83	88	88	78
Women in French- or Italian-speaking cantons				
Schools preparing for university	24	25	31	35
Other general education	20	19	17	21
Vocational education	63	79	74	66

Source: Authors.

German-speaking region enter vocational education more often than those of the French- and Italian-speaking regions.

c)   Graduates from general vs. vocational education, 1977-1993

Four out of five upper secondary graduates complete a vocational education, and one in five follow general education. The rate is slightly higher for males than for females, and the drop for females in recent years slightly more pronounced than for males.

Upper secondary vocational education

a)   Fields of study

Owing to the different duration of programmes, a comparison between all students in vocational occupation would distort the distribution of the occupational groups. Instead, a comparison is made between fields of study. The occupational groups of entrants have on the whole been remarkably stable, despite considerable economic changes and great shifts in size of the population involved in vocational education.

The four largest groups retained their relative rank up until the late 1980s. Only in the last few years has vocational education in health care overtaken "selling" in quantitative importance. Since both occupational groups are predominantly female, this change could indicate a move by women towards more prestigious occupations. There is also a move towards tertiary functions: occupations are increasing in administration, planning and communication (office work, draughting and technical work and graphics). The traditional industrial occupations (metal processing and machines, food and timber), and those in the building trade are declining, while the traditional service occupations in health care, sales, the restaurant and hotel trades, cosmetics, hairdressing and beauty care, increased during the first few years of the 1980s but – with the exception of health care – have lost some apprentices since then (Table 6).

The stability of the larger groups tends to mask any changes at the level of individual occupations. Particularly in small occupations, the number of new entrants each year tends to vary considerably.

b)   Learning sites

.   The majority of participants in vocational education are apprentices who train in two or three learning sites. The number of entrants in vocational education in full-time schools rose by one-third, from 10 to 16 per cent in 1977-1992. Programmes in part-time schools which also take place in only one formal learning

Table 6. **Entry rate in vocational education, by occupational group,
1978, 1980, 1985, 1993**

Percentage

	1978	1980	1985	1993
Total	100.0	100.0	100.0	100.0
Office	23.9	23.6	25.2	25.1
Metal-processing/machines	20.1	20.3	18.0	19.9
Health care	8.1	8.1	7.9	10.4
Selling	11.4	10.6	11.3	9.6
Draughting, technical occupations	5.4	6.1	5.6	5.9
Wood, cork	3.9	4.0	4.0	3.7
Hotel and restaurant trade, domestic science	3.9	3.5	4.8	3.6
Cosmetics, hairdressing, beauty care	3.1	3.0	3.0	3.0
Food, beverages	3.4	3.0	3.1	2.6
Construction, building trades	2.1	2.5	3.3	2.4
Horticulture	1.9	1.9	2.1	2.2
Painting	1.9	2.0	2.1	1.9
Agriculture	3.4	3.2	2.6	1.4
Graphics industry	1.1	1.2	1.2	1.3
Transport	1.5	2.0	1.1	0.8
Other fields	5.0	4.6	4.9	6.1

Source: Authors.

site are followed by 2 per cent of all students in vocational education for the whole period.

The differences between male and female and language region are quite pronounced here: in 1977, 4 per cent of males in the German-speaking cantons and 30 per cent of females in the French- and Italian-speaking cantons acquired their vocational education in a school (Figure 8). Both males and females of the French and Italian regions attend full-time vocational school more often than people in the German region, and both female groups study more often than males of the same region. All groups show an increase in participation in full-time vocational schools.

c) Duration of study

Ten years ago the percentage of students following long programmes was slightly higher. Today's changes can be explained by the trend towards tertiary occupations (Table 6) which traditionally have study programmes lasting up to three years, whereas training for industrial occupations usually lasts four years.

◆ Figure 8. **Entrants into vocational education: percentage of students in full-time schools, by gender and language region**
1977-92

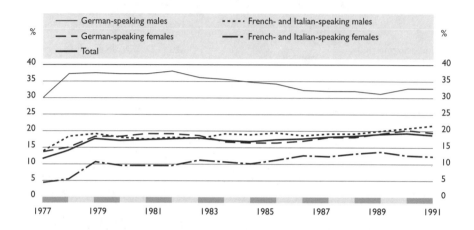

Source: Swiss Federal Statistical Office.

Pathways in evolution

Describing pathways through the system not only involves a review of the participation in a given programme but also a description of the paths taken. Unfortunately, current data allow us to depict only the single steps that make up paths. In addition, there is the problem of size of the groups: often the most interesting groups, those who leave the beaten track and implement new strategies, are quite small and therefore easily overlooked.

The step from lower secondary to upper secondary education

Most cantons divide the lower secondary level into streams with basic or wider demands. In 1993, two-thirds of students in the 8th grade were in wider-demand streams and one-third in a basic-demand stream. The step into upper secondary education or into the world of work presupposes the completion of nine years of schooling and not necessarily that of the nine-year programme of compulsory school. In actual fact, those who leave before their ninth year are almost exclusively basic-stream students; they are grouped into an "incomplete compulsory education" category.

In 1993, 85 per cent of those who had been in compulsory education in 1992 proceeded directly to upper secondary education, 54 per cent entered general education and 31 per cent vocational education. The remaining 15 per cent left the educational system, some to return to upper secondary education after an interruption in their career. Entering vocational education is almost the only choice for students from basic-demand streams, while those from wider-demand streams choose vocational and general education with almost the same frequency (Table 7). Although the overall rate of continuation of education at upper secondary level does not differ much from the streams at lower secondary level, the scope of programmes followed and their prestige is clearly different.

Students taking this first step of the pathway through upper secondary education can be divided into six main categories – those:

– leaving after lower secondary education;

– going from basic demands to vocational education;

– going from basic demands to general education;

– going from wider demands to vocational education;

– going from wider demands to general education other than *Gymnasia*;

– going from wider demands to general education in *Gymnasia*.

The evolution of the past 15 years shows a steady decrease in the proportion of students leaving the educational system after compulsory school, which would concord with the results already presented. Vocational education was at its peak in 1985 and has since declined below the 1978 rate for students leaving the lower secondary streams with wider demands. For students from lower secondary streams with basic demands, the decline between 1985 and 1993 is slight. Where there is competition between vocational and general education, it is concentrated mainly on students leaving the streams with wider demands. Of interest in this context is the small but growing number of students going from lower secondary streams with basic demands to general education other than *Gymnasia*. This group is much larger in the French- and Italian-speaking regions than in the German-speaking region and among females rather than males, which seems to indicate the strong preference for general education among these groups.

Scholastic history of entrants into upper secondary education

In this section the scholastic history of the new entrants into upper secondary education is examined, thus reversing the point of view of the previous section. In addition to those who had been in lower secondary education the year before, we also find entrants in a given programme who had attempted or followed another programme at upper secondary level.

Table 7. **Transition from lower secondary to upper secondary education, 1978, 1985, 1993**

Percentage

	Leaving after lower secondary education	Going from				
		Basic demands to		Wider demands to		
		Vocational education	General education	Vocational education	General education other than Gymnasia	General education in Gymnasia
All	14.62	24.18	1.86	30.36	7.59	21.39
Women						
German-speaking region	21.65	23.10	1.32	26.13	10.72	16.75
French- and Italian-speaking regions	11.14	10.83	5.32	27.54	12.96	32.4
Men						
German-speaking region	11.52	32.93	0.74	33.39	3.15	17.64
French- and Italian-speaking regions	9.75	19.25	2.75	34.5	5.25	29.25

Source: Authors.

a)   Scholastic history of entrants into general vs. vocational education

Seventy per cent of students in their first year of secondary education follow the "normal" track, *i.e.* they have been in school at the lower secondary level the previous year.[10] Sixteen per cent were already in upper secondary education and 14 per cent were not in school. The difference in history for students in the various programmes is quite pronounced and not very surprising (see Figure 6). The *Gymnasia* emerge as the schools with the highest rate of students from wider-demand streams, and with the lowest rate of students not having been in education the previous year. They are obviously not intended to be a mere detour. Vocational schools, however, are quite open to students who have interrupted their educational career, with one-third of their entrants having previously left the education system.

Fifteen per cent of entrants into vocational education had already been in upper secondary education; 3 per cent were repeating their first year in the same occupation, the others were probably acquiring a second upper secondary education. In this respect, the differences between the gender and language groups are important: while only 1 per cent of male German entrants had had an upper secondary general education, the figure rises to 14 per cent for French and Italian females. If there can be seen a trend towards acquiring first a general and then a vocational secondary education, it would seem to be most pronounced in the French- and Italian-speaking regions and among females. There appears to be little support for a move in the other direction – namely, acquiring general after vocational education – since there are no more than 3 per cent in any of the groups considered.

b)   Scholastic history of students in vocational education, according to fields of study, length of programme, and learning sites

The internal distinctions within VOTEC can presumably also be seen in the scholastic history of entrants into different occupations, in the length of programmes followed and in the various forms of education. We have already seen that the main difference between full-time vocational schools and apprenticeships lies in their accessibility after an interrupted educational career (Table 8). If we consider only those entrants coming from within the education system, schools receive 51 per cent coming from wider-demand streams, 25 per cent already from vocational education and only 12 per cent from basic-demand streams. Apprenticeships are taken up by 40 per cent of students from wider-demand streams and by 37 per cent from basic-demand streams. Full-time schools are generally more difficult.

The history of different occupational groups is quite varied (Figure 9). The groups also differ in the number of students coming from another upper

Table 8. **Scholastic history of entrants into upper secondary education, by programme, gender and language region, 1992**

Percentage

Education in 1992/93	Education in 1991/92					
	Incomplete compulsory education	Compulsory education, basic demands	Compulsory education, wider demands	Upper secondary general education	Upper secondary vocational education	Not in education the previous year
All						
General education	0.7	5.2	76.6	8.9	1.7	6.9
Gymnasia	0.1	0.1	91.0	7.5	0.7	0.5
Other schools	1.5	13.5	52.9	11.2	3.3	2.2
Vocational education	3.6	27.6	36.6	5.6	9.4	17.2
Vocational schools	0.7	7.9	33.1	8.2	14.8	35.3
Apprenticeships	4.2	32.2	37.3	5.0	8.2	13.1
Women						
German region						
General education	0.1	4.0	77.1	6.7	1.3	10.8
Vocational education	2.4	28.4	32.1	4.8	7.1	25.2
French and Italian regions						
General education	0.7	7.9	74.2	11.4	2.0	3.8
Vocational education	2.0	12.3	38.1	14.2	17.2	16.2
Men						
German region						
General education	0.4	2.9	83.3	5.5	1.2	6.8
Vocational education	4.9	34.6	38.5	2.3	5.9	13.9
French and Italian regions						
General education	1.9	6.5	70.6	13.7	2.7	4.7
Vocational education	4.2	21.1	40.3	8.6	17.4	8.4

Source: Authors.

◆ Figure 9. *Scholastic history of entrants into different occupational groups*
1992

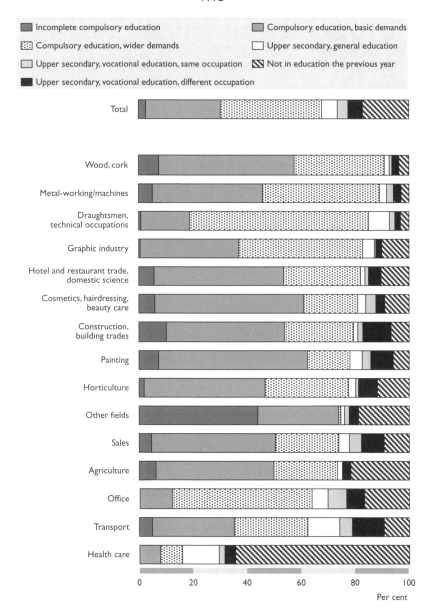

■ Incomplete compulsory education   ■ Compulsory education, basic demands

▦ Compulsory education, wider demands   □ Upper secondary, general education

□ Upper secondary, vocational education, same occupation   ▨ Not in education the previous year

■ Upper secondary, vocational education, different occupation

secondary education: they are particularly high in health care, transport, office work and in draughting and technical occupations. This comes as no surprise to the experts in the field, since some of the general education schools are set up specifically to lead to occupations, say, in transport or health care. Education for health care occupations can be entered at the age of 18 at the earliest, which would explain the large number of students coming from outside the education system. Among the occupations with the largest number of students following the straight track from lower secondary to the upper secondary are the core of the male industrial occupations in metal-working and machines, the graphics industry and in draughting and technical occupations. These occupational fields also offer good possibilities for tertiary education; their students are candidates for the *maturité professionnelle* and higher vocational education – perhaps the courses provided by vocational education are broad enough and offer such good prospects that few are tempted to make a detour via general education.

The longer a vocational education, the more scholastically qualified are the entrants (Figure 10) – the relationship between these two factors is quite direct. The shorter courses are also those more often followed after an interrupted educational career. The apprenticeships with a greater number of lessons are usually chosen by students who have had a better preparation at lower secondary level.

Pathways through upper secondary education

a) First entry into upper secondary education

The rate of first entry gives an indication of how many people of a cohort enter upper secondary education in a given programme. In 1993, vocational education was less popular among first entrants than with all other students (Table 9). The relative attraction of general and vocational education programmes since 1980 has shifted among the first entrants to an upper secondary education: general education is on the increase, while vocational education has declined.

These trends are valid for all groups, but they do not lessen the pronounced differences between genders and language regions. To begin upper secondary education in vocational education is still very much more common for males and in the German-speaking region.

b) Further steps through upper secondary education

After first entry, some students stay on to graduate in the same programme in upper secondary education, while others change programmes without completing their first, and still others return to upper secondary education after an interrup-

◆ Figure 10. **Scholastic history of entrants,**
by length of vocational education
(1992)

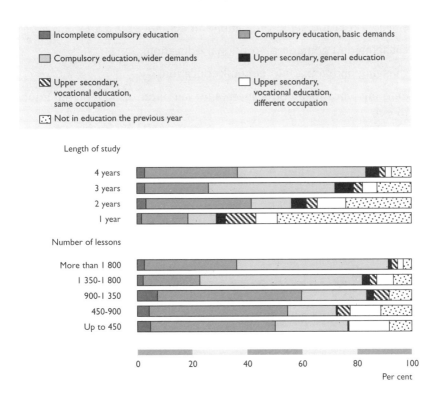

Source: Swiss Federal Statistical Office.

Table 9. **New entrants into upper secondary education,**
by programme, gender and language region, 1980, 1985, 1990, 1993

Percentage

	1980	1985	1990	1993
Schools preparing for university	16	16	19	21
Other general education	6	6	6	8
Vocational education	69	72	68	63

Source: Authors.

tion in their educational career. Further steps[11] along the pathway through upper secondary education can include:

- staying on in the same programme in vocational education;

- staying on in the same programme in general education;

- changing and going into vocational education;

- changing and going into general education;

- entering vocational education after an interruption of an educational career;

- entering general education after an interruption of an educational career;

- leaving the educational system from vocational education;

- leaving the educational system from general education.

The most common pattern is to stay on in a given programme either in vocational or in general education (Table 10). This is true for all four years (1980, 1985, 1990, 1993). What is also true for the whole of this timespan is the greater importance of vocational education in those pathways involving a change in programme or after a student has had a spell outside of the education system. Up until 1990, this tendency became even more marked, with an increase both in the changing of a programme to vocational education and in entering vocational education from outside; there has been a slight decrease in these patterns since then.

In 1993, an average of 51 per cent of the cohort stayed in the same vocational programme they had been in in 1992. This average masks the large divergence between males of the German-speaking cantons, of whom two-thirds stay on, and females of the French- and Italian-speaking regions, among whom only one-third do so. 22 per cent of the cohort stayed on in general education. Here too, German-speaking males and French- or Italian-speaking females represent the two extremes, with 16 vs. 38 per cent staying in the same programme.

Vocational education would appear to have the most positive balance (11 per cent) of this changing of programme, entering or leaving: in 1993, 20 per cent of the cohort went into vocational education and only 9 per cent left. General education, on the other hand, suffered a small net loss of 0.7 per cent after this further step through upper secondary education. The pattern of net gain for vocational education (ten percentage points) and the net loss of about one percentage point for general education has held since 1985. In 1980, the gain by vocational education had been smaller. These two extremes are also illustrated by German-speaking males giving a net gain for vocational education of three percentage points in 1993, and French- or Italian-speaking females 23 points.

Table 10. **A further step in the pathway through upper secondary education, 1980, 1985, 1990, 1993**

Percentage

Students are ...

	staying in		changing and going to		entering		leaving from	
	Vocational education	General education	Vocational education	General education	Vocational education	General education	Vocational education	General education
1980	53.7	15.2	8.7	1.2	7.7	0.9	10.0	3.0
1985	56.8	15.8	11.4	1.2	8.4	1.1	10.1	3.4
1990	53.7	19.1	12.9	1.4	8.4	1.3	10.0	3.2
1993	50.6	21.5	11.8	1.4	7.9	1.4	8.9	3.5

Source: Authors.

c) Upper secondary graduation

The number of upper secondary graduates[12] rose from 72 per cent in 1977 to 89 per cent in 1989. Since then, it has dropped to 83 per cent. The drop in the total graduation rate, which measures the number of graduates in relation to the population aged 16 to 21, is probably partly due to immigration, since the last few years have seen an immigration rate of 4 to 6 per cent for this age group. Most immigrants over the compulsory school age of 16 enter the labour market directly. There is in all probability no drop in the graduation rate of the resident population of both Swiss and foreign nationality. Another factor contributing to the drop in graduation rate is a shift in the education system: increasingly, some general education schools, which are not counted here, also give direct access to tertiary education. If their graduates were included, the rate would increase by 2 per cent in 1993, thus lowering the decrease.

d) Access to tertiary education

Access to tertiary education, especially vocational education, has been considerably on the increase. From 1985 to 1993 it rose by six percentage points to 28 per cent in higher vocational education for the whole population. University entrance increased by three percentage points to 13 per cent (Table 11). In general, the formal entry requirement for higher vocational education is graduation from initial vocational education, including apprenticehips. The high rate of entry for tertiary education is probably instrumental in keeping the interest high in vocational education at upper secondary level.

Table 11. **Entry rate in tertiary education, by type of education, 1987, 1990, 1993**

Percentage

	Higher vocational education	University
1987[1]	22	10
1990	25	11
1993	28	13

1. Earlier data not comparable.
Source: Authors.

e) Steps through upper secondary education and beyond

Figure 11 gives a simplified picture of pathways through upper secondary education, showing the situation of four steps: first entry; the situation during upper secondary education as a result of changing, crossing over, entering or leaving a given programme; graduation; and entry to tertiary education. General education expands consistently at each step, while entrance to vocational education declines slightly after 1985. The graduation rate of vocational education is on the decrease after 1990 accordingly. There is, however, no sign of a reduction in the number of entries to higher vocational education.

◆ Figure 11. **Pathways through upper secondary education**
1980, 1985, 1990, 1993

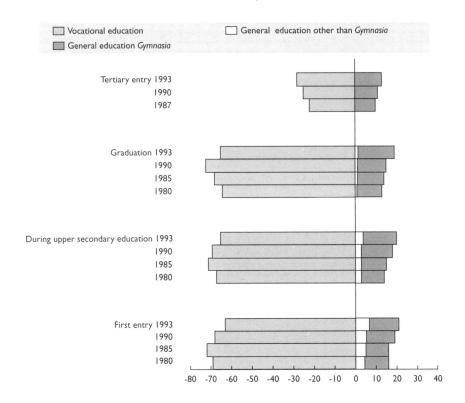

The preference for vocational education, including higher vocational education, is quite different between genders and language regions: German-speaking males have the highest rate of all four groups for first entry and graduation in vocational education and, in all training fields, for going on to higher vocational education. Further, they have a lower rate of change during upper secondary education. The opposite pattern is shown in many ways by French- and Italian-speaking females. German-speaking males also have the most stable pathways. Those from the French- or Italian-speaking regions, along with German-speaking females, hold a middle position in both respects, with French- or Italian-speaking females showing the greatest variation within pathways and the lowest participation in vocational education.

5. CONCLUSION

Current data as well as recent reforms show that the Swiss education system, including vocational and technical education, is quite stable. A strong division between general and vocational education is one of its main characteristics. Vocational education is still recognised as a valuable alternative to general education. However, the boundaries between general and vocational education have been slightly challenged by recent trends such as the *maturité professionnelle* and the increased possibility of access to "prestigious" higher education through the apprenticeship system.

An important element in the division between general and vocational education is the rigorous selectivity of lower secondary education. The achievement of young people there is the key for later choices.

An increasing trend towards upper secondary education either in a *Gymnasium* or in an apprenticeship is apparent, as is the growing percentage of young people who complete higher education. Generally, there is a trend towards the enhancement of school-based education.

Other important trends are the lower number of students leaving the system before completing compulsory education, the lower rate of students with interrupted careers, the higher rate going to *Gymnasia*, and the higher rate of those completing or attempting two different programmes of upper secondary education. Educational pathways seem at the same time to have become more widespread and less structured, with more meeting points between different programmes.

Plausible explanations cannot be derived just from the empirical data presented. Changed values of parents and young people are probably one element, with another – apart from the rising demand for more and higher education – being the increasing supply of many different educational provisions.

NOTES

1. The ordinance itself is based on the law of 1978 and the decree of 1979 (*cf.* Section 3). Ordinances are legislative means for implementing the law, or some parts of it.

2. Which will be upgraded to *Fachhochschulen* at the same time.

3. The numbering of the school years refers to the beginning of the year. School year 1993 thus means 1993/94.

4. The one-year training programmes are often part of a graduated programme.

5. Data is lacking for quite a few occupations. Information is only available for three quarters of the new entrants and for a few introductory courses.

6. 900 lessons is the equivalent of a one-year programme in compulsory school.

7. Estimation based on the fictive cohort method. Included are all entrants into upper secondary education from age 14 to 19. The rate of first entrants is calculated by deducting all students repeating their first year of the same programme or having attended another upper secondary programme in the preceding year. Further, it is estimated that only one third of those who enter upper secondary education after having interrupted their school career are first entrants.

8. Estimation based on the fictive cohort method. For the estimation of all entrants, students having attended another upper secondary programme in the preceding year are included.

9. For all estimations based on the fictive cohort method, population data by single year of age are necessary. These exist for all years for both genders and for the whole country. Regional data are available only for the years 1980, 1985, and from 1990 on a yearly basis. The earliest reference point is therefore school year 1980.

10. Detailed information is not available for the scholastic history of the first-year students who went to school in another canton or in a foreign country. However, there is no reason to suppose that they differ from those staying in the same canton and they are therefore excluded from the tables that follow.

11. Estimation based on information about the educational situation in Year *x* of those who had been enrolled in the first year of upper secondary education in Year *x*-1.

12. Estimation based on the fictive cohort method. Included are vocational education of at least two years' duration, schools leading to university entrance exams, and schools for teacher training. Omitted therefore are the one-year vocational programmes, interme-diate diploma schools and other general education schools. The omissions are made to reduce the number of double counting of graduations when estimating the number of graduates.

CONCLUSION: WHERE ARE PATHWAYS GOING?
Conceptual and methodological lessons from the pathways study

by

David Raffe, Centre for Educational Sociology, University of Edinburgh, Scotland

1. THE PATHWAYS APPROACH: A TOOL FOR RESEARCH AS WELL AS A POLICY?

Educational discourse is full of the metaphor of travel. We talk of students' origins and destinations, and the itineraries that link them. We describe tracks and streams, royal roads and alternative routes, one-way streets and dead-ends, and ladders and bridges. We apply terms such as "parking lot" to schemes where there is little progress. The pathways approach uses this metaphor to analyse education and training systems. It presents systems as networks of interconnected pathways, which may vary in the way that the pathways are structured and in the nature of their interconnections.

Policy makers try to influence participation in vocational and technical education and training (VOTEC) by changing the structure of pathways. This may take the form of:

- increasing the length of VOTEC pathways, thus providing opportunities for progression to higher levels of study and making these pathways more attractive;

- providing pathways from VOTEC to higher education, to attract students who aspire to higher education or who wish to keep their options open;

- increasing pathways between general education and VOTEC, in either direction;

- increasing the flexibility of pathways within VOTEC, making it easier to transfer between occupational areas and allowing students to keep their options open; or

- introducing new pathways.

Policy changes based on this concept of "pathways" can be observed in a wide range of countries, including those with well-developed VOTEC systems and those trying to develop systems which were formerly weak. There is a strong and widespread policy interest in pathways, and this interest was expressed at the very first policy seminar of the OECD's VOTEC activity (Raffe, 1994a). Following this seminar, several Member countries agreed to join a study in which they could learn from each others' experience of using pathways to influence participation in VOTEC.

But the very familiarity of the metaphor of pathways may make it a blunt instrument of analysis and research. We all know what we mean by pathways, or we think we do – until we apply the concept to a cross-national study such as this one and find we all use the term in different ways. A major task for the study – and the task which took the longest time – was to develop a conceptual framework which would be clear and rigorous enough to apply to countries with very different education and training systems. We had to develop the concept of pathways from a tool to support national policy development, into an instrument of cross-national research and analysis.

In this chapter we reflect on the conceptual and methodological lessons from this study. We first outline the conceptual framework developed in the study, and then address three questions:

1. How well does the conceptual framework of the pathways approach work when we apply it to each country?

2. What kinds of lessons can we learn from cross-national comparisons based on the conceptual framework?

3. What are the lessons for future research?

2.   THE CONCEPTUAL FRAMEWORK OF THE PATHWAYS APPROACH

Assumptions

The pathways approach starts from three assumptions.

The first assumption is that, in a democratic society, policy makers have an interest in participation in VOTEC. They are interested in the number of students who follow VOTEC programmes, and in the characteristics of these students – for example, their gender, social composition and prior educational attainment. They are interested in participation in VOTEC relative to participation in general education, and in different branches and levels of VOTEC. There may be economic reasons for this policy interest: for example, skills acquired through VOTEC may be perceived to contribute to national economic competitiveness. There may also be social reasons: for example, the perception that participation in VOTEC may prevent failure and exclusion, especially among disadvantaged sections of society.

The *second assumption* is that participation depends on the attractiveness of different education and training programmes to students or potential students. Modern education and training systems are increasingly diverse and complex; they are also increasingly governed by principles of democracy and individual choice. It is therefore neither feasible nor acceptable to regulate participation merely by directing students and rationing places. To an increasing extent, students choose their educational itineraries. Even when their choices are "guided" by teachers or counsellors, or influenced by family and peers, it is accepted that the main criterion should be their individual aspirations, needs and interests. We do not expect young people to select educational programmes in order to serve the interests of the state or of the economy. Instead, policy makers must find the educational equivalent of Adam Smith's "invisible hand": they must arrange things so that when individuals make the educational choices that pursue their own interests, they will also serve the economic and social interests of the society of which they are part. However, the parallel with Adam Smith stops at this point.

Our *third assumption* is that the desired pattern of participation will not necessarily be achieved by a *laissez-faire* approach. That is, it will not necessarily be achieved by letting the education system find its own equilibrium or by leaving everything to "market forces". A *laissez-faire* approach is unlikely to address issues of equity, the needs of the disadvantaged or the long-term interests of the economy. It may indeed unleash a credentialist spiral, in which the competitive scramble for high-status "academic" qualifications marginalises VOTEC. Policy makers' interest in participation in VOTEC, in other words, needs to be an active interest.

Our study did not set out to test these assumptions, although it may encourage us to reflect critically upon them. It aimed to explore *a fourth assumption*, and to test some hypotheses derived from it. This is that policy makers can influence the attractiveness of educational programmes, and consequently the level and pattern of participation in them, by changing the structure of the pathways which connect them.

Programmes and pathways

In our conceptual framework, education is provided in the form of programmes, which may be linked together in sequences to form pathways. An example may help here. Students reaching the upper secondary stage in France may enter the VOTEC programme which leads to the *Brevet d'études professionnelles* (BEP); some of these students may then follow a further programme, leading to

377

the *Baccalauréat technologique*, which in turn may lead to higher education pro-grammes such as the *Section de techniciens supérieurs* (STS). These three programmes form a pathway, although each programme also forms part of other pathways with different starting points and/or destinations. Thus, students completing the BEP may instead continue to the *baccalauréat professionnel* and thereafter enter employment.

An education system is a network of pathways. In some systems the different pathways may be separate, with few opportunities to move between them, so that each programme is a component of just one pathway (or very few); in other systems there may be numerous cross-roads, junctions and interconnecting routes, so that any programme may be entered by students travelling along a variety of different pathways.

We can therefore describe an education system and its components in terms of the characteristics of:

- *individual programmes*: their entrance requirements, content, level, learning site (school, workplace), duration, certification, and the access or entitle-ment to further education or training which they may give;
- *individual pathways*: their starting point, length, sequence (for example, sequence of general and vocational programmes and/or of programmes at different levels) and destination; pathways may also be described in terms of the characteristics of their component programmes (for example, we may talk of "general" or "work-based" pathways); and
- *systems of pathways*: the age or stage at which pathways diverge, the number and diversity of pathways, their interconnectedness, and so on; a system may also be described in terms of the characteristics of the average or typical pathways within it (for example, we may talk of a system with "long" pathways).

Opportunities, incentives, costs and constraints (OICCs)

The premise of the pathways approach is that young people's participation in a given programme may be influenced by the pathways to which the programme may lead. To put this more formally, decisions to participate are influenced by the opportunities, incentives, costs and constraints (OICCs) associated with each programme, and the OICCs in turn are influenced by the structure of pathways. For example, a country may try to increase the incentive to participate in upper secondary VOTEC programmes by creating (or strengthening) the pathways which link them to higher education.

The OICCs associated with a particular programme are also affected by fac-tors external to the education system. The most important of these is the labour market, which is an important source of incentives and constraints. Participation in a programme is influenced by the labour-market value of the qualifications to which the programme, and the pathways to which it gives access, may lead. The boundaries of our conceptual framework become untidy at this point. Many education and training systems are developing new forms of alternance, new ways of linking learning and work, and new relationships between employment and training. In such systems, as well as in longer established apprenticeship systems, it may be difficult to distinguish between educational pathways and pathways into (and within) the labour market. Ideally, our concept of pathways would be broad enough to include transitions into the labour market; however, in this study we have primarily focused on the structure of pathways within education systems.

The individual student

The next element in our conceptual framework is the individual student, or potential student, who may respond to the OICCs when making decisions. The pathways approach thus links the level of the system, with which policy makers must engage, with the level of the individual.

The OICCs associated with a particular set of pathways may vary across different categories of students. Earlier, we gave the example of new pathways from VOTEC to higher education which provide a new incentive to enter VOTEC; this incentive is stronger for students whose prior educational attainment suggests they have a good chance of qualifying for, and surviving in, higher education. OICCs may also vary between males and females or between different social groups. This may be a consequence of labour-market segmentation which creates different returns to qualifications for males and females or for different social groups.

Young people's participation in VOTEC – and their responses to a given set of OICCs – depend on their aspirations and preferences. These are also likely to vary across different categories of young people: for example, in relation to gender, social class and ethnicity or nationality. Moreover, they may change autonomously – that is, independently of the education and training system and the labour market. The pathways approach seeks to engage with the concern, expressed in many countries, about long-term changes in the occupational and educational aspirations of young people and the consequences for participation in VOTEC. Key variables include the general level of aspirations, the place of work and employment within young people's life plans, the importance of occupations as a source of identity, and the extent to which young people pursue specific objectives or seek to keep their options open (Adamski and Grootings, 1989; Banks *et al.*, 1992; Evans and Heinz, 1994).

The conceptual framework assumes that young people respond to OICCs when making decisions about participation; it therefore assumes a degree of rationality on their part. There is both a pragmatic and a theoretical justification for this assumption. The pragmatic justification is that it is easier to plan educational opportunities (or, for that matter, to construct theoretical models) on the assumption that the beneficiaries behave rationally and, therefore, predictably. Given that at least part of young people's behaviour is rational, this may be the part to which policy makers can more effectively address their efforts. The theoretical justification is that the outcomes of young people's decision-making are "rational", in the sense that they could be predicted on the assumption of rational behaviour, even if the processes which lead to those outcomes do not always resemble a model of formal rationality (Hodkinson and Sparkes, 1993; Finegold, 1995). However, the assumption of rationality is one that can, and should, be put to further test. There is a trend in some recent research to explore young people's different strategies or approaches to their educational and other transitions (Chisholm et al., 1990; Evans and Heinz, 1994); if we could link this type of research to the systems perspective of the pathways approach, we would have a powerful explanatory model indeed.

Information and guidance

Rational or not, young people's choices will depend on the information that is available to them, both about the available programmes and about the associated pathways and their OICCs. Sources of guidance – both formal and informal – have an important part to play in our conceptual framework, and one that will increase in importance as programmes and pathways become more complex.

Hypotheses

To animate our conceptual framework, and to give a focus for the country studies, we developed a set of hypotheses. These are listed in the annex to Chapter 1.

The hypotheses focus on the system level; a typical hypothesis predicts that a particular type of pathway, or system of pathways, has a particular effect on participation in VOTEC. It would equally be possible to develop hypotheses which focus on the individual level. Such hypotheses might predict trends in young people's preferences and aspirations, or in their responses to different types of OICCs, or systematic variations across categories of young people. Constructing and testing hypotheses at the individual level may be an appropriate next step in the development of the pathways framework.

3. APPLYING THE CONCEPTUAL FRAMEWORK WITHIN EACH COUNTRY

Comparative case studies

Early in the pathways study we decided on a comparative case-study approach. This gave priority to the analysis of pathways *within* rather than *between* countries, and especially to the analysis of changes in pathways and participation in each country. We did not try to describe each country's system of pathways in terms of standardised "indicators" and look for correlations between these indicators and participation in VOTEC. We used quantitative data, but mainly to analyse pathways and participation within each country, and especially to identify trends. Our comparisons across countries are made at a more qualitative level, in terms of the conceptual framework of the pathways approach and the working hypotheses developed for the study. These comparisons are presented in Claude Pair's synthesis in Chapter 1.

The case-study approach meant that we could analyse pathways more thoroughly and respect the complexity and diversity of countries' institutional structures. We could allow for the complex linkages between education, the labour market and other societal institutions (Maurice *et al.*, 1986). We could also refer to contextual information on policy and provision, and to other data available for each country, for example research on young people's reasons for choosing pathways. More practically, by choosing a case-study approach we were less constrained by the varying coverage and availability of statistical data for each country.

Applying the pathways approach to single-country studies

It should therefore be possible for each chapter in this book to stand alone, and to be read as an analysis of a single country. The conceptual framework of the pathways approach should be as valuable a tool for the analysis of a single country as for cross-national comparisons. How well has it stood up to this test?

On the whole it has worked well. The chapters in this book show that the pathways concept can be used to describe a variety of different education systems and to analyse change within these systems. Occasionally this may require somewhat arbitrary judgements; for example, when a programme includes a number of different lines or courses, it may be difficult to decide whether to count each line, or group of lines, as separate programmes; but this is the kind of judgement required in all research, in this instance the familiar trade-off between precision and parsimony of explanation.

More importantly, the pathways approach provides valuable insights into how each system works. We have learnt far more about many of the education systems described in this book than we could have learnt from any number of official reports or "organigrammes". The chapters put flesh on the bones of more formal accounts of systems, and sometimes they present rather different interpretations. They may challenge a country's image of its education system as open or flexible, or they may draw attention to pathways which have more symbolic than actual substance. They may, as in the Dutch case, show that the pathways actually travelled by students are more diverse and deviant than the conventional account supposes. Some chapters present a more reassuring picture than the public image. The chapter on Germany shows the country's relative stability and gradual pace of change compared with many other countries; this seems to contrast with German anxieties over declining VOTEC participation which have been well publicised in other countries (CEREQ, 1993).

One of the most important insights provided by the pathways approach concerns the strength and consistency of the hierarchical dimension within each education system. We discuss the hierarchical character of education systems further below.

The conceptual framework, therefore, can be applied to individual education and training systems and it can illuminate the way each system functions. But there appear to be two recurring difficulties in applying the framework within countries. The first arises from the limitations of the available statistics. The second is the problem of how empirically to identify pathways, independently of policy intentions and of the journeys that students make along them.

Limitations of available statistics

The pathways approach makes demanding requirements for statistical data. Ideally, it requires data which:

- describe flows as well as stocks – that is, data on student flows as well as on levels of participation;
- describe flows through the whole education and training system, including apprenticeship and part-time education, and into the labour market;
- compare students from different educational and social backgrounds; and
- describe the system at different points in time, using categories that allow us to make comparisons over time.

The data for most countries do not satisfy all these requirements. The countries generally have better data on stocks (numbers of students participating in programmes) than on flows (transitions between programmes). When flow data exist, they tend to be partial. In some countries, flow data are available only from one-off studies, or for particular regions, rather than on a regular, national basis. In many cases the available flow data describe particular transition points rather than flows throughout the whole system. Transitions between different full-time education programmes are relatively well described, at least in some countries, but transitions in and out of full-time education are less well covered. Most countries have poor information on flows through apprenticeship or part-time education, on entry to the labour market and subsequent outcomes, on young people returning to full-time education after a break, or on "second-chance" educational opportunities. The available data may also neglect less conventional pathways – for example, "sideways" moves between general education and VOTEC at the upper secondary level, despite the increasing frequency of such transitions in countries such as Switzerland.

In order to understand pathways, it may be necessary to know about flows across more than one transition point. For example, a new pathway may allow students to move from VOTEC to higher education; but to judge the value of this pathway we need to know whether the students who followed it had the same chances of success as other higher education students, and whether their subsequent prospects were the same. Few of the chapters in the book present data on two-stage flows of this kind. It is possible that such data exist for several countries but proved too complex to present in the space available.

The pathways approach is concerned with changes in pathways and participation, and therefore requires data on change over time. Here again the data fall short of the ideal requirements. Only a few countries have regular national information on the flows through the system of different cohorts of young people. Even data on "stocks" over time may have limitations. New methods or principles of data collection may be introduced at the same time as new pathways (for example, Australian data from 1993 onwards only cover students participating in pursuit of an award, a shift which parallels the conceptual shift towards an outcome-based system); in such cases it can be difficult to make "before/after" comparisons.

Most countries routinely record the gender of students in their national statistics; some of the most interesting conclusions of this study concern variations or (more usually) similarities in gender differences across countries. Information on other student characteristics, such as social class, ethnicity or nationality, tends only to be available from ad hoc research studies. Yet this information can be invaluable, as the Italian and German reports illustrate, because of the light they may shed on the hierarchical nature of educational pathways.

Despite these limitations, the chapters in this book demonstrate that a great deal can be achieved with the data currently available, given an appropriate conceptual framework within which to present them. In this respect, the pathways approach has proved its value. However, countries vary widely with respect to the adequacy and coverage of the available data; moreover, within each country the data need careful interpretation in the light of the specific national context. It would therefore be very difficult to make direct statistical comparisons of flows and pathways across countries, or to construct indicators to represent the key concepts of the pathways perspective. For the time being, at least, it is more appropriate to proceed on a case-study basis, and to analyse each country within the constraints of its available data.

How to identify pathways

The second difficulty in applying the framework concerns the basis on which pathways can be identified empirically. Most of the chapters in the book do so in one of two ways.

The first approach identifies pathways on the basis of the intentions of the policy makers who created them and the formal opportunities they put in place. Several chapters describe policies which are still being introduced, so there may be no other way to describe the new pathways except through the intentions of policy makers. However, "real" pathways may not precisely match these intentions. This is easiest to demonstrate in countries where formal pathways are very flexible. Our research on Scottish vocational education suggests that traditional pathways have been highly resilient despite the formal flexibility provided by a national modular framework (Raffe, 1994b); similar "informal" pathways are likely to persist in Australia after the Australian Vocational Certificate Training System (AVCTS) is introduced. Even in countries with more structured or regulated pathways, "real" pathways may differ from those intended by policy makers. An entitlement to higher education may be more symbolic than real; and we may find, as in the Dutch case, that some of the most well trodden pathways deviate from the conventional map (although this may reflect the intentions of policy makers in designing a flexible system).

The second approach describes pathways in terms of the journeys that students make along them. But this too raises problems. A pathway which is only followed by a few students may provide an incentive to many more students to enter the programmes which lead to it. For example, few VOTEC students may make use of an entitlement to higher education, but this may have attracted them to VOTEC in the first place because it let them keep their formal options open. The more general problem is circularity. The pathways approach explains participation on the basis of pathways; but what kind of explanation is it if the pathways can only be identified on the basis of the number of students who follow them?

The difficulty, then, is to identify pathways independently of policy intentions on the one hand, and of student movements on the other. This is mainly a problem when describing changes in pathways. Many of the chapters describe changes in pathways which are complex and subtle, typically comprising numerous incremental changes designed to strengthen particular pathways, or to steer young people in some directions rather than others. Even changes which appear to be more radical may be difficult to describe: for example, in England and Wales GNVQs may lead to changes in pathways but they do not introduce completely new pathways, since they replace previous programmes which occupied a similar place in the map of pathways.

In our conceptual framework pathways – and changes in pathways – may be identified on the basis of the OICCs (opportunities, incentives, costs and constraints) associated with them. The OICCs provide the motive power for the pathways perspective; pathways influence participation through the OICCs that they create. But OICCs are difficult to measure directly. Most of the chapters in this book which discuss changing OICCs, and the reasons for changes in participation, do so post hoc. Hence the problem of circularity: if we can only infer the existence of pathways (and the strength of the OICCs) from the fact that students are making journeys along them, and from the number of students who do so, our explanations may be circular.

In practice, our case-study approach means that our reasoning need not be circular. Each author has access to other information about the country concerned, and to research evidence on the reasons for the changes in participation. The practical constraints of the study have meant that authors have only made limited use of contextual evidence of this kind, but this is the logic of our methodology. By piecing together a wide variety of types of evidence we can start to construct an explanation for changes in each country, and the pathways perspective gives us a conceptual framework for doing so.

4. THE PATHWAYS APPROACH IN CROSS-NATIONAL COMPARISONS

"Degrees of freedom" and cross-national comparisons

In the previous section we discussed the pathways approach as a tool for the analysis of individual countries. There are at least three ways in which we can learn more by putting the case studies alongside each other – that is, by making the study a comparative one. We can learn more about each individual country; we can learn from the similarities in the experience of different countries; and we can learn from the differences among countries. These three types of learning are related, and we say more about them in the sub-sections that follow.

One of the most familiar problems of comparative research arises from the small number of countries typically studied (Ryan, 1991). We would not expect to gain much explanatory power from comparisons among a sample of ten individuals: in statistical terms, the "degrees of freedom" would be too small for reliable inference. A sample of ten countries might appear equally unpromising. However, our study addresses this problem in two ways.

In the first place, it increases the degrees of freedom for analysis by studying change within each country, as well as by studying differences across countries. A study of comparative dynamics has considerably more explanatory power than a study of comparative statics (Rose, 1991). As an example, let us consider the evidence on Hypothesis 2 ("delayed divergence of pathways"), discussed by Claude Pair in Chapter 1. Countries in which pathways diverge at an early stage tend to have the highest participation in VOTEC at secondary level, but this "static" comparison tells us little about the effect of pathways on participation. Cause and effect are probably in the opposite direction: only in countries with strong VOTEC systems, such as Austria, Germany, the Netherlands and Switzerland, is it politically acceptable to allow children to embark on a VOTEC programme at such an early age. However, Pair also notes that VOTEC participation (at secondary level) has declined in countries such as France and Quebec where the age at which pathways diverge has been raised; this dynamic comparison provides a stronger basis for inferring cause and effect.

Second, because our study is based on case studies, it gains degrees of freedom from the case study within each country as well as from the between-country comparisons. We can give our hypotheses a double test: we can ask whether they explain differences between countries; and using the contextual data available on each country, we can ask whether the hypotheses explain trends and patterns within each country. For example, the chapter on Austria reviews the hypotheses in the light of that country's experience.

Learning more about each country

It is a cliché, but none the less true, that one of the main benefits from comparative research is that one comes to understand one's own country much better. In this study this self-learning has come about in several ways.

First, the comparative approach makes us more competent to apply the conceptual framework to our own countries. In our study we had to reach a common understanding of the framework, and we did so by example: we observed how our colleagues applied the framework to their countries, and this helped us to apply it to our own. These chapters can be seen as an extension of the same process. Each chapter illustrates how to interpret the conceptual framework and apply it to a particular country's circumstances; it also tests the framework and helps us to develop it for future applications. If the pathways approach is used in further studies of participation in VOTEC, this volume will provide an excellent starting point.

Second, the comparative approach sensitises us to the complexity, and even idiosyncrasy, of each country's pathways; and it allows us to develop the language of pathways so that we can apply it more effectively to analyse this complexity.

We may seek to describe these systems of pathways in terms of the concepts discussed earlier (diversity, interconnectedness, flexibility, etc.); but there may be as much variation within systems as there is between them. For example, a country may have flexible pathways connecting certain programmes, but it may have rigid or restricted pathways in other parts of the system. Seeing the different systems described alongside each other helps us to resist the temptation to classify any one country in terms of an over-simplified typology. Typologies may have great heuristic value but they must be applied cautiously to any individual country.

Third, the comparative approach allows an empirical "benchmarking": each country can compare its own experience with that of others. This too must be done cautiously. Our ten case studies are not a representative sample of OECD countries. (For example, none of the case studies, with the possible exception of some Australian states, is integrating general and vocational learning within unified upper secondary education, as is the case in Scotland and Sweden and on an experimental basis in Finland.) Nevertheless, the countries cover a sufficiently wide range of systems to make the benchmark useful. Some trends revealed by this study would provide a valuable frame of reference for VOTEC policy debates within countries. For example, the study shows that participation in secondary-level VOTEC, especially in the non-technological branches, is declining in a wide range of countries; yet policy debates within countries often ignore this wide-spread decline, and focus only on national trends.

Although the studies in this book do not discuss labour-market structures in detail, they point to the importance of labour markets for understanding VOTEC systems. This is another lesson that each country can take from the comparisons. It is tempting to conclude that there are two basic kinds of education and training systems: those with a strong labour-market demand for qualifications from intermediate-level VOTEC, and those without. The logic of pathways differs between the two. In the first type of system, it may be possible to strengthen VOTEC by emphasizing the differences between VOTEC and general education. In the second type of system, VOTEC at the secondary level may be strengthened only by bringing it closer to general education, and by developing pathways between VOTEC and general education (including pathways to higher education). This logic may eventually lead to a unified system which integrates general and vocational education (Raffe, 1995).

Learning from similarities between countries

Writers on comparative methodology distinguish between studies which focus on differences between countries, and those which focus on similarities (Kohn, 1987; Scheuch, 1990). The pathways approach, we believe, is consistent with both. The current fashion in comparative research may be to focus on differences, but the similarities may be at least as important, especially if they are commonly overlooked.

There is a tendency to blame educational problems on specific features of a national education system when these problems are, in fact, symptomatic of much wider trends. In Chapter I Claude Pair concludes that VOTEC participation in all countries is being "swept along by the general expansion of education". Participation is declining in the lower-status forms of VOTEC at secondary level, and expansion is most likely to occur in technological programmes and at the post-secondary stages. The fact that such trends are widespread, if not universal, means that we should be sceptical of explanations that are specific to a single country. (And, more practically, countries trying to develop apprenticeship systems need to understand why participation in apprenticeship is tending to decline in those systems where it is the dominant mode of provision.)

Such trends in VOTEC participation could, at least in principle, be inferred from national-level indicators (although a case-study approach such as ours gives us more confidence that we have adequately understood these trends). The real contribution of this study is that it identifies similarities across countries at a more analytical level. Probably the most important of these similarities is the hierarchical nature of each education system. Programmes at each stage of education are ordered in a status hierarchy; pathways connecting higher-status programmes tend to be longest and to extend most frequently to the highest educational stages; and lateral pathways tend to connect programmes at adjacent positions in the status hierarchy. Status is correlated with the social background and prior attainment of those who participate; and VOTEC programmes (at the secondary stage) have lower status than general programmes. It is impossible to explain the dynamics of educational systems without at least implicit reference to their hierarchical nature.

These generalisations appear to hold true for all countries in the study. It is not surprising that the status of VOTEC and the need for "parity of esteem" are almost universal themes of national policy debates. But our study makes us sceptical about such debates. Can we trust the good sense, or even the good faith, of policies which aim at parity of esteem, if these policies are not based on an analysis which explains why they will achieve something which has eluded other systems? And to what extent do these policies rest on country-specific explanations of the problem, when our analysis suggests that the explanation transcends countries?

The hierarchical character of education systems may vary in subtle ways across countries, although our study does not provide sufficient evidence to judge this. It does, however, point to the room for manoeuvre which is still available to the national policy maker. In the first place, although VOTEC occupies the same relative position in each country's status hierarchy, its absolute position may depend on the size and accessibility of the general education programmes above it in the hierarchy. Second, even if VOTEC has low status in secondary education, it may have higher status than general education at the higher education level. It remains to be seen whether further expansion will cause this last observation to be revised: as higher education increasingly comprises two or more stages, will VOTEC come to have low status at the first of these stages?

Learning from differences between countries

The third type of learning made possible by our comparative methodology is in respect of differences between countries. Each country's education system may be represented as a network of pathways. Is there evidence that national differences in pathways result in variations in participation in VOTEC? Our research design focuses on comparative dynamics, so we can re-phrase this question: do differential changes in national pathways lead to differential changes in participation in VOTEC? One way to answer this question takes change in the independent variable (pathways) as its starting point; another way takes change in the dependent variable (participation).

The first approach starts by identifying countries in which pathways have changed in a particular way, and tries to identify common effects on participation. For example, what can we learn from the experience of countries which have introduced "long pathways" in VOTEC, and especially those which have introduced or strengthened pathways to higher education?

The answer, as Claude Pair points out in Chapter 1, is that long pathways appear to be associated with higher participation in the relevant VOTEC programmes. Our study provides evidence in support of the hypothesis but falls short of proving it. The evidence of our study, on this as on the other hypotheses, is subject to two main limitations.

The first arises from the problem, discussed earlier, of identifying changes in pathways independently of changes in journeys along them. The Danish study provides an illustration. Participation in full-time upper secondary VOTEC (HHX/HTX) programmes has increased; over the same period the number of students progressing from these programmes to higher education has also increased. But from the evidence presented in the Danish study it is not possible to say whether there has been an independent change in pathways from VOTEC to higher education, resulting in stronger incentives (OICCs) to enter VOTEC. The increased flows to higher education may simply be a consequence of the increased number of VOTEC students and of their educational backgrounds. We need additional contextual evidence, for example on the entrance arrangements for higher education or on the motives of young people entering VOTEC programmes, before we can say whether the pathways themselves have changed. But even if there were no change in pathways over the period covered by our study, it would be significant that participation increased in the sector of VOTEC which already gave access to higher education. It would be reasonable to conclude (on the evidence of the other case studies) that Danish participation in VOTEC would not have increased had there been no such sector.

The second reason for caution is more basic: at present there is not enough variation in the independent variable to draw strong empirical conclusions. Innovations such as the GNVQ in England and Wales and the reforms of VOTEC in Quebec are too recent for their long-term effects on participation to be assessed. Other changes in pathways, such as the Swiss *Berufsmatura*, the Austrian *Fachhochschulen* and the AVCTS in Australia, are still being introduced. Other possible reforms, notably in Italy and Germany, are still under discussion. Perhaps inevitably, the case studies contain as much speculation on the effects of pathways as direct evidence on those effects. The speculation is none the less fascinating. These countries will provide valuable evidence for a further study of pathways when these changes have all taken effect. However, we must be patient. Educational changes tend to be slow to introduce and slow to take effect. The policies described here aim to influence participation in VOTEC programmes by shaping pathways which may extend many years ahead. These policies will only be "reality-tested", and perhaps gain credibility among the young, once people have travelled along them and demonstrated their viability. The long-term effects of changes in pathways may only be observable over a lengthy period.

The second approach to comparative dynamics takes a change in the dependent variable – participation – as its starting point. Participation in VOTEC at the secondary level increased significantly in just two of the countries studied, Denmark and the Netherlands. We have already discussed the Danish trend; what can we learn from the case study of the Netherlands about the reasons for its exceptional trend in participation?

There seem to be two main reasons for the increase in participation in the MBO, the main upper secondary VOTEC programme in the Netherlands. The first, and possibly more important, concerns the labour market. As de Bruijn notes, MBO graduates "have a strong labour market position, they find a job quite easily and they have good career perspectives". This is not true of graduates of full-time vocational programmes in many other countries. The second reason is the position of MBO in relation to the pathways in the Dutch system. Specifically:

- there are multiple, flexible, pathways leading to the MBO;

- many of the (alternative) pathways through general education tend to be relatively inaccessible and/or unattractive to a large proportion of young people;

- short MBO (KMBO) courses were introduced to accommodate less qualified and disadvantaged school leavers without devaluing the MBO;
- there are good pathways through MBO to vocational higher education
  (HBO), which in turn leads to good labour-market opportunities.

Can we learn lessons from the Netherlands which can be transferred to countries with different labour markets and educational systems? With respect to educational pathways, we believe that it may be possible to draw transferable lessons from the Dutch experience, but only at a certain level of abstraction. The lesson is that Dutch pathways are so arranged in relation to the educational status hierarchy as to offset the downward pressure on VOTEC participation that this hierarchy generates elsewhere. We do not know to what extent this has been conscious in Dutch policy thinking, but it helps to explain the high (and rising) participation in MBO programmes.

With respect to the labour-market value of VOTEC, we are less sure of the scope for learning practical lessons from the Netherlands, or from any other country. The different structures of national labour markets may help to explain why VOTEC qualifications are more valued in some countries than others (Ryan et al., 1991); but these differences are not within the power of VOTEC policy makers to influence. Recent comparative research has emphasized the "societal" perspective. A country's education and training system must be understood in relation to other societal institutions such as its labour market and economy, its industrial relations system and its system of government (Maurice et al., 1986; Finegold, 1995). The societal perspective is consistent with our case-study approach. However, it warns us against explanations which focus on a single set of factors such as pathways or the labour market; and it warns us against using simple causal models to study the complexities of education systems and their place in society.

The Netherlands also illustrates how much it is possible to learn about pathways even in a system where there has been no single large change in them.

5. WHAT NEXT?

As an analytical tool the pathways approach is still at an early stage of development. The chapters in this book have demonstrated its value, but there is more that could be done. We conclude by proposing four areas for further work.

First, there is a need to develop the data sources on participation and flows, ideally so that each country can present data which satisfy the requirements which we listed earlier.

Second, the conceptual framework needs further development. We need a richer language to describe and compare systems of pathways, while respecting the complexity of each system. In due course this language might become the basis for country-level indicators and/or typologies.

Third, we need to develop the conceptual framework at the individual (student) level, and to give more attention to this level in national case studies. This study has necessarily focused primarily on pathways and participation at the system level. A next step could be to review the student-level evidence within each country: for example, on young people's preferences and aspirations, on how they perceive and respond to OICCs, on information and guidance, and on changes and variations in all of these. The pathways approach, and its conceptual framework, would provide a basis for this review because it links the individual and system levels. Young people do not form preferences in the abstract but in relation to a particular structure of opportunities. The pathways approach enables us to analyse individual preferences and aspirations in the context of the system within which they are formed.

Finally, pathways continue to change; we need research to make sure that we learn as much as possible from the experience of these changes. In many of the countries described here the most important changes in pathways are still in progress. Other countries are also introducing major reforms which affect pathways. It would be regrettable if the strong policy interest shown when these reforms are introduced wanes before it is possible to assess their impact. There is a continuing need for pathways studies, and they must be planned and started as soon as possible if the necessary data collection is to be set in motion. This book demonstrates the value of the pathways approach; it also demonstrates the crucial role of the OECD in mobilising and co-ordinating such studies.

BIBLIOGRAPHY

ADAMSKI, W. and GROOTINGS, P. (1989), *Education and Work in Europe*, Routledge, London.

BANKS, M., BATES, I., BREAKWELL, G., BYNNER, J., EMLER, N., JAMIESON, L. and ROBERTS, K. (1992), *Careers and Identities*, Open University Press, Buckingham.

CEREQ (Centre d'Études et de Recherches sur les Qualifications) (1993), "Allemagne : la formation professionnelle en question", *Céreq Bref*, No. 88.

CHISHOLM, L., BUCHNER, P., KRUGER, H.H. and BROWN, P. (eds.) (1990), *Childhood, Youth and Social Change: A Comparative Perspective*, Falmer, London.

EVANS, K. and HEINZ, W.R. (eds.) (1994), *Becoming Adults in England and Germany*, Anglo-German Foundation, London.

FINEGOLD, D. (1995), *The Low-Skill Equilibrium*, Oxford University Press.

HODKINSON, P. and SPARKES, A.C. (1993), "Young people's choices and careers guidance action planning: a case study of training credits in action", *British Journal of Guidance and Counselling*, No. 21, pp. 246-261.

KOHN, M.L. (1987), "Cross-national research as an analytic strategy", *American Sociological Review*, No. 52, pp. 713-731.

MAURICE, M., SELLIER, F. and SILVESTRE, J.-J. (1986), *The Social Foundations of Industrial Power*, MIT Press, Cambridge, MA.

RAFFE, D. (1994a), "Compulsory education and what then? Signals, choices, pathways", in OECD and US Department of Education, *Vocational Education and Training for Youth: Towards Coherent Policy and Practice*, OECD, Paris.

RAFFE, D. (1994b), "The new flexibility in vocational education", in W.J. Nijhof and J. Streumer (eds.), *Flexibility in Training and Vocational Education*, Lemma Uitgeverij, Utrecht.

RAFFE, D. (1995), "One system at 16+ years", *ACE Scotland Briefing*, No. 5, BP International, Poole.

ROSE, R. (1991), "Prospective evaluation through comparative analysis: youth training in a time-space perspective", in P. Ryan (ed.), *International Comparisons of Vocational Education and Training for Intermediate Skills*, Falmer, London.

RYAN, P. (1991), "Introduction: comparative research on vocational education and training", *International Comparisons of Vocational Education and Training for Intermediate Skills*, Falmer, London.

RYAN, P., GARONNA, P. and EDWARDS, R.C. (eds.) (1991), *The Problem of Youth*, Macmillan, London.

SCHEUCH, E.K. (1990), "The development of comparative research: towards causal explanations", in E. Øyen (ed.), *Comparative Methodology*, ISA/Sage, London.

MAIN SALES OUTLETS OF OECD PUBLICATIONS
PRINCIPAUX POINTS DE VENTE DES PUBLICATIONS DE L'OCDE

AUSTRALIA – AUSTRALIE
D.A. Information Services
648 Whitehorse Road, P.O.B 163
Mitcham, Victoria 3132   Tel. (03) 9210.7777
                          Fax: (03) 9210.7788

AUSTRIA – AUTRICHE
Gerold & Co.
Graben 31
Wien I   Tel. (0222) 533.50.14
                   Fax: (0222) 512.47.31.29

BELGIUM – BELGIQUE
Jean De Lannoy
Avenue du Roi, Koningslaan 202
B-1060 Bruxelles Tel. (02) 538.51.69/538.08.41
                          Fax: (02) 538.08.41

CANADA
Renouf Publishing Company Ltd.
5369 Canotek Road
Unit 1
Ottawa, Ont. K1J 9J3   Tel. (613) 745.2665
                          Fax: (613) 745.7660

Stores:
71 1/2 Sparks Street
Ottawa, Ont. K1P 5R1   Tel. (613) 238.8985
                          Fax: (613) 238.6041

12 Adelaide Street West
Toronto, QN M5H 1L6   Tel. (416) 363.3171
                          Fax: (416) 363.5963

Les Éditions La Liberté Inc.
3020 Chemin Sainte-Foy
Sainte-Foy, PQ G1X 3V6 Tel. (418) 658.3763
                          Fax: (418) 658.3763

Federal Publications Inc.
165 University Avenue, Suite 701
Toronto, ON M5H 3B8   Tel. (416) 860.1611
                          Fax: (416) 860.1608

Les Publications Fédérales
1185 Université
Montréal, QC H3B 3A7   Tel. (514) 954.1633
                          Fax: (514) 954.1635

CHINA – CHINE
Book Dept., China National Publications
Import and Export Corporation (CNPIEC)
16 Gongti E. Road, Chaoyang District
Beijing 100020   Tel. (10) 6506-6688 Ext. 8402
                          (10) 6506-3101

CHINESE TAIPEI – TAIPEI CHINOIS
Good Faith Worldwide Int'l. Co. Ltd.
9th Floor, No. 118, Sec. 2
Chung Hsiao E. Road
Taipei   Tel. (02) 391.7396/391.7397
                          Fax: (02) 394.9176

**CZECH REPUBLIC –
RÉPUBLIQUE TCHÈQUE**
National Information Centre
NIS – prodejna
Konviktská 5
Praha 1 – 113 57   Tel. (02) 24.23.09.07
                   Fax: (02) 24.22.94.33
E-mail: nkposp@dec.niz.cz
Internet: http://www.nis.cz

DENMARK – DANEMARK
Munksgaard Book and Subscription Service
35, Nørre Søgade, P.O. Box 2148
DK-1016 København K   Tel. (33) 12.85.70
                          Fax: (33) 12.93.87

J. H. Schultz Information A/S,
Herstedvang 12,
DK – 2620 Albertslung   Tel. 43 63 23 00
                          Fax: 43 63 19 69
Internet: s-info@inet.uni-c.dk

EGYPT – ÉGYPTE
The Middle East Observer
41 Sherif Street
Cairo   Tel. (2) 392.6919
                          Fax: (2) 360.6804

FINLAND – FINLANDE
Akateeminen Kirjakauppa
Keskuskatu 1, P.O. Box 128
00100 Helsinki

Subscription Services/Agence d'abonnements :
P.O. Box 23
00100 Helsinki   Tel. (358) 9.121.4403
                          Fax: (358) 9.121.4450

*FRANCE
OECD/OCDE
Mail Orders/Commandes par correspondance :
2, rue André-Pascal
75775 Paris Cedex 16 Tel. 33 (0)1.45.24.82.00
                   Fax: 33 (0)1.49.10.42.76
                   Telex: 640048 OCDE
Internet: Compte.PUBSINQ@oecd.org

Orders via Minitel, France only/
Commandes par Minitel, France
exclusivement : 36 15 OCDE

OECD Bookshop/Librairie de l'OCDE :
33, rue Octave-Feuillet
75016 Paris   Tel. 33 (0)1.45.24.81.81
                      33 (0)1.45.24.81.67

Dawson
B.P. 40
91121 Palaiseau Cedex   Tel. 01.89.10.47.00
                          Fax: 01.64.54.83.26

Documentation Française
29, quai Voltaire
75007 Paris   Tel. 01.40.15.70.00

Economica
49, rue Héricart
75015 Paris   Tel. 01.45.78.12.92
                          Fax: 01.45.75.05.67

Gibert Jeune (Droit-Économie)
6, place Saint-Michel
75006 Paris   Tel. 01.43.25.91.19

Librairie du Commerce International
10, avenue d'Iéna
75016 Paris   Tel. 01.40.73.34.60

Librairie Dunod
Université Paris-Dauphine
Place du Maréchal-de-Lattre-de-Tassigny
75016 Paris   Tel. 01.44.05.40.13

Librairie Lavoisier
11, rue Lavoisier
75008 Paris   Tel. 01.42.65.39.95

Librairie des Sciences Politiques
30, rue Saint-Guillaume
75007 Paris   Tel. 01.45.48.36.02

P.U.F.
49, boulevard Saint-Michel
75005 Paris   Tel. 01.43.25.83.40

Librairie de l'Université
12a, rue Nazareth
13100 Aix-en-Provence   Tel. 04.42.26.18.08

Documentation Française
165, rue Garibaldi
69003 Lyon   Tel. 04.78.63.32.23

Librairie Decitre
29, place Bellecour
69002 Lyon   Tel. 04.72.40.54.54

Librairie Sauramps
Le Triangle
34967 Montpellier Cedex 2 Tel. 04.67.58.85.15
                          Fax: 04.67.58.27.36

A la Sorbonne Actual
23, rue de l'Hôtel-des-Postes
06000 Nice   Tel. 04.93.13.77.75
                          Fax: 04.93.80.75.69

GERMANY – ALLEMAGNE
OECD Bonn Centre
August-Bebel-Allee 6
D-53175 Bonn   Tel. (0228) 959.120
                          Fax: (0228) 959.12.17

GREECE – GRÈCE
Librairie Kauffmann
Stadiou 28
10564 Athens   Tel. (01) 32.55.321
                          Fax: (01) 32.30.320

HONG-KONG
Swindon Book Co. Ltd.
Astoria Bldg. 3F
34 Ashley Road, Tsimshatsui
Kowloon, Hong Kong   Tel. 2376.2062
                          Fax: 2376.0685

HUNGARY – HONGRIE
Euro Info Service
Margitsziget, Európa Ház
1138 Budapest   Tel. (1) 111.60.61
                          Fax: (1) 302.50.35
E-mail: euroinfo@mail.matav.hu
Internet: http://www.euroinfo.hu//index.html

ICELAND – ISLANDE
Mál og Menning
Laugavegi 18, Pósthólf 392
121 Reykjavik   Tel. (1) 552.4240
                          Fax: (1) 562.3523

INDIA – INDE
Oxford Book and Stationery Co.
Scindia House
New Delhi 110001   Tel. (11) 331.5896/5308
                          Fax: (11) 332.2639
E-mail: oxford.publ@axcess.net.in

17 Park Street
Calcutta 700016   Tel. 240832

INDONESIA – INDONÉSIE
Pdii-Lipi
P.O. Box 4298
Jakarta 12042   Tel. (21) 573.34.67
                          Fax: (21) 573.34.67

IRELAND – IRLANDE
Government Supplies Agency
Publications Section
4/5 Harcourt Road
Dublin 2   Tel. 661.31.11
                          Fax: 475.27.60

ISRAEL – ISRAËL
Praedicta
5 Shatner Street
P.O. Box 34030
Jerusalem 91430   Tel. (2) 652.84.90/1/2
                          Fax: (2) 652.84.93

R.O.Y. International
P.O. Box 13056
Tel Aviv 61130   Tel. (3) 546 1423
                          Fax: (3) 546 1442
E-mail: royil@netvision.net.il

Palestinian Authority/Middle East:
INDEX Information Services
P.O.B. 19502
Jerusalem   Tel. (2) 627.16.34
                          Fax: (2) 627.12.19

ITALY – ITALIE
Libreria Commissionaria Sansoni
Via Duca di Calabria, 1/1
50125 Firenze   Tel. (055) 64.54.15
                          Fax: (055) 64.12.57
E-mail: licosa@ftbcc.it

Via Bartolini 29
20155 Milano   Tel. (02) 36.50.83

Editrice e Libreria Herder
Piazza Montecitorio 120
00186 Roma   Tel. 679.46.28
                          Fax: 678.47.51

OECD PUBLICATIONS, 2, rue André-Pascal, 75775 PARIS CEDEX 16
PRINTED IN FRANCE
(91 98 01 1 P) ISBN 92-64-15368-3 – No. 49191 1998